Abstracts

of

Pittsylvania County, VA.

Deeds

1783-1790

Compiled By:
Gayle Austin

Book Publishers

Southern Historical Press, Inc.
Greenville, South Carolina

Please direct all correspondence and orders to:

www.southernhistoricalpress.com
or
SOUTHERN HISTORICAL PRESS, Inc.
PO BOX 1267
375 West Broad Street
Greenville, SC   29601
southernhistoricalpress@gmail.com

ISBN #0-89308-711-4

Printed in the United States of America

Introduction

This book is a translation of Deed Book 7 and 8 of Pittsylvania County, Virginia and a part of Deed & Wills No 11 which was included on the microfilm of Deed Book 8. The period of time covered in Deed Book 7 and 8 is from January 1783 through April 1790. The period from May 1790 to April 1791 is from Deed & Wills No 11. It contains a partial listing of the deeds. Deed Book 9, which has already been published, has May 1791 to April 1794

In an effort to save space, I have used the abbreviation "P" for Pittsylvania County. To designate the signer or signers of the deeds, I have used s/ and then the name(s). The date under the signatures of the witnesses is the date the document was recorded.

This transcription was verified by the original documents in the Court House in Chatham, Virginia. The names and geographical locations are indexed in the back of the book.

Table of Contents

Deed Book 7 Pittsylvania County
1783-1786

Page 1
Reynalds from Kreek Deed
April 15, 1783 between Killien Kreeke of P and Hugh Reynolds of P for
15 pounds, a parcel of land on the Waters of Tomahawk Creek containing
105 acres
s/ Jullian Kreech
Wit: none
April 15, 1783

Page 3
Hewlett from Mosley Deed
April 15, 1783 between Samuel Mosley of P and William Hewlet of P for
50 pounds on south fork of Sandy River containing 102 acres being part of
the above said Samuel Mosley's Patent or Survey of 215 acres
Bounded: beginning at a bank or hill of the above said fork of Sandy
river, Zachariah Groom, the Patten Line
s/ Sam'l Mosley
Wit: none
April 15, 1783

Page 4
Shaw from Terry Deed
April 12, 1783 between Henry Terry of P and Thomas Shaw of P for 40
pounds, a parcel of land on the Waters of Sandy Creek containing by   '
estimation 200 acres
Bounded: the Order Line, Parishes Line, Bartons Branch
s/ Henry Terry
Wit: John Atkinson, Barton Terry, David Parish
April 15, 1783

Page 6
Martin from Echoles Deed
August 17, 1782 between Benjamin Echols and Peter Martin of P for 30
pounds, a parcel of land containing 150 acres
Bounded: John Waller's line, Wetherford's Order line, Wolfhole Branch,
Waller's line, being part of the Tract the said Echols lives on
s/ Benja Echols
Wit: Richard Hands, Soloman (X) Seal, Joseph Flippin, John Watkins
April 15, 1783

Page 7
Flippin from Echoles Deed
August 17, 1782 between Benjamin Echols and Joseph Flippin of P for 50
pounds, a parcel of land containing 150 acres being the same plantation
the said Echoles now lives on
Bounded: Absalom Hendrick's line, John Waller's line, Wolfhole branch,
Wetherford Order Line, Hendrick's line
s/ Benja Eckoles
Wit: Richard Hans, Solomon (X) Seal, John Watkins, Peter (X) Martin
April 15, 1783

Page 8
Ingrum from Henry Deed
September 25, 1782 between James Henry of King and Queen County and
William Ingram of P for the rents and covenants hereafter to be performed,
Parcel of land containing 400 acres
Bounded: Beginning at Thomas Hill's corner pine at the road to Rawley
Dodson's line where it crosses Bare Branch, Shaw's line, Parrishes path,
road. During the term of 17 years from the January 1 paying the taxes or
quit rents of the divised premises the first three years as they become due,
and the next seven year the sum of 30 shillings by the year and the taxes or
quit rents likewise and for the last seven years the sum of three pounds by
the year and the quit rent taxes, if any, as they become due. Said Ingram to
build a good square logg dwelling house 20 feet by 16 with a good plank
floor, overhead covered with hart of pine shingles put on with nails and a
barn built in the same manner 30 feet by 20, to plan and to raise 200 apple
trees of good grafted fruit, and 500 peach trees in three years from the
commencement of the lease hereof, and leave the plantation fencing and
other improvements in good tenantable repair at the experation of the term.
If the rents shall at anytime be unpaid for six months and no distress to be
had on the premises to pay the rent, it shall be lawful for the said Henry to
enter the premises and this lease decease and be void for the future.
s/ William Ryburn for James Henry
Wit: William Russell, Thos Hill, William Hamlin and Reubin Hill
April 15, 1783

Page 9
Deer from Huse Deed
April 15, 1783 between Samuel Huse of P and John Dier of P for 50
pounds, a parcel of land containing 370 acres on both Sides of Bareskin
Creek
Bounded: Owen Atkins corner, Pigg line, said Owen Atkins line
s/ Samuel Hughs
April 15, 1783

2

Page 11

Exceen from Mosley Deed

April 15, 1783 between Samuel Mosley of P and Daniel Exceen of Henry
County for 6 pounds, 9 shillings, a parcel of land containing 21 acres on
the South fork of Sandy River, being part of 215 acres Surveyed on April
9, 1762 and Patented September 1, 1780 in the name of the above Mosley
Bounded: crossing said fork of Sandy Creek, Patten line, crossing the
county Line to an Oak in Henry County, crossing said fork of Sandy River,
crossing the County line
s/ Sam'l Mosley
Wit: none
April 15, 1783

Page 12

Duncan from Kreek Deed

April 15, 1783 between Killin Kreek of P and Samuel Duncan of P for ten
pounds, a Tract of Land on the Waters of Tomhawk Creek containing 172
acres
Bounded: Corner of William Hills, a new line, corner of Roberts, the old
line
s/ Juillian Jering?
Wit: None
April 15, 1783

Page 14

Hamblin from Henry Release

September 1782 between James Henry of King and Queen County,
Virginia and William Hamlin of P in consideration of the Rents and
Covenants hearafter Covenanted to be performed, paid and done doth grant
a tract of Land bounded by Thomas Hills Corner, McLaughlans Line,
Fitzgeralds Line, Snead's line on Ye lick Branch, up the Branch to Hills
Corner, to hold for nineteen years from January 1 next, paying the Taxes or
Quit Rents of any kind which is supposed to be 400 acres for the first five
years and for the next seven yers the sum of 30 shillings by the year and
for the last seven years the sum of three pounds by the year during the
whole Term. Said Henry to build a good Square logg Dwelling House 20
feet by 16 with a good Plank floor over head Covered with hart of Pine
Shingles put on with nails and a Barn built in the same manner 30 feet by
20, plant and raise 200 apple trees of good grafted fruit and 500 peach
Trees in five years from the Commencement of this Lease. Therefore to
leave the Plantation fencing and other improvements in good Tennantable
repair at the Experation of the Term
s/ Wm Ryburn for James Henry

3

Wit: Thos Hill, William Russell, Reuben Hill, Wm (X) Ingram
April 15, 1783

Page 16
Worsham from Beard Deed
January 3, 1783 between Martin Baird of P and John Worsham of P for
225 pounds Current Money of Virginia, a parcel of land on both sides of
Rutleges Creek containing 200 acres
Bounded: Samuel Bynum's Corner, crossing the N Fork of Said Creek,
crossing a branch, Jacob Stillwell junr's Corner, crossing the Creek,
William Traveses Corner, crossing the south fork of said Creek and a
Branch
s/ Martin Beard
Wit: George (X) Surtherland, George Lumpkin, Samuwell Jones, Joseph
Farguson
April 15, 1783

Page 18
Hill from Henry Release
September 1782 between James Henry of King & Queen County, Virginia
and Thomas Hill of P in consideration of the Rents and Covenants to be
paid and done hath granted to the said Hill a tract of Land beginning at the
road, fork of the lick branch, up south East fork of the sd Branch to a large
heap of rocks, Hearth Stone Branch, down Timber Tree Branch to the lick
Branch & down sd Branch, up a small Branch to the road, supposed to be
400 acres. For the term of 14 years from January 1 next paying thirty
shillings by the year the first seven years and the taxes or Quit Rents and
the sum of three pounds for the year the next seven years and the Taxes
and Quit Rents. Said Hill to build a good Square logg Dwelling House 20
feet by 16 with a good Plank floor over head Covered with hart of Pine
Shingles put on with nails and a Barn built in the same manner 30 feet by
20, plant and raise 200 apple trees of good grafted fruit and 500 peach
Trees in five years from the Commencement of this Lease. Therefore to
leave the Plantation fencing and other improvements in good Tennantable
repair at the Experation of the Term.
s/ Wm Ryburn for James Henry
Wit: William Russell, William Hamlin, Wm (X) Ingram, Reubin Hill
April 15, 1783

Page 20
Bergar from Ward Deed
April 14, 1783 between Jeremiah Ward of P and Jacob Bergar of P in
consideration of three hundred pounds hard Money, a parcel of land on
both sides the frying Pan Creek containing 600 acres

4

Bounded: said Bergars lines by James Mitchell's Land and by David Ross's dividing Line till it comes to the Back Line and the other part.
s/ Jeremiah (X) Ward
Wit: James Mitchell, Lemmuil Gwyne, James (X) Flanagan
Anne, Wife of the said Jeremiah, relinquished her right of Dower
April 15, 1783

Page 22
Hendrick from Vaughan Deed
April 15, 1783 between John Vaughan of P and Obadiah Hendrick of P for 100 pounds Current Money of Virginia, a certain Tract containing 100 acres on Strate Stone Creek
Bounded: said Hendicks Line, Thomas Collins Line, straight Stone, a new line
s/ John Vaughan
Wit: None
April 15, 1783

Page 24
Hunt's Bond for Finishing the Court House
I, David Hunt of P, am firmly bound unto James Roberts, John Wilson, Benjamin Lankford and Crispin Shelton, they being appointed to take bond of me for the compleating of a Courthouse which I have undertaken to build in the penal sum of 300 pounds. April 15, 1783
The Condition of the above Obligation is such that whereas the above bound David Hunt doth agree to Build a Court House agreeable to the last plan which was in Nov 1782 Signed by Abraham Shelton & William Todd now know ye that if the above bound David Hunt shall will and truly compleat the said House before the last day of November next, then this obligation to e Void or else to remain in full force.
s/ D Hunt
Wit: Haynes Morgan, R Williams
April 15, 1783

Page 25
Sutherland from Gibson Deed
February 7, 1778 between Valentine Gibson of Surry County, North Carolina and William Sutherland of P for the sum of 50 pounds, a parcel of Land being on both sides of a large fork of Cascade Creek containing 100 acres.
Bounded: Old Line, the Creek of Sell, across the Old Survey to the Old back Line, crossing the creek
s/ Vallintine (X) Gibson, Elizabeth (X) Gibson

Wit: Joseph Harris, Elijah (X) Pyears, Gerret Gibson, David Harris,
Joseph Macmillion
April 15, 1783

Page 28
Tucker from Tucker Deed
April 3, 1783 between William Tucker of P and Robert Tucker of P for
five pounds, a parcel of land containing 200 acres by Estimation lying on
the Draughts and Branches of Mill Creek
Bounded: Phebe Tucker's line, new marked line, Arch'd Gordon's line,
Thomas Payne's line, Payne's Branch, below said Robert Tucker's Spring,
Phebe Tucker's line
s/ William Tucker
Wit: None
April 15, 1783

Page 29
Ward from Polley Deed
March 2, 1783 between David Polley of P and Jermiah Ward of P for 20
pounds, a parcel of land containing 440 acres on both sides of the
Widemouth Creek
Bounded: Jeremiah Ward's corner, Witcher's line, s'd Polly's Line,
Branch, Ward's line, crossing the wide mouth Creek
s/ David Polley
Wit: None
Agness, Wife of the said David Polley, relinquished her right of Dower.
April 15, 1783

Page 31
Adams from White Deed
April 15, 1783 between Benjamin White of P and Sylvister Adams of P for
the sum of 50 pounds, a parcel of land on the South side of Sandy Creek
containing 200 acres
Bounded: Where Isaac Dodson's Line crosses the River, up the River to
the mouth of a Branch below the Waggon ford, up the said Branch that
runs Square of as it meanders to the head where the said Benja White's line
crosses it , along said White's line until joyns Dodson's line, Sandy River
s/ Benj'm White
Wit: None
April 15, 1783

Page 33
Hendrick from McDonald Deed

November 23, 1782 between Moses McDonanld of Mongomary County and Agness Vaughan of Henry County and Obediah Hendrick of P for 100 pounds, a parcel of land containing 400 acres on both sides Strait Stone Creek adjoining the Land of John Vaughan, John Ballinger, Gilbord Hunt, Joseph West and Thomas Collins and being the Land and plantation whereon the said Obediah Hendrick now lives
s/ Agness (X) Vaughan
Wit: John Craddock, Thos Davis, Nathaniell Hendrick
April 15, 1783

Page 35
Buckley from Boaz Deed
February 18, 1783 between James Boaz of P and John Buckley of P for 100 pounds, a parcel of land containing 363 acres on both sides of the grasy fork of Stewarts Creek
Bounded: Maxwell's line, said James Boaz's former line, crossing the said Grassey fork, Thomas Boaz's old Line, Maxwell's Line aforesaid, crossing said Grassey fork
s/ James Boaz
Wit: John Owen, John Wilson, William Clarke
April 15, 1783

Page 37
Williams from Stratton Deed
April 15, 1783 between Thomas Stratton of P and Robert Williams of P for 18 pounds Current Money of Virginia, a parcel of land containing by Estimation 12 acres
Bounded: Robert Williams and Jeremiah White's Corner, corner between said Ro Williams and Francis Wisdom and along a line that was Lacy's Land
s/ Thomas Straton
Wit: G Strothers, John Williams, Jo Williams, Benja (X) Straton
April 15, 1783

Page 39
Seal from Echoles Deed
August 17, 1782 between Benj Echols and Soloman Seal of P for 24 pounds, a parcel of land containing 100 acres
Bounded: Abselom Hendrick's Line, James Danels and Wetherford Order, then new line, new line between said Solomon Seal and Joseph Flippen being part of the said Tract the said Echols now lives on
s/ Benj Echols
Wit: Richard Hands, Peter (X) Martin, Joseph Flippin, Jessee Man, William Slatyen

April 15, 1783

Page 40
Wilson from McDaniel Exor Deed
October 20, 1782 between Ann McDaniel and William McDaniel, Ex'tr
and Executor of William McDaniel, the Elder, Dec'd of the County of
Halifax, Virginia and John Wilson, Esq'r of P for 1850 pounds Current
Money of Virginia, a parcel of land containing 482 acres on the upper
Sandy Creek of Dann River, it being the Lands the said William McDaniel,
Dec'd, purchased in his Life Time of Alexander Gordon by Deed dated
April 12, 1772 and the said William McDaniel left in his Last will and
Testament to be sold by his Executors which said Land agreeable to the
Testators will advertise the ab'v Lands and sold to the highest bidder for
the af'd consideration December 5, 1779
s/ Ann McDaniel, William McDaniel
Wit: R Williams, William Rice, Cloe McDaniel, Clem't McDaniel
April 15, 1783

Page 42
McDaniel from Wilson Deed
April 15, 1783 between John Wilson of P and Ann McDaniel of Halifax
County for 1850 pounds Current Money of Virginia, a parcel of land
containing 482 acres on the upper Sandy Creek of Dann River, it being the
Land the said John Wilson purchased of the Executors of William
McDaniel, Dec'd at Publick Auction which Lands the said McDaniel
purchased of Alexander Gordon by Deed dated April 20, 1772
s/ John Wilson
Wit: None
April 15, 1783

Page 44
Denton Junr from Grisham Deed
October 25, 1782 between Thomas Grisham of Washington County, North
Carolina and James Denton junr of P for 65 pounds, a parcel of land
containing 142 acres on the Branches of the south fork of Sandy River and
the Branches of Sugar Tree Creek
Bounded: Lumkin's Corner in Shield's Line, Lumpkin's line, Thomas's
corner, crossing a Branch of Sugar Tree Creek, said Grisham's line,
crossing a Branch of the said fork of Sandy River in Shield's Line
s/ Thomas Gresham
Wit: Robert Bullington, Richard (X) Shores, Mary Scales, Martha Sneed,
David Scales
April 15, 1783

Page 46
Harrison from Denton Deed
October 29, 1780 between Joseph Denton of P and William Harrison of P
for 12,000 pounds Current Money of Virginia, a parcel of land containing
449 acres by a Survey made by James Denton and transferred to the said
Joseph Denton and being all the lands whereon the said Joseph Dinton now
lives & also including all the Lands whereon John Norton now lives.
s/ Joseph (X) Denton
Wit: William Wadlow, Drury Pulliam, William Watson, Nathan Watson,
Joshua (X) Nelson
April 15, 1783

Page 48
Ward from Polley Deed
April 15, 1793 between David Polley fo P and Jeremiah Ward of P for 40
pounds hard money, a parcel of land on Reedey's Creek containing 57 ½
acres
Bounded: North side of the said Creek, said Ward's line, Watery Branch,
crossing Reedeys Creek, Ridge Path, Old Dividing Line, crossing the
Creek
s/ David Polley
Wit: None
April 15, 1783
Agness, Wife of said David Polley, relinquished her right of Dower

Page 50
Toler from Cato Dedimus
To Dan'l Hankins & Jos Morton, Esq'r or any two of them of P, Whereas
Stirling Cato by his Indenture hath conveyed unto John Toler a parcel of
Land containing by Estimation 741 acres and Abbigail, wife of the said
Sterling Cato, cannot conveniently travel to the County Court of P, do
examine her to see if see willingly relinquish her right of Dower. March
18, 1783
s/ Will Tunstall
Abbigail Cato relinquished her right of Dower. March 21, 1783
s/ Daniel Hankins, Joseph Morton
April 15, 1783

Page 51
Johnson from Wimbish Deed
May 20, 1783 between John Wimbish of P and Archebald Johnston of P
for 75 pounds, a parcel of land on both sides of the Rackoon run, a Branch
of Elkhorn Creek containing by Estimation 188 Acres, it being the Land
granted to John Cheswell by Patent dated September 10, 1755 by the said

John Cheswell conveyed to Henry McDaniel by Deed dated July 1, 1762 and by said Henry McDaniel conveyed to said John Wimbish by deed dated March 4, 1772
s/ Jno Wimbish
Wit: None
May 21, 1783

Page 53
Stockton from Tunstall Deed
May 10, 1783 between James Roberts of P and William Tunstall of Henry County and John Stockton of P for the sum of 300 pounds Current Money, two certain parcels of land on the head of Sandy River, one tract containing 333 acres agreeable to bond given to the said John Stockton by James Roberts to make him a right in fee simple, it being the said tract of Land whereon the said James Roberts now Lives and where the Courthouse formerly stood and bounded on the Lines of James Smith, George Jefferson, Abraham Aaron and Joining a anew Survey of the said James Roberts, also on the Lines of William Roberts . The other Tract joining the former Containing by Estimation 232 acres
Bounded: Daniel Prewitt's Line, new Lines, William Lovell's Line, crossing the creek, crossing a branch, Abraham Aaron's Line, crossing the River to Prewitt's Line
s/ James Roberts, Will Tunstall
Wit: Wm (X) Oliver, John (X) Smith, Eliz'a (X) Smith, Sam'l Tenant, Reubin Tarrant
May 21, 1783
Elizabeth, wife of the said James Roberts, relinquished her right of Dower.

Page 55
Brown from Williams Deed
May 19, 1783 between Lewis Williams of P and Nathan Brown of P for 30 pounds, a parcel of land containing 302 acres on both sides of the head Branches of Bannister River
Bounded: James Divin's Corner, crossing Banister River, Branch in James Devins line, crossing Bannister, crossing a Branch
s/ Lewis Williams
Wit: None
May 21, 1783

Page 57
Owen from Sutherlin Deed
November 1, 1782 between George Sutherlin Senr of P and Thomas Owen of Guildford County, North Carolina for 200 pounds, a parcel of land containing 395 acres

Bounded: James Duncan's corner, Stone's line, Duncan's line
s/ George (X) Sutherlin
Wit: Edw'd Warren, Thomas Casey, John (X) Cox
May 21, 1783

Page 59
Worsham from Pankey Deed
May 19, 1783 between Stephen Pankey of Hallifax County and Henry
Worsham of Amelia County for 1500 pounds, a parcel of Land Containing
by Estimation 200 acres on the Branches of Burches Creek, it being a Tract
of Land granted the said Stephen Pankey by Patent dated July 20, 1780
s/ Stephen Pankey
Wit: John Pankey, Fredrick Ragsdale
May 21, 1783

Page 60
Prestage from Terry Deed
April 15, 1783 between Thomas Terry of P and Jno Prestige of P for 1000
pounds, a parcel of land on the Branches of Birches Creek containing by
Estimation 100 acres, being the same tract of Land the said Terry
purchased of said Prestige
Bounded: Corner in said Prestriges Line, Thomas Terry's line
s/ Thomas Terry
Wit: John Atkinson
May 21, 1783

Page 62
Lovell from Riding Bill Sale
I, William Riding of King George County in consideration of the sum of
375 pounds paid by Daniel Lovell of P do sell the said Daniel Lovell the
following Negro Slaves, to wit: David, Sall, Rachal, Harris, Pinn, Nane,
Peter & Charles
s/ Wm Riding
Wit: James Johnson, Daniel Peryman, Geo Phillips
May 21, 1783

Page 62
Motley from White Deed
January 28, 1782 between Daniel White of P and Joseph Motley of P for
10 pounds a parcel of land containing 10 acres by Estimation near Ecolses
fork
Bounded: said Motley's corner, Kidd's line
s/ Daniel White
Wit: Webb Kidd, Daniel Motley, Samuel Motley

11

May 21, 1783

Page 64
To all to whom these present shall Come Greeting, Know Ye that I,
George Rouff of P being Possessed of a Negro Boy named John Roff that I
purchased of Sarah Worsham for 1000 pounds which said slave I am now
Possessed of. I do hereby these presents agreeable to an act of Assembly
in this Case made and provided set him free to be as a Natural Born
Subject of the State of Virginia. May 2, 1783
s/ George Ruoff
Wit: R Williams, G Strother
May 21, 1783

Page 65
Treasurer for Owen Bond
We, John Owen, Sylvester Adams, Wm Todd, Thos Harden Perkins, Robt
Wynne, George Southerland, Jeremiah White, Thos Tunstall Senr & James
Johnson, Charles Burton & William Lynch of P are Bound unto Jacquelin
Ambler Esq, Treasurer of this Commonwealth in the sum of Ten Thousand
pounds Current Money.   May 21, 1783
The Condition of the above Obligation is such that if the above bound John
Owen do shall, will and Truly Collect, Account for and pay unto the
Treasurer according to Law, all the Taxes from each and every Taxable
person and article within the County imposed by virtue of an Act of the
General Assembly.
s/ John Owen, Sylvester Adams, Will Todd, Thos H Perkins, Robt Wynne,
Geo Southerland, Jere White, T Tunstall, Jas Johnson, Chs Burton, Wm
Lynch
Wit: None
May 21, 1783

Page 66
Adams from Lynch Deed
May 21, 1783 between William Lynch of P and Sylvester Adams of P for
50 pounds, a parcel of land on a Branch of Fall Creek containing 164 acres
Bounded: William Framan's Corner, Beryman Porter's Line, Donelson's
corner, Donelson's line, Burgeses Line
s/ William Lynch
Wit: None
May 21, 1783

Page 68
Williams from Burgess Deed

12

May 20, 1783 between Thomas Burgess of P and Robert Williams of P for 25 pounds, a parcel of land containing by Estimation 92 acres on the North fork of Pooding Creek, the same being granted to the aforesaid Thomas Burgess as by Paten dated June 12, 1780
Bounded: north fork of the said Creek, said Thomas Burgesses Line, crossing the said creek
s/ Thomas Burgess
Wit: None
May 21, 1783

Page 69
Bleakley from Bleakley Deed
May 23, 1783 between James Bleakley of P and John Bleakley of P, said James Bleakely hath given John Bleakley a parcel of land containing by Estimation 161 acres
Bounded: Hickeys Road, crossing Strawberry Creek
s/ James Bleakley
Wit: Griffith Dickinson, Mel Spraggins
May 21, 1783

Page 70
Watson from Justice Bond
I, Simon Justice of P am held and bound unto John Watson Senr in the full and just sum of 900 pounds
March 11, 1783
The Condition of the above Obligation is such that the above bound Simon Justice shall ever interrupt the said Watson in 90 acres of land agreeable to an antient Line now by John Justice Senr, it being part of the Land where the said Watson now lives then this Obligation to be Void. Otherwise to Remain in full force and Virtue. March 11, 1783
s/ Simon Justice
Wit: Dan'l Lovell, Sam'l Hughs, John Watson Senr
May 21, 1783

Page 72
White from Challis Deed
January 4, 1783 between Hugh Challis of the County of Guilford, North Carolina and Jeremiah White of P for 450 pounds, a parcel of l and on Wolf Den Branch containing by Estimation 680 acres
Bounded: north side of Wolf Den Branch, crossing three branches, up side of the said Wolf Den Branch
s/ Hugh Challis
Wit: John Owen Sen, James Buckley jr, Wm White, Wm Clark
June 17, 1783

13

Page 72
Wright from Lacy Release
Whereas Theophilus Lacy, Gent, Dec'd in his Life Time at the request of
WilliamWright did enter a friendly Court in the Council and Secretarys
Office against the said William Wright for 800 acres of land on Bacon
Branch of Cherrystone Creek and Prosecuted the same to a Decree, as by
the Records of the General Court will appear and sometimes afterwards
departed this Life intestate Leaving Batts Cocke Lacy Party to these
payment, his Eldest Son and Heir at Law, to whom the right and Interest of
his said Father in the said Land Descended and the said Batts Cocke Lacy
well knowing the intention of his said Father Not to Deprive the said
William Wright of the said Land doth by these present for himself his heirs
release, exonerate and forever quit Claim to all his Right, Title and Interest
which he hath or can on may have or Claim by Descent as aforesaid unto
the said William Wright. March 23, 1783
s/ B C Lacy
Wit: Mel Spragins, G Shother
June 17, 1783

Page 73
Tweddle from Bates Deed
March 13, 1783 between Fleming Bates of Halifax County and Benjamin
Twedel of P for 70 pounds, a parcel of land containing 205 acres by
Estimation
Bounded: William Wilkinson's Lines, James Nelson's line, William
Twedel's Line, a new line hereafter to be made Between Charles Harris
and the said Benjamin Twedel agreeable to a Bond the said Fleming Bates
gave to William Twedel for the said 205 acres
s/ Flm Bates
Wit: Homes Gwin, Wm Rice, Charles Harris, Humphrey Hendrick
June 17, 1783

Page 74
Harris from Bates Deed
March 13, 1783 between Fleming Bates of Halifax County and Charles
Harris of P for 70 pounds, a parcel of land containing 405 acres by
Estimation
Bounded: William Wilkinson's Line, William Twedel's Line, a new line
to be hereafter Run Between the said Harris and Benjamin Twedel to
Wilkinson's line
s/ Flm Bates
Wit: Benjamin Twedel, Homes Gavin, Wm Rice, Humphrey Hendrick
May 21, 1783

Page 75
Weatherford from Burnett Deed
March 26, 1783 between Benjamin Burnett of P and John Weatherford of
P for 40 pounds, a parcel of land containing 50 acres on the north side of
Banister River
Bounded: Chamberlin's Order Line near John Emerson's corner, fork of
the great Branch, Twedel's Line, Old Order Line
s/ Benjamin Burnett
Wit: None
June 17, 1783

Page 76
Prewitt from Burton Deed
June 17, 1783 between Charles Burton of P and John Prewitt of P for five
pounds, a parcel of land containing 100 acres Joining of Colo John
Wilson's Line on the Branches of Sandy Creek running down the Old
Road and Joing of the said Charles Burton's Line to the Rockey Branch,
down said Branch to the mouth, up the said Creek along Nathan
Ashworth's line to Colo John Wilson's Line
s/ Charles Burton
Wit: Lemuel Smith, Benjamin White, William (X) Quinn
June 27, 1783

Page 78
Conneley from Crowley Deed
June 17, 1783 between Benjamin Croley of P and Enock Conley of P for
60 pounds, a parcel of land on both sides of Sugar Tree Creek containing
by Estimation 140 acres
Bounded: crossing the Creek above the fork, Old Line, a little Branch
s/ Benjamin (X) Croley
Wit: None
June 17, 1783

Page 79
Walrond from Short Deed
June 17, 1783 between John Short and Elizabeth, his wife of P and
Benjamin Walrond of Halifax County for 425 pounds, a parcel of land on
the south side of Banister River joining the Lines of John Adams &
Thomas Adams being part of two Tracts of Land, One purchased of James
Pigg called the River Tract, the other called the mountain Tract containing
by Estimation 300 acres

Bounded: old Waggon ford on Banister River opposite to John Park's house, said John Shorts's land to his Back Line of the Mountain Tract to River Tract

s/ John (X) Short, Elizabeth (X) Short

June 17, 1783

Elizabeth, wife of said John Short relinquished her right of Dower

Page 82

Mecbray from Colley Deed

July 15, 1783 betweeb John Colley of the county of Henry and Hugh Mulinay of P for 100 pounds, a parcel of land containing 106 acres being part of a Tract of Land formerly granted to Dutton Lane lying on both sides of Sugar Tree Creek and bounded on the west by John Macks line and on the east by James Cox's line, on the South by Land entered by John Oakes. Also one other Tract of Land containing 252 acres and bounded by the lines of John Mack, James Burnett, John Cox and by the above mentioned Tract of Land.

s/ John Colley

Wit: None

July 15, 1783

Page 83

Barksdale from Gray Deed

March 27, 1783 between James Gray of P and Lucy his wife and Beverly Barksdale of P for 200 pounds, a parcel of land on the north side of Sandy Creek being the same Land the said Gray purchased of Thomas Buckingham containing by Estimation 400 acres

Bounded: north side of Sandy Creek, Old line dividing the said Grays and Adkinsons land, Adkinson's line, David Terry's line

s/ James Gray

Wit: Wm Ryburn, Thos Linthicum, Beverly (X) Miller

July 15, 1783

Page 84

Shockley from Shockley power Atto

I, James Shockley of P, appoint my son Chalton Shockley of P my true and Lawful Attorney to dispose and Sell a Tract of Land on or near the head of Nantice River containing 150 acres and was granted unto me December 20, 1741, also to Recover all Legacis or Sums of Money that may be due me from my Father David Shockly, Deceased either by will or otherwise.

July 14, 1783

s/ James (X) Shockley

Wit: Sam'l Calland, Jerimiyrie Doss

July 15, 1783

Page 85

Warren from Perkins, Marr Deed

November 20, 1782 between Peter Perkins of P and John Marr of Henry County, Virginia and Edward Warren of P for 900 pounds, a parcel of land containing 490 acres on the East side of Mountain Creek

Bounded: Mountain Creek, Langford's line, County Line

s/ Peter Perkins, John Marr

Wit: Lemuel Smith, Philip Jenkins, Joseph Scales

June 17, 1783

Susanna, wife of John Marr, relinquished her right of Dower

Page 87

Shelton from Parsons Deed

August 19, 1783 between George Parsons of P and Amistead Shelton of P for and in consideration of a Track of Land containing 200 acres lying on White thorn Creek, a parcel of land containing 285 acres

Bounded: Richard Parson's Line to Samuel Parsons to Richard Farthing's line to Jonathan Griffithe's line to William Easley

s/ George (X) Parsons

Wit: None

August 19, 1783

Page 88

Jenkins from Warren Deed

August 19, 1783 between Edward Warren of P and Philip Jenkins of P for 100 pounds, a parcel of land containing 145 acres on the East side of Mountain Creek

Bounded: Stone on Mountain Creek, up the creek, Beach on the Creek

s/ Edward Warren

Wit: None

August 19, 1783

Page 89

Black from Young Deed

June 25, 1783 between Archibald Young of Henry County and Thos Black of P for 100 pounds, a parcel of land containing 100 acres on both sides of Snow Creek part in P and part in Henry County

Bounded: Thos Black's line formerly belonging to Archibal Grayham, said Black's line, crossing Snow Creek to George Jefferson's line, Archabale Graham's Corner

s/ Archerball Young

Wit: Nathan Swanson, Tar Lewis, Milton Young

August 19, 1793

Page 90
Clement from Carleton Deed
September 9, 1779 between Thomas Carlton Junr & Martha, his wife, of
the county of Mecklenburg and Isaac Clements of P for 110 pounds, a
parcel of land containing by Estimation 370 acres
Bounded: James Hunt's line, crossing a branch, Benjamin Clement's line
s/ Thos Carleton, Martha Carlton
Wit: Henry Carlton, Sam'l Harris, R Williams
September 17, 1782

Page 92
Keezee from Cocke Deed
July 5, 1783 between Andrew Cocke of the county of Montgomery and
Arthur Keesee of P for 250 pounds, a parcel of land on both sides of the
north fork of frying Pan Creek containing 400 acres
Bounded: Woodding's line, crossing frying pan Creek, John Goad's Line,
crossing two branches
s/ Andrew Cocke
Wit: James (X) Downen, Robert (X) Martain, Mary (X) Madcarf, George
Marlow
August 19, 1783

Page 93
Flowers from Vance Deed
August 18, 1783 between Mathew Vance of Surry County, North Carolina
and Edward Flowers of P for 60 pounds, a parcel of land on the Lower side
of the South fork of Straight Stone Creek containing 400 acres
Bounded: Frances Pollard's Corner, crossing three Branches
s/ Mathew (X) Vance
Wit: None
August 19, 1783
Anne, wife of the said Mathew Vance relinquished her right of dower

Page 95
Swinny from Lackey Deed
August 19, 1783 between Alexander Lackey of P and Moses Swinney of P
for 20 pounds, a parcel of land containing by estimation 150 Acres on
Cherry Stone Creek
Bounded: Wilson's line, Charles Rigney's line, Lackey's line, Wilson's
line
s/ Thomas (X) Leckie
Wit: None
August 19, 1783

Hannah, wife of Alexander Lackey, relinquished her right of Dower

Page 96
Carter from Hutchings Deed
July 31, 1783 between Christopher Hutchings & Elizabeth, his wife, of P
and Thomas Carter of the county of Cumberland, a parcel of land on both
sides of Green Rock Creek, it being a part of an Order of Council of 3000
acres purchased by the said Hutchings containing by Estimation 389 acres
Bounded: said Order Line, crossing Piggs Road, John Pigg's line, lick
Branch, said Hutchings Order Line, crossing Green Rock Creek, crossing
the head of Green Rock.
The second tract being part of the aforesaid Order of Council and lying on
Lick Branch in P and Joining the forementioned Tract containing by
Estimation 78 acres
Bounded: Pigg's Old Road, the Order line
s/ Christopher (X) Hutchings, Eliz'a Hutchings
Wit: Jesse Carter, Jeduthun Carter, Hopkins Lacy, John Chattin
August 19, 1783

Page 99
Sheilds from Brawner Deed
June 10, 1783 between Benjamin Brawner of P and Thomas Shields of P
for 30 pounds, a parcel of land lying on Elkhorn Creek containing by
Estimation 80 acres
Bounded: Winders line, Rich'd Baynes line, crossing Elkhorn Creek
twice, Leak's line
s/ Benjamin (X) Brawner
Wit: None
August 19, 1783

Page 100
Moore from Moore Deed
August 13, 1783 between James Moore of P and Thomas Moore of P for
50 pounds, a parcel of land on the head of the South fork of Allen Creek
containing 112 acres
Bounded: John Pemberton's line, crossing Allen's Creek, up the said
creek to the head, a new line to Chisam's Corner, near head of Camp
Branch, Vance's line, Pemberton's Line, Allen's Creek
s/ James (X) Moore
Wit: Benj'a Lankford, Thos Lankford, John (X) Perkins
August 19, 1783

Page 102
Anderson from James Deed

August 18, 1783 between Enock James of Hallifax County, Virginia and Mathew Handason of P for 40 pounds, a parcel of land on the Waters of Burches Creek containing by Estimation 232 acres
Bounded: William Walter's corner, William Walter's line
s/ Enock James
Wit: Rotherick McDaniel, Thomas Bennett, John Hall, Thomas Dodson
August 19, 1783

Page 104
Dyer from Dourrough Deed
August 15, 1783 between James Durrugh of P and James Dyer of P for 50 pounds, a prcel o f land on Tomahawk Creek containing 206 acres
Bounded: John Balls Corner, crossing two branches, John Ball's line,
s/ James Durraugh
Wit: None
August 19, 1783

Page 106
Cook Senr from Cook Junr Deed
August 9, 1783 between George Cook Senr of P and George Cook Junr of P. The said George Cook Junr and Ruth, his wife, in consideration of 20 pounds, a parcel of land on Sandy Creek of Dan River and adjoins the land of James Callaway and is part of the same Tract the said George Cook Junr purchased of Electus Musick being by Estimation 100 acres
s/ George Cook Junr
Wit: Lem'r Hedgpeth, Joseph Flippin, James Holloway, Elijah Cook, Orlando Smith
August 19, 1783

Page 108
Stockton from Swipson Deed
September 9, 1782 between Richard Swipson of the county of Meckg, Virginia and John Stockton of P for 100 pounds, a parcel of land on Sandy River containing by Estimation 525 acres
Bounded: Cox's former line
s/ Rich'd Swepson
Wit: Robt Hyde, Sam'l Harris, H Carlton, R Williams
July 15, 1783

Page 109
Clark from Walker Deed
May 20, 1783 between Joseph Walker of P and Frances Clark of P for 120 pounds, a parcel of Land containing 100 acres

Bounded: North side of the great Road at the head of John Watson's Still House Branch, crossing Harmon Cook's fence to the Creek, crossing the Great Road on an Old dividing Line which is not run by an instrument dividing Between the said Land of John Watson and as the Courses often Varies is thought proper not to insert them trees are all marked fore & aft is the Line that has always been known as the Boundaries of the Land, crossing the Creek to Watson's fence, near the Old Road to the fork, along the Great Road
s/ Joseph (X) Walker
Wit: Peyton Smith, Fortinus Doss, Hundley Vaughan
July 15, 1783

Page 111
Thornton from McBee Deed
June 2, 1782 between William McBee Junr of Washington Syllivan County, North Carolina and Presley Thornton of P, a parcel of land on the Waters of Mountain Creek containing 250 acres
Bounded: Joseph Cons Lines on the Eastward and by William Mitchell's lines South Westwardly thence touching Edward Cahalls and Joined by unpatented Land Northward
s/ William Macbee
Wit: Will Tunstall, William Mitchell, Wat. Lamb, David Scales, Clement Nance
June 21, 1783

Page 113
Williams from Gwin Deed
July 30, 1779 between Richard Gwin of P and Robert Williams of P for 3020 pounds, a parcel of land containing 381 acres
Bounded: Creek side, Jackson's line crossing both Branches of Sandy Creek, it being the middle Survey of a larger Tract of Land on Sandy Creek that the said Gwinn had of William Kennon. Esq
s/ Rich'd Gwinn
Wit: Geo Strother, Jere White, Benja (X) Stratton
August 19, 1783

Page 114
Bobbitt from Peak Deed
September 16, 1783 between George Peek of P and John Bobbitt of P for 100 pounds, a parcel of land containing by Estimation 100 acres on the South Side of Pigg River
Bounded: Mouth of a Branch called Little Hungry Camp, up the Branch
s/ George Peek
Wit: None

21

September 16, 1783

Page 116
Finley from Posey Deed
September 4, 1783 between John Price Posey as Guardian to the Heirs of
Richard Chamberlayne, Dec'd of New Kent County and Robert Finley of P
for 30 pounds, a parcel of land containing 163 ¾ acres on both sides of
Strawberry Creek being Part of an Order of Council of Rich'd
Chamberlayne, Dec'd
Bounded: Lines of Epaphroditus White, James Blakely, Joshua Cantrall &
along the new line
s/ Jon'o Price Posey
Wit: Epa White, Jas Johnson, Letty Johnson
September 16, 1783

Page 117
Kay from Stone Deed
September 16, 1783 between Joshua Stone of P and Henry Kay of P for
100 pounds, a parcel of land containing 300 acres on both sides of Mill
Creek
Bounded: Will Tucker's Line, crossing Mill Creek and a Branch, William
Payne's line, crossing a Branch and Mill Creek
s/ Joshua Stone
Wit: None
September 16, 1783

Page 119
Brooks from Bates Deed
April 7, 1783 between Daniel Bates of P and Samuel Brooks of P for 60
pounds, a parcel of land containing by instimation baring date April 15,
1774 at Richmond Town with 115 acres on the South side of Banister
River
Bounded: Samull Mathases Corner, Tornors Corner
s/ Daniel Bates, Betsy (X) Bates
Wit: John Watkins, Benjamin Watkins, Hennery (X) Blankes, Jeremiah
Keesee, Jacob Nickols
April 15, 1783

Page 120
McHaney from Hurt Deed
January 17, 1783 between Joel Hunt and Tabitha, his Wife of P and Terry
McHaney of P for 100 pounds, a parcel of land on the Draughts of Strait
Stone and Buffelow Creek containing 152 acres

Bounded: Nathaniel Hendricks corner, William Pollard's line, James Mitchell's line, Hendrick's line
s/ Joel Hurt, Tabitha (X) Hurt
Wit: John Luck, Edward (X) Prier, Cornelius Mchaney
July 15, 1783

Page 122
Bruce Jr from Cocke Deed
August 21, 1783 between Natha'l Cocke of the county of Hallifax and James Bruce Junior of P for 30 pounds, a parcel of land containing 695 acres in two Surveys, one lying on both sides of the north fork of George's Creek containing 350 acres. The other lying on the Branches of Stinking River and Sycamore containing 345 acres beginning at Jones's corner in Talbot's line
s/ Nath Cocke
Wit: Ben Lankford, David (X) Irby, Saml (X) Irby
September 16, 1783

Page 124
Harris from Harris Deed
April 14, 1783 between John Harris Senr of P and Joseph Harris of P for 100 pounds, a parcel of land containing 200 acres
Bounded: Russel's Corner, up both sides of Cascade Creek
s/ John (X) Harris
Wit: Joseph Minter, William Southulin, John Prewett, William Winstead
August 19, 1783

Page 126
Astin from Perkins Deed
August 30, 1783 between Peter Perkins of P and William Astin of P for 5000 pounds, a parcel of land containing, by Survey made November 3, 1774, 697 acres on the head Branch of Sandy Creek
Bounded: John Hall's corner, new line, crossing four branches, crossing two branches, Ashworth's line, head of a Branch, Robert Adams corner, crossing the Branch in said Adams line
s/ Peter Perkins
Wit: Lemuel Smith, Allen Stokes, Daniel Perkins
September 16, 1783

Page 128
Williams from Dalton Power of Attorney
I, James Dalton of P, Eldest Son & Heir to Timothy Dalton, Dec'd, , also an Executor of the Last Will and Testament of said Deceased do appoint Nathaniel Williams, Esq of Guilford County, North Carolina my Lawful

23

Attorney to enter into and take Possession of all my rights & Title that I claim to a certain Messuage of Land as Heir & Executor, the land in P on both sides of Stanton River known by the land and place whereon my said Father, Timothy Dalton dyed and claimed by John Chiles and others by their getting Possession and Standing a Suit for the same Reference to the Records in the high Court of Chancery will more fully appear and also to prosecute against any Persons any Writs or Actions to him shall summeet for the Recovery or obtaining Possession of the Premises or any Part thereof. January 1, 1783

s/ James Dalton

Wit: Wm Arthur, Randolph Dalton, Jos Cook

September 16, 1783

Page 129

Parsons from Shelton Deed

October 21, 1783 from Armistead Shelton of P and William Parsons of P for 4 pounds, twelve shillings, a parcel of land containing 25 acres being part of a Tract of Land the said Shelton had of George Parsons

Bounded: Richard Parson's line, new line to a Branch, Curry's Order Line

s/ Armistad Shelton

Wit: None

October 21, 1783

Page 130

Muse from Mckenzie Deed

September 25, 1783 between Aron Mckinzie of P and John Muse of P for 150 pounds, a parcel of land containing by Estimation 162 acres on both sides of Turky Cock Creek

Bounded: Arthur Hopkins corner, new line, said Hopkins Line

s/ Aaron MacKenzie, Jemima Mackenzie

Wit: None

October 21, 1783

Jemima, wife of Aaron McKensey, relinquished her right of Dower

Page 131

Mineas from Meneas Deed of Gift

I, James Minus of P in consideration of the Love, good will and affection which I have and bear towards my son, Benjamin Minus of P, at my Decease and my Wife's, one Negro Fellow named Sam and 60 pounds of Hard Money, April 4, 1783

N.B. the above Negro at Benjamin Menus his Decease is to belong to his Oldest Son James Minus

s/ James Minus Senr

Wit: Peter Field, Jefferson Zackara, Fuller, Field Jefferson

October 21, 1783

Page 132
Dodson from Dodson Deed
December 14, 1782 between Jesse Dodson of P and George Dodson of P
for 60 pounds, a parcel of land on Jeremiah fork of Birches Creek
containing by Estimation 250 acres.
Bounded: John Mading's Corner, Madding's line
s/ Jesse Dodson
Wit: George Dodson, Thomas Chelton, Elisha Dodson, John Bennett,
Charles Lewis
December 21, 1783

Page 134
Dodson from Dodson Bill of Sale
I, Thomas Dodson of P, have sold unto Jesse Dodson of P one Negro
Named Swirnah for 50 pounds
s/ Thomas (X) Dodson
Wit: Rawleig Dodson
October 21, 1783

Page 134
Davis's Emancipation to Negroes
I, Samuel Davis of Campbell do emancipate and Liberate the following
Slaves in my Possession which now reside in this County, to wit, Jack
Sampson and his Wife, Mary and their two Children Martain and Abram
and Mathew Birgess, this I deliver as my act and Deed and desire that a
October 21, 1783
Jack Sampson   37 Years old
Wife Mary   21 Years old
Martin 5
Abram 3
Matt 23
s/ Sam'l Davis
October 21, 1783

Page 135
Duncan from Duncan Deed
August 19, 1783 between Samuel Duncan of P and Benjamin Duncan of P
for 30 pounds, a parcel of land on the Waters of Tomahawk Creek
containing 182 acres
Bounded: Robert Neely, corner of Roberts
s/ Samuel Duncan
Wit: John Campbell, Hugh Reynolds, Noton Dickinson

October 21, 1783

Page 137
Lumkins from Jones Deed
July 30, 1783 between Nathan Jones of P and George Lumpkin of P for
150 pounds, a parcel of land containing 60 acres on the South side of Dan
River
Bounded: Samuel Jones and George Lumpkin's corner, a Branch, Robt
Lumpkins line, Larkin Dix's line, George Lumpkins line
s/ Nathan Jones
Wit: Joseph Lumpkin, Samuel (X) Jones, Robt Lumpkins, John Worsham
October 21, 1783

Page 138
Kelley from Walters Deed
July 26, 1783 between Robt Walters of P and Hugh Kelley of P for 50
pounds, a parcel of land containing 176 acres
Bounded: near the road on Elijah Walters line, Andersons and Ponds
Lines crossing two Branches, crossing the creek
s/ Robert (X) Walters
Wit: Robt Clopton, Mathew Anderson, Wm Herring
October 21, 1783

Page 140
Stewart from Irby Deed
October 16, 1783 between John Stewart of P and Charles Irby of P for 100
pounds, a parcel of land joining Elkhorn Creek containing by Estimation
100 acres including the Plantation where on James Singleton now lives
Bounded: Elkhorn Ck in Fisher's Line, Fisher's line, Farmer's Corner,
Stewart's line, Elkhorn in Stewart's line
s/ Charles Irby
Wit: None
October 21, 1783

Page 142
Lumkins from Jones Deed
July 30, 1783 between Nathan Jones of P and Joseph Lumpkin of P for 140
pounds, a parcel of land containing 140 acres on the south side of Dan
River
Bounded: Samuell Jones corner on Jacksons Creek, along Creek to Robt
Lumpkins Line, to the Land I sold George Lumpkins, along new line to
Samuell Jones Corner, on Jacksons Creek
s/ Nathan Jones

Wit: George Lumpkins, Samuel Jones, Robt Lumpkins, Robert Wynne,
John Worsham
October 21, 1783

Page 143
Hall from Waller Deed
October 20, 1783 between Zachariah Waller of P and Henry Hall of P for
55 pounds, a parcel of Land on the East side of Polleys Branch it being part
of a Tract of Land where Zachariah Waller now lives containing by
Estimation 50 acres
Bounded: Theoderick Carter's line, Polleys Branch running west down
said Branch to Finies Order Line
s/ Zachariah (X) Waller
Wit: Jesse Carter, Thomas Carter, Thomas Carter, W M Allen
October 21, 1783

Page 145
Waller from Waller Deed
October 20, 1783 between Zachariah Waller of P and John Waller of P for
50 pounds, a parcel of land containing by Estimation 100 acres
Bounded: South side of Polleys Branch, running up said Branch to the Old
Line
s/ Zachariah (X) Waller
Wit: Jesse Carter, Thos Carter, Thos Carter, Henry Hall
October 21, 1783

Page 147
Anderson from James Deed
October 4, 1783 between Enock James of Hallifax County, Virginia and
Mathew Anderson of P for 40 pounds, a parcel of land on the Branches of
Burches Creek containing 356 acres
Bounded: William Walters Corner, crossing a branch & Road, Thomas
Walters corner, Robert Walters corner, crossing a branch, William Walters
line
s/ Enoch James
Wit: John Hall, John (X) Haris, Thomas Dodson
October 21, 1783

Page 149
Bridgewater from Bailey Deed
Between Peter James Bailey of P and Fanny Bridgewater of P for 50
pounds, a parcel of land containing by Estimation 50 acres
Bounded: Walker's line, up the Miry Branch, Summerses Line

s/ Peter James Bailey
Wit: Jesse Carter, Thos Carter, Thos Carter, Henry Hall
October 21, 1783

Page 150
Waller from Waller Deed
October 20, 1783 between Zachariah Waller of P and Pleasant Waller of P
for 50 pounds, a tract of land containing by Estimation 100 acres
Bounded: Finney's Old Order Line, Adam's line, Thompson's line,
Abraham Cammels Line to Polleys Branch
s/ Zachariah (X) Waller
Wit: Jesse Carter, Thos Carter, Thos Carter, Henry Hall
October 21, 1783

Page 152
Davis from Chiles Deed
November 18, 1783 between Rowland Chiles of the County of Henry and
Richard Davis of P for 400 pounds, a parcel of Land on the south side and
joining Stanton River, it being the lower Part of the Land the said Chiles's
Father formerly lived on and which he Devised to him the said Rowland
Chiles is his Last Will and testament containing by Estimation 126 acres
Bounded: South Bank of the said River just below the mouth of a Small
Branch, John Ward's Dividing Line, Back Line, said Old Line, just by the
House until it Strikes a Branch, down the Branch, up Stanton River
s/ Rowland Chiles, Nancy (X) Chiles
Wit: None
November 18, 1783
Nancy, wife of Rowland Chiles, relinquished her right of Dower

Page 154
Morton from Sheilds Deed
November 18, 1783 between Samuel Shields, Planter, of P and John
Morton for 30 pounds, land granted by Patent dated April 14, 1770 on the
Waters of Sandy River containing 340 acres
Bounded: John Morton's line, Elizabeth Reeds Line, crossing a branch,
crossing two Branches in the aforesaid Morton's Line
s/ Samuel Shields
Wit: None
November 18, 1783

Page 155
Fearn from Wynne Deed

November 14, 1783 between John Wynne of P and Thomas Fearne of P for 150 pounds, a parcel of land on the south side of Dan River containing by a deed 208 acres
Bounded: East on Thomas Fearn's Line, North by the Meanders of Dan River, West by Robert Wynne Line & South by Charles Wynne Line, it being the Land & Plantation whereon the said John Wynne now occupies.
s/ John Wynne
Wit: John Wilson, Jno Dix, Joseph Farguson, George (X) Southerland
November 18, 1783

Page 156
Williams from Kirby Deed
September 12, 1783 between Joseph Kirby, Heir at Law of Richard Kirby, Dec'd of county of Halifax, Virginia and Robert Williams of P for 700 pounds, a parcel of land containing 367 acres as by Patent granted to Richard Kirby, farther to the aforesaid Joseph Kirby dated September 1, 1780 on the Branches of the North fork of Sandy Creek
Bounded: William Astin's Corner in Kennon's Line, Astin's line, crossing Three Branches, Kennon's line
s/ Joseph Kirby
Wit: G Strother, Richard Kirby, Edward (X) Wall
November 18, 1783

Page 157
Stokes from Adams Deed
May 16, 1783 between Robert Adams of P and Sylvanus Stokes of P for 300 pounds, a parcel of land containing by Estimation 200 acres lay'd off in the lower end of Robert Adams 400 acres on White Oak Creek
Bounded: said Stokes line on the said Creek, Adams Line, crossing the said Creek, Adams Back Line, said Stokes Line.
Also the Courses of 50 acres Lay'd off out of the upper end of the above said Land
Bounded: upper end of the said Adams Line, head of a Branch, down the said Branch, Adams Back line
s/ Robert (X) Adams
Wit: Jesse Carter, John Adams, Sally Adams
September 16, 1783

Page 159
Weatherford from Burnett Deed
November 18, 1783 between Benjamin Burnett of P and Jno Weatherford of P for 20 pounds, a parcel of land containing by Estimation 100 acres
Bounded: Chamberlayne's Line at the Long Branch, said Weatheford's line, the Long Branch

s/ Ben Burnett
Wit: None
November 18, 1783

Page 160
Tunstall from Tunstall Deed
November 10, 1783 between Thomas Tunstall of P and Thomas Tunstall
Junr of P for the Natural love and affection which he the said Thomas
Tunstall hath to the said Thomas Tunstall Jr, a parcel of land whereon the
said Thomas Tunstall jr now lies and which the said Thomas Tunstall, the
Elder purchased of Samuel Cox lying on both sides of Stinking River
containing by Estimation 200 acres
s/ T Tunstall
Wit: None
November 18, 1783

Page 161
Birks from Hardin Deed
November 18, 1783 between Henry Hardin of P and James Birk of P for 60
pounds, a parcel of land on the Branches of Sweeting fork of Sandy Creek
containing 182 acres
Bounded: Thomas Hardies Corner, crossing Sweetings fork, crossing the
Middle of the Land
s/ Henry Hardin
Wit: Jonas Lawson, Thomas Hardy, Joshua Welch
November 18, 1783
Alce, wife of said Henry Hardin, relinquished her right of Dower

Page 162
**Abraham Shelton's Bond for the Collection of the Taxes for the year
1784**
We, Abraham Shelton, William Todd, Joseph Morton, Lodowick Tuggle,
John Parks & Daniel Hankins are bound unto the Commonwealth of
Virginia for 10,000 pounds   November 17, 1783
The Condition of this Obligation is such that the above bound Abraham
Shelton is appointed Sheriff of P who shall collect, account for & pay the
Several Taxes due for the year 1784
s/ Abra Shelton, William Todd, Joseph Morton, Lodowick Tuggle, John
Parks, Daniel Hankins
Wit: None
November 18, 1783

Page 163
Abraham Shelton's Bond for Sheriff

30

We, Abraham Shelton, William Todd, Joseph Morton, Lodowick Tuggle, John Parks & Daniel Hankins are bound unto the Commonwealth of Virginia for 500 pounds   November 17, 1783

The Condition of this Obligation is such that the above bound Abraham Shelton is appointed Sheriff who shall collect all Quitrents , account for & pay the same to the Officers of the Commonwealth Revenue

s/ Abra Shelton, William Todd, Joseph Morton, Lodowick Tuggle, John Parks, Daniel Hankins

Wit: None

November 18, 1783

Page 164

Abraham Shelton's Bond for Sheriff

We, Abraham Shelton, William Todd, Joseph Morton, Lodowick Tuggle, John Parks & Daniel Hankins are bound unto the Commonwealth of Virginia for 1000 pounds   November 17, 1783

The Condition of this Obligation is such that the above bound Abraham Shelton is appointed Sheriff

s/ Abra Shelton, William Todd, Joseph Morton, Lodowick Tuggle, John Parks, Daniel Hankins

Wit: None

November 18, 1783

Page 165

A Commission to Examine MrsYoung and Deed from her said Husband to Thomas Black

To Peyton Smith, Lodowick Tuggle, Gent. Justices of P, Whereas Archibald Young by his certain Indenture of Feaffment has conveyed to Thomas Black of P one tract of Land containing 100 acres & whereas Sarah Young, wife of said Archibald Young cannot travel to our County Court, Know ye that we Trusting to faithful and Provident Circumspection in Examining her apart from her Husband, Archibald, whether she does freely Relinquish her right of Dower   September 1783

s/ Will Tunstall

By Virtue of the above Dedimus we have Examined Sarah, wife of the said Archibald Young, who relinquished her right of Dower   October 11, 1783

s/ Peyton Smith, Lodowick Tuggle

November 18, 1783

Page 166

Williams from Jones Power of Attorney

Samuel Jones of Caswell County, North Carolina do shortly intend to remove, do and have made Robert Williams, my true and Lawful Attorney

31

to ask, demand, levy, sue for and by all Lawful ways and means to recover all Sums of Money, Goods, wares, Merchandizes, Effects or Estate which shall hereafter be due in the province of North Carolina.   Nov 17, 1783
s/ Samuel (X) Jones
Wit: R Williams, Geo Phillips, G Strother
November 18, 1783

Page 167
Casey from Duncan Deed
December 16, 1783 between John Dunkin, Son of the Late Charles Dunkin, of P and Thomas Casey of Guilford County, N C for 20 pounds, a parcel of land containing 282 acres
Bounded: James Duncan's Line, McGriff's Line, Perkin's Line. Said Dunkin's former line
N.B. The above Tract was granted to Charles Dunkin, Deceased on the Branches of the open ground fork of Beens Creek
s/ John Duncan, Sarah Duncan
Wit: None
November 16, 1783

Page 168
Bayes from King Deed
December 15, 1783 between James King of P and Isaiah Bays of P for 100 pounds, a parcel of land containing 184 acres
Bounded: Marsens Branch of Sandy River, crossing a branch, crossing the said Morsons Branch
s/ James King
December 16, 1783

Page 169
Bass from Mullins Deed
December 15, 1783, John Mullins of P doth make a free Deed of Gift to Philip Bass of P of 50 acres of Land on a Branch of Sandy River
Bounded: Nathan Asher's Line on the road & along his Line & joins John Smith's Line, thence joining Branch, down Branch to the Road, Asher's Line
s/ John Mullins
Wit: None
December 16, 1783

Page 170
Porter from Doss Deed

December 16, 1783 between Thomas Doss of P and William Porter of P
for 50 pounds, a parcel of land on the Branches of the Long Branch of the
Timbred fork of White thorn Creek containing 220 acres
Bounded: Hugh Innises Corner, Crossing the Timbred fork, crossing the
creek, Inneses line
s/ Thomas Doss
Wit: None
December 16, 1783

Page 172
Goad from Witcher Deed
August 14, 1783 between Ephraim Witcher of Mongumry County and
William Goad of P for 10 pounds, a parcel of land containing 150 acres on
both sides of Reddy's Creek
Bounded: David rosses Lines on the North side of Reddys Creek, crossing
a branch, Thomas Ramsey's Corner, crossing Redes Creek, up a Branch
s/ Ephraim Witcher
Wit: William Young, John Witcher, James Witcher
December 16, 1783

Page 173
Hewlett from Hodges Deed
December 15, 1783 between Moses Hodges of P and Martin Hewlett of P
for 100 pounds, a parcel of land on the Waters of Bareskin Creek
containing 140 acres, it being Part of a grater Tract containing 800 acres,
the 140 acres aforesaid was Willed to me by my Father, Edmund Hodges,
Dec'd in his Last Will & Testament
Bounded: Corner on Jesse Hodges Line near the Round pond and bounded
by the Lines of the Jesse Hodges, John Hodges & Thomas Hodges
s/ Moses Hodges
Wit: Sam'l Mosley, Arthur Nash, Zac (X) Grum
December 16, 1783

Page 175
Craine from Askey Deed
September 3, 1783 between Sam'ee Askey of P and James Craine of P for
30 pounds, a parcel of land on the Waters of fall Creek containing by
Estimation 247 acres
Bounded: John Kirby's Corner, new line, Crossing a Branch, Crossin main
fork, John Kirby's Corner
s/ Sam'l (X) Askey
Wit: Silly's Stokes
December 16, 1783

Page 176
Short from Hutchings Deed
December 16, 1784 between Christopher Hutchings of P and William
Short of P for 20 pounds, a parcel of land containing 125 acres
Bounded: Short's Corner, Crosses the Great Branch, said Hutching's Line,
crossing a branch, James Allin's Line
s/ Christopher Hutchings
Wit: None
December 16, 1783

Page 178
Linthicum from Shackleford Deed
December 8, 1783 between John Shackleford of P and Thomas Linthicum
of P for 60 pounds, a parcel of land on the Branches of Shockgo and Sandy
Creek containing by Estimation 112 acres
Bounded: Branch, crossing the Road
s/ John Shackleford
Wit: Jno Corbin, Thos Tanner
December 16, 1783

Page 179
Crane from Burks Deed
December 16, 1783 between James Burks & Susanna, his Wife of P and
John Crane of the County of Cumberland for 60 pounds, a parcel of land
on the fork of White Oak Creek containing by Estimation 100 acres
s/ James Birk
Wit: James Craine, Sillvs Stokes, James Lawless
December 16, 1783
Susannah, wife of James Burks relinquished her right of Dower

Page 181
Allin from Roberson Deed
December 12, 1783 between Jesse Roberson and Elizabeth, his wife of P
and Francis Allin of P for 100 pounds, a parcel of land on Strawbery Creek
containing by Estimation 165 acres
Bounded: Bank of the Creek in Jonathan Thomas's line, head of a branch,
Jos Meguyhus, Ridge of rocks, Bank of the Creek
s/ Jesse Roberson, Elizabeth Robinson
Wit: Thos Hardy, John Davis, John Allin
December 16, 1783

Page 183
Ragsdale from Birks Deed

December 16, 1783 between James Burks of P and Frederick Ragsdale of
P for 50 pounds, a parcel of land near the White Oak Mountain containing
by Estimation 100 acres
Bounded: Frances Luck's line, new line
s/ James Burks
Wit: None
December 16, 1783
Susannah, wife of James Burks relinquished her right of Dower

Page 184
Southerland from Duncan
December 10, 1783 between John Duncan of P and George Southerland of
P for 60 pounds, a parcel of land on the Branches of Sandy River
containing by Estimation 390 acres
Bounded: Constant Perkins line, Gammons line, crossing a branch, Mill
road, Chadwick's corner, Perkins line
s/ John (X) Duncan
Wit: Rich'd Harrison, Sylvester Adams, John Ross, George Southerland
December 16, 1783

Page 186
Commission to Examine John Southerland from Thornton
To William Thornton and James Marshall Esqs or any two Justices of the
County of Brunswick, Greetings. Whereas James Thornton by his
Indenture of feoffment hath hath conveyed unto John Southerland a parcel
of land containing 270 acres and Elizabeth Thornton, wife of the said
James Thornton cannot travel to County court of P. Know ye that we ask
that you examine Elizabeth apart from her husband. March 21
s/ Will Tunstall
By virtue of the above Dedimus directed to me, we have Examined
Elizabeth, the wife of James Thornton. She relinquished her right of
Dower   October 14, 1783
s/ William Thornton, James Marshall
Wit: None
December 16, 1783

Page 187
Womack from Martin Bill of Sale
I John Martin of P agree to let Wm Womack one Negro Boy named Aaran
& one Negro Girl named Alse, one Negro Woman named Beck for the
right of a Peace of Land Sold the said Womack containing 50 acres which
the said Martin is to make a good & lawful right on or before June 1, 1785
June 3, 1783
s/ John Martin

35

Wit: Chas Womack, Agness Womack, Salley Womack, Luke Williams
December 16, 1783

Page 188
Dunn from Burnett Deed
January 28, 1783 between Benjamin Burnett of P and John Dun of P for 30 pounds, a parcel of land on the N side of the long Branch containing by Estimation 100 acres
Bounded: Spring Branch, John Smith's line, crossing the road
s/ Benjamin Burnet, Frances Burnett
Wit: John Hodges, Barnet Burnett, Benjamin Burneet
February 17, 1784

Page 189
Dunn from Roberson Deed
October 15, 1783 from Jesse Roberson of P and John Dunn of Luingbergh County for 30 pounds, a parcel of land between Banister River and little Bairskin containing by Estimation 200 acres being the Tract of Land that said Robinson bought of Jesse Roberson
Bounded: John Smith's line on the south side of a Small Branch, along Smith's line
s/ Jesse Robinson
Wit: Benjamin Burnett, Thos Smith, Rich'd Pigg
February 17, 1784

Page 190
Bates from Robinson Deed
December 24, 1783 between Jesse Robinson of P and Daniel Bates of P for 40 pounds, a parcel of Land on the Branches of Mill and Middle Creek containing 162 acres
Bounded: Hutchingses Corner in Payne's Line, Payne's Line, crossing two branches, crossing the Road, corner in William Tuckers Line, crossing two Branches, Richard Farthings line, corner Hutchingses Line aforesaid, crossing the Rode
s/ Jesse Robinson
Wit: William Porter, John Dyer, Henry Shackleford, Susanna Porter
Feby 17, 1784

Page 191
Watlington from Vaughan Deed
December 20, 1783 between William Vaughan of the county of Halifax and John Watlington of P for 300 pounds, a parcel of land on both sides of both forks of allins Creek containing by Estimation 300 acres

Bounded: Joseph Farris's Line to head of his Spring Branch and Down the Stream as it meanders to the said fork of the said Creek & across running Still on Farrises line to where it Joins Col Morgan's Line, Benjamin Hendrick's Corner, said South fork of Allin's Creek, down said Creek on the Lines of the old Pattent granted to John Hamilton Augt 15, 1784, Joshua Stone's line, a new line Crossing the said Creek
s/ William Vaughan
Wit: John Buckley, Jas Buckley, Joshua Stone, James Buckley Senr
February 17, 1784

Page 193
Ulias from Dickinson Deed
Feby 17, 1783 between Noton Dickinson of P and Philip Ulias of the State of Pensylvania for 30 pounds, a parcel of land on the Branches of Bareskin Creek containing 104 acres
Bounded: Atkins Line on a Branch, Hughes line, crossing a Branch
s/ Noton Dickinson
Feby 17, 1784

Page 195
Barrey from Burton Deed
January 4, 1784 between Charles Burton of P and John Berrey for 30 pounds, a parcel of land on the Branches of Mountain Creek and the Branches of Sandy Creek of Dan River containing by affirmation 200 acres
Bounded: Corner in John Wilson's Line made by Bartholenimus Baker and James Brumfeald Senor, a new line, Thomas Billings old Line, Branch in Wilson's line,
s/ Charles Burton
Wit: None
Feby 17, 1784

Page 196
Tomlin from Burton Deed
January 8, 1784 between Charles Burton of P and Joseph Tomlin for 40 pounds, a parcel of land on the Dry fork of Sandy Creek of Dan River containing by affirmation 500 acres
Bounded: Clay's Order Line, Hall's line, Aston's line, crossing a Branch twice
s/ Charles Burton
Wit: None
Feby 17, 1784

Page 198
Burton from Rose Deed

January 10, 1784 between Frances Rose of P and Charles Burton for 25
pounds, a parcel of land on Sandy Creek of Dan River containing 50 acres
Bounded: the said Creek on the Bank of the said Creek, said Burton's line,
Clay's Order Line to head of a Branch
s/ Frances (X) Rose
Wit: None
Feby 17, 1784

Page 199
Wyer from Burton Deed
January 5, 1784 between Charles Burton of P and John Wyer for 50
pounds, a parcel of land on the Branches of Sandy Creek of Dan River
containing by affirmation 300 acres
Bounded: Billing's old line, a new Line, Wilson's line, the old road to the
Rocke Branch, down said Branch, near the mouth of the said Branch made
by the said Burton and Wyir , said Burton's old line
s/ Charles Burton
Wit: None
Feby 17, 1784

Page 200
Rose from Burton Deed
January 10, 1784 between Charles Burton of P and Francis Rose for 5
pounds, a parcel of land on the Branches of Sandy Creek of Dan river
containing by affirmation 50 acres
Bounded: Corner made between Thomas Billings & Frances Rose, Rose's
old line
s/ Charles Burton
Wit: None
Feby 17, 1784

Page 201
Price from Burton Deed
January 15, 1784 between Charles Burton of P and William Price of
Louisa County for 1000 pounds, a parcel of land on the Dry fork of Sandy
Creek of Dan River containing 300 acres
Bounded: Crossing the said Branch and the Creek, Hughe's line, crossing
the said Creek to a corner in John Tomlin's Line, Hall's Line, a new line
Also one other Tract of Land on the Branch of Sandy River being 352
acres
Bounded: Evins Stokes Line, Robert's Line, said Burton's former Line,
crossing a Branch to a Corner near Piggs Road, Billings old Line
Also one other tract of Land on Both sides of Sandy Creek of Dan River
containing 600 acres

38

Bounded: Stokes Line, Rockey Branch near the mouth of the said Branch, Hughes and Wimbush Line, Crossing the Creek, crossing the Creek twice, Quinn line, main county Road, head of a Branch, Down said Creek and up the Creek, crossing the creek, Roses Line, Stokes line
s/ Charles Burton
Wit: None
Feby 17, 1784

Page 204
Worthy from Terry Deed
February 17, 1784 between Stephen Terry of P and Thomas Worthy of Virginia for 86 pounds, a parcel of Land containing 202 acres
Bounded: Banister river at colonel John Donelson's Corner, said Donelson's line, Banister River
s/ Stephen Terry
Wit: None
Feby 17, 1784

Page 205
White from Tanner Deed
February 12, 1784 between Joel Tanner Senr of the County of Amelia and Reubin White of P for 150 pounds, a parcel of land containing 150 acres on Johns run Being the same Land conveyed by Deed from the said White to the said Tanner 1782
Bounded: John Gwins patent Line, Johns Run, up the other side of the said Run, crossing the said run again, mouth of the said White's spring Branch
s/ Joel Tanner
Wit: Floyd tanner, Creed Tanner, Jeremiah Ellington
Feby 17, 1784

Page 207
Ross from Ward Deed
February 10, 1784 between Jeremiah Ward of P and David Ross of Chesterfield County for 100 pounds, a Tract of Land containing 200 acres, on the south side of Pigg River
Bounded: said Jeremiah Ward's lines, by Pigg river, by Jacob Barger's Lines and by said David Ross Lines
s/ Jeremiah Ward
Wit: James Mitchell, Jesse Duncan, George Herndon
Feby 17, 1784

Page 208
Seal from Ayres Deed

December 3, 1783 between Moses Ayers and James Seals for 60 pounds, a parcel of land on the Branches of Sandy Creek containing 304 acres
Bounded: James Woody's Line, Harrison's Line, Tunus Coles Senr Line, Hardy's line, Tunis Coles Line, Wynne's Line, Hammock's line, Durrot's line
s/ Moses Ayres
Wit: Pertin (X) Morton, William (X) Maary, Solomon (X) Seal, William Combs
Feby 17, 1784

Page 209
Samuel from Glaspey
February 16, 1784 between James Glaspey of Caswell County, North Carolina and Edmond Samuel of same county for 60 pounds, a parcel of land on the Waters of Dan river containing by survey 400 acres
Bounded: John Owen's corner, crossing two branches, William Thomases line, John Owen's line
s/ James Gillasby
Wit: Wm Dix, Jas Benton, Joseph Fargerson
Feby 17, 1784

Page 210
Adams from Rose Deed
February 17, 1784 between Francis Rose of P and Sylvester Adams for 50 pounds, a parcel of land containing 40 acres which the said Rose purchased of Charles Burton together with the Land and Plantation that the said Rose now lives upon containing 100 acres
Bounded: South side of Sandy Creek, down the Creek unto Thomas Drake's line
s/ Francis Rose
Wit: None
Feby 17, 1784

Page 211
Ward from Kreek Deed of Trust
I Killian Kreek of P being indebted to Jeremiah Ward in the sum of 34 pounds and being desirous to Secure the payment of the debt and for the further consideration of five shillings have sold unto Jeremiah Ward a certain parcel of land on both sides of Pigg River Road containing 400 acres
Bounded: Bowker Smith's Land, Harmon Cook's Land, John Watson's Land, David Dalton's land, Brian Ward Nowlin's land & by William Thompson's Land
s/ Killian Kreey?

40

Wit: James Mitchell, Benja Tarrant, Peyton Wade, John (X) Keesee
Feby 17, 1784

Page 213
Epperson from Hendrick Deed
February 17, 1784 between Benjamin Hendrick & Judith, his wife, of P
and William Epperson of P for 100 pounds, a parcel of land on the north
side of Banister River containing by Estimation 100 acres
Bounded: John Watlington's corner, south fork of Allins Creek, Joshua
Short's line, Banister River, and down said river as it meanders to the
mouth of Allins Creek and up the said Creek as it meanders to the fork, up
south fork of said Creek
s/ Benjamin Hendrick
Wit: None
Feby 17, 1784

Page 214
Adams from Conn Deed
January 12, 1784 between Joseph Conn of P and Silvester Adams for 100
pounds, a parcel of l and on Waters of Cascade Creek
Bounded: Morgan's Corner, Beach on a creek, crossing four branches,
Hampton's line, Morgan and Hampton's corner
s/ Jo Conn
Wit: Wm White, Simon Adams, John ross, John Conn
Feby 17, 1784

Page 216
Baker from Caldwill Deed
February 18, 1784 between James Caldwell of P and James Baker of P for
200 pounds, a parcel of land containing 300 acres
Bounded: west side of the Creek, crossing the creek
s/ Jas Caldwell
Wit: None
Feby 17, 1784
Jeane, wife of James Caldwell, relinquished her right of dower

Page 217
Atkins from Duncan Deed
December 16, 1783 between Benjamin Duncan of P and Joseph Atkins of
P for 80 pounds, a parcel of land, it being part of the Tract of Land which
William Neeley now lives on, on Tomahawk Creek
Bounded: across from said Creek from George Smith's line, said Smith's
outward line, which is the lower part of said Smiths Tract and bounded by
said Neeley's Pattant which from the said Cross Line which is part of 200

41

acres which was obtained from Colo John Chiswell and conveyed by Deed
by Record shall appear containing 100 acres
s/ Benjamin Duncan
Wit: None
Feby 17, 1784

Page 219
Keezee from Stone Deed
January 14, 1784 betrween Joshua Stone of P and Jeremiah Keesee of P for
20 pounds, a parcel of land on both sides of Panther Creek containing by
Estimation 260 acres granted to the said Joshua Stone September 1782
Bounded: John Payne's line, new lines, crossing the creek, Wades line,
Dodd's path
s/ Joshua Stone
Wit: None
Feby 17, 1784

Page 221
Humphrey from Wynn Power of Attorney
I John Wynne of the County of Lincoln, North Carolina do appoint George
Humphrey of Caswell County, North Carolina my true and lawful attorney
to act for me & in my behalf to demand and Recover a Certain Negro Boy
Named George which said Boy was given me by my grand Father William
Wynne which said Negro Boy was sold by the Sheriff of P by Virtue of an
attachment of one Sylvester Adams to Capt John Pigg   January 1, 1784
s/ John (X) Wynne
Wit: Thos Tiffin, Jacob Stillwell, Nance Stillwell
Feby 17, 1784

Page 222
Barr from Fulton Deed
March 15, 1784 between John Fulton of P and the Reverend David Barr,
his Son in Law in consideration of the natural love and affection which he
the said John Fulton hath unto said David Barr, a parcel of land containing
248 acres on both sides of little Stuarts Creek of Sandy River
Bounded: James Booze's line, Frances Mabary's Corner, crossing two
Branches, Booze's line, crossing the said creek
s/ John Fulton
Wit: None
March 15, 1784

Page 224
Parish from Pigg Deed

March 1, 1784 between Wm Pigg and Abrahm Parish of the county of
Flewanah? in consideration of six Negroes, a parcel of land containing 360
acres on both sides of Bare Skin Creek
s/ William Pigg, Molley (X) Pigg
Wit: John Bailey, Stout Brinson, Allin (X) Adams
March 15, 1784
Mary, wife of said William Pigg relinquished her right of Dower

Page 225
Kay from Stone Dedimus
To Stephen Coleman and David Hunt, Gent or any two Justices of P,
whereas Joshua Stone hath conveyed to Henry Kay a parcel of land
containing 300 acres, and whereas Mary the wife of the said Joshua Stone
cannot conveniently travel to the County Court, Know ye that we trusting
to your faithful and provident circumspection in examining Mary apart
from her husband whether she does freely relinquish her right of Dower.
January 19, 1783
s/ Will Tunstall
By Virtue of the above Dedimus to us directed we have examined Mary,
the wife of the said Joshua Stone and she relinquished her right of Dower
February 25, 1784
s/ Stephen Coleman, D Hunt
Wit: None
March 15, 1784

Page 226
Stockton from Oliver Bill of Sale
I William Oliver of P have sold and delivered unto John Stockton of P for
100 pounds the following articles: (Viz) Six head of Neat Cattle, three
cows, one yearling, two claves, thirty head of Hogs, three head of hoarse
biast beads and furniture, two chests, one pot and dutch oven, one long
Iron and hXXX swin head of sheep, one Rifle gun, two puter dishes, four
Basons, twelve plates, six spoons, one cutting nife and Steel one guilted
Trunk, twenty barrels of corn   October 3, 1783
s/ William (X) Oliver
Wit: Aaron Mackenzie, John Muse
March 15, 1784

Page 227
Atkins from Hopper Deed
March 15, 1784 between Luther Hopper of P and Jesse Atkins of P for 30
pounds, a parcel of land on the Waters of Bareskin Creek & bounded by
the meadow fork of Said Creek on the East side and a line made by Owen

Atkins on the west side containing 30 acres, it being all that the said
Hopper ever claimed on the west side of said Creek
s/ Luther Hopper
Wit: None
March 15, 1784

Page 228
Young from Farrar Deed
October 1, 1783 between Raynard Farrar, Executor of the Last Will &
Testament of Shadrick Farrar, Dec'd, Elizabeth Farrar & Seth Farrar of P
and John Young of P for 200 pounds, a parcel of land containing by
Estimation 200 pounds
Bounded: Lansford's corner, crossing sandy River, Gray's line, Lansford's
corner, crossing the creek
s/ Raynard (X) Farrow, Elizabeth (X) Farrow, Seth (X) Farrow
Wit: John Tarrant, Rich'd Farrar, George Young, Stephen (X) Farrow
March 15, 1784

Page 229
Callaway from Callaway Deed
June 5, 1783 between John Callaway and Agatha, his wife of Campbell
County and Charles Callaway of the county of Beadford for 5000 pounds,
a parcel of land containing 394 acres on the south side of Stanton River
s/ John Callaway, Agatha Callaway
Wit: Haynes Morgan, Harry Innes, John Ramcy
March 15, 1784

Page 231
Shelton from Shelton Deed of Gift
December 29, 1783 between Daniel Shelton of P and Leroy Shelton of P
for the love and affection he bears to the said Leroy and the sum of 100
pounds, three Negroes, to wit, Randolph, Luchy and Janey, Silvar and their
future increase, a gray mare, a Black Mare and ten head of neat cattle, nine
head of sheep, twin head of Hogs and the other half of the said Daniel's
House hold furniture
s/ Daniel Shelton
Wit: None
March 15, 1784

Page 232
Shelton from Shelton Deed of Gift
December 29, 1783 between Daniel Shelton of P and Young Shelton of P
for love and affection he bears to the said Young and 100 pounds, three
Negroes, to wit, Bobb, Easther, and Isaac, also a Black mare & colt, Bay

horse, ten head of neat cattle, nine head of Sheep, 20 head of hogs, and half the said Daniel's Household furniture of all sorts
s/ Daniel Shelton
Wit: None
March 15, 1784

Page 233
Mackley from Holland Deed
September 20, 1783 between Benjamin Holland of the county of Montgomery and Thomas Shockley of P for 50 pounds, a parcel of land on Sycamore Creek running each side of Sycamore Creek and bounded by Wm Evins and Joshua Abston's lines, then along the old survey
s/ Benjamin (X) Holland
Wit: James (X) Doss, John Doss, James (X) Flanagan, Joshua Abston
March 15, 1784

Page 234
Mann from Slayton Deed
March 27, 1784 between Daniel Slayden of P and Jesse Mann of P for 50 pounds, containing 150 acres by estimation on the waters of the lower double creek
s/ Daniel Slaton
Wit: George Dodson, Thomas Chalton, Charles Collie, William Slayden
April 19, 1784

Page 236
Shelton from Shelton Deed
April 2, 1784 between Armistead Shelton of P and Thomas Shelton of P for 50 pounds, a parcel of land being the greater part of a tract the said Armistead Shelton purchased of George Parsons containing 265 acres Bounded: Richard Parson's line, Samuel Parsons line, Richard Farthing's line, Jonathan Griffith's line, Curry's order line, William Parson's corner, said William Parsons new line
s/ Armistead Shelton
Wit: None
April 19, 1784

Page 237
Murray from Martin Deed
April 17, 1784 between Peter Martin of P and William Murray of P in consideration of the said William Murray having served a tour of eight months in the militia service in the room of the said Peter Martin, a parcel of land containing 165 acres adjoining to the land whereon the said Peter Martin now lives on the waters of Sandy Creek and of the double Creek

45

and joining to Thomas Wynn, Robert Scott, Zachariah Seal and Nathaniel Murray's and Sarah Dupee's lands
s/ Peter (X) Martin
Wit: Wm Dix, Nathaniel Murray, Wm Durrett, Wm Richardson
April 19, 1784

Page 238
Colley from Slayton Deed
March 27, 1784 between Daniel Slayden of P and Charles Colley of P for 50 pounds, a parcel of land containing 100 acres by estimation on the Waters of the lower double creek
Bounded: said Daniel Slayden's line
s/ Daniel Slaten
Wit: George Dodson, Thomas Chelton, William Slayden, Jesse Mann
April 19, 1784

Page 240
Slaton from Slaton Deed
March 27, 1784 between Daniel Slayden of P and William Slayden of P for 50 pounds, a parcel of land containing 150 acres by Estimation
Bounded: said Daniel Slayden's line
s/ Daniel Slaten
Wit: George Dodson, Thomas Chelton, Charles Collie, Jesse Mann
April 19, 1784

Page 242
Flippin from Seal Deed
April 17, 1784 between Solomon Seal of Hallifax County and Joseph Flippin of P for 20 pounds, a parcel of land containing by estimation 100 acres
Bounded: Weatherford's order line, Anna Daniel's line, Absolom Hendrick's line, to the lands the said Flippin now lives on and adjoining the same
s/ Solomon (X) Seal
Wit: Wm White, Wm Durett, Peter (X) Martin, Robert Walters
April 19, 1784

Page 244
Holloway from Martin Deed
April 19, 1784 between Peter Martin of P and James Holloway of P for 38 pounds, a parcel of land containing 150 acres on Kane Creek of Dan river
Bounded: John Waller's line, Weatherford's order line, wolf hole branch
s/ Peter (X) Martin
Wit: None

April 19, 1784

Page 246
Madding from Hall &c
December 23, 1783 between John Hall and James McMurdey of P and
Robert Mading of P for 100 pounds, a parcel of land containing 100 acres
by estimation on the waters of the double creeks and birches creek
Bounded: John Bennett's corner, Stampses line, Hardies line, Madings
line
s/ John Hall, James (X) McMurday
Wit: Geo Dodson, William Mading, Rotherick McDaniel
April 19, 1784

Page 248
Elliott from McColough Deed
January 28, 1781 between Barnett McColough of P and Richard Elliott for
60 pounds, a parcel of land containing 324 on the branches of Sandy river
Bounded: James Fulton's line
s/ Barnett McColough
Wit: none
April 19, 1784

Page 249
Oakes from Orr Deed
March 15, 1784 between Robert Orr of P and Daniel Oakes of P for 40
pounds, a parcel of land on both sides of tomahawk creek containing 228
acres
Bounded: James Smith's corner, Chessel's old line
s/ Robert Orr, Jean (X) Orr
Wit: None
April 19, 1784
Jane, wife of said Robert Orr, relinquished her right of Dower

Page 251
Thomas from Owen Deed
April 12, 1784 between William Owen of P and Asa Thomas of P for 50
pounds, a parcel of land containing 200 acres
Bounded: John Lewises line, James Graspy's line, Aryres's line
s/ William (X) Owen
Wit: Benjamin Thrasher, Peyton Thomas, John Thomas
April 19, 1784

Page 253
Herndon from Atkinson Deed

October 22, 1774 between William Atkinson Senr of P and George
Herndon of P for 80 pounds, a parcel of land containing 50 acres on the
north side of Pigg river
Bounded: said Atkinson's line, Zacheous Dosses line, Pigg River to
Daniel Witcher's fish trap up the river
s/ Will (X) Atkinson, Sarah (X) Atkinson
Wit: Henry Atkinson, George Peak, John Peak
April 17, 1784

Page 255
Mchaney from Pryor &c
December 11, 1783 between Edward Pryor and Mary Pryor, his wife, of P
and Cornelius Mchaney of P for 130 pounds, a parcel of land on little
straight stone creek containing 150 acres
Bounded: Edward Burton's, Thomas Davis's, and the said Cornelius
Mchaney's lines
s/ Edward (X) Pryor, Mary Pryor
Wit: Will Todd, D Hunt, John Buckley
April 19, 1784

Page 257
Nash from Barksdale Deed
April 16, 1784 between Beverly Barksdale of P and John Nash of P for 35
pounds, a parcel of land containing 55 ½ acres
Bounded: Justises spring branch, line between said Barksdale and Wm
Martin crossing said branch, Justis spring branch
s/ Beverley Barksdale
Wit: Wm Walrond, Joseph Terry, Joab Meadows
April 19, 1784

Page 258
Thomas from Thomas Deed of Gift
April 17, 1784 between William Thomas of P and Nathaniel Thomas of P
in consideration of the love and affection which he has for the aforesaid
Nath'l Thomas hath given to said Nath'l Thomas a parcel of land
containing 216 acres
Bounded: Byrd's corner on the county line, County line,
Also one other tract adjoining the first & on the branches of dan river
Bounded: James Glasby's corner, said Thomas line, Cargill's line,
crossing a branch to a corner on a branch, Jno Owens line, James Glasby's
line containing by patent dated March 22, 1775, 320 acres
Also one other tract joining the two others being the land purchased of
Samuel Harris containing 112 acres lying on Cane Creek the couresas by
reference to Halifax records will fully appear

s/ Wm Thomas
Wit: None
April 19, 1784

Page 260
Smith from Smith Deed
April 20, 1784 between John Smith of P and Drury Smith of P for 100
pounds, a parcel of land on both sides of Sandy River on Crooked Creek
Bounded: Clouds and Wallens corner, crossing two forks of Sandy river
including 400 acres beginning at Yarington's corner, hickies road, John
Morton's line, Yarington's line including 104 acres
s/ Jno Smith
Wit: Wm Harrison
April 19, 1784

Page 262
Richards from Stokes Deed
May 15, 1784 between Silvanus Stokes & Christopher Hutchings of P and
Joseph Richards of P for 5 shillings, a parcel of land whereon the said
Richards now lives containing 150 acres on both sides of white oak creek
Bounded: Stokeses & Hutchings back line, new line, crossing the creek,
Ragsdale's field
s/ Silv's Stokes, Christopher Hutchings
Wit: Allin Stokes, John Ragsdale, James Hutchings, Silv's Stokes
May 17, 1784

Page 263
Pigg from Lawson Deed
April 7, 1784 between Jonas Lawson of P and Mary, his wife and
Hezekiah Pigg of P for 120 pounds, a parcel of land containing by
estimation 399 acres lying on both sides of white oak creek
Bounded: Paynes line, head of Charleses Spring branch, Stokeses line
s/ Jonas Lawson
Wit: Wm Short, David Hodges, John Adams
May 17, 1784

Page 265
Miller from Ragsdale Deed
May 14, 1784 between John Miller of P and William Ragsdale of the
county of Halifax, Virginia for 100 pounds, a parcel of land on elkhorn
creek containing by estimation 171 acres
Bounded: Farmers & Rosses corner, Rosses line, Dudgeon's corner,
Ellington's line, Yates's line, Farmer's corner
s/ William (X) Ragsdale

49

Wit: Rawley White, Jno Justiss, James Farmer
May 17, 1784

Page 266
Carter from Kirby Deed
May 15, 1784 between Henry Kirby of P and Theoderick Carter of Halifax
County for 30 pounds, a parcel of land on the waters of Sandy Creek
containing by estimation 220 acres
Bounded: by the lines of Thomas Burgess, Robert Williams, William
Price, and the said Theo Carter
s/ Henry Kirby
Wit: None
May 17, 1784

Page 267
Adams from Hardin Deed
May 17, 1784 between Mark Hardin and Thomas Adams of P for 40
pounds, a parcel of land containing 150 acres on the branches of Johns Run
and Short's Creek
Bounded: Line of the Patent on a branch, down said branch crossing Johns
run and the road both at one place, up to the mountain a straight line to the
back line of the patent, near Dennys fence, down the mountain, along the
mountain towards Dennys, down the mountain to the said old path, to a
branch near Dennys fence, down the said branch to the mouth crossing
John Run to the line of the patent, road
s/ Mark Hardin
Wit: Jno Corbin, Moses (X) Childriss, William Corbin
May 17, 1784

Page 269
Cook from Brewer Deed
May 17, 1784 Between James Brewer of P and Harmon Cook of P for 30
pounds, a parcel of land containing 373 acres on both sides of bold branch
of Cherry stone creek
Bounded: William Wright's corner, William Wright's line, John Swinny's
corner, John Swinny's line, Taylor's line, crossing the aforesaid branch
s/ James Brewer
Wit: None
May 17, 1784

Page 271
Ellington from Ellington Deed

May 17, 1784 between Enoch Ward Ellington of P and Jeremiah Ellington of P for 200 pounds, a parcel of land on the branches of Sandy Creek containing by estimation 430 acres
Bounded: Dudgeon's corner in Ellington's line, Dudgeon's line, Joseph Motley's line, crossing a branch to a beach on a bold branch, Webb Kidd's line, crossing several branches, Tucker Woodson's line, John Yates's corner, John Yates's line, William Ragsdale's line, head of a branch, down the said branch, Ragsdale's new line, Dudgeon's line aforesaid
s/ Enoch W Ellington
Wit: None
May 17, 1784

Page 273
Johns from Stockton Deed
April 20, 1784 between John Stockton of P and Thomas Johns of P for 350 pounds, two parcels of land on the branches of Sandy river, one parcel being a certain remainers of 455 acres of land surveyed for Thos Harget which land is divided between Jacob Clevland and the said Thomas Johns by a nominal line concluded upon by the contracting parties of which the said Johns is computed to hold 200 acres, the other parcel of land is a certain parcel of land that was conveyed by John Cox unto Thos Harget by Indenture June 23, 1769, the quantity of land being 400 acres by that Indenture of which said Johns has the whole excepting a mority of the same of 45 acres that said Harget conveyed to Joseph Balinger by Indenture
s/ John Stockton
Wit: None
May 17, 1784

Page 274
Keatts from Greggory Deed of Gift
I, William Gregory of P, for divers consideration and good causes to me known, do hereby relinquish to John Keatts a Negro Man Slave named Timmy who the said John Keatts holds in possession in right of his Wife, my Mother, being part the estate of my deceased Father. And also in like manner I do relinquish all my rights or claim to a certain Negro woman named Lucy and her former increase, to wit, Essez, Lucy, Phillis & Tener
October 4, 1783
s/ William Greggory
Wit: Wm Keatt, Mary (X) Keatt, Tavinor Shelton, Isaac Motley
May 17, 1784

Page 275
Coleman from Whitworth Deed

51

February 5, 1784 between Jacob Whitwith of P and William Coleman of P
for 50 pounds, a parcel of land between The Waters of Sandy River &
Sandy Creek bounded on the South by Southerland's line, on the west
Gwin's line, on the north by Clay's line containing 50 acres being the said
land Jacob Whitwith's formly lived on
s/ Jacob (X) Whitwith
Wit: None
May 17, 1784
Susanna, wife of said Jacob Whitworth, relinquished her right of Dower

Page 276
Burch from Clements Deed
November 17, 1783 between John Clements & Hanna, his wife, of P and
Henry Burch of Henry County, Virginia for 250 pounds, a parcel of land
containing by estimation 533 acres on both sides of the north & south forks
of Sycamore Creek
Bounded: James Callaway's corner, a new line, along the old line,
crossing two branches, crossing the south fork, crossing Sycamore Creek
just below the fork
s/ John Clement
Wit: John Martin, Joel Short, Moses (X) Childres, Joseph (X) Hancok
May 17, 1784

Page 279
Thomas from Meriwether Bill of Sale
I, Thomas Meriwiather of Hallifax County, Virginia in consideration of
130 pounds paid by William Thomas Senr of P do deliver to him one
Negroe Slave named Abraham
s/ Thos Meriwether
Wit: Wm Thomas, Asa Thomas
May 17, 1784

Page 280
Miller from Hundley Deed
June 21, 1784 between Caleb Hundley of P and Henry Miller of P for 9
pounds, a parcel of land containing 200 acres lying on the branches of
bares creek
s/ Caleb Hundley
Wit: None
June 21, 1784

Page 281
Briscoe from Harris Deed

January 8, 1784 between Peter Harris and Honour, his wife, of North Carolina and John Briscoe of Virginia for 250 pounds, a parcel of land on the north side of Caskade Creek and on a branch of said creek called Mountain Run and on one other branch of said creek called Cow Branch, it being part of a tract granted to Peter and Tyrey Harris by patent which part containeth 400 acres
Bounded: Carolina line, the Mountain Run, the Cow Branch, mouth of the same, Cascade Creek, Carolina line
s/ Peter Harris, Honour (X) Harris
Wit: Thos Henderson, T Coldwell
Sullivan County, North Carolina-We Thos Coldwell & Thos Henderson two Justices of the peace for Sullivan County, do certify to the Justices of the court of P that Peter Harris & Honour his wife signed & acknowledged the within Deed, and that Honour, wife of the said Peter, relinquished her right of Dower
January 8, 1784
s/ T Coldwell, Thos Henderson
June 21, 1784

Page 284
Doss from Bates Deed
June 21, 1784 between Daniel Bates of P and Thomas Doss of P for 50 pounds, a parcel of land on both sides of Hickies road containing by estimation 130 acres
Bounded: Payne's line, William Tucker's line, crossing the road, Benjamin Shelton's line, Richard Farthing's line, Christopher Hutchings line, crossing the said road again
s/ Daniel Bates
Wit: None
June 21, 1784

Page 285
Motley from Kidd Deed
May 17, 1784 between Webb Kidd of P and Joseph Motley of P for 20 pounds, a parcel of land on the south side of Eacolses fork containing 30 acres by estimation
Bounded: head of the bottom, new line, Motley's old line near Eacolses fork,
s/ Webb Kidd
Wit: None
June 21, 1784

Page 287
Tuggle from Robinson Power of Attorney

I, Alexander Robinson of the state of South Carolina of the District of
Camden for divers good causes do appoint my trusty friend Lodowick
Tuggle of P my true and lawfull Attorney to rent, sell or dispose of a
certain tract of land on Pigg River containing 322 acres to receive the rent
purchase money, to make a Deed of Conveyance and transact every thing
concerning the sale of the said land
s/ Alexander (X) Robinson
Wit: Thos Black, John Breden, Mary Black
June 21, 1784

Page 287
Thurston from Thurston Deed
March 19, 1784 between John Thurston of P and Plummer Thurston of
Campbell County for 100 pounds, a parcel of land containing 260 acres on
beach branch of Straitstone Creek
Bounded: Thomas Dillard's line now John Wards at a corner agreed on
between John Dillard and Thomas Dillard, a path that leads from said
Thomas Dillard's towards James Dosses thence with the said path as it
meanders to the said line mentioned in the patent for part of the said land
to Jno Dillard, said Dillard's line, Beach on a branch, fork called the
Musterfield fork
s/ John Thurston
Wit: W Pace, William Payne, Jos Crenshaw, Samuel Irby, Walter
Hutchingson
June 21, 1784

Page 289
Kidd from Motley Deed
May 17, 1784 between Joseph Motley of P and Web Kidd of P for 20
pounds, a parcel of land on the north side of the south branch of Eacols
fork containing by estimation 30 acres
Bounded: head of a bottom, said branch first mentioned, Thomas Tanner's
new line, said Motley's old line
s/ Joseph Motley
Wit: None
June 21, 1784

Page 291
Linthicum Jr from White Deed
December 13, 1783 between Daniel White of P and Thomas Linthicum
junr of P for 110 pounds, a parcel of land on Eacolses fork containing 260
acres
Bounded: Ellington's line, Woodson's line, Motley's line, Mabry's line,
Kidd's line

s/ Daniel White
Wit: Benjamin Terry, John Corbin, Webb Kidd
June 21, 1784

Page 292
Watkins from Flippin Deed
March 3, 1784 between John Watkins of P and Joseph Flippin of P for 50
pounds, a parcel of land containing **125** acres being part of a tract of land
whereon the said John Watkins now living.
Bounded: John Waller's line, Jonathan Hill's line and John Halls and so
on to the lines of the old tract
s/ Joseph Flippin
Wit: John Walters, Mordica Burgess, John Stamps
June 21, 1784

Page 293
Ward from Dalton Deed of Trust
I, Robert Dalton of P, being indebted to Jeremiah Ward of P for 45 pounds
and being desirous to secure the payment and for the further consideration
of five shillings, I do hereby acknowledge have sold unto the said Jeremiah
Ward three tracts of land containing by estimation 120 acres being the land
I bought of Soloman Dalton and part of another tract of which I sold the
said Ward a part and a tract of vacant land on which I have lad a warrant
and bounded by Pigg River, by James Mitchells and William Thompson's
lines
April 9, 1784
s/ Robert Dalton
Wit: Thomas Ward, John Bobbitt, Joseph (X) Polley, Wm Witcher
June 21, 1784

Page 295
Easley from Turner Deed
June 21, 1784 between John Turner of Henry County and William Easley
of P for 50 pounds, a parcel of land on Cherry Stone and Green Rock
Creek containing by estimation 300 acres
Bounded: great Cherrystone Creek in the said John Turner's old line, John
Watson's line, Turner's former line, crossing cherry Stone
s/ John Turner
Wit: None
June 21, 1784

Page 297
Cooke from Mitchell Deed

June 21, 1784 between James Cook of P and Harmon Cook of P for 30 pounds, a parcel of land on the branches of Harping Creek containing 294 acres
Bounded: Pigg river road, Harmon Cook's line, Shockley's line, Williams's line, Watson's line, Pigg River road
s/ James Mitchell
Wit: None
June 21, 1784

Page 298
Smith from Burton Deed
June 21, 1784 between Charles Burton of Louisa County, Virginia and Thomas Smith of P for 50 pounds, a parcel of land on the Branches of Sandy Creek containing 400 acres
Bounded: Little's corner, new line, crossing a branch, crossing three branches, Little's corner, Little's line
s/ Chas Burton
Wit: James Fulton, William Cunningham, Thomas Smith
June 21, 1784

Page 301
Adams from Ware Deed
March 10, 1784 between Edward Ware of P and Sylvester Adams of P for 50 pounds, a parcel of land containing 252 acres granted to the said Ware dated June 12, 1780 on the head branches of Sandy Creek
Bounded: John Anglin's Corner, crossing a bold branch, said John Anglin's line
s/ Edward (X) Ware
Wit: Simon Adams, John Elliot, Elizabeth Yates
July 19, 1784
Nancy, wife of said Edward Ware, relinquished her right of Dower

Page 302
Oakes from Bushby Deed
June 28, 1784 between William Bushby in the town of Alexandria, Virginia and James Oakes of P for 200 pounds, a parcel of land on the south side of dan river containing 404 acres
Bounded: County line crosses dan river, crossing green's creek five times, Yates' line, river aforesaid
s/ William Bushby
Wit: Sylvester Adams, William Summers, William Ross
July 19, 1784

Page 304

Adams from Ware Deed

March 10. 1784 between Edward Ware of P and Sylvester Adams of P for 100 pounds, a parcel of land containing 238 acres as by patent dated October 25, 1774 on both sides of the west fork of White Oak creek Bounded: James Lawson's corner, crossing the creek several times, Lawson's line
s/ Edward (X) Ware
Wit: Simon Adams, John Elliot, Elizabeth Yates
July 19, 1784
Nancy, wife of the said Edward Ware, relinquished her right of Dower

Page 306
Adams from Givins Deed

March 22, 1784 between Jno Givins of P and Syl Adams of P for 50 pounds, a parcel of land containing 150 acres whereon the said Givins now lives lying between the lines of William Sutton and the land formerly belonging to Jno Grissom joning Samuel Lewis & John Brawner
s/ John (X) Givins
Wit: Simon Adams, Edwin Hammonds, Drury Pulliam, William Ross, George Adams
July 19, 1784

Page 307
Adams from Pigg Deed

July 19, 1784 between Richard Pigg and Elizabeth, his Wife, of P and William Adams of P for 100 pounds, a parcel of land on the miery branch containing 100 acres and is part of the same land that was formerly assigned and laid off for Allen Adams by his Father, John Adams Bounded: Symmond's line on the east, Nathan Adam's line on the north, John Adams Senr line, John Adams junr's line
s/ Rich'd Pigg
Wit: None
July 19, 1784
Elizabeth, wife of said Richard Pigg, relinquished her right of Dower

Page 309
Davenport from Worsham Deed

April 6, 1784 between Jeremiah Worsham of P and William Devinport of the County of Cumberland for ten pounds, a parcel of land containing by estimation 72 acres
Bounded: on the great road side, crossing a branch, the great road that crosses Cherrystone Creek
s/ Jeremiah (X) Worsham
Wit: Jos Akin, Jos Morton, D Hunt

July 19, 1784

Page 310
Perkins from Hodges Power of Attorney
I, John Hodges of P, appoint Daniel Perkins of P my true and lawful
attornery to recover or receive any sums of money due to me in the state of
South Carolina, also to recover and obtain a right to a parcel of negroes &
household furniture and also a track of land and other property formerly
belonging to John Hodges, Deceased which I claim a right to being heir at
law to the said John Hodges, deceased and when recovered sell and
dispose of the same   July 19, 1784
s/ John Hodges
Wit: None
July 19, 1784

Page 312
Smith from Givins Deed
April 23, 1784 between Edward Givins of P and Hezekiah Smith for 100
pounds, a parcel of land on the south side of Sandy river containing by
estimation 296 acres
Bounded: Watson's line, branch, new line, the river, Merick's line
s/ Edward Givan
Wit: Robt Astin, Jacob Dotson, Benjamin White
July 19, 1784

Page 313
Pigg from Short Dedimus
To John Salmon, George Wallin & John Rentfro, Gent , or any two
Justices of the county of Henry, whereas James Pigg hath conveyed unto
John Short of Henry county a parcel of land containing 186 acres and
whereas Sarah, wife of said James, cannot conveniently travel to our
county court of P, we trusting to your faithfull provident circumspection in
examining Sarah apart from her husband whether she does freely
relinquish her right of Dower to the said land.   May 19, 1784
s/ Will Tunstall
By Virtue of the above dedimus to us directed we have examined Sarah,
wife of said James Pigg, and she relinquished her right of Dower
June 24, 1784
s/ Geo Waller, Jno Rentfroe
July 19, 1784

Page 314
Welch from Hall Deed

July 19, 1784 between Henry Hall of P and Joshua Welch of P for 60
pounds, a parcel of land containing by estimation 100 acres
Bounded: Jesse Carter's line, joining George Mierses line, order line
s/ Henry Hall
Wit: None
July 19, 1784

Page 316
Crenshaw from Pace Deed
July 19, 1784 between John Pace of Henry County and Joseph Crenshaw
of P for 100 pounds, a parcel of land containing by estimation 280 acres
lying on both sides of White thorn Creek and bounded by William Pace's
lines, Sterling Willis's line, Wm Paynes lines, Newsom Pace's lines &
Robert Boatman's line, it being the land conveyed from William Pace and
William Pain to the said John Pace
s/ Jno Pace
Wit: None
July 19, 1784
Elizabeth, wife of said John Pace, relinquished her right of Dower

Page 318
Miller from Gray Deed
July 15, 1784 between James Gray and Lucy, his wife and Beverly Miller
for 150 pounds, a parcel of land on the South side of Sandy Creek, partley
in the County P and partly in the County of Halifax containing by
estimation 480 acres
Bounded: Ingram's line, Fitzgarrald's line, Sandy Creek, mouth of the
Ditchers branch, up the branch as it meanders to Sloans corner, Solin's line
s/ James Gray, Lucy Gray
Wit: Wm Ryburn, Thos Beech, Mary (X) Ryburn
July 19, 1784
Lucy, wife of said James Gray, relinquished her right of Dower

Page 319
Keezee from Martin Deed
August 4, 1783 between Samuel Martin and Jeremiah Kezee, both of P, for
100 pounds, a parcel of land containing 400 acres on the waters of
Tomahawk creek
s/ Samuel Martin, Jan (X) Martin
Wit: Noton Dickinson, John Cook, John (X) Parsons
July 19, 1784

Page 322
Keeling from Childress Deed

59

December 13, 1783 between Armajah Childress of P and Leonard Keeling
of P for 40 pounds, a parcel of land on the branches of straight stone creek
containing by estimation108 acres
Bounded: Frances Luck's corner, Cornelius Mchaney's line
s/ Armajah (X) Childress
Wit: John Luck, James Baber, Wm (X) Pemberton
July 19, 1784

Page 323
Gray from Ryburn Deed
April 20, 1782 between William Ryburn and Mary his wife of P and James
Gray of P for 135 pounds, a parcel of land whereon the said William
Ryburn now lives, it being part of the tract of land given him by James
Henry with an addition purchased by said Ryburn of Nathaniel Dickerson
containing by estimation 480 acres
Bounded: Fitzgarrald's corner, Sandy Creek, mouth of ditchers branch,
John Sloan's corner, Ingram's line, Henry's order line, Fitzgarrel's line
s/ William Ryburn, Mary (X) Ryburn
Wit: Elijah King, Wyatt (X) King, John Sloan
July 19, 1784

Page 326
George from Johnson Deed
August 16, 1784 between James Johnson of P and John George of P for
250 pounds, a parcel of land containing 299 acres by estimation
Bounded: on the said John George's line, Joseph Farrisses line, James
Henderson's line, William Vason's line, Thomas Carter's line
s/ Jas Johnson
Wit: None
August 16, 1784
Letty, wife of said James Johnson, relinquished her right of Dower

Page 327
Walker from Mineus Deed
August 16, 1784 between Benjamin Menus of P and Elisha Walker of P for
350 pounds, a parcel of land containing 500 acres on both sides of
Turkycock Creek
s/ Benjamin Mences
Wit: None
August 16, 1784

Page 328
Callaway from Talbott Deed

August 14, 1784 between John Talbot and James Callaway for 60 pounds, a parcel of land containing 82 acres on the south side of Stanton river
s/ John Talbot
Wit: None
August 16, 1784

Page 330
Reynolds from Brewer Deed
August 7, 1784 between James Brewer of P and Joseph Rynolds of P for 40 pounds, a parcel of land on tomahawk Creek containing 240 acres
Bounded: Chisel's old line, Hugh Rynold's corner, crossing the creek, Chisel's old line, crossing buck horn branch to John Savory's corner, crossing the said creek
s/ James Brewer, Jemnenance Brewer
Wit: Robert Orr, Hugh Rynolds, John Stockton
August 16, 1784

Page 332
Beekells from Adams Deed
April 26, 1784 between Absolom Adams of P and Edmond Beekells of P for 40 pounds, a parcel of land containing by estimation 181 acres lying on the west side of the rockey branch
Bounded: Thos Hardy's corner, Donelson's line, new line, the rocky branch, Robert Adams line, Finney's order line, Thomas Hardey's line
s/ Absolon (X) Adams
Wit: Jesse Carter, James Craine, Thomas C Carter, Wm Allin
August 16, 1784

Page 333
Sheilds from Lewis Deed
March 20, 1783 between William Lewis of P and Pleasant Shealds for 50 pounds, a parcel of land on the waters of the upper double creek containing by estimation 230 acres
Bounded: on he east by the Lands of John Moore, Daniel Payne and James Grvce?, on the west by the lands of John Hall and Nimrod Scott, on the north by the lands of Jonathan Hill, south by the land of James Grover and the said William Lewis
s/ William (X) Lewis
Wit: Chs Kennon, Flm Bates, Benja Twedel, Wm Seal, Zacheous Seale, Jarrut Grace
August 19, 1783

Page 335
Mayes from Atkins Deed

August 16, 1784 between Richard Atkins of P and Elisabeth Mays of P for 30 pounds, a parcel of land on the waters of barskin Creek containing 50 acres
Bounded: branch above her plantation, down the branch, a new line to the Haystack branch as it meanders to the head, along a new line
s/ Rich'd Atkins
Wit: None
August 16, 1784

Page 336
Cook from Smith Deed
August 15, 1784 between George Smith of P and Harmon Cook of P for 100 pounds, a parcel of land on the branches of Harping Creek
s/ George Smith
Wit: None
August 16, 1784

Page 338
Hendrick from Thacker Deed
June 28, 1784 between Nathaniel Thacker and Cassy, his wife, of P and Obediah Hendricks of P for 30 pounds, a parcel of land containing by estimation 60 acres on the branches of Banister river
Bounded:Piggs road on William Davis's line, Nathaniel Thacker's line, Pigg's road
s/ Nathaniel Thacker, Cassy Thacker
Wit: Elisha Burton, Henry Hall, Joseph (X) Thacker
August 16, 1784
Cassy, wife of said Nathaniel Thacker, relinquished her right of Dower

Page 340
Hodnett's heirs from Hutchings Deed
September 25, 1782 between Thomas Hutchings of Lincoln county and the heirs of Harris Hodnett, deceased of P for 20 pounds, a parcel of land containing 356 acres
Bounded: King's line, to Wisdoms, to Terrys, White's lines
s/ Thomas Hutchings
Wit: Samuel Dillard, James Hutchings, Joseph (X) Jackson
August 16, 1784

Page 341
Youlace from Prosize Deed
July 26, 1784 between William Prosise of P and Philip Youlce of P for 30 pounds, a parcel of land containing by estimation 310 acres on both sides of bear skin Creek

Bounded: Richard Atkinson's corner, crossing a branch several times, said
Atkinson's corner
s/ Wilm Prosise
Wit: James Walker, James Hinson, Jonathan Griffe Junr, Irvin Yong?
August 16, 1784

Page 343
Henry from Shockley Deed
August 2, 1784 between Charlton Shockley of P and Francis Henry of P
for 30 pounds, a parcel of land containing by estimation 165 acres
Bounded: James Shockley's corner, crossing a branch, crossing turkey
cock creek, crossing a branch
s/ Charlton Shockley
Wit: Jno Bobbitt, Thomas Black, Lodock Tuggle
August 16, 1784

Page 346
Irby from Wilcox Deed
August 9, 1784 between George Wilcox of Lincoln County and Francis
Irby of P for 10 pounds, a parcel of land containing 149 acres of a tract
granted to the said George Wilcox wife by patent dated May 1, 1780 on the
branches of blow creek joining Thomas Vaughans & Thomas Farrises
lines
Bounded: Vaughan's corner in Farrises line, Vaughan's line, Anderson's
Line, Farrises line
s/ George Wilcox
Wit: Thomas Vaughan, David Irby, Peter Irby
August 16, 1784

Page 348
Glassco from Cheatham Deed
February 20, 1784 between Abia Cheatham and Frances his Wife of
Hallifax County and John Glasco of P for 200 pounds, a parcel of land on
the waters of fall creek
Bounded: Harris's and Clay's lines, Harris's line, Finns branch, Clay's
corner
s/ Abia Cheatham
Wit: Henry Mickelburrough, Abraham Pistole, Robert Glasco, Thos
Mown

Page 350
Johnson from Maples Deed

August 16, 1784 between William Maples of P and James Johnson of P for 100 pounds, a parcel of land on both sides the north fork of Cherry Stone Creek containing 163 acres
Bounded: Creek, Willisses corner, Willis dividing line, creek then up bar branch to the head, Bynum's corner, John Donelson's order line, creek
s/ William Maples
Wit: None
August 16, 1784

Page 351
Johnson from Watson & Hughs Deed
August 17, 1784 between John Watson Senr and Sam'l Hughes of P and James Johnson of P for 10 pounds, a parcel of land containing 43 ares
Bounded: George Curre's order line to the little branch, down little branch to my line, said Johnson's line
s/ John Watson
Wit: Rich'd Johnson, Gabriel Shelton, William Easley
August 17, 1784

Page 353
Brewer from Walker Deed
August 14, 1784 between Joseph Walker of P and James Brewer of P for 100 pounds, a parcel of land containing by estimation 500 acres on the waters of Turkey cock creek being part of Winsor Forrest which the said Joseph Walker purchased of John Philpott by a Deed dated December 17, 1782
Bounded: little round mountain in the old line, a new line, the old line
s/ Joseph (X) Walker
Wit: Sam'l Calland, Robert Orr, Peter Fields Jefferson
August 16, 1784

Page 355
Smith from Campbell Deed (*Deliv'd Jabez Smith Augt 1811*)
July 22, 1784 between William Campbell heir of Archibald Campbell, deceased of the County of Botteart and George Smith Of P for 40 pounds, a parcel of land on Tomahawk creek containing by estimation 168 acres which land was conveyed from Archibald Campbell to William Campbell by will
Bounded: Isaac Cloud's line, crossing two branches and a creek, a new line, said Cloud's upper line
s/ Wm Campbell
Wit: John Bobbitt, Benja Tarrant, Susanna Doss
August 16, 1784

Page 358
Ellington from Ellington Deed
August 16, 1784 between Jeremiah Ellington of P and Enoch Ward
Ellington of P for 200 pounds, a parcel of land on the branches of Elkhorn
Creek, it being the land the said Jeremiah Ellington bought of Thomas
Terrry containing by estimation 200 acres
Bounded: Atkinson's line, Stephen Coleman's line, Joseph Terry's line,
Atkinson's line
s/ Jeremiah Ellington
Wit: None
August 16, 1784

Page 360
Petty from Turner Deed
April 15, 1783 between Shadrick Turner of the County of Henry and
Frances Moor Petty for 5 shillings a part of larger tract of land the said
Shadrick Turner survaid on green rock creek of both sides of said creek
containing by estimation 162 acres
Bounded: Joseph Fargeson's new line, down the old line to Easley's new
line, crossing green rock
s/ Shadrick Turner
Wit: Jeremiah Worsham, William Parsons, Nathan Thurman
August 16, 1784

Page 361
Henderson from Tunstall Deed
August 16, 1784 between Thomas Tunstall of P and James Henderson of P
for 50 pounds which the said Thomas Tunstall is justly indebted to the said
Henderson. Said Tunstall hath sold one Negro man Slave named Peter to
Henderson
s/ T Tunstall
Wit: Rich'd Todd, William Henderson, John George
August 16, 1784

Page 363
Adams from McDaniel Deed
August 6, 1784 between Henry McDaniel of the County of Greenbrier and
John Adams of P for 160 pounds, a parcel of land containing 203 acres
Bounded: Corner between Rawley Corbin 7 the aforesaid John Adams Jr,
down dividing line, head of the Branch at the River
s/ Henry McDaniel
Wit: Rawley Corbin, Sarah (X) Corbin, Liney (X) Corbin, Molley (X)
Poor
October 18, 1784

65

Page 365
Pigg from Owen Deed
February 25, 1785 between William Owen and Edey, his wife, of P and
Hezekiah Pigg of P in consideration of a Certain Satisfaction made unto
said William Owen and his wife Edey, a parcel of land on both sides
Banister River containing by estimation 100 acres
Bounded: Little bear Skin, William Pigg's former corner, Jesse
Robinson's corner, new corner in John Pigg's old line of the mill Survey,
Jesse Robinson's corner, crossing the Mill Pond, south side of the Mill
Pond, Hezekiah Pigg's line, corner near Hezekiah Pigg's Spring, corner in
Bickums Line, Banister river, the old field, south side of Banister
s/ William Owen
Wit: None
Feby 21, 1785
Edey, wife of said William, relinquished her right of dower

Page 366
Robertson from Beale
October 18, 1784 between William Beale of P and Samuel Robertson of
the County of Halifax for 100 pounds, a parcel of land on the Banister
River containing by estimation 100 acres
Bounded: Glascock's line, the River
s/ William Beale
Wit: None
October 18, 1784
Ann, wife of said William Beale, relinquished her right of Dower

Page 367
Sawyers from Rogers
October 16, 1784 between Joseph Rogers of P and James Soyer of P for 30
pounds, a parcel of Land on the Waters of Fall Creek containing by
estimation 100 acres
Bounded: Donaldson's line (it being part of that Land), the old line
s/ Joseph Rogers
Wit: None
October 18, 1784

Page 367
Nelson from Rogers
October 16, 1784 between Joseph Rogers of P and William Nelson of
(Blank) for 30 pounds, a parcel of land on the Waters of Fall Creek
containing by estimation 100 acres
Bounded: Donaldson's line, new line

s/ Joseph Rogers
Wit: None
October 18, 1784

Page 368
Clever from Mays
April 26, 1784 between Joseph Mays Senior and John Clever for 150
pounds, a parcel of land containing 150 acres on Banister River on the
South side
Bounded: Henry Blank's corner on the river, Blank's Path, new line to
Worthy's line, the River
s/ Joseph Mays
Wit: Richard (X) Worthy, Fany (X) Roberts, Joseph Mays
October 18, 1784

Page 369
Chelton from Taylor
February 22, 1783 between William Taylor of the County of Guilford,
North Carolina and William Chelton of P for 50 pounds, a paracel of land
containing 200 acres by estimation on the Waters of Sandy Creek and
Birches Creek
Bounded: Thomas Chelton's corner, Thomas Terry's line
s/ William Taylor
Wit: Thomas Chelton, Thomas Lomax, William (X) Lomax
October 18, 1784

Page 370
Motley from Atkinson
October 13, 1783 between Roger Atkinson Esq of Dinwiddie County and
Joseph Motley of P for 60 pounds, a tract of land containing by Estimation
80 acres on the lower side Echolses fork
Bounded: said Motley's corner, Duging's line, said Motley's old line,
crossing a branch
s/ Roger Atkinson
Wit: Thos D Brown, Wm B Price, Mathew Farmer, John Buckley
October 18, 1784

Page 371
Linthicum from Mabry
May 4, 1784 between Braxton Mabry of P and Thomas Linthicom Senr of
P for 150 pounds, a parcel of land containing 306 acres on the branches of
Sandy and Shocko Creek

Bounded: Hugh Henry's former corner in a former line of David Walker, dec'd, along said Hugh Henry's line, Willias's line, David Gwin's former line, crossing a branch, the old line
s/ Braxton Mabry
Wit: Jere White, Thomas Linthicum jr, John White, Wm Clark
October 18, 1784

Page 372
Anderson from Turner
June 19, 1784 between Meshach Turner of P and Richard Anderson Senior of P for 1223 pounds, three certain tracts on both sides of Banister River and the mouth of Stinkin River containing 1223 acres as per patent including the plantation whereon I now live and my Mill
Bounded: South side of Banister River, new lines south, crossing the River, Canon's corner, Canon's line, Stinking River, Banister river, crossing River containing 354 acres including my Home Plantation and Mill.
Item of second tract which lyeth on South side of Banister is Bounded: Joseph Roger's corner on said River, Joseph Roger's line, Order Line, down a branch as it meanders to the Creek, , said Turner's line, River containing 557 acres as per Pattent will appear
Item of third tract of land containing 312 acres on the north branches of Banister River is Bounded: Bolton's corner, new lines, head of a small branch, Bolton's line
s/ Meshack Turner
Wit: J Preston, Moses Hendrick, James (X) Brewis
November 15, 1784

Page 374
Conway's Heirs from Terry
June 28, 1784 between James Conway, Son and heir of James Conway, deceased, late of P and Joseph Terry Senr of P for 80 pounds, a parcel of land containing 420 acres as by Grant under the Seal of this Commonwealth dated February 1, 1781
Bounded: said Terry's order line, crossing a branch, new lines south, Henry's Order line, Ingram's line, Lazarus Dodson's line, crossing three branches
s/ Joseph Terry
Wit: R Williams, Sarah Williams, Mary Williams
November 15, 1784

Page 375
Hendrick from Moore

May 30, 1784 between John Moore of Halifax County, Virginia and John H Hendrick of P for 40 pounds, a parcel of land containing 400 acres on Burches Creek, it being the Lands that my Father Hugh Moore had Granted him by Patent dated September 26, 1760, reference being thereunto had may more fully appear, it being the Lands my Father have to my Sister Ann Moore who intermarried with the said John H Hendrick
s/ John Moore
Wit: R Williams, Mary Williams, Sarah Williams
November 15, 1784

Page 376
Piat from Moore
October 29, 1784 between Jas Moore of P and Claude Piat of P for 20 pounds, a parcel of land on the head branches of allens Creek containing by Estimation 100 acres
Bounded: James Mackbee's line where it crosses Clements old road, Daniel Jenkins line, Thomas Vaughan's line, Chisum's line, crosses Clements old Road aforesaid, along the Road
s/ James (X) Moore
Wit: Joshua Stone, John George, Ben Bailey
November 15, 1784

Page 377
Marler from Madkiff
November 15, 1784 between Joseph Madkiff of P and Able Marler of P for 35 pounds, a parcel of land containing 100 acres on the Glady fork of White thorn Creek
Bounded: Branch that is Henry Pieron's line to mouth of said Branch, along the Glady fork of White thorn Creek to John Neel's line
s/ Joseph Madkiff
Wit: None
November 15, 1784

Page 378
Hill from Dodson
October 5, 1784 between George Dodson of P and Thomas Hill of P for 100 pounds, a parcel of land containing 250 acres by estimation
Bounded: John Mading's corner, crossing Jeremiah's fork in the head of a hollow
s/ George Dodson
Wit: Reubin Hill, Moses Hanks, Anne (X) Dodson,
November 15, 1784

Page 379

Bates from Farthing
November 15, 1784 between Richard Farthing of P and Daniel Bates of P
for 25 pounds, a parcel of land containing 40 acres on the Waters of Little
Cherry Stone Creek
Bounded: Personses line, Hoskinses new corner, up the Branch, Hoskins
line,
s/ Rich'd Farthing
Wit: None
November 15, 1784

Page 380
Willis from Maples
November 15, 1784 between William Maples of P and Major Willis of P
for 50 pounds, a tract of Land on both sides of the North fork of Great
Cherry Stone Creek containing by estimation 100 acres
Bounded: North side of the said creek, Hill's line, crossing the creek, new
lines south, Bynum's corner, head of Bas Branch, Cherry Stone Creek,
crossing the Creek
s/ William Maples
Wit: None
November 15, 1784
Prudence, wife of said William Maples, relinquished her right of Dower

Page 381
Madkiff from Buckner
August 15, 1784 between William Buckner of P and Joseph Madkiff of P
for 100 pounds, a parcel of land containing 100 acres being part of a
greater quantity that James Taylor bought of George Ridle
Bounded: Slone's branch on the East side of the Creek, crossing the creek,
new Road, back line
s/ William (X) Buckner
Wit: Francis Bucknall, Thomas Bucknall, John (X) Neck, Cha Rigney,
Stephen Yates, Arth'r Keesse
November 15, 1784

Page 382
Watson from Watson
I, John Watson Senr of P, in consideration of the love, good will and
affection which I have towards my loving Son, William Watson of P have
granted him a certain parcel of land containing by estimation 140 acres on
the South side of Cherrystone Creek
Bounded: the on the said Creek, up the Hill to Pigg's road, Francis
Polley's line, Josiah Farguson's line, Davenport's line, said creek, said
road again including all the Land on the South side of the said Creek

November 15, 1784
s/ John Watson
Wit: None
November 15, 1784

Page 382
White from Tucker
I, Robert Tucker of P, have made and appoint John White of P my true and Lawful Attorney to ask, demand, sue fro, levy, recover and receive all such Sums of Money, damages, Debts, rents, Negroes, Goods, Warrents, dues, Accounts whatsoever which are or shall be due, owing, payable to me
November 15, 1784
s/ Robert Tucker
Wit: None
November 15, 1784

Page 383
Barr from Fulton
October 22, 1784 between James Fulton of P and Rev'd David Barr of P for 50 pounds, a parcel of land containing by estimation 195 acres
Bounded: Thomas Harget's corner in Morton's line, new line, crossing two branches, Thomas Harget's line
s/ James Fulton, Martha (X) Fulton
Wit: John Fulton, Thomas Smith, Thos Robison
November 15, 1784

Page 384
Dyer from Henry
July 10, 1784 between Watson Henry of P and Joseph Dyer of P for 50 pounds, a parcel of land containing 380 acres
Bounded: John Pig's Road, new lines, Devan's corner, Twedwell's corner on Robin's Branch
s/ Watson Henry
Wit: John Dyer, Isaac Martin, Elizabeth (X) Martin
December 20, 1784

Page 386
Johnson from Doss Deed
September 20, 1784 between Thomas Doss of P and James Johnson of P for 30 pounds, a parcel of land on both sides of Hickies Roade containing by Estimation 130 acres
Bounded: Payne's line, William Tucker's line, crossing the Road, Benjamin Shelton's line, Richard Farthing's line, Christopher Hutching's corner

s/ Thomas (X) Doss
Wit: Richard Johnson, Tho Hoskins, Henry Easley
December 20, 1784

Page 387
Walters from Ayres Deed
October 24, 1784 between Thomas Ayres of Surry County, North Carolina
and Moses Ayres of P and John Walters of P for 100 pounds, a parcel of
land on the Waters of Dan River adjoining the Land of Benjamin Thrasher
and James Woody being formerly a part of the Land the said Woody now
lives on containing by Estimation 161 acres
s/ Thomas (X) Ayres, Moses Ayres
Wit: Eliher Ayres, William (X) Yourk
December 20, 1784

Page 387
Smith from Lawson Deed
September 3, 1784 between John Lawson and Delphey, his Wife, of P and
John Smith of Bedford County for 60 pounds, a parcel of land containing
277 acres
Bounded: Peter Bennet's line, crossing a Branch, the river, Peter Bennet's
line
s/ John (X) Lawson, Delphey (X) Lawson
Wit: John Roberson, Sam'l Smith, Sam'l Calland, Jas Johnson, Rich'd
Johnson
December 20, 1784

Page 389
Wilson from Anderson Deed
November 3, 1784 between Mathew Anderson of P and John Wilson of P
for 100 pounds, a parcel of land on the Branches of Burches Creek
containing by Estimation 356 acres
Bounded: William Walter's corner, crossing a branch and road, Thomas
Walter's corner, Robert Walter's corner, William Walter's line
s/ Mathew Anderson
Wit: None
January 17, 1785

Page 390
Warren from Livingston Deed
August 21, 1784 between Thomas Leventon and Margaret, his wife, of P
and Henry Warren of Henry County for 80 pounds, a parcel of land on the
Waters of Sandy River containing 747 acres
Bounded: Hankins line, Cleavelan's corner, said Hankins line

s/ Thomas Livingston, Margret (X) Livingston
Wit: Rozel Hill, John Warren, John Smith, John Livingston
January 17, 1785

Page 391
Davis from Hutchings
February 1, 1785 between Christopher Hutchings of P and Samuel Davis
of Cambell County for five shillings, a parcel of land being part of a Tract
once Deeded to Samuel Dillard containing by estimation 22 acres
Bounded: Chamberlin's corner, Johm Hutching's line, John Chattwin's
line, Eaklos line
s/ Christopher Hutchings
Wit: None
February 21, 1785

Page 392
Pierson from Jones Deed
September 2, 1784 between John Jones of Lincoln County and Richard
Pierson of P for 100 pounds, a parcel of land containing 200 acres
Bounded: Mouston's corner, lines of the former Survey, Read's corner, it
being part of 400 acres surveyed by my Father on the branches of Sandy
River
s/ John Jones
Wit: John Stockton, John Pigg, Absolam Crem
February 21, 1785

Page 394
Thomas from Samuel Dec'd Deed
February 21, 1785 between Edmund Samuel of Caswell County, North
Carolina and Jacob Thomas of P for 80 pounds, a parcel of land containing
400 acres lying on the Branches of Dan
Bounded: John Owen corner, Lewis's line, crossing two branches,
William Thomas's line, John Owen's line
s/ Edmund Samuel
Wit: None
February 21, 1785

Page 395
Pigg from Owen Deed
February 21, 1785 between William Owen of P and Hezekiah Pigg of P in
consideration of a certain satisfaction made unto them the day and date
above written by said Hezekiah Pigg doth hereby acknowledge and said
William Owen and his wife, Edey, hath granted unto said Hezekiah Pig a

73

parcel of land on both sides Bannister river containing by estimation 100 acres

Bounded: little Bare Skin, William Pigg's former corner, Jesse Robinson's corner, new corner in John Pigg's old line of the Mill Survey, said line to Jesse Robinson corner, crossing the Mill pond, south side of the mill pond , Hezekiah Pig line, corner near Hezekiah Pigg's Spring, said Pigg's line, corner in Bukkoms line, Bucomes line, Banister River, up said river, old fieald, new line including along he South side of Bannister to Gether with a certain Piece of Ground allowed for a Grave Yard between four corner Stones

s/ William Owen

Wit: None

(No recording date given)

Page 395

Gray from Barksdale Deed

Feby 16, 11785 between Beverley Barksdale and Ann, his wife, of P and James Gray of P for 200 pounds, a parcel of land containing by Estimation 265 acres

Bounded: John Wimbishes Corner, new line to Mans corner, Nashes corner, Justice's Spring branch, Wimbishes lines

s/ B Barksdale, Anne Barksdale

Wit: Wm Walrond, Joseph Terry, Joab Meadows

February 21, 1785

Page 396

Dalton for Dyer Deed

February 21, 1785 between John Dyer of P and James Dalton of P for 30 pounds, a parcel of land on both sides of Bearskin Creek being part of a greater Tract of 400 acres granted unto John Pigg and by the said Pigg conveyed the 100 acres of land to Daniel Mchensey by a Deed dated February 22, 1773 lying at the lower end of the said 400 acres

Bounded: runs with the said Patent North, across the whole original Tract, the great road, along the patent

s/ John Dyer

Wit: None

February 21, 1785

Page 397

Harrison from Harrison Deed of Gift

In consideration of divers good causes but more especially for the love and parental Affection I have and do bear towards my Son, Robert Harrison, I give unto him on parcel of land adjoining on the North side of Dan River containing by Estimation 500 acres

74

Bounded: River Bank, mouth of a branch, up the said Branch at the foot of the River Hills, Hardimans Corner on the top of the Hill, Hardimans lines, Bounded by William Harrison, William Wodlow, Jonathan Church and Nicholas Perkins to the River Bank at the said Perkins corner, down Dan River

Also I give unto the said Robert Harrison the following Slaves named Jack, Aggy, Tom, George, Mary and Sam   February 18, 1785

s/ Wm Harrison
Wit: None
February 21, 1785

Page 398
Barger from Payne Deed
July 19, 1784 between Ledford Payne of P and Jacob Barger of P for 500 pounds, a parcel of land where the said Jacob Barger now lives on Buck branch, a branch of the Frying Pan Creek on the south side of said Creek and joyning David Rosses and William Mitchell's lines containing 100 acres
s/ Ledford Payne
Wit: James Mitchell, Benj'a Henson, James (X) Henson
February 21, 1785

Page 398
Carter from Hutchings Dedimus
To William Short and John Parks, Gent or any two Justices of P, Whereas Christopher Hutchings hath conveyed unto Thomas Carter of P two parcel of land containing by Estimation 467 acres and whreas Elizabeth, wife of the said Christopher cannot conveniently travel to and from our said County Court of P, we trusting in your faithful and provident circumspection in Examining Elizabeth, the wife of said Christopher, apart from her said Husband whether she does voluntarily relinquish her right of Dower.
November 6, 1784
s/ Will Tunstall
By Virtue of the above Commission to us directed we have examined Elizabeth, wife of said Christopher Hutchings and she relinquished her right of Dower   February 4, 1785
s/ William Short, John Parks
February 21, 1785

Page 399
Watlington from Vaughan Dedimus

To James Bates and E Hunt and Edmund King, Gent or any two Justices of Halifax, Whereas William Vaughan hath conveyed unto John Wadlington of P a parcel of land containing by Estimation 300 acres and whereas Frances, wife of the said William Vaughan cannot conveniently travel to and from our said County Court of P, we trusting in your faithful and provident circumspection in Examining Frances, the wife of said William Vaughan, apart from her said Husband whether she does voluntarily relinquish her right of Dower.
June 24, 1784
s/ Will Tunstall
Halifax County
By Virtue of the above Dedimus to us directed we have examined Frances, wife of said William Vaughan and she relinquished her right of Dower
October 27, 1784
s/ Jas Bates, E Hunt
February 21, 1785

Page 400
Anderson from Turner Dedimus
To Stephen Coleman and Joshua Stone, Gent or any two Justices of P, Whereas Meshack Turner hath conveyed unto Richard Anderson of P a parcel of land containing by Estimation 1223 acres and whereas Rebecca, wife of the said Meshack Turner cannot conveniently travel to and from our said County Court of P, we trusting in your faithful and provident circumspection in Examining Rebecca, the wife of said Meshack apart from her said Husband whether she does voluntarily relinquish her right of Dower.
November 17, 1784
s/ Will Tunstall
By Virtue of the above Commission to us directed we have examined Rebecca, wife of said Meshack Turner and she relinquished her right of Dower   November 17, 1784
s/ Stephen Coleman, Joshua Stone
February 21, 1785

Page 401
Chelton from Jackson Deed
September 11, 1784 between Joseph Jackson of P and Mark Chilton of P for 200 pounds, a parcel of land containing 335 acres on two Branches of Sandy Creek of Banister River
Bounded: Isham Kennons former line now Colo Robert Williams's line, crossing both branches aforementioned, crossing two small branches
s/ Joseph (X) Jackson
Wit: John Wright, David Tanner, John Chelton

February 21, 1785

Page 402
White from Harden Deed
February 21, 1785 between Mark Hardin of P and Jeremiah White of P for
100 pounds, a parcel of land on the branches of Shoco Creek and Johns
Run of Sandy Creek containing 275 acres
Bounded: top of Banister Mountain, branch, crossing Johns Run and the
road, crossing Johns Run, branch of Shoco
s/ Mark Harden
Wit: Wm White, Simon Adams, George Wright
February 21, 1785
Hannah, wife of said Mark Harden, relinquished her right of dower

Page 403
Shelton from Innes Deed
February 22, 1785 between Hugh Innes of Henry County and Abraham
Shelton of P for 60 pounds, a parcel of land containing 400 acres on the
Waters of Stinking River (being part of a larger Tract Granted to the said
Hugh Innes by Patent dated August 3, 1771)
Bounded: Thomas Mustain's line, Peter Irby's line, Joel Shelton's line,
Benjamin Shelton's line, Thomas Davis's line, Benjamin Fambrough's line
to the said Thomas Mustain's line, it being the Tract of land whereon
Moses Hurt now lives
s/ Hugh Innes
Wit: None
February 22, 1785

Page 404
Witcher from Ward Deed
February 21, 1785 between Jeremiah Ward of P and William Witcher Senr
of P for 180 pounds, a parcel of land on both sides of Reddies Creek
containing 337 acres
Bounded: Bowker Smith's line, Watice branch, crossing Radys Creek,
Ridge path
s/ Jeremiah(X) Ward
Wit: None
February 21, 1785

Page 405
Tost from Barger Deed
February 16, 1785 between Jacob Barger of P and Jacob Tost of P for 300
pounds, a parcel of land on the Frying pan Creek containing by estimation
600 acres

Bounded: the old line by the old Cabbin, Robert Goad's line, a new line, crossing a branch to the old line, Jacob Bargers dividing line, the old line, Pigg River at Peyton Wade's Fish trap, river on Ross's line. the old line, crossing the Popplar branch, crossing the Mill path, crossing the road, crossing the road back, crossing the Mill path, the old line
s/ Jacob Barger
Wit: Thomas (X) Bennet, John Smith, Richard (X) Bennet
February 21, 1785

Page 406
Johnson from Johnson Deed of Gift
March 29, 1785 between James Johnson and Richard Johnson for the love and affection that he haith for his Son Richard Johnson do give to him a parcel of land containing 130 acres
Bounded: Benj'a Shelton's line, Christopher Hutchings line, William Parks line, Phillip Payne's line, William Tucker's line
s/ Jas Johnson
Wit: Hannah Hoskins, Wm Easley, Thos Hoskins, Jas Harkins
April 18, 1785

Page 407
Burgess from Jackson Deed
September 13, 1784 between Joseph Jackson of P and Thomas Burgess of P in consideration of value recev'd and paid by him said Burgess to Henry Kirby commonly called Hanover paid before the seeling and delivering, a parcel of land containing by estimation 224 acres on the South fork of Sandy Creek
Bounded: the Creek at Orlando Smith's line, the Order line, a new line to the old line of said Survey, old line, creek including the Plantation whereon the said Henry Kirby lived
s/ Joseph (X) Jackson
Wit: John Kearby, John Harvey, Henry (X) Kiarby
April 18, 1785

Page 408
The said Tucker Woodson for and in consideration of 50 pounds paid by the said Allen Woodson is hereby acknowledged and hath Granted unto the said Allen Woodson a parcel of landon both sides Elkhorn Creek containing by Estimation 100 acres
Bounded: road in the said Woodson's Patent line, new line, crossing the Creek, old Patent line, a branch, John Yates line, Jeremiah Ellington's line
s/ Tucker Woodson
Wit: None
April 18, 1785

Page 409
Tunstall from Mosely Deed
March 21, 1785 between William Tunstall of the County of Henry and
Sam'l Mosly of P for 150 pounds, a parcel of land lying on both sides of
the south fork of Sandy River being the land one Thomas Callaway
formerly lived upon containing by estimation 200 acres and bounded by
the lines of William Hewlet and Isbell Nash
s/ Sam'l Mosley
Wit: None
April 18, 1785

Page 409
Cook from Kreek Bill of Sale
I, William Creek of P, in consideration of the sum of 200 pounds paid by
Harman Cook, the receipt whereof I do hereby acknowledge sell unto the
said Harmon Cook all the Land I posses in P, a Waggon and six horses, all
my Cattle and all my other Estate real and personal. The Condition of the
above Bill of Sale is such that if the above Killian Creek shall pay to
Jeremiah Ward his bond 34 pounds for which the above Harmon Cook is
security on the first day of March 1786 then the above Bill of Sale to be
void, else to remain in full force   February 25, 1785
s/ Killian Creek
Wit: James Mitchell, John Cook, John Wright
April 18, 1785

Page 410
Thacker from Parsons Deed
November 1, 1784 between William Parsons of P and Joseph Thacker of P
for consideration of a Mare, a parcel of land containing 25 acres being a
tract of Land that said William Parson had of Armistead Shelton
Bounded: Richard Parson's line, a new line to a branch, Curry's Order
line, Richard Parsons former line
s/ William Parsons
Wit: None
April 18, 1785

Page 411
Walters from Mathews &c
November 20, 1784 between Chitester Matthews and James McMurdey of
P and Thomas Walters of P 100 pounds, a parcel of land containing 400
acres by Estimation
Bounded: said Thomas Walters corner, branch, a Beech
s/ Chichester Matthews, James McMurdey

79

Wit: Archer Walters, Samuel Walker, Obadiah Walters
April 18, 1785

Page 412
Isaac from White Deed
November 15, 1784 between John White of P and Jacob Isaac of P for 150
pounds, a parcel of land on the waters of Strawberry and Wetsleeve Creeks
containing by estimation 250 acres
Bounded: Richard Prewet's line, wetsleave Creek at a crossing place at the
mouth of a Branch, up the Creek as it meanders to the great bend, a new
line, his back line, said John Biswell's line, Richard Prewet's lines
Also one certain Tract of Land on the branches of Banister and bounded:
said White's line, William Devins line, crossing a little Creek, said Devins
line
s/ John White, Milley White
Wit: Thomas Johns, Joseph Austin, James Biggar, Joseph Morton
April 18, 1785

Page 413
Rieger from Webb Deed
August 15, 1783 between Martin Webb and his wife of P and Jacob Rieger
of P for 100 pounds, one certain parcel of land containing 200 acres on
both sides the Glaidy fork of Sandy River
Bounded: east side line, branch to Joseph Alsup's Spring, down the Spring
branch to the Glady fork, Garrenton's line,
s/ Martin Webb, Judith (X) Webb
Wit: John Morton, James Deer, Daniel Johnson, Joseph Allsup
April 18, 1785

Page 414
Kelly from Short Deed
April 18, 1785 between William Short of P and Jacob Kelley of Halifax
County for 350 pounds Gold or Silver Coin, a parcel of land on both sides
of Banister River containing by estimation 425 acres
Bounded: Elijah Beckums line, crossing the river, James Allin's line,
corner Beech on the great branch, John Chattens corner, Buckum's line
s/ William Short
Wit: None
April 18, 1785
Winefred, wife of said William Short, relinquished her right of Dower

Page 415
Wilson from Crowley Deed

80

November 3, 1784 between Benjamin Crowley of P and Peter Wilson of P
for 100 pounds, a parcel of land on both sides the South fork of Sandy
Creek containing 48 acres
Bounded: North side of the river, crossing a branch, crossing a small
branch to Henry Lansford's corner, crossing the river
s/ Benjamin (X) Crowley
Wit: Sillv Stokes, Hezekiah Smith, James Boaz, Robt Lumkin, Jno Wilson
April 18, 1785

Page 417
Adams from Hamblin Deed
October 15, 1784 between George Hamblin and Sylvester Adams of P for
100 pounds, a parcel of land containing by Estimation 300 acres
Bounded: Jonas Lawson's corner, crossing a branch, crossing the Creek
several times, Lawson's line aforesaid
s/ George (X) Hamblin
Wit: Daniel Tompkins, Dav'd Lay Senr, Thomas Whelan, Simon Adams,
Joab Hamblin
April 18, 1785

Page 418
Wilson from Crowley Deed
December 4, 1784 between Benjamin Crowley and Peter Wilson of P
receipt whereof he the said Benjamin Crowley doth hereby acknowledge,
one certain piece of land on both sides of the south fork of Sandy River
containing by Estimation 300 acres
Bounded: Thomas Gresham's corner, Gray's line, crossing the river,
Beach on the said river
s/ Benjamin (X) Crowley
Wit: Sillv Stokes, Hezekiah Smith, Robt Lumkin, James Boaz, Jno Wilson
April 18, 1785

Page 419
Clark from Shelton Deed
April 18, 1785 between Armisted Shelton of P and William Clark of P for
173 pounds, a parcel of land on both sides of Banister River containing 252
acres
Bounded: James Mades corner near Banister River, his line, William
Wright's line, Simmons line, Middle Creek, Rubin Payne's line, Banister
River, crossing the said river, Martain's line, dividing line between said
Shelton and Braxton Mabry, middle of Banister River
s/ Armistead Shelton
Wit: None
April 18, 1785

81

Susannah, wife of said Armistead, relinquished her right of Dower

Page 421
Mosely from Lansford Deed
April 18, 1784 between Isham Lansford, Executor of Henry Lansford, deceased and Samuel Moseley of P for 180 pounds, a parcel of land containing by estimation 263 acres, one acre excepted for a burying place, on both sides of the south fork of Sandy River
Bounded: George Young's line, Clay's Order, David Harris's line, John Cummings
s/ Isham Lansford
Wit: None
April 18, 1785

Page 421
Herring from Terry Deed
September 16, 1784 between Joseph Terry of P and William Herring of P for 600 pounds, a parcel of land on the Waters of Birches Creek containing 484 acres by estimation
Bounded: his corner in Moor's line, Chelton's line, John Prestidge's line, Joseph Terry's former line. a branch called Prestidges Branch, Joseph Terry's former line
s/ Joseph Terry
Wit: George Dodson, Forten Dodson, John H Hendrick, Lankford Herring
April 18, 1785

Page 423
Norton's emancip'd Negroes
I, Nehemiah Norton of P, being fully convinced of the inequity of keeping Negroes in a Slavish bondage do by these presents emancipate, discharge and give the following Negroes all the priviledges of the free Citizens of this State agreeable to an Act of Assembly in that case made and provided, there names are as followeth: Toney, Priss, Isaac, William, Shadrick, Sam, Mesheck, Janny   April 18, 1785
s/ Nehemiah Norton
Wit: None
April 18, 1785

Page 423
Jones from Stephens Deed
January 1, 1785 between Thomas Stephens of P and George Jones of P for 60 pounds, a parcel of land being the lower end of the Tract patten'd by Henry Lansford, deceased and sould to Charles Oakes and Oakes sould same Land to said Stephens containing 100 acres which was taken out of

the Survey formerly Granted to Henry Lansford now deceas'd of 404 acres and sould to Charles Oakes
Bounded: Lansford's lower corner where joyn'd by Southerland, crossing Cascade Creek, joining David Stephens
s/ Thomas (X) Stephens, Sarah (X) Stephens
Wit: Isaiah Watkins, Henry Lansford, David (X) Stephens, Isham Lansford
April 18, 1785

Page 424
Echols from Echols Deed
September 17, 1784 between Joseph Echols of Halifax County and Elkaner Echols of Halifax County for 500 pounds, a parcel of land on both sides of stinking River containing by estimation 400 acres
Bounded: crossing the river, crossing a branch of flyblow Creek, crossing the same branch and the river
s/ Jos Echols
Wit: Samuel Calland, Wm Short, Wm Wilkinson, Spenc'r Shelton
April 18, 1785

Page 426
Duff from Motley Deed
March 18, 1785 between Joseph Motley of P and Laurence Duff of P for 20 pounds, a parcel of land on the branches of Eacholus fork containing by estimation 50 acres
Bounded: side of the road, old pattern line, the road
s/ Joseph Motley
Wit: Reubin Pain, John Parks, John Adams
April 18, 1785

Page 426
Chelton from Creel Deed
November 22, 1784 between John Creel of P and John Chelton P for 50 pounds, a parcel of land containing 100 acres by estimation on the north side of Birches Creek
Bounded: bank of the said Creek, said Creel's line, side of a Mountain, near a road and near the edge of the said Creel's old field, bank of the south side of the said Creek
s/ John Creel
Wit: Thos Hill, James (X) Donelson, Samuel Morris
April 18, 1785

Page 428
Merrick from Givens Deed

1785 between Edward Givens of P and John Merrick of P for 20 pounds, a parcel of land containing 431 acres
Bounded: Wm Watson's line, crossing Stone's branch, south side of Sandy river, Shadrick Seace, Rocky Branch, Satel branch, Gamon's line
s/ Edward Given
April 18, 1785

Page 429
Slone from Wright Deed
September 20, 1784 between William Wright and Mary, his wife of P and James Slone of Bedford County for 100 pounds, a parcel of land containing 404 acres on both sides of rockey fork of Harping Creek
Bounded: Thomas Shockley's line near the said Rocky fork, crossing Rocky Fork, aforesaid Shockley's line
s/ William Wright, Mary Wright
Wit: Reubin Pain, James Made, Edmond Fitzherald, John Chattin, Dan'l Tompkins
April 18, 1785

Page 430
Lester from Bruas Deed
April 10, 1785 between James Bruas of P and William Lester of P for 50 pounds, a parcel of land on the Waters of Stinkin River and Sycamore containing by estimation 344 acres
Bounded: Charles Tolbart's line, Owen West's line, James Bruas's line, Tolbert's line, it being the Land formerly the property granted to Nathaniel Cock
s/ James Bruas
Wit: Moses Hurt, Frederick Shelton, Wm Herring
April 18, 1785

Page 431
Stonestreet from Vincent Deed
March 21, 1784 between Moses Vincent of P and Butler Edelen Stonestreet of P for 50 pounds, a parcel of land containing 159 acres granted to Moses Vincent by Patent dated March 13, 1777 on the Branches of Sandy river
Bounded: John Smith's line
s/ Moses Vincent
Wit: Elisha Thomas, Moses Vincent junr, Jesse (X) Vincent junr,
April 18, 1785

Page 432
Farmer from Robertson Deed

October 25, 2784 between Thomas Robertson and Margrett his wife and John Robertson and Stasee his wife of P and Thomas Farmer fo the County of Campbell for 165 pounds, a parcel of land containing 575 acres on both sides of Sycamore Creek and its branches
Bounded: William Mobly's line, Thomas Robertson's line, Mobley's line, Mobley's old line
s/ Thomas (X) Robertson, John Roberson, Margret (X) Robertson, Stasie (X) Robertson
Wit: Ra Smith, John Smith, John Baber, Walter Urquart
April 18, 1785

Page 434
Madding from McMurdy Deed
November 27, 1784 between James McMurdy of P and Champness Mading of P for 100 pounds, a parcel of land on the Waters of the lower Double Creek containing 84 acres
Bounded: Robert Mading's line, said McMurdy's line, said McMurdy's fence
s/ James (X) McMurdy
Wit: Geo Dodson, John Bennet, Jesse Bennet
April 18, 1785

Page 435
Laney from Simons Power of Att'o
We, John Simons and Jean, his wife of P do make our trusty friend William Laney of P our lawful Attorney to recover a tract of land in the County of Cumberland, state of Pensilvania that was given to my wife by her father, Joseph Laney
s/ John Simons, Jeane (X) Simons
Wit: Hezekiah Pigg. Jeremiah Eckhols, Hezekiah Pigg
April 18, 1785

Page 436
Nance from Cahall Deed
March 11, 1785 between Edward Cahall of P and Clement Nance for 2 pounds, a parcel of land, containing by estimation 4 acres on a branch of Cascade Creek being part of the tract of Land whereon the said Edward Cahell now lives bounded on Waltons Order land on the North west by Swelins Survey on the south west and by the said branch on South east
s/ Edward (X) Cahall
Wit: Robert Bullington, David Scales, William (X) Mitchell, Martha (X) Jones, Giles Nance, Jos Rice
April 18, 1785

85

Page 437
Stimson from Stimson Deed
November 17, 1784 between Benjamin Stimson of P and Jeremiah Stimson
of P for 20 pounds, a parcel of land on the little dubble Creek near the head
whereon the said Jeremiah Stimson now lives containing 122 acres
including the Plantation according as John Stamps has marked of already
s/ Benjamin (X) Stimson
Wit: John Stamps, William Stamps, Joseph Flippin
April 18, 1785

Page 437
Tanner from Bailey Deed
September 20, 1784 between John Bailey of P and Dav'd Tanner of P for
185 pounds, a parcel of land containing 150 acres on Sandy Creek of
Banister
Bounded: John Kerby's line on the north side of Sandy Creek, Lacy's line,
Poynor's line crossing the Mill pond, Hardin's line, Kerby's line
s/ Jno Bailey
Wit: Thomas Tanner, Fred Ragsdale, Bazel Nelson
May 16, 1785

Page 438
Waddill from Wynne Deed
December 30, 1784 between Thomas Wynne of P and Noel Waddill of
Halifax County for 350 pounds, a parcel of land on both sides of Sandy
Creek of Dan River containing 606 acres
Bounded: James Seal's line, Hammock's, Robert Williams's line, James
Wooddin's line, Roger Atkinson's line, Edward Burgess line John Seal's
line, James Seal's line
s/ Thos Wynne
Wit: Solomon (X) Seale, Jas Seale, Nath'l Waddill, Noel Waddill junr,
George Hardey
May 16, 1785

Page 439
Hunt from Thurman Deed
October 1, 1784 between Pleasant Thurman of Chesterfield and David
Hunt of P for 120 pounds, a parcel of land on both sides of the south fork
of Straight stone Creek containing 300 acres
Bounded: Pollard's corner on the south side of the creek, William Short's
dividing line, Thomas Lester's line
s/ Pleasant Thurmon
Wit: Joshua Stone, Isaac Clement, Aaron Clement, John Martin
May 16, 1785

Magdaline, wife of said Pleasant, relinquished her right of Dower

Page 441
The Commonwealth of Virginia to Abraham Sallie, Bernard Markham &
David Patterson, Gent or any two Justices of Chesterfield County, Whereas
Pleasant Thurman by his certain Indenture hath conveyed unto David Hunt
of P a parcel of land containing 300 acres and whereas Madgelin, the wife
of the said Plesent Thurman cannot conveniently travel to and from our
County Court of P, we trusting to you faithful and provident
circumspection in examining Magdeline, wife of said Thurman, apart from
her husband that you certify to our Justices
s/ William Tunstall
October 20, 1784
Chesterfield County- By Virtue of the above Dedimus to us directed, we
have examined Magdaline, wife of said Plesent Thurman. She
relinquished her right of Dower   November 1, 1784
s/ Bernard Markham, David Patteson
(No recording date given)

Page 441
Marcer from Ball Deed
May 17, 1785 between John Ball of P and Richard Marcer of
Notochuckey, North Carolina for 55 pounds, a parcel of land which was
Granted to me by Pattant dated April 10, 1781 on the waters of Tye Creek
containing 233 acres
s/ John Ball, Mary Ball
Wit: None
May 16, 1785
Mary, wife of said John Ball, relinquished her right of Dower

Page 443
Crenshaw from Hawkins Deed
December 12, 1777 between John Hawkins and Mary his wife of Saint
Martins Parish and County of Hanover and Charles Crenshaw of the said
Parish and County for 500 pounds, a parcel of land containing by
estimation 745 acres on Banister and Stinking Rivers
Bounded: north side of Stinking river, Roger's line, line run by Drury
Stith for Henry Isham Kennon, Banister River, mouth of Stinking River
s/ John Hawkins, Mary Hawkins
Wit: Jane Hawkins, Martin Hawkins, Wm Wadsy, Milley Hawkis, John
(X) Genty, Christopher Curtis, John Sims
May 16, 1785

Page 445
Payne from White Deed
December 20, 1784 between Reubin White of P and Reubin Pain of P for
50 pounds, a parcel of land on the drafts of John Chapman's Run and
Shockoe Creek containing by estimation 50 acres
Bounded: John Shackelford's corner in the said Reubin White's line, said
White's line, a new line marked John Shackelford & Edmund Fitzgarield
to Shackelford's line
s/ Reuben White
Wit: Edmund Payne, Philimon Payne, Leucrecy Payne, Urirah (X)
Camron
May 16, 1785

Page 446
Cunningham from Clever Deed
December 17, 1784 between John Clever of P and Bridget Cunningham of
P for 200 pounds, a parcel of land on Banister River on the south side sid
Land that John Clever bought of Joseph Mays Jur, Deeded to the said
Clever by Joseph Mays Senr containing by estimation 150 acres
Bounded: Henry Blankes corner on the river, along Blank's and Mattox
Mayses line under the Mountain, Blankses path, Thomas Worthy's line to
the river
s/ John Clever
Wit: Faney (X) Roberts, Mattox (X) Mays, Thomas Worthy
May 16, 1785

Page 447
Roberts from Mays Deed
September 20, 1784 between Joseph Mayes Senr and Marget my wife and
Faney Roberts, it is my desire that the said Marget my wife and Faney
Roberts should posses 100 acres of my land, the senter of my Patant, the
Plantation where on I now live computed to be 100 acres. I do hereby give
unto John Roberts and Thos Roberts the above mentioned 100 acres as is
bounded by Patent   September 20, 1784
s/ Joseph (X) Mayes
Wit: John Clever, Bridget (X) Cunagam, Mattox (X) Mays
I, Joseph Mays Senr, It is my desire that Faney Roberts should Recive one
Feather bed and furniture and that I do hereby give and grant to her the said
Faney Roberts the same out of my Estate and it is my desire that Moly
Roberts should Receve ten pounds current money out of the profits of my
estate   Sept 20, 1784
s/ Joseph (X) Mays
Wit: Jno Clever, Bridget (X) Cunagam, Mattox (X) Mays
May 16, 1785

Page 448
M Mays from Mayes Deed
August 31, 1784 between Joseph Mayes Senr and Mattox Mayes of P for
50 pounds, a parcel of land containing 170 acres
Bounded: Coleman's path, Claybrock's line, Markham's line, Stephen
Terry's corner, the old line, mountain, Worthy's Path, along a branch to its
mouth
s/ Joseph (X) Mayes
Wit: Richard (X) Worthy, Faney (X) Bingam, Jno Clever
May 16, 1785

Page 449
Ryburn from Kidd Deed
December 9, 1784 between Webb Kidd of P and Elizabeth his wife and
William Ryburn of P for 150 pounds, a parcel of land which the said Kidd
purchased of Daniel White bounded Easterly and Southerley by the Lands
of Joseph Motley and Jeremiah Ellington, Northerley by the Lands at
present held by Thomas Linticomb and by the Land of Thomas Tanner and
others being the same place where the said Kidd now dwells containing by
estimation 190 acres
s/ Webb Kidd, Betty Kidd
Wit: John Yates, Ben Terry, Amstead Shelton
June 20, 1785

Page 450
Bobbitt from Bobbitt Deed
May 5, 1785 between John Bobbitt of P and James Bobbitt, his Son, of P
for 10 pounds, a parcel of land containing by estimation 100 acres
Bounded: mouth of Hugry Camp Branch on the south side Pigg River
s/ John Bobbitt
Wit: None
June 20, 1785

Page 451
Devan from Devan Bill of Sale
I James Devan of P have have sold unto William Devan Senr of P one
black stone Horse, Saddle & Bridle abough fore feet eight inches high both
hind foot lacks whight and one feather beed and furniture in consideration
of nine pence   June 20, 1785
s/ James Diven
Wit: Sam'l Calland, Thomas Terry, Jeremiah Cleaverland, William (X)
Olliver
June 20, 1785

Page 451
Ross from Clement Deed
December 6, 1784 between Martha Clement of P and David Ross of
Chesterfield County for 50 pounds, a parcel of land on both sides the
frying pan containing 80 acres
Bounded: Henry Croft's line, dividing line made by John and James
Clement dividing Field Robinson's Land and the said Martha Clement's
land, Croff's line on the other side of the Creek, dividing line the said
Croff's land and said Martha Clement's land
s/ Martha Clement
Wit: James Mitchell, Killian Giong, George Herndon, Benjamin
Townson
June 20, 1785

Page 453
Motley from Motley Deed
March 18, 1785 between Jos Motley of P and Daniel Motley of P hath
granted and given unto said Dan'l Motley one certain Tract of land
containing 281 acres on the south side of Banister River together with the
back lands adjoining the same that the said Jos Motley purchased of John
Markham by a pattern dated 1781
s/ Joseph Motley
Wit: None
June 20, 1785

Page 453
Cook from Martin Deed
June 4, 1785 between Peter Martin of Halifax County, Virginia and Elijah
Cook of P for 10 pounds, a parcel of land on Sandy Creek where Elijah
Cook now lives containing by estimation 50 acres
Bounded: Jeremiah Stimson's line by the side of the Sawpitt branch,
Rosamon Stimson spring branch, John Walter's line, George Cooks Senr
corner, along his line to John Walters corner formerly called James Collies
s/ Peter (X) Martin
Wit: Zachariah Butt, Uriah (X) Owen, George Cook, Senr, John Everett
June 20, 1785

Page 454
Ryan from Clack Deed
1785 between Spencer Clark of the County of Henry and William Ryon of
the same County for 20 pounds, a parcel of land containing 270 acres on
the branches of Strawberry Creek

Bounded: Henry Hall's corner on the Long branch, Joshua Cantrel's line, along the Order line, crossing three branches
s/ Spencer Clack
Wit: None
June 20, 1785

Page 455
Smith from Smith Deed of Gift
I, Drewry Smith in consideration of the sum of one shilling and six pence which I the said Drewry Smith do owe and am indebted unto Wm Smith, the son of John Smith, deceased, of P do give unto the said William Smith all a certain parcel of Land of 412 acres on the branches of pudding Creek and Banister River a Joyning Hezekiah Pigg and Isaack Clemmence and Chamberlain's Order, also a Negro boy named James, about three years ould   1785
s/ Drury Smith
Wit: Joseph Morton, Jacob Reiger, Henry Burnett
June 20, 1785

Page 456
Eckhols from Short Deed
September 20, 1784 between John Short of P and Joseph Eccols of Halifax county for 175 pounds, a parcel of land whereon said Short now lives containing 157 acres
Bounded: old Wagon ford on Banister, Waldrons, Clabrook's line, Finney's line, Banister River
s/ John (X) Short
Wit: Wm McCraw, Spencer Shelton, Wm Short, Sam'l Calland
April 18, 1785

Page 457
Motley from Motely Deed
July 17, 1785 between Joseph Motley and Elizabeth his wife of P and Samuel Motley of P for 500 pounds, a parcel of land on Donelsons Run by estimation 400 acres
s/ Jos Motley, Elizabeth Motley
Wit: None
July 18, 1785

Page 458
Burton from Burton Deed
February 22, 1785 between John Burton and Mary his wife of the County of Mecklenburg and John Burton of the County of Cumberland for 400

pounds, a parcel of land on both sides of Banister River containing by
estimation 800 acres
Bounded: Jesse Carter's corner, on his dividing line, crossing the river,
Hardy's line, William Davis's lines, Joshua Welch's corner in a great
Meadow of Cherrystone Creek, crossing the said Meadow
s/ Jno Burton
Wit: Robt Smith, John Burton junr, Harry Smith, Benjamin Burton, Jesse
Burton, Geo Craghead, R Williams, D Burton
July 18, 1785

Page 459
Tuggle &c from Black Bill of Sale
I Thomas Black of P in consideration of the sum of 250 pounds which I
acknowledge myself to be indebted unto Lodowick Tuggle and Samuel
Calland of P hath this day sold unto them all my personal Estate, to wit,
one traveling Waggon not yet finished, my Stock of Cattle consisting of 14
head marked with a crop in the left Ear and a slit in the right Ear, one bay
Horse branded on the Shoulder & Buttock T, one Desk, 17 pewter Dishes,
17 pewter plates, one looking glass, four ploughs and 4 pole axes, one
Brandy Still, Cap and Worm, four feather Beds and furniture and one bald
faced Horse branded T on the near Shoulder & Buttock
s/ Thos Black
Wit: Sam'l Tompkins jr, Bowker Smith
July 18, 1785

Page 460
Quinn from Burton Deed
July 16, 1785 between Charles Burton Senor of the County of Louisa and
William Quinn of P for 100 pounds, a parcel of land on the middle fork of
Sandy Creek of Dan River containing by Estimation 200 acres
Bounded: a new line that was made by Charles Burton and John Hall,
middle fork of Sandy Creek, Hall's line, ajoyning the Land called the burnt
Cabbin, William Aslain's line
s/ Charles Burton
Wit: None
July 20, 1785

Page 461
Swinney from King Deed
June 20, 1785 between James King and Winney his Wife of P and Joseph
Swinney of P for 25 pounds, a parcel of land containing 130 acres on the
branches of the middle fork of Cherrystone Creek
Bounded: Hix's line, Charles Rigney's line, Hix's corner
s/ James King

Wit: None
July 18, 1785

Page 462
Hardy's B'd for building the prison
We Thomas Hardy and Abraham Shelton are firmly bound unto Colo John
Wilson preciding Justice of P for 240 pounds, ten shillings   July 18, 1785
The Condition of the above obligation is such that the abovebound Thomas
Hardy hath this day agreed to build a Prison at Pittsylvania Courthouse
agreeable to a plan which is in the hands of John Parks of P
s/ Thos Hardy, Abr'a Shelton
Wit: John George, John Davis
(No recording date given)

Page 463
Carter from Burton Deed
July 13, 1785 between John Burton of the county of Mecklenburg and
Jesse Carter of P for 4500 pounds a parcel of land on both sides of Banister
River containing by estimation 1302 acres being part of a Tract of 4485
acres as appears by patent obtained by William Finney dated October 17,
1753
Bounded: Easley's line
s/ John Burton
Wit: R Williams, Tho Carleton junr, H Carleton, Simon Williams, Ben
Lankford, Peter Field Jefferson, John Burton, Geo Craghead
(No recording date given)

Page 464
Carter from Burton Ded's
To John Speed, Lewis Parkam & William Starling Esq of nay two Justices
of the County of Mecklenburg, Whereas John Burton hath conveyed unto
Jesse Carter of P a parcel of land containing 1302 acres and whereas Mary,
wife of the said John Burton cannot conveniently travel to and from our
said County Court of P, we trusting to your faithful and provident
circumspection in examining Mary, wife of said John Burton, whether she
does freely and voluntarily relinquish her right of Dower   The 11th day of
December in the 6th year of the Commonwealth
Mecklenburg County-By Virtue of the above Dedimus to us directed, we
have examined Mary, the wife of John Burton and she relinquished her
right of Dower 15th day of April in the 8th year of our independence
s/ John Speed, Lewis Parham
July 18, 1785

93

Page 465
Clark from Mackbee Deed
January 15, 1785 between James Mackbee of P and Joseph Clark of
Halifax County for 35 pounds, a parcel of land containing 200 acres
s/ James Mackbee
Wit: Joshua Stone, Jno Ramey, John Buckley, Richard Anderson
July 18, 1785

Page 466
Cook from Grayham Deed
July 18, 1785 between Archibald Grayham and Margret his wife of Henry
County and Harmon Cook of P for 240 pounds, a parcel of land containing
by estimation 400 acres on both sides of Pye Creek
s/ Archibald Grayham
Wit: Thos Dyer, Hugh Reynolds, John Wright

Page 467
To Swinfield Hill and Moses Greer Esq Justices of the County of Franklin,
Whereas Archibald Graham of P hath conveyed unto Harmon Cook of P a
parcel of land containing 400 acres and whereas Margret Graham, wife of
the said Arch'd Graham cannot conveniently travel to and from our said
County Court of P, we trusting to your faithful and provident
circumspection in examining Margret, wife of said Archibald Graham,
whether she does freely and voluntarily relinquish her right of Dower   The
12th day of February 9th year of the Commonwealth
s/ Will Tunstall
By Virtue of the above Dedimus to us directed, we have examined
Margret, the wife of Arch'd Graham and she relinquished her right of
Dower   February 18, 1786
s/ Swinfield Hill, Moses Greer
July 18, 1785

Page 468
Roach from Robinson Deed
August 10, 1785 between Jesse Robinson of P and Thomas Roch for 15
pounds, a parcel of land on both sides Mill Creek being by Estimation 100
acres
Bounded: north side the said Creek, John Midkiff's line, south side of said
Creek, John Thompson's former line
s/ Jesse Robinson
Wit: John Midkif, Gidion roach, John Parsons
August 15, 1785

Page 469

Motley from Tanner Deed

August 15, 1785 between Floyd Tanner of P and Samuel Mottley of P for 95 pounds, a parcel of land on Donelson branch
Bounded: head of a bottom belonging to Donelson branch, head spring of Donelson Branch, said Tanner's line
s/ Floyd Tanner
Wit: None
August 15, 1785

Page 470
Weatherford from Burnet Deed

October 8, 1784 between Benjamin Burnett of P and John Weatherford of P for one dark bay Mare, a parcel of land containing by estimation 50 acres on the south side of the long branch
Bounded: John Weatherford's line, William Easley's line, the long branch
s/ Benjamin Burnet
Wit: Mary Prise, John Emmerson, Tho Boas
April 18, 1785

Page 471
Chattin from Hardy Deed

August 15, 1785 between Thomas Hardy of P and John Chattin of P for 50 pounds, a parcel of land containing by estimation 200 acres on Christopher Hutchings old order line
Bounded: near Green Rock Creek, Pigg's line, Pettey's line, Jeremiah Worsham's corner in Pettey's line
s/ Thos Hardy
Wit: None
August 15, 1785

Page 472
George from Short Deed

August 13, 1785 between Joel Short of P and John George of P for 140 pounds, a parcel of land on the north side of Banister River containing by estimation 100 acres
Bounded: Morgan's line, Drean above Short's Spring and including half the propery and privilege of the said Spring, Banister River, Morgan's line
s/ Joel Short
Wit: Joshua Stone, Will Todd, Dudley Glass, Will George
August 15, 1785
Lucy, wife of the said Joel, relinquished her right of Dower

Page 473
Adams from McDaniel Com &c

To James Henderson and William Hutchison Gent, Justices of the County
of Greenbrier, Whereas Henry McDaniel hath conveyed unto John Adams
junr of P a parcel of land containing 203 acres and whereas Mary Ann,
wife of the said Henry McDaniel cannot conveniently travel to our county
court, we trusting to your faithful and provident circumspection in
examining Maryann, wife of said Henry McDaniel apart from her said
husband whether she does freely and voluntarily relinquish her right of
Dower
January 20, 1785
s/ Will Tunstall
GreenBrier-By virtue of the above Commission to us directed, we have
examined Mary Ann, the wife of the said Henry McDaniel apart from her
husband, and she relinquished her right of Dower.
July 30, 1785
s/ Jas Henderson, Wm Hutchison
August 15, 1785

Page 474
Woodie from J Owen Deed
August 1785 between John Owen of Halfax County and John Woodie, son
of James Woodie of P for 20 pounds, a parcel of land on the Branches of
Dan river containing by estimation 320 acres
Bounded: corner of the land that formerly was of said Owen, Adkinson's
line, Noel Waddill's line, Williams's line
s/ John Owen
Wit: James Woody, Solmon (X) Lett, John Walters
August 15, 1785

Page 475
Woodie from Owen Deed
February 13, 1785 between William Owen of P and John Woody junr for
50 pounds, a parcel of land on the Waters of Sandy Creek containing by
Estimation 200 acres
Bounded: McDaniel's line
s/ William Owen
Wit: John Walters, James Woody
August 15, 1785

Page 476
Hunt from Hoskins Bill of Sale
I William Hoskins of P for 46 pounds sell to David Hunt one Waggon and
Team consisting of five Horses, to wit, one light bay Horse about four feet
nine or ten inches high with a blaze face and Glass eyes and some saddle
spots, One white Horse said to be thirteen years old next Spring and

branded on the near buttock I W, one lare bay Horse said to be about six years old with a srain in his forehead and snip on his Nose some whit on his off fore foot and som Saddle spots and branded S Pon the near Shoulder and J C on the near buttock, One bay Horse said to be seven years old (pretty large) with sundrey white spots about on his back. Also on dark bay Mare said to be eight years old with some large Saddle Spotts and some white on her hind feet.   August 9, 1785
s/ Wm Hoskins
Wit: James Purcel, Thomas Lawson, John Craddock
I, Joel Eastess of Henry County, do promise and oblige myself to see the within Waggon and Team delivered to David Hunt in P at Mr John George's in the said County within ten days from this day under the penalty of 50 pounds   August 9, 1785
s/ Joel Eastes
Wit: Thomas Lawson, John Craddock
I discharge the above Joel Eastes from the above Obligation
August 14, 1785
s/ D Hunt
August 15, 1785

Page 477
Calland from Smith Power of Att'o
I James Smith late of P now of the Borough of Norfolk, Merchant have made Mr. Samuel Calland Merchant in P my true and lawful Attorney to ask, receive, demand and sue for and recover all debts or Sums of Money which may be due to me in the United States of America. August 13, 1784
s/ James Smith
Wit: George Smith, John Smith, Thomas Townsen, James Brewer
August 15, 1785

Page 478
Innes &c from Smith & Co Power of Att'o
We James Smith and Company of P, Merchant, have appointed Hugh Innes of Henry County Esq, Harry Innes of Bedford County, Esq and Mr Samuel Calland, Merchant in P our true and lawful Attorney for us and in our Name to ask, demand, sue from and recover all Debts or Sums of Money which may be due to us in the United States of America
August 13, 1784
s/ James Smith & Co
Wit: George Smith, John Smith, Thomas Townsen, James Brewer
August 15, 1785

Page 478
George from Owen Shf Deed

97

August 15, 1785 between John Owen, Gent late Sherif for P and John George of P for 3 pounds, 8 shillings and one penny, hath by virtue of an Act of assembly passed at the October Session 1782 entitled and Act to amend and reduce the several Acts of Assembly for ascertaining certain Taxes and duties and for establishing an perminant Revenue into one Act, hath Sold unto the said John George 49 acres of Land being part of 469 acres of Land said to be the property of Peter Pucket of Prince Edward County for the Taxes due for the year 1783 that being the smallest quantity of Land that any person present at the sale thereof would pay the taxes together with the Charges of Distress Sale &c on the West fork of Allins Creek
Bounded: Joseph Clark's line on the said fork
s/ John Owen
Wit: None
August 15, 1785

Page 479
Scales from Conley Deed
April 20. 1785 between Enoch Conley of P and David Scales and Joseph Rice of P for 80 pounds, a parcel of land on both sides of Sugar tree Creek containing by Estimation 140 acres
s/ Enoch (X) Conley
Wit: Clement Nance, Wm (X) Mitchell, John (X) Payne, James Oakes
August 15, 1785

Page 481
Burnet from Cox Deed
December 25 1784 between James Cox of P and Henry Burnet of P for 13 pounds, a parcel of land containing 145 acres on the Waters of Sugar tree
Bounded: above Cox's patent line of which this is a part, Crowley's line
s/ James Cox
Wit: James Burnet, John Cox, Prudence Cox
August 15, 1785

Page 482
Chattin from Hutchings Deed
August 15, 1785 between Christopher Hutchings of P and John Chattin of P for 1200 pounds, a parcel of land containing by Esttimation 50 acres
Bounded: Line between John Chattin and Samuel Davis, red oak between John Chattin, Samuel Davis and Ann Hutchings, it being part of a tract of Land that was once Deeded from Christopher Hutchings to Joshua Wealch before there was a proper right obtain
s/ Christopher Hutchings
Wit: None

98

August 15, 1785

Page 483
Buckley from Owen Deed
August 16, 1785 between John Owen of P and John Buckley of P for three
pounds, ten shillings and eleven pence hath sold unto said John Buckley 49
acres of Land part of 400 acres said to be the property of William
Claybrook of Henrico County for the Tax's due on the said Land for the
year 1783 that being smallest quantity of land any person present at the
Sale thereof would pay the taxes for, together with the charges of susing,
selling &c lying on the draughts of Shocko Creek
Bounded: Mattox Mays's corner in the said Claybrook's line, Brown's
corner, his line, said May's line aforesaid
s/ John Owen
Wit: None
August 16, 1785

Page 483
Mead from Pigg Deed
July 12, 1785 between Richard Pigg of Henry County and Mary Meade of
P for 20 pounds, a parcel of land containing 100 acres, being part of a tract
laid of for Allen Adams out of a tract formerly belonging to William Peters
Martin
Bounded: William Adams corner in Peter Legrand's line, James Mead's
line, Eleanor Adams's line, line of John Adams junr, William Adams
corner, his line
s/ Richard (X) Pigg
August 15, 1785

Page 484
Laws from Dalton Deed
January 17, 1785 between Robt Dalton and Mary Dalton of P and Joeph
Laws of P for 80 pounds, a parcel of land on the south side of Pig river
containing 40 acres
Bounded: Jeremiah Wards and Peyton Wades lines on the north side of
said pigg River, cross the river to Jacob Barger's line, James Mitchell's
lines, a Survey made by the said Robt Dalton , William Thompson's lines,
the river, across the river
s/ Robert Dalton, Mary (X) Dalton
Wit: James Mitchell, Daniel (X) Witcher, Randolph Bobit
August 15, 1785

Page 485
Morton from Vaughan Deed

August 15, 1785 between John Vaughan and Sarah his wife and Hezekiah
Morton of the county of Prince Edward for 115 pounds, a parcel of land on
Straitstone Creek containing by estimation 282 acres
Bounded: Obadiah Hendricks lower corner on Straight Stone Creek, lines
of the said John Vaughan's new patent, Straightstone Creek aforesaid
s/ John Vaughan
August 15, 1785
Sarah, wife of the said John Vaughan, relinquished her right of Dower

Page 487
Wimbish from Hughes Deed
May 20, 1785 between Archelous Hughes of the County of Henry and
John Wimbish of P for a consideration of the said Archelous Hughes and
John Wimbish being as partners in Trade, and having purchased divers
Tracts of Land and obtained titles to the same on their joint accounts, and
now having mutually agreed on equal division of the said Lands and are
desirious to relinquish titles each toth other for their respective Allotments
as also for and consideration of the sum of 20 shillings to the said
Archelous Hughes in hand paid by the said John Wimbish, a parcel of land
on Sandy Creek containing by Estimation 400 acres which said 400 acres
was granted to the said Archelous Hughes and John Wimbish by Patent
dated June 15, 1773
Bounded: Billings line
s/ A Hughes
Wit: Thos (X) Brady, Armistead Brown. Patrick (X) Brady, John Wimbish
Jr, John (X) Brown
August 15, 1785

Page 488
McAlister from Wooding Deed
May 23, 1785 between Robert Wooding of the county of Halifax and
William McAlister of the County of Chambell for 30 pounds, a parcel of
land containing by estimation 400 acres on the branches of Swan Creak
Bounded: John Chisum's line, James Hancock's corner, his line
s/ Ro Wooding
Wit: James Childress, John McAlister, William McAlister, Thomas H
Wooding, Glover Craine
August 15, 1785

Page 489
Chelton from Crenshaw Deed
January 26, 1785 between Joseph Crenshaw of P and Armistead Shelton of
P for 150 pounds, a parcel of land containing 286 acres on both sides
White thorn Creek

Bounded: William Paien line, Newsum Paces line, Robert Botemas line, Wm Paynes line, Stirling Willis's line
s/ Joseph Crenshaw
Wit: Daniel Shelton, Henry Kay, Robert (X) Boatman
September 19, 1785
Betty, wife of said Joseph Crenshaw, relinquished her right of Dower

Page 490
Gregory from Latimer Deed
August 31, 1785 between Samuel Lattimer of P and William Gregory of P for 150 pounds, a parcel of land on both sides of the North fork of Stinking river containing by estimation 100 acres, it being part of a greater Tract granted to Jonathan Jones by Patent dated September 22. 1766 and by him conveyed to George Keesee and by said Kesee conveyed to Samuel Lattimer
Bounded: Abram Payne's corner in the old line, in Jacob Faris's line, Jesse Kesee's dividing line, the old line, Abram Paynes dividing line
Also 85 acres of Land adjoining the above mentioned Tract which the said Lattimer purchased of Abram Payne and has a Deed recorded in the County Court of P reference thereto had may more fully appear
s/ Samuel Latimer
Wit: Will Todd, Thos Tunstall jur, John George
Sept 19, 1785
Lydia, wife of said Samuel Lattamore, relinquished her right of Dower

Page 491
Lattimore from Gregory Deed
August 31, 1785 between William Gregory of P and Samuel Lattimer of P for160 pounds, a parcel of land containing 63 acres lying on the South side of Banister river
Bounded: the River Banister on the North and William Beal on the West and Glascockes order of Council on the South
s/ Wm Griggory
Wit: Will Todd, Tho Tunstall Jr, John George
September 19, 1785
Martha, wife of said William Griggory, relinquished her right of Dower

Page 492
Corbin from Pain Deed
March 12, 1785 between Reubin Pain of P and Ambrose Corbin of P for 80 pounds, a parcel of land containing by Estimation 226 acres being part of a tract Granted to the said Reubin Pain by Setters Pattent dated June 1, 1782 on the South side of John Chapmans run

101

Bounded: Guynes corner on John Chapmons Run, Dudging's line,
Claybrook's line, Hickses line,
John Chapmans Run, Guynes line
s/ Reubin Pain
Wit: William Pigg, William Parks, Allen (X) Adams, Edmond Fitzgerald
September 19, 1785

Page 493
Stone from Stone Deed
September 19, 1785 between John Stone of Halifax County and Joshua
Stone of P for 20 pounds, a parcel of land on the draughts of Allins Creek
containing by Estimation 64 acres, being part of the Tract the said John
Stone lives on
Bounded: Logan's corner, said John Stone's former line
s/ John Stone
Wit: None
September 19, 1785
Dolly, wife of said John Stone, relinquished her right of Dower

Page 494
Watkins from Watson Power of Atto
I, John Watson of P, make my trusty friends Isaiah Watkins and Alice his
wife, for me and in my name, to pay or deliver such Negroes or Cash
promed me by his Honour the Governor of South Carolina by his
Proclamation for ten months service as a Soldier in General Sumters
Brigade and under the command of Col Wade Hampton my Complianet
agreeable to an Act of General Assembly, the Certificate placed in hands
and purchased by them my said Attorney. I also appoint and impower my
said Attornies my debt of ten Months Service or to receive the said Negros
promised or Cash in lue thereof according to Custom
Sept 20, 1785
s/ John Watson
Wit: None
September 19, 1785

Page 495
Johnson from Watkins Power of Att'o
I, Isaiah Watkins of P, appoint my trusty friend John Johnson Farmer of ye
County of Bedford, Virginia my true and lawful attorney to ask, demand,
reieve and recover of and from any and every person and persons that is
indebted to me by virtue of a Letter of Power of Attorney granted to me by
Anne Miller, Widow of John Laws, Blacksmith of Wilks County, North
Carolina, the same Power of Attorney being entered in the records of P and
Bedford County especially to recover and receive all the Estate of John

102

Miller, dec'd, in the County of Bedford now belonging to me by a purchase by me made of the above mentioned Ann Miller and John Laws and transfer'd by them to me and recorded as above mentioned. I also appoint and impower my said Attorney to sell the said above mentioned estate particularly the Land 127 acres lying on Magatty Creek in Bedford County which appears to be their third parts of the moveable Estate
Sept 19, 1785
s/ Isaiah Watkins
September 19, 1785

Page 496
Hampton from Watkins Power of Att'o
I, Isaiah Watkins of P, Blacksmith, appoint my trusty friend Col Henry Hampton of South Carolina in Camden District my lawful Attorney to ask, demand, recover from any persons that is indebted or that shall be indebted to me relative to a Sale of Land intended to be made lying the State of South Carolina in Camden District. I also appoint my said attorney to sell the said Land and Mill according to my said Deed granted to me by James Smith and Ester his wife, the said Land lying on Little Sedar Creek
September 20, 1785
s/ Isaiah Watkins
September 19, 1785

Page 497
Motley from Pendleton Deed of Gift
I, Philip Pendleton of P for divers good causes as well as for the natural love and affection which I have and do bear unto my daughter, Elizabeth Motley, have given to said Elizabeth one Negro fellow Charles now in my possession to be held by the said Elizabeth free and clear
September 19, 1785
s/ Philip Pendleton
Wit: None
September 19, 1785

Page 497
Witcher from Witcher Deed
September 15, 1785 between James Witcher of P and Ephraim Witcher of P for 100 pounds, a parcel of land on Reddys Creek containing 160 acres, it being the upper part of a larger Tract of 302 acres convey'd by Deed to the said Ephraim Witcher by David Polley and by said Ephraim Witcher convey'd by Deed to the aforesaid James Witcher divided from the lower part of the Tract by a straight line crossing the said Creek
s/ James Witcher
Wit: None

September 19, 1785
Mary, wife of said James Witcher, relinquished her right of Dower

Page 498
Witcher from Young Deed
February 24, 1785 between William Young of P and Daniel Witcher of P
for 30 pounds, a parcel of land containing by Estimation 100 acres
Bounded: James Cares corner in John Reeces line, Corn Branch
s/ William Young
Wit: John Witcher, John Bobbit, Milton Young
September 19, 1785

Page 499
Smith from Givens Ded 'm
To Stephen Coleman & Lodowick Tuggle, Gent, Justices of the Court of P,
Whreas Edward Givens hath conveyed unto Hezekiah Smith of P a parcel
of land containing 296 acres and whereas Elinor, Wife of the said Edw
Givens cannot conveniently travel to and from our said county of P, we
trusting to your faithful and provident circumspection Examining Elinor,
wife of said Edward Givens apart from her said Husband
January 210, 1785
s/ Will Tunstall
Pittsylvania-By Virtue of the above Commission to us directed, we have
Examined Elinor, wife of the said Edward Givens apart from her said
Husband and she relinquished her right of Dower   Sept 19, 1785
s/ Stephen Coleman, Lodowick Tuggle
September 19, 1785

Page 500
Cristian from Mullings Deed
October 21, 1784 between John Mullings of P and John Christain of P for
25 pounds, a parcel of land containing 100 acres on the Branches of Sandy
Creek of Dann River
Bounded: south side of a Branch of Sandy Creek, Tomlins line
s/ John (X) Mullins
Wit: Hezekiah Smith, Nathan (X) Baker, Jonas Cook
September 19, 1785

Page 502
Hall from Burton Deed
September 19, 1785 between Charles Burton Senor and Mary his wife of
the county of Louisa and John Hall of Amelia County for 40 pounds, a
parcel of land on the Middle fork of Sandy Creek of Dan River containing
by Estimation 200 acres

104

Bounded: Tomlins line, along the line of the Land called the Burnt
Cabbin, mouth of a small branch, John Mays line
s/ Charles Burton, Mary Burton
Wit: William Burton, Nathaniel Burton, Cutbird (X) Burton
September 19, 1785

We, Jno Buckley, James Buckley, & Richard Bayne are held and Bound
unto the Commonwealth for 50 pounds   September
20, 1785
The condition of this Obligation is that the above bound John & James
Buckley hath Obtained a License to keep an Ordinary at his house in P if
the said John & James doth constantly fine & provide in his Ordinary good
wholesome and Cleanly Lodging and Diett for Travellers and stabbage
fodder and provinder & provinder as the Season shall Require for their
horses for the term of one year and shall not permit any unlawful haming
in his house nor on the Sabbath Day Suffer any person to lepple or drink
any more than is necessary
s/ John Buckley, James Buckley, Rich'd Baynes
Wit: None
(No recording date given)

Page 504
Parsons from Robertson Deed
August 10, 1785 between Jesse Roberson of P and John Parsons of P for
15 pounds, a parcel of land containing by Estimation 100 acres
Bounded: a Branch on the South side of Mill Creek called the persimmon
Branch wheare Roches new line strikes this Branch, Woiddow Martins
Line, John Thomson's line, Roches formerly called new line
s/ Jesse Robinson
Wit: John Midkif, Gideon Roach, Thos Roach
September 19, 1785

Page 505
Calland from Grayham Deed
February 16, 1786 between Archibald Graham Senior of the County of
Franklin, Virginia and Samuel Calland of P for 300 pounds, a parcel of
land on the south side of Pigg river containing by Estimation 180 acres
being part of a greater Tract of 280 acres, being the Land & Plantation
whereon Thomas Black now lives
Bounded: the River, crossing Snow Creek, crossing Turkey Cock near the
Mouth thereof, east side of Snow Creek, Pigg River
s/ Arch'd Graham
Wit: Sam'l Tompkins jr, Arch'd Graham Jun, Arthur Graham, William
Graham

105

April 17, 1786

Page 507
Adams from Adams Deed
September 16, 1785 between John Adams of P and Ethaner Adams of P for
200 pounds, a parcel of land containing 175 acres part of a Survey that was
granted to John Hix Letters Pattent dated August 3, 1771
And conveyed by Deed by said John Hix to said John Adams
Bounded: Robert Woodings line, John Park's line, William P Martin's line
Marked by the said John Adams and Ethaner Adams
s/ John Adams Junr
Wit: Spenc'n Shelton. Gabriel Tucker, Benja Shelton
September 19, 1785
Sarah, wife of said John Adams jr, relinquished her right of Dower

Page 509
**Chelton's Bond in the Collection of Tax's for the year 1785 due in
hand Money**
We Abraham Shelton, William Todd, William Dix, John Parks and Reubin
Payne of P are bound unto Jacquelin Ambler Esq,
Treasurer of the Commonwealth of Virginia in the sum of 10,000 pounds
September 20, 1785
The Condition of the above Obligation is the above bound Abraham
Shelton shall collect and account for and pay unto the said Treasurer all the
taxes which shall or may Become due and paiable from Each and Every
Taxable Person in P and other Articles also Taxable which were imposed
by Virtue of an Act of Assembly made and passed October 1784
s/ Abra Shelton, Will Todd, Wm Dix, John Parks, Reubin Pain
September 19, 1785

Page 510
Dodson's Bond for Marr'ge License
We Lazarus Dodson, Reubin Payne, & Jeremiah White are held & firmly
bound unto Patrick Henry, Esq Governor of the Commonwealth of
Virginia for the Sum of 500 pounds   September 19, 1785
The Condition of the above Obligation is such that the above Bound
Lazarus Dodson this Day produced Credentials of his Regular ordination in
the Communion of the Society of Christians called Baptists & obtained a
Certificate to impower him to perform the Rites of Matrimony
s/ Reubin Pain, Jere White
September 19, 1785

Page 510
Roberson License Bond

We James Roberson & Jesse Carter of P are bound unto his Excellency
Patrick Henry Esq in the sum of 500 pounds   September 19. 1785
Whereas the above bound James Roberson having produced to Court of P
Credentials of his Ordination to solemnize Marriages agreeable to an Act
of Assembly
s/ James Roberson, Jesse Carter
Wit: None
September 19, 1785

Page 511
Chattin from Welch Deed
October 17, 1785 between Joshua Welch of P and John Chattin of P for 65
pounds, a parcel of land containing by Estimation 100 acres
Bounded: Jesse Carter's line, George Miers's line, the Order Line
s/ Joshua Welch
Wit: None
October 17, 1785
Jemima, wife of said Joshua Welch, relinquished her right of Dower

Page 512
Dodson from Dodson Deed
April 20, 1785 between William Dodson of the county of Halfax and Caleb
Dodson of Halifax County for 71 pounds, five shillings, a parcel of land
containing by Estimation 280 acres
s/ William Dotson
Wit: None
October 17, 1785

Page 514
Wooten from Hendrick Deed
July 18, 1785 between Humphrey Hendrick of P and Nathaniel Wooton of
P for 100 pounds, a parcel of land containing by estimation 252 acres being
part of a greater Tract of 352 acres which was Granted to the said
Humphrey Hendrick by a grant from The Land Office dated June 21,
1780
s/ Humphrey Hendrick
Wit: W Wright, Benj Lawless, William Twedel, James (X) Nelson
October 17, 1785

Page 515
Boaz from Cantrell Deed
October 17, 1785 between Joshua Cantrell of P and Thomas Boaz of P for
100 pounds, a parcel of land containing by Estimation 293 acres on both
sides of Strawberry

Bounded: Johnsons branch, crossing the creek sundrey times, near the
Long Branch, near the Still house Branch, Edward Adkins line
s/ Joshua Cantrall, Ann Cantrall
Wit: None
October 17, 1785
Ann, wife of said Joshua Cantrall, relinquished her right of Dower

Page 517
Holder from Adams Deed
April 29, 1785 between Thomas Adams of P and William Holder of P for
25 pounds, a parcel of land containing by Estimation 75 acres it being part
of a tract of land granted as by patent to Mark Hardin for 378 acres of Land
on the branches of Johns run and Shocko
Bounded: south side of the Road in Johns run, path under the mountain,
Denny's fence, crossing the Road
s/ Thomas Adams
Wit: Ambros Corbin, Burrel (X) Boden, William Wright
October 17, 1785

Page 518
Rice from Walters Deed
October 14, 1784 between Robert Walters of P and William Rice of for 80
pounds, 300 acres part of that tract on the waters of Fall Creek containing
by Estimation 504 acres granted to the said Walters by Patent dated June
13, 1785
Bounded: Orlando Smith corner, crossing two branches, Robert Walters
line, William Russel's line
N.B. 204 acres part of the said patent for 504 acres the said Walters had
sold to William Reynolds the remaining 300 acres to Reynolds's line I the
said Walter do sell to the said Rice
s/ Robert (X)Walters
Wit: None
October 17, 1785

Page 520
Payne from Payne Deed of Gift
April 27, 1785 between Josias Payne of P and Robert Payne of P for
consideration of the Natural Love and Affection that I Bear to my Son
Robert Payne and also in consideration of the sum of 50 pounds, a parcel
of land in Goochland County on Licking hole Creek containing by
Estimation 800 acres, it being the Land and Plantation whereon I lately
lived
s/ Josias Payne
Wit: Robert Burton, Robt Harrison, Robert Payne Jr

October 17, 1785

Page 521
Twedwell from Hendrick Deed
July 18, 1785 between Humphrey Hendrick of P and William Twedell of P
for 100 pounds, a parcel of land containing by Estimation 200 acres, part
of a greater tract of 400 acres which was granted to the said Humphrey
Hendrick by a grant from the Land Office of this State for 400 acres dated
June 1, 1784
s/ Humphrey Hendrick
Wit: W Wright, Nath (X) Wooton, James (X) Nelson
October 17, 1785

Page 523
Pendleton from Pendleton Deed of Gift
I, Philip Pendleton of P, for divers good Causes as Well as for the natural
love and affection which I have unto my son, James Pendleton, have given
him three Negroes, Viz, Harry, Sue & Jeremiah
October 15, 1785
s/ P Pendleton
Wit: David Mottley, Rawley Corbin, Edm'd Fitzherreld
October 17, 1785

Page 523
Price from Quinn Deed
October 17, 1785 between William Quin and Ann Quin his wife of P and
William Price Senr for 100 pounds, a parcel of land on the waters of Dan
River containing by Estimation153 acres
Bounded: Thos Billings's line, crossing the Road, Billings's Line
s/ William (X) Quin, Ann (X) Quin
Wit: William Price Junr, James Robison, John Adams
October 17, 1785
Ann, wife of said William Quinn, relinquished her right of Dower

Page 524
Holder from Hardin Deed
May 1, 1785 between Mark Hardin of P and Davis Holder of P for 10
pounds, a parcel of land containing by Estimation 40 acres, being part of a
tract of Land granted to the said Mark Harden as by Patent
At the head of Johns run
Bounded: Clabrooks corner on the top of Banister mountain, Denny's
fence
s/ Mark Hardin

Wit: George Wright, William Corbin, Ambros Corbin, John Holder, John Denny
October 17, 1785

Page 526
Westbrook from Burks Deed
October 17, 1785 between James Burks and Susanna his wife of P and Henry Westbrook of P for 75 pounds, a parcel of land on the dry fork of White Oak containing 118 acres
Bounded: Nelson's corner, Tompson's line, Clay's line, said Nelson's line
s/ James Birk, Susana Birk
Wit: None
October 17, 1785
Susanna, wife of said James Burks, relinquished her right of Dower

Page 527
Shields from Shields Deed
October 17, 1785 between Thomas Shields of P, Planter and Patrick Shield, son and heir at law of James Shields, Dec'd of P for 35 pounds, a parcel of land on the south side of Sandy River containing by Estimation 27 acres being part of a tract granted Richard Womack by patent
Bounded: the old line, Dividing line Between James Shields and Thomas Shields
s/ Tho Shields
Wit: None
October 17, 1785

Page 528
Hall from Atkinson Deed
August 8, 1785 between Roger Atkinson of the County of Dinwiddie and Benjamin Hall of the county of Halifax for 187 pounds, a parcel of land on a branch of Johns run containing by Estimation 250 acres
Bounded: Dudgion's line, William Walrond's Line
s/ Roger Atkinson
Wit: George Camp, Samuel Mottley, James Purcel
November 21, 1785

Page 529
Todd's B'd for his Shff atty
We, William Todd, Thos Worthy, Charles Lewis Jr, Abra Shelton & Vincent Shelton of P are firmly bound unto the Commonwealth of Virginia for the Sum of 500 pounds   November 21, 1785

The Condition of the above Obligation is such that whereas the above Bound William Todd is Constituted and approinted Sheriff of P by Commission from his Excellency the Governor.
s/ Will Todd, Thomas Worthy, Chas Lewis, Abra Shelton, Vincent Shelton
Wit: None
November 21, 1785

Page 530
Todd B'd for his Shff atty
We, William Todd, Thos Worthy, Charles Lewis Jr, Abra Shelton & Vincent Shelton of P are firmly bound unto the Commonwealth of Virginia for the Sum of 1000 pounds   November 21, 1785
The Condition of the above Obligation is such that whereas the above Bound William Todd is Constituted and approinted Sheriff of P by Commission from his Excellency the Governor. If therefore the said William Todd shall well and truly Collect all Officers Hus? and dues pertint to the Office to whom such Hus are due Respectively at such time as are by Law prescribed and Limited and well and truly pay and Satisfy all sums of money and Tobacco by him Collected and in all other things shall truly and faithfully perform the Office of Sheriff during the time of his Continuance therein, then the above Obligation to be Void
s/ Will Todd, Thomas Worthy, Chas Lewis, Abra Shelton, Vincent Shelton
Wit: None
November 21, 1785

Page 531
Hughes from Roberts Deed
To Hugh Innes and John Salmon Esq or any two of them Justices of the Peace of Henry County, James Roberts whereas by his certain Indenture hath conveyed unto Arch'd Hughes & John Wimbish a tract of Land in P containing by estimation 200 acres and whereas Eliza Wife of the said James Roberts cannot conveniently travel to and from our said Court of P, Know that we trustin to your faithful and provident Circumspection in Examined Elizabeth, the wife of said James from and apart from her husband wheather she does freely and Voluntarly relinquish her right of Dower   October 17, 1785
s/ Will Tunstall
Henry Cty-By Virtue of the above Dedimus to us directed we have Examined Elizabeth, Wife of said James Roberts, and she relinquished her right of Dower   October 27, 1785
s/ Hugh Innes, Jno Salmon
November 21, 1785

Page 532

111

Corbin from McDaniel Deed
September 5, 1785 between Henry McDaniel and his Wife of the County
of Greenbrier and Rawley Corbin of P for 90 pounds, a parcel of land
containing by Estimation 100 acres
Bounded: Beginning at a corner to Philip Pendleton in the Division of
Land made between the said Rawley Corbin and John Adams Junr,
Banister River, Mouth of the big meadow branch, North fork of the branch
to the head
s/ Henry McDaniel
Wit: Reubin Pain, Edmond Fitzharreld, Edmund Paine, William Pigg
November 21, 1785

Page 534
Devin from Leak Deed
November 21, 1785 between Francis Leak of Anson County, North
Carolina and William Devin Senr of P, Parcel of land containing by
Estimation 400 acres
Bounded: William Gray and Ansford Hughes their corner, crossing
Banister River
s/ Francis Leak
Wit: None
November 21, 1785

Page 535
Peak from Adkins Deed
November 21, 1785 between Joel Adkinson of the County of Henry and
William Peak of P for 30 pounds, a parcel of land on the branches of
Bariskin Creek containing 110 acres
Bounded: Twedell Corner on Robins Branch, John Pigg's road
s/ Joel Atkinson
Wit: None
December 19, 1785

Page 536
Terry from Terry Agreem't
This is to certify that in the year 1765 I sold unto my Son David Terry one
Negro Girl named Kate for which I have received full satisfaction. My
desire is that she nor none of her increase should be apprais'd as my Estate
for I have no right to none of them   November 5, 1785
s/ Joseph Terry
Wit: Thos Terry, Samuel Sloan
December 19, 1785

Page 537

112

Ebert from Oar Deed
December 19, 1785 between Robert Oar and Jean his wife of P & Ann,
Mary, Eve, Michail, Jacob, John, Jonas, Suzanah & Martin Ebert Heirs of
Michael Ebert, Dec'd of York County, Pennsylvania for 50 pounds, a tract
of land which was granted to the said Robert Oar by the Commonwealth of
Virginia, the pattans dated September 1, 1780 and June 21, 1784 on both
sides of Tomahawk Creek containing 900 acres
Bounded: Larery's line, Jefferson's line, Robert's line, Ellot's line, Ball's
line, Chissel's line
s/ Robert Orr
Jean (X) Oar
Wit: John Campbell, Benj Sampson, John Ball
December 19, 1785
Jane, wife of said Robert Orr, relinquished her right of Dower

Page 539
Lattamore from Watkins Deed
February 23, 1785 between John Watkins of P and Samuel Lattimar of P
for 20 pounds, a parcel of land containing 100 acres on Squirrill Creek
Bounded: James Bakirs, Richard Baynes, Roger Adkinson & Glasscocks
Lines
s/ John Watkins, Martha Watkins
Wit: Samuel Robertson, James Baker, Henry Terry, John (X) Freeman
December 19, 1785

Page 541
Blagrave from Davis Deed
July 24, 1785 between Samuel Davis of the County of Camel and Henry
Blagrave of P for 300 pounds, a parcel of land on the North side of
Bannister River & Bareskin Creek containing by Estimation 152 acres
Bounded: Bearskin Creek, John Hutchinges line, the river, Mouth of
Bareskin Creek
s/ Sam'l Davis
Wit: Aaron Hutchings, Nancy Hutchings, Ann Hutchings
December 19, 1785

Page 543
Shelton from Roberson Deed
December 9, 1785 between Richard Johnson of P and Benjamin Shelton of
P for 30 pounds, a parcel of land containing 130 acres by Estimation
Bounded: said Benjamin Shelton's line, Christopher Hutching line, Peter
Legrand, William Tucker's line
s/ R Johnson
Wit: Ja Johnson, Daniel Lowell, Thomas Hoskins

113

December 19, 1785

Page 544
Lovell from Richards
I Joseph Richards of P hath agreed to with Daniel Lovell and Rich'd Todd
of P to Deliver unto the said Lovell and Todd for the consideration of 16
pounds 8/5 Dish mold and plate molds, frying pan and Table, two feather
Beds   Aug't 17, 1785
s/ Jos Richards
Wit: Sam'l Moon Lovell, Thomas Hutchings
December 19, 1785

Page 544
Wright from Mead Deed
November 14, 1785 between John Mead and Joseph Wright of P for the
Natural love and effection that he bears for the Joseph Wright and for the
consideration of five shillings, a parcel of land containing 100 acres, it
being part of a tract laid of for Allen Adams out of a tract belonging to
William Peters Martin which said Land was conveyed by Richard Pigg of
P to Mary Mead which was my wife
Bounded: William Adams corner in Peter Legrand's line, James Mead's
line, Ellinar Adams line, line of John Addams Junr, William Addams
corner
s/ John (X) Maid
Wit: James Murphy, Mary (X) Maid, Elizabeth Denney, John Denney
December 19, 1785

Page 546
Gowing from Gowing Deed
Septmeber 24, 1781 between Daniel Gowing of the state of So Carolina
and Suffiah Gowing of P for 30 pounds, a parcel of land containing 400
acres
Bounded: the county line
s/ Daniel (X) Gowing
Wit: James Gillasby, James Landon, William (X) Gilliasby
December 19, 1785

Page 547
Cook from Hinsley Deed
December 10, 1785 between John Henslee of P and Harmon Cook of P 50
pounds, a parcel of land containing by Estimation 100 acres on both sides
of Potters Creek
s/ John Henslee
Wit: None

114

December 19, 1785

Page 549
Dejarnette from Crenshaw Bill of Sale
I Joseph Crenshaw of P in consideration of a certain tract of land lying in
Charlotte County, Virginia containing 100 acres have sold to Daniel
Dejarnatt of Charlotte County, Virginia one Negro boy, Ned, and one
Negro woman named Diley and one Negro Child named Hannah, one mare
branded on the Near buttock with a Swivel Sturup Iron, One Black roan
Mare branded on the Near Buttock thus IC, Two feather Beds and
furniture, one Chest, two Skillets, two Jugs, two Butter Pots
s/ Joseph Crenshaw
Wit: Thomson Harris, John Whitworth, Joseph Atkins
December 19, 1785

Page 549
Tuggle from Lucus Deed
January 10, 1780 between John Lucas of Charlotte County and Lodowick
Tuggle of P for 200 pounds, a parcel of land containing 100 acres
Bounded: Mouth of Rocky Creek on the North side of Pig River, Justices
line, Pig River, Joining Joseph King's Land
s/ John (X) Lucas
Wit: William (X) Stegall, William Jameson, John Montgomery, Francis
Henry
August 15, 1780

Page 551
Morgan from George Deed
January 15, 1786 between John George of P and Haynes Morgan of P for
100 pounds, 100 acres being the said land the said John George purchased
of Joel Short lying on the north side of Bannister River
Bounded: Said Haynes Morgan, Joshua Short
s/ John George
Wit: none
January 16, 1786

Page 552
Lovell from Johnson Deed
January 16, 1786 between James Johnson late of the county of P, now of
Lunenburg, and Samuel Lovell son of Daniel Lovell of P for 410 pounds,
60 pounds to be paid on demand, 175 pounds on or before February 1,
1787 and 175 pounds on or before February 1, 1788 containing by
estimation 200 acres

Bounded: the lines of John Watson Senr, Thomas Watson, and Curries
Order including the Court House of the said County with the Ordinary and
adjacent buildings thereon, being the same land and appertenances
purchased of the said James Johnson of Colo John Wilson and Samuel
Hughes
s/ Jas Johnson
Wit: none
January 1786

Page 554
Seal from Payne Deed
July 26, 1784 between Charles Payne of the County of Washington and
state of North Carolina and Solomon Seal of the County of Halifax,
Virginia for 60 pounds, a parcel of land on the branches of Sandy Creek
containing by estimation 147 acres
Bounded: Robert Willliams line, Reubin Payne's line, Hammock's line,
William Durrett's line
s/ Charles Payne
Wit: Nimrod Scott, Jesse Davis, Zachory (X) Seal, Gabriel Richards
February 21, 1785

Page 555
Sparks from Roberson Deed
June 3, 1786 between Thomas Robison of P and Samuel Sparks of P for 5
pounds, a parcel of land containing 100 acres of patented land
Bounded: Thomas Roberson's line, William Shelds line, old Shildes line,
Roberson's corner
s/ Thomas Robison, Catherine Robison
Wit: none
January 16, 1786

Page 556
Thorp from Hamblin Deed
January 16, 1786 between George Hamblin of P and William Thorp of
Henry County for 70 pounds, a parcel of land contain ing 167 acres
George (X) Hamblin
Wit: none
January 16, 1786
Persey, wife of said George, relinquished her right of Dower

Page 557
Barksdale from Linthicum Deed

116

January 14, 1786 between Thomas Linthicum and Mary his wife of P and
Beverley Barksdale of P for 110 pounds, a parcel of land containing 360
acres
Bounded: Motley's line, Kidd's line, Ellington's line
Thos Linthicum Junr
Wit: none
January 16, 1786

Page 558
Watson from Clark Deed
December 19, 1785 between Francis Clark of P and John Watson of P for
200 pounds, a parcel of land which was granted to John Justice Senr by
patent February 14, 1761 on both sides of Harpin Creek containing 100
acres
Bounded: said John Watson's corner, Dividing line that formerly Divided
Between John Justice Senior and John Justice Junr to the Back Line on the
Great Road, patent line
s/ Francis Clark
Wit: Sam'l Calland, Sam'l Smith, Sam'l Tompkins Jr
January 16, 1786
Anne, wife of said Francis Clark, being privately examined, relinquished
her right of Dower

Page 561
Crider from Ward Deed
Januray 16, 1786 between Jeremiah Ward of P and Daniel Crider of P for
50 pounds, a parcel of land on the North Side of Pigg River containing 40
acres
Bounded: Pigg River on Bouker Smith's line, Peyton Wade's new line,
Peyton Wade's old line to Pigg River
s/ Jeremiah (X) Ward
Wit: James Mitchell, James (X) Bennett, Peyton Wade
January 16, 1786

Page 562
Johnson from Wilson Deed
January 16, 1786 between John Wilson of P and James Johnson of
Lunenburg County for 50,000 pounds of Inspected Crop Tobo, a parcel of
land containing by Estimation 150 acres
Bounded: by the lines of John Watson Sr, Thos Watson, and Curries order
including the Court House of the said County with the Ordinary and
adjacent buildings thereupon being the same Lands purchased of the said
John Wilson of Jeremiah Worsham.
s/ Jno Wilson

117

Wit: none
January 16, 1786

Page 564
January 14, 1786
Shelton from Moore Deed
Janurary 14, 1786 between William More of Pand Benjamin Shelton of P
for 27 pounds, a parcel of land on the Branches of Mill Creek, it being part
of a greater tract which was granted to Christopher Gorman by patent dated
September 15, 1762 and conveyed Watson Henry to the said More by
Deed containing by Estimation 100 acres
Bounded: Branch in Adams line, Hicks line
s/ William Moore
Wit: Jas Taylor, Eliz'a Taylor, Wm Taylor
January 16, 1786
Mable, wife of the said William Moore, relinquished her right of Dower

Page 566
Price from Burton Deed Ded's
To John Wilson and William Harrison, Gent, Whereas Charles Burton by
his certain Indenture has conveyed to William Price one certain parcel of
land containing by Estimation 1250 acres and whereas Mary, the wife of
the said Charles Burton, cannot conveniently travel to and from our County
Court of P, Know ye that we trustin to your faithful & provident
Circumspection in Examining Mary, wife of said Charles Burton, whether
she does freely and voluntarily relinquishe her right of Dower
March 23, 1786
s/ Will Tunstall
Pittsylvania-By virtue of the above Commission to us directed we have
examined Mary, apart from her said husband and she relinquished her right
of Dower   March 27, 1786
s/ Jno Wilso, Wm Harrison
January 16, 1786

Page 567
Elliott from Hamblin Deed
October 22, 1785 between George Hamlin of P and Thomas Elliott of P for
100 pounds, a parcel of land whereon I now live containing 167 acres
Bounded: Adams back line, path from Hamlin to Pigg's Mill, Corners
between Stokes and Hamlin, Adamses Old line
s/ George (X) Hamlin
Wit: Silv's Stokes, Moses Vincent, James Elliott, Daniel Hamblin
January 16, 1786
Perbey, wife of George Hamlin, relinquished her right of Dower

Page 568
Payne from Payne Deed
March 26, 1784 between Elizabeth Paine, widow and relict of John Paine
of P and Charles Paine of Washington County, North Carolina for 10
pounds hath sold all her right of Dower in and to a tract of land containing
by estimation 250 acres, being the land belonging to the said Elizabeth's
husband, the said John Payne, the same whereas he lived and died.
Bounded: By the land of Robt Williams, Wm Durrett, the Widow
Hammuck
s/ Elizabeth (X) Payne
John Ayers, Elihu Ayers, Gabriel Richards
January 16, 1786

Page 569
Neal from Terrel Deed
February 18, 1786 between John Terrell of Henry County and Stephen
Neal of P for 140 pounds, a parcel of land on both sides of Byrds Creek
containing by estimation 400 acres
Bounded: Terry's Order line
s/ John Terrell
Wit: John George, Will George, Edward (X) Prior, Samuel Robertson, Jno
Ramey
February 20, 1786

Page 570
Tompkins from Tompkins Deed
October 26, 1785 between Samuel Tompkins of Halifax and Daniel
Tompkins of P for 100 pounds, a parcel of land containing 320 acres by
Estimation
Bounded: Charles Lynch corner, crossing rhe North fork of Reed Creek,
crossing the south fork
s/ Sam'l Tompkins
Wit: Will Todd, Abra Shelton, Wm Clark, Tavinor Shelton
February 20, 1786

Page 572
Blackburn from Wilson Deed
August 15, 1785 between John Wilson of P and James Blackburn of P for
28 pounds, a parcel of land on the Waters of Cheristone Creek containing
100 acres
Bounded: Lackey's line
s/ Jno Wilson
Wit: Joshua Stone, Waller Lamb

119

February 20, 1786

Page 574
Johnson from Stott
August 9, 1785 between Solomon Stott of Halifax County and Isham
Johnson of Halfax County for 150 pounds, a parcel of land on the Draughts
of Straitstone Creek containing 245 acres
Bounded: at the head of the school house, Spring Branch in a dividing line
between James Dejarnette and said Isham Johnson, Hubbard's line,
Cornelius Machaney's corner, William Collins line, Vaughan's line into
Dejarnette's line
s/ Solomon Stott
Wit: Thomas Vaughan Junr, Edward Burton, Thoms Vaughan Senr
February 20, 1786

Page 576
Richardson from Davis Bill of Sale
We, William Davis and John Davis of P, do deliver unto Holt Richerson of
King William County one Negro man by name of Rubin
s/ William Davis, John Davis
February 18, 1786
Wit: Samuel Parks, John Rowden
February 20, 1786

Page 577
Johnson from Echols Deed
January 11, 1786 between Richard Echols of P and James Johnson of P for
200 pounds, a parcel of land containing 476 acres on the main fork of
Sandy Creek and it was granted to the said Richard Echols by patent dated
November 11, 1779
s/ Rich'd Echols
Wit: Absalom Hendrick, Samuel Pruitt Junr, Zackariah (X) Pruitt
February 20, 1786

Page 578
Adams from Swan Power of Atto
I, George Swan of P, appoint John Adams Junr of P my True and Lawful
Attorney to demand and recover any sums of money due to me in the state
of Virginia and also to recover a right to a certain tract of land in P which
said tract of land was given to me by my mother, Susannah Swan by a
Deed of Gift and also being the land willed to my mother Susanna Swan by
James Weeding and when recovered to sell the same
George (X) Swan
Wit: Jos Atkins, Tho Hodges, Jesse Hodges

120

February 20, 1786

Page 579
Swan from Swan Deed of Gift
January 28, 1786
Between Susanna Swan of P and George Swan of P in consideration of the natural love and affection that I bear for my son, George Swan, and for 10 pounds, a parcel of land that was willed to me by James Weeding in his Last Will and Testament
s/ Susanna (X) Swan
Wit: Jos Akin, Tho Hodges, Jesse Hodges
February 20, 1786

Page 580
Tuggle from Breeden Bill of Sale
I, John Breden Senr of P, for 50 pounds sell unto Lodowick Toggle eleven head of cattle, ten of which are marked with a crop and half crop in each Ear, the other one branded on Cushion with a VV, seven head of sheep marked with the same mark of the Neat Cattle, three feather beds
s/ John Bredin
Wit: John Breden Junior, Thos Tuggle, Rob't Tuggle
February 20, 1786

Page 581
Mahue from Bird Deed
February 4, 1786 between John Bird of P and Samuel Mahew of the County of Charlotte for 60 pounds, a parcel of land on George's Creek containing 200 acres
Bounded: John Payne's line
s/ John (X) Bird
Wit: Arther Keezee, James Mitchell, George Marlow, Ranbart Martin
February 20, 1786

Page 583
Williams's inform'n of a Negro Slave
I have in my possession a Negro man slave named Jacob belonging to the estate of Joseph Williams, deceased, of North Carolina which said slave I request may be received and admitted to the laws of this county To Jer White. I am sir
s/ R Williams
December 14, 1785
NB Information of the above was given me the 14th of December 1785
Wit: Jere White
February 20, 1786

Page 583

Harp from Fulton Deed

August 15, 1785 between John Fulton and Rosanna his wife of P and
Bednigo Harp for 400 pounds, a parcel of land on the Waters of Sandy
River containing by Estimation 311 acres
Bounded: Billings line
s/ John Fulton, Rosna (X) Fulton
Wit: Nathan (X) Frizel, Richard (X) Watts, John (X) Berry
February 20, 1786

Page 584

Easley from Bailey Deed

February 21, 1786 between John Bailey of the County of Kentucky and
William Easley of P for 20 pounds that divided tract of land containing 100
acres being part of a greater tract of 350 acres granted to the said John
Bailey the 10th day of October 1784 by the said Grant of record
Bounded: said Grant line, Williams Peaks line formerly Joel Atkinsons's
s/ John Balley
Wit: none
February 20, 1786

Page 586

Nowlin from Dalton Deed

February 18, 1786 between David Dalton of P and Bryan Ward Nowlin of
P for 75 pounds, a parcel of land on both sides of Potters Creek containing
126 acres
Bounded: Robinson's corner, dividing line made by John Hinskee &
Bryan Ward Nowlin, Surveyed line of the Said Land
s/ David (X) Dalton
Wit: W Young, Sam'l Hughs, John Hinslee
February 20, 1786

Page 589

Adams from Owen Deed

February 4, 1786 between Thomas Owen Senr of Guilford County, North
Carolina and George Adams of P for 300 pounds, a parcel of land 395
acres on the Branches of Dan River
Bounded: James Duncan's corner, Stone's line
s/ Thomas Owen
Wit: John Wilson, Simon Adams, David Owen, Rob't Wynne
March 20, 1786

Page 590

Brawner from Nelson Deed
1786 between John Nelson of P and John Brauner of P for 50 pounds, a parcel of land on the fork of the Double Creek or Now called Beens Creek containing by Survey 154 acres
s/ John Nelson
Wit: None
March 20, 1786

Page 591
Burton from Willis Deed
March 21, 1786 between Sherwood Willis of P and William Burton of P for 3000 weight of Inspected Tobacco, a parcel of land containing 153 acres (Exclusive of two acres in Bounds of the said tract)
Bounded: spring called Ardens Spring, crossing the road, Spencer Shelton's corner, James Taylor's line, Henry Key's line, Sterling Willis's line, Gabriel Shelton's corner
s/ Sherwood (X) Willis
Wit: None
March 20, 1786

Page 592
Willis from Shelton Deed
March 20, 1786 between Armistead Shelton of P and Sherwood Willis of P for 6000 pounds of inspected Tobacco, a parcel of land containing 312 acres
Bounded: north side of the old road on Spencer Shelton's line, James Taylor's line, Henry Keys line, Sterling Willises line, Gabriel Shelton's corner, the old road, Leroy Shelton's new chopped line
s/ Armistead Shelton
Wit: None
March 20, 1786

Page 594
Adams from Hix Ded's
To William Leftwich and William Trigg, Gent, or any two Magistrates of the County of Bedford, whereas John Hix by his Indenture hath conveyed unto John Adams Junr a certain tract of land on Cherrystone Creek containing by estimation 400 acres and Elizabeth, the wife of the said John Hix, cannot conveniently travel to and from our said County Court, Know ye that we trusting to your faithful and provident Circumspection in Examining Elizabeth, Wife of said John Hix, whether she does freely and voluntarily relinquish her right of Dower   December 6, 1785
s/ Will Tunstall

Bedford-Pursuant to the within order we have examined Elizabeth, Wife of John Hix, and she relinquished her right of Dower
s/ W Leftwich, William Trigg
March 20, 1786

Page 595
Wilson from Adams Deed
March 20, 1785 between George Adams of P and John Wilson of P for 40 pounds, a parcel of land containing 204 acres more or less
Bounded: on the Draughts of Stones Spring Branch , Wilson's line, Stone's line, Stone's Spring branch aforesaid
s/ George Adams
Wit: none
March 20, 1786

Page 596
Lewis from Jones Deed
February 18, 1786 between Thomas Jones of P and Edward Lewis for 100 pounds, a parcel of land containing 190 acres on Panter Creek
Bounded: Mouth of the Dry Fork, crossing the north fork of said Creek, Col Lightfoot's line, fourth fork of said Creek
s/ Thomas Jones
Wit: William Jones, Henry Doyl
April 17, 1786

Page 598
Roberson from Emberson Deed
September 19, 1784 between Samuel Emberson and Jesse Robinson for 110 pounds, a parcel of land containing 400 acres
Bounded: Edmond Hodges corner, last fork Barskin Creek, Pigg's Road
s/ Samuel Emberson
Wit: John Hodges, William Pigg, Jesse Hodges, Joseph (X) Dyer
April 17, 1786

Page 600
Dodson from Terry Deed
November 28, 1785 between Joseph Terry of P and David Dodson of P for 100 pounds, a parcel of land containing 150 acres by Estimation on the Waters of Sandy Creek of Bannister River
Bounded: Henry's line, Henry Terry's line, Lazarus Dodson's line, Thomas Madings line
s/ Joseph Terry
Wit: Rawleigh Dodson, Thomas Madding, Thomas Shaw
April 17, 1786

Page 601
Merrick from Lawless deed
April 10, 1786 between James Lawless Sr of P and John Merrick for 95
pounds, a parcel of land containing by Estimation 138 acres on the Head
Branches of Fall Creek
Bounded: Charles Clay's corner, top of White Oak Mountain, said Clay's
line
s/ James Lawless, Mary (X) Lawless
Wit: George Adams, Hezekiah Smith, William Price Junr, D Tompkins
April 17, 1786

Page 603
Dodson from Terry Deed
November 28, 1785 between Joseph Terry of P and Lazarus Dodson for
150 pounds, a parcel of land on the Waters of Sandy Creek of Bannister
River containing by Estimation 100 acres
Bounded: Lazarus Dodson old line
s/ Joseph Terry
Wit: Thomas Madding, David Dodson, Thomas Shaw
April 17, 1786

Page 605
Fitzgerreld from Nowlin Deed
January 16, 1786 between Bryant Ward Nowlin of P and Edmund
Fitzgarreld of P for 20 pounds, a parcel of land containing by Estimation
150 acres, being a tract of land granted unto the said Bryant Ward Nowlin
by Patent dated December 14, 1785 on the draughts of Horseshoe fork of
Whitethorn Creek
s/ Bryan Ward Nowlin
Wit: None
April 17, 1786
Lucy, wife of the said Bryan Ward Nowlin, relinquished her right of
Dower

Page 606
White from Gammon Deed
March 15, 1784 between John Gammon of P and Benjamin Wight of P for
six pounds, a parcel of land on the Waters of Sandy River containing 56
acres more or less
Bounded: Said Gammon corner on William Barker's line, Benjamin
Wight's line, Gammon's line
s/ John Gammon
Wit: Edward Legg, William (X) Barker, John (X) Pearce

April 17, 1786

Page 608
Hoskins from Farthing Deed
April 17, 1786 between Richard Farthing of P, Planter, and Grissell
Farthing, his wife, and Thomas Hoskins of P for 125 pounds, the land
whereon the said Richard Farthing lately dwelt containing by a plan or
Survey 100 acres
Bounded: Parson's old line, said Farthing's Pattent line
s/ Richard Farthing, Grissell Farthing
Wit: Geo Craghead (R F), Jas Johnson (Do), R'd Johnson (Ditto)
April 17, 1786

Page 610
White from Barker Deed
March 15, 1783 between Wm Barker of P and Benjamin Wight of P for
five pounds, three shillings, thre pence, a parcel of land on the south side
of Sandy River containing 44 acres more or less
Bounded: Jno Gammon's corner, Sandy River
s/ William (X) Barker
Wit: John Gammon, Edward Legg, John (X) Pearce
April 17, 1786

Page 612
Dodson from Terry Deed
November 28, 1785 between Joseph Terry of P and Rawleigh Dodson of P
for 100 pounds, a parcel of land on the Waters of Sandy Creek containing
by Estimation 100 acres
Bounded: Thomas Madding's line, James Conney line
s/ Joseph Terry
Wit: Thomas Madding, David Dodson, Thomas Shaw
April 17, 1786

Page 613
Jones from Hammond Deed
1786 between John Hammond of P and Thomas Jones of P for 80 pounds,
a parcel of land on the Waters of Shocko Creek containing by survey 245
acres which was granted to said John Hammock by a Grant bearing date
May 1, 1780.
s/ John Hammond
Wit: none
April 17, 1786

Page 615

Burgess from Chambers Deed
January 18, 1786 between Thomas Chambers of Pand William Burgess of
P for 15 pounds, a parcel of land containing by Estimation 100 acres on
Swedens fork
Bounded: line of the Pattern to the mouth of a branch near the old path,
Burrels Vodins line
s/ Thomas Chambers
Wit: John Wright, Thomas (X) Burgess Snr, Martin Hardin, Henry
Cambell, John Ballard, John Holden
April 17, 1786

Page 616
Boaz from Buckley
April 17, 1786 between John Buckley of P and Thomas Boaz of P for
seventeen pounds ten shillings, a parcel of land containing by Estimation
181 ½ acres on both sides of the Grassey fork of Stewarts Creek
Bounded: James Boaz's line, crossing the said Grassey fork to a Corner in
Thomas Boaz's old line
s/ John Buckley
Wit: None
April 17, 1786

Page 617
Parks from Adams Jr Deed
March 17, 1786 between John Adams Junr of P and John Parks of P for
115 pounds, a parcel of land containing 185 acres on the Waters of
Bannister River and Little Cherrystone
Bounded: Said Parks corner, Nathan Adams's line, Robt Woodings line,
Mary Wright's line
s/ John Adams Jr
March 17, 1786
Sarah, wife of said John Adams Jr, relinquished her right of Dower

Page 619
Boaz from Buckley Deed examined
April 17, 1786 between John Buckley of P and Shadrack Boaz of P for
seventeen pounds, ten shillings, a parcel of land containing by Estimation
181 ½ acres on both sides the Grassey fork of Stewarts
Bounded: Thomas Boaz's old line, Maxwell's line, said Grassy fork,
James Boaz's line
s/ John Buckley
Wit: None
April 17, 1786

Page 620
McDonnald from Brawner Deed
April 15, 1786 between John Brawner of P and Randolph McDonald of P
for 55 pounds, a parcel of land containing by estimation 77 acres, the land
whereon the said Randolph McDonald now lives
Bounded: Beach on the Bank of the Double Branches on Yorks fork, a
new line now mark'd, a Boundary line Between the said John Brawner and
the said McDaniel, Bank of the Double Creek
s/ John Brawner
Wit: Ignatius Wilson, John Davis, William Brawner
April 17, 1786

Page 622
Goodman from Thompson Deed
April 17, 1786 between John Tompson of P and William Goodman of P for
ten pounds, a parcel of land containing 100 acres on White Thorn Creek
Bounded: Said William Goodman's line where it crosses the said Creek,
William Paus line, William Hopwood's line, White thorn Creek
s/ John Tompson
Wit: none
April 17, 1786
Mary, wife of said John Thompson, relinquished her right of Dower

Page 623
Echols from Hubbard Deed
April 17, 1786 between John Hubbard and Kezziah his wife of P and
Joseph Eckhols of Halifax,
Whereas John Pigg, Dec'd, late of the county of P did by his Last Will and
Testament give to his daughter, Keziah Hubbard, one tract of land being
part of the land whereon he lived in P and bounded as the said will
describes and in the consideration of 250 pounds
s/ John Hubbard, Kezea Hubbard
April 17, 1786
Kiziah, wife of said John Hubbard, relinquished her right of Dower

Page 625
Towler from Tarrant Deed
April 17, 1786 between Benjamin Tarrant and Martha his wife of P and
Joseph Towler of Bedford County for 300 pounds, a parcel of land
containing 645 acres on the South Side of Stanton River
Bounded: Lynn on the River, crossing a Branch of Lynches Creek, David
Terry's line, the River
s/ Benja Tarrant, Martha (X) Tarrant

Wit: None
April 17, 1786
Martha, wife of said Benjamin Tarrant, relinquished her right of Dower

Page 626
Owen from Martin Deed
January 4, 1786 between Peter Martin of Halifax and Uriah Owen of P for
50 pounds, a parcel of land on the Branches of Sandy Creek containing
235 acres
Bounded: Hardy's line, Simpson's line, Samps line, Wilson's old road,
Williams road
s/ Peter (X) Martin
Wit: Zachary (X) Seal, James (X) Seale, Adam (X) Davis
April 17, 1786

Page 628
Pigg from McDonald Deed
September 5, 1785 between Henry McDaniel of Greenbrier County and
William Pigg of P for 130 pounds, a parcel of land containing 218 acres on
Bannister River
s/ Henry McDaniel
Wit: Rubin Pain, Edmond Fitzhgarreld, Edmund Paine
November 21, 1785

Page 629
Cook from Bobbit Deed Trust
July 14, 1785 between John Bobbitt of P and Harmon Cook of P for 39
pounds, a parcel of land on the South side of Pigg River where the said
Bobbit now lives containing 100 acres
s/ John Bobbit
Wit: Thos Dyer, Anthony Rybsen, John H Millner
July 18, 1785

Page 631
Duncan from Robertson Deed
April 4, 1786 between Jesse Robinson and Elizabeth his wife of P and
Jesse Duncan of P for 250 pounds, a parcel of land on both sides of
Strawberry Creek containing by estimation 252 acres
Bounded: Thomas Hargett's line, crossing three Branches of Strawberry
Creek, crossing Strawberry Creek, Thomas Harget's line
s/ Jesse Robinson, Betty Robinson
Wit: Jos Akin, Edward Popjoy, Thos Price
April 17, 1786

Page 633
Hubbard from Robinson Deed
April 3, 1786 between Jesse Robinson and John Hubbard for 200 pounds, a parcel of land containing 400 acres
Bounded: Edmund Hodges corner, east fork of Bearskin Ck, Pigg Road
s/ Jesse Robinson
Wit: Hezekiah Pigg, Edey Owen, Thos Dickerson
April 17, 1786

Page 634
Rawlings from Cantrall
July 20, 1785 between Joshua Cantrall and Anne his wife of P and Henry Rolling of P for 60 pounds on both sides the West fork of Strawberry Creek, it being part of a Survey of four acres containing 150 acres
Bounded: Jonathan Thomas's line, William Rickey's former line, said Thomases corner
s/ Joshua Cantrall, Ann Cantrall
Wit: Elisha Thomas, Jonathan Elliott, Constantine Clerkson, William Elliot, John Elliot, James Blakeley
April 17, 1786

Page 636
Davis &c from Gross Power of atto
Isaac Gross of P appoint Jacob Davis and Waller Guild both of P True and Lawful Attorneys and in my name to ask, demand and receive from Anthony Asher all the land and other property which is in the County of Baltimore, Maryland to recover the same
s/ Issac (X) Gross
Wit: James Gallaway, D Tompkins, Simon Adams
April 17, 1786

Page 637
Bradley from Adams Deed
November 2, 1785 between Thomas Adams of P and William Bradley of P for 40 pounds, a parcel of land on Bannister Mountain containing 75 acres
Bounded: up the Mountain to the line of the patent, corner near Denny's fence, down the Mountain
s/ Thomas Adams
Wit: George Dodson, Seaton Beadles, W W A
April 17, 1786

Page 638
Ward Junr from Patey Deed

November 9, 1785 between Jesse Patey of P and John Ward junr of P for
20 pounds, a parcel of land lying on the Branches of Stanton River
containing 159 acres more or less
Bounded: John Dillard's line
s/ Jesse Patty, Delliah (X) Patty
Wit: Henry Ward, David Pulliam, Samson (X) Martin
April 17, 1786
Delliah, wife of said Jesse Patty, relinquished her right of Dower

Page 639
Ward from Patey Deed
April 17, 1780 between Jesse Patey and Deliah his wife of P and John
Ward of the County of Campbell for 250 pounds, a parcel of land on the
South side of Stanton River, one tract granted to James Patey for 27 acres,
150 granted to James Dinny, 45 acres granted to said Jesse November 16,
1779. Also one other tract granted to said Jesse Patey for 260 acres with
eight acres purchased of James Doss, containing in the whole by
Estimation 486 acres
Bounded: Thomas East's corner on said River Bank, Buck tree Creek,
James Doss's line, Stanton River
s/ Jesse Patty
Wit: none
April 17, 1786
Deliliah, wife os said Jesse Patty, relinquished her right of Dower

Page 641
Boaz from Contrall Deed
March 18, 1786 between Joshua Cantrall and Abednego Boaz both of P for
100 pounds, a parcel of land containing 293 acres
Bounded: Thos Boaz's line on the west side of Strawberry, on the Long
branch, Chamberlin's line
s/ Joshua Cantrall
Wit: Robert Devin, William Robison, Jonathan (X) Elliott
April 17, 1786

Page 642
Hatchett from Johnson
February 7, 1786 between James Johnson of Lunenburg County and
Edward Hatchett of P for 125 pounds, a parcel of land on both sides of the
North fork of Cheristone Creek containing 163 acres by Estimation
Bounded: Willises dividing line, the Creek, up Bar Branch to the head,
Bynum's corner, John Donelson's order line
s/ Jas Johnson
Wit: Benson Tisdall, Ro Johnson, William Tisdale

April 17, 1786

Page 643
Tanner's From Mottley Deed
March 12, 1786 between Joseph Motley and Daniel Motley of P and Floyd
Tanner of P for 300 pounds, a parcel of land on the South side of Bannister
River on both sides of Shocko Creek
Bounded: Bank of Bannister River, old patent line, Clay Brook's corner,
near Shocko Creek on the upper side, old Patent line, Thomas Jones line in
said Banister River, Mouth of the spring branch, crossing Shocko Creek,
Banister River
s/ Joseph Motley, Daniel Motley
Wit: Thos Linthicum, Joel Willis, James Walker
Eliz'a and Sarah the wifes of the said Jos Motley and Daniel Motley
relinquish their right of Dower
April 17, 1786

Page 646
Motley from Tanner Deed
January 11, 1786 between Floyd Tanner of P and Daniel Motley of P for
300 pounds, a parcel of land containing 280 acres on Johns Run a branch
of Sandy Creek
Bounded: Dugins line, old Road, Donelson Branch as it meanders to the
first principle fork, up the left hand fork to the head spring, west side of
Johns run
s/ Floyd Tanner
Wit: David Motley, Samuel Motley, William (X) Walker
(No recording date given)

Page 647
Duff from Motley Deed
March 10, 1786 between Joseph Motley and Larance Duff both of P for 60
pounds, a parcel of land containing 5 acres
s/ Jos Motley
Wit: None
April 17, 1786

Page 648
Tanner from Motley Deed
March 24, 1786 between Joseph Motley and Daniel Motley of P and
Thomas Tanner of P for 200 pounds, a parcel of land containing 200 acres
on the South side of Bannister River
Bounded: Bank of the said River, the old Patent line
s/ Joseph Motley, Daniel Motley

Wit: Thos Linthicum, Joel Willis, James Walker
Elizabeth and Sarah, the wives of the said Joseph and Daniel, relinquish
their right of Dower
April 17, 1786

Page 650
Motley from Tanner Deed
1785 between Thomas Tanner of P and Daniel Motley of P for 125 pounds,
a parcel of land containing 125 acres on the North Branches of Sandy
Creek
Bounded: Floyd Tanner's corner, crossing a bold branch, an old line,
crossing said branch several times
s/ Thomas Tanner
Wit: None
Elizabeth Motley and Sarah Motley came into court and relinquished their
right of dower

Page 651
Motley from Motley Deed
February 17, 1786 between Samuel Motley of P and Daniel Motley of P
for 6600 weight of Crop Inspected Tobacco, a parcel of land containing 92
acres on Donelson's branch
Bounded: Said Daniel Motley's corner on Donelson Branch, head spring
on Donelson Branch
s/ Samuel Mottley
Wit: None
April 17, 1786
Elizabeth Motley and Sarah Motley came into Court and relinquished their
respective right of Dower

Page 652
Johnson from Morton Deed
October 16, 1784 between John Morton of P and Daniel Johnson of P,
Planter, for 100 pounds, a parcel of land said Daniel Johnson granted by
patent dated September 1, 1780 containing 735 acres more or less on the
Waters of Sandy River
Bounded: John Morton's line, Mitchel's line, Samuel Sheilds line
s/ John Morton
Wit: James (X) Blackley, Edmon (X) Covington, John Allsup
April 18, 1785

Page 654
Shelton Jr from Shelton Deed

133

March 10, 1786 between Abraham Shelton of P and Crispin Shelton Jr of P
for the love and affection Abraham Shelton do bear to the said Crispin
Shelton Jr, a parcel of land containing 400 acres by Estimation on the
branches of Stinking River
Bounded: By the Lines of Joel Shelton, Benjamin Shelton, Joseph Mays,
Benjamin Fambrough, and Thomas Murtains line, being the land conveyed
from Hugh Jones to the said Abraham Shelton by Deed, the plantation
whereon the said Crispin Shelton Jr now lives being part of the same.
s/ Abraham Shelton
Wit: None
April 17, 1786

Page 655
Hall from Betterton Deed
November 4, 1785 between William Betterton of P and Moses Hall of P
for 12 pounds, a certain Divident Tract containing 50 acres more or less
Bounded: James King's corner on the Rock Branch on Thomas
Dougherty's line, head of Flat Rock Branch
s/ William Betterton
Wit: John Buckly, Jno Raney, Jno Watlington
April 17, 1786

Page 657
Terrel from Flowers Deed
February 15, 1786 between Edward Flowers of P and Richard Terrel of P
for 50 pounds, a parcel of land lying on the North Side of Stinking River
containing 200 acres more or less
Bounded: Land of the said Edward Flowers, bounded by lines of David
Hunt, Thomas Leister, Edward Munford
s/ Edward Flowers
Wit: Thos Tunstall, jr, William Tunstall, William George, T Tunstall, Jno
Tunstall
April 17, 1786

Page 658
Buckley from Mayes Deed
June 19, 1786 between Mattox Mayes of P and John Buckley of P for 47
pounds, four shillings, eight pence, a parcel of land on the Draughts of
Byrd and Shocko Creeks containing by estimation 109 acres more or less
Bounded: Stephen Neal's line, Brown's line, said Buckley's corner, his
former line, Claybrook's line to Mays Corner, Mays line, on the Mountain
s/ Mattox Mayes
Wit: None
June 19, 1786

Page 660
Adams from Watson Deed
June 19, 1786 between William Watson of P and George Adams of P for 250 pounds, a parcel of land on both sides of a Branch of Sandy River containing 266 acres more or less, being part of a larger tract granted to the said William Watson by patent dated October 24, 1785
Bounded: south of said branch in the said William Watson's line, Montoney's line, Thomas Sparkes's line, Nehemiah Norton's line
s/ William (X) Watson
Wit: None
June 19, 1786

Page 661
White from Holder Deed
April 6, 1786 between William Holder of P and Jeremiah White of P for 30 pounds, a parcel of land containing 87 acres on the Waters Shocko Creek and Johns Run of Sandy Creek
Bounded: a path it being a Conditional line Between said White and Bradley, said White's former line, crossing the road, Conditional line Between said White and Davis Holder Jr
s/ William (X) Holder
Wit: Braxton Mabry, William Pigg, George Wright, Jesse Carter
June 19, 1786
Susannanh, wife of William Holder, relinquishes her right of Dower

Page 663
Cunningham from Shields Deed
November 5, 1785 between Thomas Shields of P and John Cunningham of Henry County, Planter for 150 pounds, parcel on land upon which he now lives, on both sides of Sandy River containing 85 acres by Estimation
Bounded: the mouth of the south fork at James Shield's Corner, Henry Burnett's line, James Gallaway's line, John Begely's line, Mathew Sparks corner, William Shield's corner, Sandy River
s/ Thomas Shields
Wit: William Cunningham, William Shields, Joseph Shields, Samuel Read
June 19, 1786

Page 664
George from Davis Deed
June 17, 1786 between Thomas Davis of P and John George of P for 300 pounds, a parcel of land on both Sides of Stinking River containing by estimation 250 acres more or less

Bounded: Benjamin Fambro's corner in Crispin Shelton Jr's line, lines of John Barber's Survey, crossing Stinking River several times, Joshua Stone's line, head of a Branch, Benjamin Fambrough's corner to said Branch, along his Dividing line crossing the said River
Thom (X) Davis
Wit: None
June 19, 1786

Page 665
Roberts from May Deed
June 19, 1786 between Mattox Mays and Anne his Wife of P and Daniel Roberts of P for 50 pounds, a parcel of land on the upper Side of Byrd Creek containing by estimation 100 acres more or less
Bounded: said Mattox Mays line, Thomas James line, Byrd Creek, up the creek to John Ferrel's line
s/ Mattox Mays, Nancy (X) Mays
Wit: none
June 19, 1786

Page 667
Watson from Watson Deed of Gift
I, John Watson Senr of P, Know ye that I, for and in the consideration of the love, good will and affection that I do bare towards my loving son Thomas Watson of P, have given and granted to him a parcel of land containing 100 acres
Bounded: South Side of Great Cherry Stone Creek on said John Watson's old line, Pigg's Road, Pettey's line, Easley's line, Thomas Watson's line
s/ Thomas Watson Senr
Wit: Major Willis, Jonathan (X) Rigney, John Hall
June 19, 1786

Page 668
Thaxton From Clay Deed
May 2, 1786 between Charles Clay of the County of Powtan and William Thaxton of the the County of Halifax for 10 pounds, a parcel of land containing by Estimation 336 acres
Bounded: joining of Christofor Hudging, ajoining Ragdale's line, Whiteoak Mountain
s/ Charles Clay
Wit: Robert Wynne, George (X) Southerland, Tavinor Shelton, John Southerlin
June 19, 1786

Page 669

Watlington from Mays Deed
May 12, 1786 between Mattox Mays of P and John Wattington of P for 55 pounds, a parcel of land on the South side of Bannister River containing 210 acres
Bounded: Henry Blank's corner upon said river, Samuel Mathews line, Byrd Creek, up said Creek to John Owen's corner, Thomas James' line, Joseph Mays line
s/ Mattox Mays, Ann (X) Mays
Wit: Joshua Stone, John Buckley, John Dugless
June 19, 1786

Page 670
Yuille and Company from Griggory Deed of Trust
March 4, 1786 between John Griggory of P and Thomas Yuille Junr of Halifax County for 57 pounds, 10 shillings which is justly indebted to Yiille Barksdale & Company, Merchants and Partners of the County of Halifax, and honestly desires to Licence and pay & in the further consideration of five shillings in hand paid unto the said John Griggory by the said Thomas Quille Junr, the said John Greggory hath granted, Bargained and Confirmed unto the said Thomas Yuille Jurn one Negro named Alley, Sicily, Molly, George, Orange, Jacob, John
s/ John Griggory
Wit: Thoms Murdock, R Fargurson, Samuel Pryor
June 19, 1786

Page 672
Williams from Lovell Bill of Sale
I, David Lovell of P, in consideration of 100 pounds paid by Robert Williams of P for the hire of two Negroes to wit: Dick and Vinna have sold to said Robert Williams four feather beds and furniture, 14 head of cattle marked with an under kill in each ear, five head of hogs, three head of horses named Fox, Kate, a bay mare, and Citty Fisher a bay mare, two tables, 12 chairs together with all the rest and residue of my household and kitchen furniture   June 8, 1786
s/ Daniel Lovell
Wit: Leroy Johnson, Eliz Dodson
June 20, 1789?

Page 673
Reynolds from Lynch Deed
January 23, 1786 between William Lynch of P and John Reynolds of P for 12 pounds, a parcel of land containing 125 acres more or less, part of a greater tract granted to the said William Lynch by Patent dated November 6, 1783 on the Waters of Fall Creek

Bounded: Charles Harris's line, William Twedwell's line now Richard
Hintons, Harrises line aforesaid
s/ William Lynch
Wit: none
July 17, 1786

Page 675
Neal from Bayes &c Deed
June 19, 1786 between Stephen Neal of P and John Bayes Senr and Lucy
his wife, John Bayes Junr and Vicey his wife of P for 90 pounds, a parcel
of land on Byrd Creek containing by Estimation 135 acres
Bounded: said Neals corner in Terry's Order line, Byrd Creek, Isham
Farmer's corner, his line, crossing tow branches to Terry's Order line
s/ John (X) Bayes, Lucy (X) Bayes, John (X) Bayes Jr, Vicey (X) Bayes
Wit: Thomas (X) James, John (X) Owen, Rich'd (X) Worthy, William (X)
Bayes
July 17, 1786
Lucy Bayes & Vicey Bayes relinquished their right of Dower

Page 677
Owen from Pigg Bill of sale
I ,Hezekiah Pigg of P, sold unto William Owen my land and Negroes and
all my cattle and horses and my household furniture   March
4, 1786
s/ Hezekiah Pigg
Wit: William Bayes, John Hollon Owen, Richard (X) Pigg, Thomas (X)
Dickerson
July 17, 1786

Page 677
Roberson from Pigg agreem't
I lend unto Jesse Robinson and Elizabeth his Wife two Negroes, to wit:
Fisher and Jude as long as I live and then to be his property during their
Life for their own, but they are not to sell or Dispose of them on no terms
Which he receives as his Property for his Estate Willed to him by John
Pigg Except a Watch will to him by said Pigg
April 3, 1786
s/ Jesse Robinson, Ann (X) Pigg
Wit: John Hubbard, Edey Owen, Thos Dickerson
July 17, 1786

Page 678
Hodges from Hewlett Deed

138

April 10, 1786 between Martin Hewlett of P and John Hodges of P for 35 pounds, a parcel of land containing by Estimation 60 acres more or less on the Waters of Little Bearskin Creek
Bounded: In a bottom in Edward Atkins line, corner between said John Hodges Path and the Old Courthouse Road, James Dalton's corner, his line to said John Hodges line, Edward Atkins line
s/ Martin Hewlett
Wit: none
July 17, 1786
Jean, Wife of Martin Hewlett and Molly Hodges, wife of Moses Hodges, relinquished their right of Dower

Page 679
Eggleston From Tunstall Deed
February 26, 1786 between Thomas Tunstall of P and Joseph Eggleston Hailey of County of Halifax for 150 pounds, a parcel of land on south Side of Stinking River containing 352 acres more or less which said parcel of land was Granted to the said Thomas Tunstall by Patent dated July 20, 1780
Bounded: Kezee's line, Coxes line
s/ T Tunstall
Wit: John Chandler, Caty Chandler, William Chandler, Diana Chandler
July 17, 1786

Page 681
Robinson from Pigg Power of Atto
I, Hezekiah Pigg of P, make my true friend Jesse Robinson of P my Lawful Attorney for me that he may receive from Elizabeth Pigg, Exor of Hezekiah Pigg, deceased, or any other persons in possession of the Lands and other Property which I lay any claim in or to, by virture of my Father Hezekiah Pigg's Last Will and Testament.
s/ Hezekiah Pigg
Wit: Alin Gray, Miller, Elizabeth Pigg
July 17, 1786

Page 682
Jones from Russell Bill of Sale
I, William Russell of P, for the consideration of 19 pounds six shillings, have sold unto John Jones two horses, two beds, and six head of cattle
s/ William Russell
Wit: Thomas Adams, Tavinor Shelton, William Jones
July 17, 1786

Page 682

Rickett from Poiner Deed
June 20, 1786 between John Poyner of the County of Halifax and William
Rickett of P for 35 pounds, a parcel of land on the Dry fork of White Oak
Creek containing 150 acres more or less
Bounded: John Gee's line on the dry fork of White Oak, William Rickett's
line, Crossing a Beanch, Bazel Nelson's line
s/ John Poynor, Elinor (X) Poynor
Wit: Joseph Rogers, William Nelson, James Soyars, Abolom (X) Adams
July 17, 1786

Page 683
Elliott from Cantrall Deed
July 13, 1786 between Joshua Cantrall and Jonathan Elliott Senr both of P
for 10 pounds, a parcel of land containing 100 acres beginning at the new
road Vincins Corner, head of a Branch of Sandy Creek, New rode Vinson
Corner
s/ Joshua Catrall
Wit: Joseph Morton, Rob't Devin, Wm Nash
July 17, 1786

Page 684
Vincent from Cantrall
July 13, 1786 between Joshua Cantral and Joshua Vinson both of P for 20
pounds, a parcel of land containing 150 acres
Bounded: Edward Atkins corner maple on Vals fork of Strawberry Creek,
Pigg's Road, Adkins line aforesaid,
s/ Joshua Cantrall
Wit: Rob't Devin, Joseph Morton, Wm Nash
July 17, 1786

Page 685
Bailey from Willis Deed
July 16, 1786 between Sherwood Willis and Mary his wife of P and
Benjamin Bailey of P for 110 pounds, a parcel of land containing 158 acres
on the South side of White thorn Creek joining the mane county Rode
Bounded: Gabriel Shelton's line, the road, Spencer Shelton's line, Gabriel
Shelton's line aforesaid
s/ Sherwod (X) Willis, Mary (X) Willis
July 17, 1786

Page 687
Matherly from Lynch Deed
January 23, 1786 between William Lynch of P and Israel Matherly of P for
12 pounds, a parcel of land containing 100 acres, being part of a greater

tract Granted to the said William Lynch by Patent dated November 16, 1783 on Waters of Fall Creek
Bounded: Charles Harris's line, William Wilkinson's line
s/ William Lynch
Wit: Joseph (X) Hughes, Jacob Rhoades, Joshua Stone
July 17, 1786

Page 688
Crider from Wade Deed
January 16, 1786 between Peyton Wade of P and Daniel Crider of P for 150 pounds, a parcel of land on the North side of Pigg River containing 260 acres
Bounded: Jeremiah Ward's line, Bowker Smith's line, William Witcher's line, Top of the Ridge, David Ross's line, up the river to J Ward's line
s/ Peyton Wade
Wit: James Mitchell, James (X) Bennett, Jeremiah (X) Ward
September 18, 1786
Molly, wife of Peyton Wade, relinquished her right of Dower

Page 689
Moore from Shelton Deed
March 18, 1786 between Gabriel Shelton and Elizabeth his wife of P and Thomas Moore of P for 30 pounds, a tract of land containing 322 acres on the Branches of the Long Branch
Bounded: Hugh Innes's corner, John Payne's line, Innes's line
s/ Gabriel Shelton
Wit: W Pace, Vincent Shelton, R'd Todd, William Clark
September 18, 1786

Page 691
Neal from Wimbish Deed
March 29, 1786 between John Wimbish of P and Stephen Neal of P for 47 pounds, a parcel of land on Elkhorn Creek containing by Estimation 47 acres
Bounded: Stephen Coleman's line, said Neal's former line, crossing a fork of the said Creek, Stuart's line, crossing the said fork to Where it Mouths into the Main Creek
s/ Jno Wimbish
Wit: John Nash, John Wimbish Junr, Jno Stewart Jr, Joseph T Williams, M Goode
September 18, 1786

Page 692
Dix Jr from Walters Deed

141

September 18, 1786 between John Walters of P and William Dix Junr of P
for 50 pounds, a parcel of land on the Branches of Sandy, Burches, and
Fall Creek on both Sides of the main road that lead from Peytons Burg to
Dixes Ferry and joining the Lands of Robert Walters Junr, the order line,
Amy Daniel & Humphey Hindrickess, it containing 157 acres, it being one
half of the tract of land that John Walters Surveyed and Patent obtained in
1780
s/ John Walters
Elinor, wife of John Walters, relinquished her right of Dower
Wit: none
September 18, 1786

Page 693
Walters from Walters Deed
April 15, 1786 between John Walters of P and Robert Walters of P for 200
pounds, a parcel of land containing 200 acres, being the land the said John
Walters hath deeded to him on the lower Double Creek
Bounded: John Watkins line, Jonathan Hill's line, Wilson's line, crossing
the creek to Atkinson's line, Thomas Walters's line, Rob't Walters line
s/ John Walters
Wit: none
September 18, 1786
Ellinor, wife of John Walters, relinquished her Dower

Page 694
Thacker from Griffith Deed
September 18, 1786 between Jonathan Griffith of P and Randol Thacker of
P for 14 pounds, a parcel of land on the branches of Cherrystone Creek
containing 158 acres
Bounded: Martin's corner, his line, Richard Perryman's line, Person's
line, Curreys Order line, the New Road. Griffith's former line, Sith
Coldwell's line
s/ Jonathan (X) Griffith
Wit: none
September 18, 1786

Page 696
Shelton from George Deed
October 13, 1786 between John George of P and Abraham Shelton of P for
100 pounds, a parcel of land on both Sides of Stinking River containing by
Estimation 250 acres
Bounded: Benjamin Fambrough's corner in Crispin Shelton Jr's line, lines
of John Barber's Survey, crossing Stinking River several times, Joshua

Stone's Line to the head of a Branch,,Benjamin Fambrough's corner in said Branch
s/ John George
Wit: D Roberts, Will George, Fred Shelton, Crispin Shelton Jr
October 16, 1786

Page 698
Hodges from Clack Deed
October 16, 1786 between Spencer Clark of County of Franklin and Moses Hodges of P for 15 pounds, a parcel of land containing 80 acres Granted to the said Spencer Clark June 1, 1784
s/ Spencer Clark
Wit: None
October 16, 1786

Page 699
Franks from Barrot Deed
September 13, 1786 between Jno Barret Senr of P and Richard Frank commonly called Rich'd Barret of P for 15 pounds, a parcel of land on both Sides of Magotty Creek containing by estimation 50 acres
s/ John Barret
Wit: Jesse Lester, John Martin
Elizabeth, the wife of the said John Barret, relinquished her right of dower
October 16, 1786

Page 700
Reynolds from Neal Ded
To Abraham Penn and John Dilliard of Henry County, Greetings, Whereas Benjamin Neal by his certain Indenture hath conveyed unto George Reynolds 397 acres of land in Pittsylvania and Eliz'a Neal, wife of said Ben Neal cannot conveniently travel to the County to make Acknowledgm't of the said conveyance, We therefore Command you or any two or more of you, that you do personally repair to the said Eliz Neal and take her Acknowledgement of the said Indenture and examine her privately.   May 15, 1786
s/ Will Tunstall
Henry County to wit: Agreeable to the within Dedimus to us directed, we personally Applyed to said Elizabeth Neal, wife of the within mentioned Benjamin Neal, who relinquished her right of Dower.
Abrah'm Penn, Jno Dillard
October 18, 1786

Page 701

Garner from Shields Ded'm
To Daniel Hankins and Joseph Morton Esq, or any two Justices of the
Peace of Pittsylvania County, Whereas Samuel Shields by his certain
Indenture hath conveyed unto William Garner of Prince Edward County
two certain tracts of land in Pittsylvania County containing by estimation
475 acres and whereas Sarah, the wife of the said Samuel Shields, cannot
travel to the said County, know that we command you or any two of you
do personally examine the said Sarah and take her Acknowledgement of
the said Indenture.
December 10, 1786
s/ Will Tunstall
Pittsylvania-By virture of the above Dedimus to us directed, we have
examined Sarah, the wife of Samuel Shields, who relingusishes her right of
Dower
s/ Daniel Hankins, Joseph Morton
October 16, 1786

Page 702
Robertson from Westbrook Deed
May 9, 1786 between Henry Whitbrook and Mary his wife of P and
Edward Robertson of Amelia County
For 75 pounds Current Money, a parcel of land on Dry Fork Creek
containing by estimation 118 acres
Boundaries: corner where said Westbrook & Baswell Nelson makes a
corner, Thomson's Line, Frederic Ragsdale's line, Atkinson's line,
Nelson's line, It being the same tract of land which the said Westbrook
purchased of James Burk
s/ Henry (X) Westbrook
Wit: Mathew Anderson, James Bagby, John Dejernatt
October 16, 1786
Mary, wife of said Henry Westbrook, relinquished her right of Dower

Page 703
Martin from Stamps Deed
October 25, 1784 between Timothy Stamps of state of Georgia and Peter
Martin of P for 150 pounds Current Money of Virginia, s parcel of land
containing 576 acres on Branches of Sandy Creek and Upper Double
Creek
Bounded: William Payne's corner, Parrishes line, Elecllous Musick's line,
William King's line, William Russell's line, Thomas Hardy's line, Payne's
corner
s/ Timothy Stamps
Wit: Zachaus Seale, Uriah Owen, John Stamps
June 20, 1785

Page 705
Wright Jr from Hall Deed
March 4, 1786 between Henry Hall of P and John Wright Jr of P for 50
pounds, a parcel of land on the north Side of White Oak Mountain
containing by Estimation 50 acres
Bounded: Polley's Branch, Hardin's line, Carter's line, Pollys Branch
s/ Henry Hall
Wit: John Wright Senr, Thomas Wright, Peter Bailey, Henry Wesbrook
October 16, 1786

Page 706
Wright from Hardey Deed
June 17, 1786 between Thomas Hardy of P and Charles Wright of Henrico
County for 20 pounds, a parcel of land on the Branches of Cheristone
Creek containing 42 acres
Bounded: Currys order Line, a new line of Hardy's Orphan, Curry's line,
a new line of Thomas Hardy, to Finis Order, Finis Old line to a new line of
Wm Hardy's Orphan
s/ Thos Hardy
Wit: Arch Campbell, John Parks, Jesse Duncan
October 16, 1786

Page 707
Ford from White Deed
December 2, 1784 between Reubin White of P and Richard Ford of
Buckingham County for 110 pounds, a parcel of land on both Sides of
Chapman Branch containing by supposition 400 acres
Bounded: said Branch, Pains line, a new line made by John Shackleford
and Edmond Fitzgarreld, Shackleford's old line, Fitzgarrel's line, Ben
Terry's School House, Terry's said line, Pain's line
s/ Reubin White
Wit: Jere White, Jno Corbin, Linzy (X) Shumaker, Susanna (X)
Shumaker, Sally (X) Stanton
October 16, 1786

Page 708
Smith's Indenture from Southerland
August 21, 1786 between William Witcher, Ledowick Tuggle and
Jeremiah Keesee, Overseers of the Poor of the Parish of Cambden in the
County of Pittsylvania, and William Smith of P. Said Overseers by Order
of the County Court of Pittsylvania, bearing date 17th of July past, have
placed and bound by those present James Southerland, an apprentice, unto
William Smith, and with him to dwell continually from the date of those

145

present until he arrives at the age of 21 years, he being now 5 years old, during all which time the said James Southerland, his said master, faithfully shall serve his secrertts, keep his Lawful Commands, gladly obey him &c. During the four years and in consideration thereof, the said William Smith do covenant and agree that he, the said William Smith, that he will teach and instruct to read and write the said James Southerland and further agrees that he will teach or cause to be taught the said James Southerland some trade whereof he may get a livelihood and shall provide sufficient meat, drink, washing, lodging and apparent fit for such an apprentice.
s/ William Witcher, Lodd'r Tuggle, Jeremiah Keesee, William Smith
Wit: Thos (X) Bennet
(No recording date given)

Page 709
Tinley's Indenture from Moore
August 21, 1786 between William Witcher, Lodowick Tuggle and Jeremiah Keesee, overseers of the Poor for Pittsylvania County and John Turley Sen of P. By Order of the County Court of P bearing date 17th day of July past doth bind William Moore on pain of William Moore, deceased, Apprecitice unto John Turley and to dwell and serve with him until he arrives at the age 21 years, he being now five years old the 25th day of March last, during which time said William Moore shall serve his secrett, keep his Lawful Commands, gladly obey him &c. Shall not embezzle, nor absent himself day or night from his service without obtaining leave of his said master, and he shall not play for any sums of money or neither shall he contract matrimony during the term aforesaid. The said John Turley doth agree to teach and instruct to read and write the said John Moore and teach him some trade where he may get a liveyhood and shall provide sufficient meat, drink, washing, lodging and apparel, At the termination of the term aforesaid give and allow Moore what the Assembly allowed an Apprentice.
s/ William Witcher, Lodo'k Tuggle, Jeremiah Keesee, John Turley
Wit: Thos (X) Bennett

Page 710
Smith from Smith Deed
August 26, 1786 between William Smith of Franklin County and Martha his wife and Ralph Smith of P for 20 pounds, a parcel of land on Sycamore Creek and on the Waters of said creek containing 244 acres
Bounded: Near John Smith Co on west side of said creek, crossing both forks of Wheelers Branch to Pointers in Robinson's line, crossing Sychamore Creek
s/ William (X) Smith, Martha (X) Smith

146

Wit: Jno Smith, William Anderson, John Smith, Robt (X) Foster, Sam'l
Smith
December 18, 1786

Page 713
McMillion from Young
August 18, 1786 between George Young Sen of P and Stephen
Meckmillion of P for 40 pounds, a parcel of land containing 50 acres on
the South fork of Sandy River
Bounded: John Morton's line below the Mill, secon Branch, Main fork, up
the left fork of the said Branch to Back line to Isaiah Morton's line, John
Morton's line
s/ George (X) Young
Wit: Sam'l Mosley, Arther Nash, David Harris
December 18, 1786

Page 714
Wilson from Benion Deed
December 18, 1786 between William Binion Senior of P and John Wilson
of P for 500 pounds, for two tracts of land containing 350 acres on North
side of Dan River viz: one tract containing 180 acres by Patent granted to
Edmund Floyd dated June 25, 1757 and other other tract of land Granted
by patent to William Cornelius containing 170 acres dated July 15, 1774,
land where the said William Benion now dwells and lying on Dan River
s/ William Binion
Wit: none
December 18, 1786

Page 715
Shelton Jr from Shelton Deed
December 1, 1786 between Joel Shelton of P and Crispin Shelton Jr of P
for 10 pounds, a parcel of land on waters of Stinking River containing by
Estimation 38 acres
Bounded: Samuel Irby's corner in Joel Shelton's line, said Irby's line,
Thomas Mustain's line, Crispin Shelton Jr's line
s/ Joel Shelton
Wit: None
December 18, 1786

Page 717
Shelton Jr from Fambough Deed
July 4, 1786 etween Benjamin Fambrough of P and Crispin Shelton Jr of P
for 35 pounds, a parcel of land on both sides Stinking River containing by
Estimation 80 acres

Bounded: Joshua Stone's corner in Crispin Shelton's line, said Stone's line crossing Stinking River to the Mouth of a branch, crossing the said River again, Shelton's line aforesaid
s/ Benjamin (X) Fambrough
Wit: Joseph Mays, Tavinor Shelton, Fred Shelton, Abra Shelton
December 18, 1786

Page 719
Bradley from Davis Deed
December 18, 1786 between William Davis of P and Daniel Bradley of P for 5 shillingsand for divers good causes, a parcel of land on the North side of Bannister River containing 100 acres
Bounded: Adamses Corner in the river, his line, the River, being part of the same tract whereon the said William Davis now lives
s/ William Davis
Wit: Thos H Woodings, Sam'l Parks, William Miers
December 18, 1786

Page 720
Short from Kelly Deed
November 20, 1786 between Jacob Kelly of Halifax County and William Short of P for 300 pounds, a parcel of land on both sides of Bannister River containing by Estimation 425 acres
Bounded: Elijah Beckam's line, crossing the river, James Allin's line, the Great Branch, John Chattin's corner on the river, up the river, Beckum's corner, along his line
s/ Jacob Kelley
Wit: John Rowden, Aaron Hutchings, Daniel Bradley, Henry Easley
December 18, 1786

Page 722
Price from Roberson Deed
October 30, 1786 between Jesse Roberson of P and Thomas Price of P for 120 pounds, a parcel of land containing 410 acres beginning at John Dunn Senr's corner
Bounded: John Dunn senr's corner, Smith's line, John Pigg's line, Hezekiah Pigg's line, Thomas Price's line, David Weatherford's spring branch, corner of the Deed of said Land made by Jesse Robertsn
s/ Jesse Robinson
Wit: Arch Weatherford, Thomas Price, John Weatherford
December 18, 1786

Page 723
Parsons from Griffith Deed

148

December 18, 1786 between William Griffith of P and David Parsons of P
for 8 pounds, a parcel of land containing 100 acres on Branches of
Cherrystone Creek, it being part of a tract formerly the property of William
Griffith, deceased
Bounded: crossing a Branch, new line marked by Jonathan Rigney, down
said Branch to the Old line
s/ William (X) Griffith
Wit: None
December 18, 1786

Page 724
Fergusson from Worthey Deed
November 18, 1786 between Thomas Worthy of P and Henry Ferguson of
Amelia County for 200 pounds, a parcel of land containing 202 acres on
the South side of Bannister River
Bounded: John Donelson's line on the south side of Banister River,
s/ Thomas Worthy, Elizabeth Worthy
Wit: None
December 18, 1786
Elizabeth, wife of said Thomas Worthy, relinquished her right of Dower

Page 726
Stone from Shelton Deed
December 18, 1786 between Abra Shelton, Gent, late Sheriff for the
County of Pittsylvania, and Joshua Stone of P, a parcel of land containing
200 acres of land charged by said Commissioners of said County to
Ignatius Nevil Tenison for one pound, three shillings, and seven pence half
penny, taxes due on the said land for 1785 on the the Rocky Branch of
Sandy Creek
Bounded: John Bruis's corner in Thomas Clay's line, Charles Clay's line,
John Bruis's corner, his line
s/ Abra Shelton
Wit: None
December 18, 1786

Page 727
Owen from Pigg Deed
June 14, 1786 between Hezekiah Pigg of P and William Owen of P for 800
pounds, a parcel of land containing 400 acres
Bounded: Edge of the Mill Pond, William Owen's line, Bareskin Bank,
John Smith deceased line, Jesse Robinson former line, Banister river,
Thomas Price's line on the South side of Bannister River, John Pigg
deceased line, said Thomas Price's line, crossing the river aforesaid
s/ Hezekiah Pigg

149

Wit: Jos Akin, Thomas M (X) Dickinson, Samuel (X) Hughes, John
Watson
October 16, 1786

Page 729
Todd's B'd for the Collection of the Specie tax due for the year 1786
Know all by those present that William Todd, Abraham Shelton, Vincent
Shelton, Crispin Shelton Jun, Gabriel Shelton, Beverley Shelton, William
Shelton, David Hunt, Thomas Hardy, Edmund Fitzgerrall, and Daniel
Tompkins of the County of P are held and firmly bound unto Jackquelin
Ambler Esq, Treasurer of the Commonwealth of Virginia for the time
being, for the sum of 10,000 pounds on 18th day of December 1786.
The Condition of the above Obligation is such that if the above bound
William Todd shall collect, account for and pay to the said Treasurer all
the taxes which shall or may become due and payable in specie from each
and every taxable person
s/ Will Todd, Abra Shelton, Vincent Shelton, Crispin Shelton, Gabriel
Shelton, Beverly Shelton, Wm Shelton, D Hunt, Thomas Handey, Edm'd
Fitzgarald, Dan'l Tompkins
Wit: None
December 18, 1786

Page 730
Todd's Bond for Certf'e Tax due for 1786
Know all by those present that William Todd, Abraham Shelton, Vincent
Shelton, Crispin Shelton Junr, Gabriel Shelton, Beverley Shelton, William
Shelton, David Hunt, Thomas Hardy, Edmund Fitzgerrall, and Daniel
Tompkins of the County of P are held and firmly bound unto Jackquelin
Ambler Esq treasurer of the Commonwealth of Virginia for the time being
for the sum of 10,000 pounds on 18th day of December 1786. The
condition of the above obligation is such that if the above bound William
Todd shall not and truly collect, account for and pay to the said treasurer
all the taxes which shall or may become due and payable in Certificate
from each and every taxable person in Pittsylvania County
Will Todd, Abra Shelton, Vincent Shelton, Crispin Shelton, Gabriel
Shelton, Beverly Shelton, Wm Shelton, D Hunt, Thomas Handey, Edm'd
Fitzgarald, Dan'l Tompkins
Taken in Open Court
Wit: None
December 18, 1786

Page 730
Todd's Bond for Certf'e Tax due for 1785

150

Know all by those present that William Todd, Benjamin Lankford, Abraham Shelton, and Richard Todd, of the County of P, are held and firmly bound unto Jackquelin Ambler Esq Treasurer of the Commonwealth of Virginia for the time being, for the sum of 10,000 pounds on 16th day of May1786.

The Condition of the above obligation is such that if the above bound William Todd shall and truly collect, account for and pay to the said Treasurer all the taxes which shall or may become due and payable in certificate from each and every taxable person in Pittsylvania County and other articles which also were taxable which were imposed by an Act of Assembly made October session 1785

s/ Will Todd, Ben Langford, Abra Shelton, R C Todd
Taken in Open Court
May 16, 1786

Page 731
White's Bond for Coroner's Office
We, Jeremiah White, William White and William Clark, are bound unto the Commonwealth for the sum of 500 pounds. The condition of the above Obligation is that the above bound Jeremiah White is constituted and appointed Coroner of the County of Pittsylvania by a Commissioner from his Excellency, the Governor
s/ Jer White, Wm White, Wm Clark
March 19, 1787

Page 731
Dyers Deed from Hardy
April 18, 1785 between John Bailey of state of Virginia and George Dyer of P, Whereas the Power of Attorney dated the 15th day of Septmeber 1784 and recorded in P, the said John Bailey did appoint Thomas Hardy of P his Lawful Attorney to acknowledge and make a Deed of Conveyance to a certain tract of land in the County to the said George Dyer for 80 pounds on the head branches of Little Bearskin Creek, part of a greater tract granted unto the said John Bailey by Patent bearing date the 10th of October 1784 containing 300 acres
Bounded: Edward Atkins' line which corner white oak stnds on the Branch side about 200 yards below the Plantation, up the Branch on the South side to Jesse Roberson's line, Samuel Emmerson's line, Henry Atkinson's path, John Pigg's Road, Edward Atkinson's line
s/ Thomas Hardy
Wit: Thomas Maid, Thomas Hardy, Rhoda (X) Hardy
June 20, 1785

Page 732

Stone's List of Surveys

A List of Surveys made by Joshua Stone Senr, Pittsylvania County between the 14th day of June 1784 and 14th day of June 1785

July 20	John Chattin 1 Survey
	400 acres 250 lbs tobacco
July 23	Thomas Read & John Coleman Esq 1 ditto
	400 acres
	250 "
Oct 5	Benjamin Lankford Esq 1 Ditto
	404 acres
	250 "
Oct 16	William Harrison 1 Ditto
	300 acres
	250
Oct 19	Reubin Payne 1 Ditto
	485 acres
	262 "
Jan 18 1785	John Colwell 1 Ditto
	300 acres
	250 "
Jan 20	John Talbot 1 Ditto
	429 acres
	256"
Jan 20	John Doss 1 Ditto
	290 acres
	250"
Jan 28	Blizzard McGruder 1 Ditto
	326 acres
	250 "
Jan 29	John Ashworth 1 Ditto
	107 acres
	250 "
Jan 31	Blizzard McGruder 1 Ditto
	170 acres
	250 "
Feb 2	Francis Rose a Dividing line
	100"
Feb 4	George Southerland 1 Survey
	144 acres
	250 "
Feb 4	Ditto Dividing line
	100 "

Mar 29	William Witcher 1 Survey
	120 acres
	250"
Mar 31	William Irvin 1 Ditto
	575 acres
	274 "
Apr 1	William Burditt 1 Ditto
	230 acres
	250 "
Apr 15	Stephen Coleman a Dividing line
	100 "
Apr 15	Allen Woodson 1 Ditto
	100 "
Apr 20	Lodowick Tuggle 1 Survey
	2500 acres
	250 "
	John Bobbit Do
	375 acres
	250 "
	Francis Henry 1 Ditto
	267acres
	250 "
Apr 22	Joseph Martin 1 Ditto
	107 acres
	250 "
Apr 23	Thomas Livesay 1 Ditto
	210 acres
	250 "
Apr 25	George Phillips 1 Ditto
	990 acres
	322 "

Joshua Stone S.P.C.
Total 57640
July 18, 1785

Page 733
A List of Surveys made by Joshua Stone, Surveyor of Pittsylvania County since his last list rendered that is since July Court 1785

July 28 1785   John Buckley 94 Acres lay'd off from Claybrooks Track acres

Aug 1   John George 49 Acres Ditto laid off from Peter Pucket's Tract   49

acres

Aug 10   William Jenkins 1 Survey made per Warrant
         260 acres

Aug 16   William Clark 1 Ditto per Ditto
         400 acres

Nov 12   Joseph West Senr 1 Ditto per Ditto
         300 acres

Jan 7 1786   Daniel Jenkins 1 Ditto per Ditto   75
acres

         John George 1 Ditto per Ditto   50

acres

Jan 10   Crispin Shelton 1 Ditto per Ditto
         240 acres

Jan 11   William Pigg 1 Ditto per Ditto
         100 acres

Jan 17   Thomas Clay 1 Ditto per Ditto
         267 acres

Jan 23   William Twidwell 1 Ditto per Entry
         316 acres

Feb 7   John Grant 1 Ditto per Warrant   32
acres

         David Irby 1 Ditto per Ditto   24

acres

Feb 8   James Bruce Jr 1 Ditto per Ditto
         380 acres

Feb 9   Daniel Mitchell 2 ditto per Entry
         666 acres

Feb 10   Samuel Tompkins 1 Ditto per Ditto
         400 acres

Feb 22   Ephraim Witcher 1 Ditto per Warrant   68
acres

Feb 11   David Ross 1 Ditto per Ditto   14
acres

Feb 24   George Phillips 1 Ditto per Ditto
         100 acres

Feb 28   Edward Bybee 1 Ditto per Ditto   90
acres

Mar 1   Littleberry Patterson 1 Ditto per Entry
         185 acres

Mar 6	John Watkins 3 Ditto per Warrant	
	966 acres	
Mar 8	John Markham 1 Ditto per Ditto	24
acres		
May 16	John Hubbard 2 Ditto per Entry	
	550 acres	
May 17	William Divan 1 Ditto per Warrant	
	430 acres	
May 18	James Biggars 1 Ditto per Ditto	91
acres		
May 19	Charles Matlock 1 Ditto per Entry	
	251 acres	
May 22	James Crane 1 Ditto per Warrant	
	150 acres	

Signed Joshua Stone S.P.C.
July 18, 1786

Page 734
This Indenture this 27th day of October 1780 between George Adams
Adm't of Sylv't Adams of P and Henry Simmons of Southhampton County
for 50 shillings, a parcel of land containing 279 acres by Survey bearing
date the 17th day of January 1781 on the Waters of Cascade Creek
Bounded: Morgan's corner, beach on a Creek, Hampton's line, Morgans
and Hampton's corner, Morgan's line,
s/ George Adams
Wit: D Tompkins, Jonathan (X) Elliott
December 18, 1786

Deed Book 8 Pittsylvania County
1787-1790

Page 1   **Williams from Seal Deed**
December 20, 1786 between Solomon Seal of P and Robert Williams of P
for 75 pounds a parcel of land containing 145 acres by estimation, it being
the land of said Solomon Seal purchased of Charles Payne that was
formerly John Paynes that was granted him by patent the 28th of July 1780.
Bounded: Robert Williams' line, Hammock's line
s/ Solermon (X) Seal
Wit: James Lucas, Polly Williams, Lusinda Williams, William (X)
Lawson, Thomas (X) Davis, Tavinor Wisdom
January 15, 1787

Page 2   **Herndon from Duncan Deed**
January 15, 1787 between Jesse Duncan of P and George Herndon of P for
250 pounds a parcel of land on both sides of Strawberry Creek containing
by estimation 255 acres together with the Water Grist Mill and being said
land that said Jesse Duncan purchased of Jesse Robinson and was by said
Jesse Robinson, bearing date the 4th day of April 1786, conveyed to the
said Jesse Duncan
s/ Jesse Duncan, Nancy Duncan
Wit: None
January 15, 1787

Page 3   **Jones from Willis Deed**
September 1, 1786 between Major Willis of P and Thomas Jones of P for
75 pounds a parcel of land on both sides of Great Cherry stone Creek
containing by estimation 100 aces
Bounded: Edward Hatcher's line, James Blackburn, Thomas Linthicum on
the south, Benjamin Jennings on the east and William Watson on the west
s/ Major Willis
Wit: Thomas Linthicum, Junr, William Watson, John Tompson, Daniel
Taylor, James Taylor, Seth Caldwell
January 15, 1787

Page 4   **Tanner from Chelton**
November 23, 1786 between George Chelton of P and Lucias Tanner of P
for 50 pounds a parcel of land containing 213 acres
Bounded: Mark Chelton's line
s/ George Chelton
Wit: John Wright Sen, John (X) Davidson, Mark (X) Chelton
January 15, 1787

Page 6   **Adams from Shelton Deed**
November 15, 1786 between Spencer Shelton of P and Elkannah Adams of
P for 127 pounds a parcel of land containing 127 acres on south side of
Bannister River
Bounded: William Clark and Robert Martin's line, Bannister River, Allen
Adams' line, William Clark's line
s/ Spencer Shelton
Wit: George Prosize, George Wright, John Adams
January 15, 1787

Page 7   **Shelton from Shelton Deed**
October 10, 1786 between Abraham Shelton, Sheriff of Pittsylvania
County and William Shelton of P at public auction 350 acres, part of a tract
of 400 acres of land charged by the Commission of the County to Edward
Mumford for the sum of 2 pounds, 11 shillings and 11 pence, taxes due on
the said 400 acres of land for the year 1785, that being the least quantity of
land that any person present at the sale would pay for the said taxes and
their expenses, on the branches of Flyblow and Straitstone Creek
s/ Abra Shelton
Wit: None
January 15, 1787

Page 8   **Lewis from Keatts Deed**
October 12, 1786 between Charles Keatts and Archen his wife of P and
William Lewis and Jane his wife of Amelia County for 400 pounds a
parcel of land containing 400 acres on both sides of Panther Creek
Bounded: Lightfoot's line, north side of Panther Creek, John Waller's line,
John Shelton's line, it being a certain tract of land that Charles Keatts
purchased of Hall Hudson
s/ Charles Keatts
Wit: Vincent Shelton, William Griggory, R'd Todd
January 15, 1787

Page 9   **Cunningham from Watlington Deed of Gift**
I, John Watlington of P for the natural love and affection I have and bear
unto Stephen and Washington Cunningham, have given Stephen Cunagam
and Washington Cunagam one certain bay horse with a blaze in his face,
six years old this summer, said horse I bought of John Redmond
s/ John Watlington
Wit: John Clever, Joshua Stone
January 15, 1787

Page 10   **Wells from Ballinger Deed**

157

December 13, 1786 between Joseph Ballinger of Amherst County and
Mathew Wells of P for 265 pounds a parcel of land on both sides of north
branch of Sandy river containing 350 acres
s/ Joseph Ballington
Wit: Joseph Morton Junr, Joseph Austin, Thomas Johns, Thomas Clift
January 15, 1787

Page 10   Clark from Shelton Deed
January 15, 1787 between Abra Shelton, Gent late Sheriff of P, and
William Clark of P, sold at auction to said William Clark 110 acres, part of
804 acres charged by the Commission of the said County to Peter Legrand
of Prince Edward County for the sum of four pounds, 18 shillings and 2
pence taxes and cost due thereon for the year 1785 on both sides of Middle
Creek
Bounded: William Jones' line, Clark's former line,
s/ Abra Shelton
January 15, 1787

Page 11   Wright from Wade Deed of Trust
January 10, 1787 between James Wade of P and John Wright of Bedford
County for sum of 75 pounds current money of Virginia bearing interest
from the date above mentioned which the said James Waid is indebted unto
the said John Wright for five shillings for track of land containing by
estimation 391 acres, being land whereon I now live, the land I purchased
of William Peters Martin
s/ James Wade
Wit: William Esley, Joseph Carter, John Adams, John Hoskins, Fanny
Wright
January 15, 1787

Page 12   Young from Young
February 7, 1787 between George Young Senr of P and James Young of P
for 200 pounds, 150 acres on the south fork of Sandy river
Bounded: Stephen McMillion's line, James Currey's line, Jesse
Robertson, said James Young
s/ George (X) Young
Wit: William Nance, John Young, Henry Potter, Isham Williams, Seth (X)
Farrar
April 16, 1787

Page 13   Young from Young
February 6, 1787 between George Young Senr of P and John Young for
200 pounds current money of Virginia, a parcel of 130 acres on the south
fork of Sandy River

Bounded: Gray's line, Robert Williams, Isaiah Morton and Seth Farrow
s/ George Young
Wit: Isiah Morton, James Cunningham, Seth Farrar, Thomas Grisham,
James Young, William Nance
April 16, 1787

Page 14   Harris from Williams

January 9, 1787 between John Williams of Granville County, N C and
David Harris of P for 40 pounds a parcel of land on both sides of the south
fork of Sandy River containing by estimation 200 acres
Bounded: Lansford's old line, it being part of the land on which Henry
Lansford, deceased, did live
s/ John (X) Williams, Anne (X) Williams
Wit: Isham Lansford, Isham Williams, Thomas (X) Harris, Robert (X)
Williams, Elijah Williams, William W Glover
April 16, 1787

Page 15   Nance from Ricketts &c Deed

November 3, 1786 between William Ricketts of Henry County and John
Harris of P for 61 pounds a parcel of land on south fork of Sandy River
being that tract of land whereon the said John Harris lately lived containing
100 acres
Bounded: Clays line, John Brown, an Entry of Roberts
s/ William (X) Rickels, John Harris
Wit: Mathew Raney, George Fuller Harris, Seth (X) Farrer, David Scales
April 16, 1787

Page 16   Witcher From Polley

April 16, 1787 between Edward Polley and Agness Polley both of P and
Daniel Witcher of P for 100 pounds a parcel of land on both sides of
Redies Creek containing 250 acres
S/ Edward (X) Polley, Agness (X) Polley
Wit: None
April 16, 1787

Page 17   Garner from Shields

December 1785 between Samuel Shields of P and William Garner of
Prince Edward for 195 pounds a parcel of land on both sides of Sandy
River containing by estimation 130 acres bounded by Elizabeth Read's
corner. Also another tract containing 345 acres on the branches of Sandy
River bounded by Thomas Binson's corner, William Shields' new line,
Thomas Robinson's line
s/ Samuel Shields
Wit: Daniel Hankins, Joseph Morton, James Garner, Joseph Cunningham

April 16, 1787

Page 19   Polley from Witcher
March 20, 1787 between Daniel Witcher and Susannah his wife of P and
Agness Polley of P for 25 pounds a parcel of land containing 100 acres part
of a tract of land surveyed by William Young
Bounded: James Carr's line, John Reese's line
s/ Daniel (X) Witcher, Susannah (X) Witcher
Wit: John Witcher, John Rees, Robert Dalton
April 16, 1787

Page 20   Reynolds from Reynolds
April 16, 1787 between William Reynolds of P and Jesse Reynolds son of
the said William of P, Planter, for 25 pounds, a parcel whereupon the said
Jesse Reynolds now dwells containing by estimation 100 acres being part
of a great tract of 200 acres the said William Reynolds purchased of Robert
Walters and was by said Robert Walters by Indenture dully recorded.
s/ William (X) Reynolds
Wit: Thomas Shelton, Arch'd Campbell, W Wright
April 16, 1787

Page 21   Blanks from Bates
April 16, 1787 between Daniel Bates of P and Henry Blanks of P for 3
pounds a parcel of land on Bannister River containing by estimation 37
acres joining the lower part of Henry Blanks' land granted to the said
Daniel Bates by Patent dated at Richmond and joined Sam Matthesses line
and Bates Junr line
s/ Daniel Bates, Elizabeth Bates
Wit: none
April 16, 1787

Page 21   Elliott's Deed from Elliott
April 16, 1786 between Thos Elliott of P and James Elliott of P for 50
pounds a parcel of land on White Oak Creek containing 80 acres
Bounded: Stokes upper line where it crosses White Oak Creek, Adams old
line, Billenses Branch, in the fork of White Oak Creek
s/ Thomas Elliott
Wit: none
April 16, 1787

Page 22   Tanner's Deed of Gift from Motley
I Joseph Motley of P for natural affection that I bear towards my beloved
daughter Elizabeth Tanner, the wife of Floyd Tanner, I do give unto the
said Floyd Tanner two Negro slaves to wit named: Boswin and Charity,

160

being the very same two Negro slaves which I have put in possession of
the said Floyd Tanner ever since he married my said daughter Elizabeth.
March 1787
s/ Joseph Motley
Wit: None
April 16, 1787

Page 23   McCubbins from McClane Ded and rept
To John Wilson and William Harrison, two Justices of the county of
Pittsylvania. Whereas John McClane by his Indenture hath conveyed unto
William McCubbins 335 acres of land in P and where Ann McClane, wife
of the said John McClane cannot travel to and from our Court House.
Know that we trust to your fidelity and providence circumspection in
privately examining Ann Mclane, wife of said John McClane apart from
her said husband. January 12, 1787
s/ Will Tunstall
Pittsylavania County
By virtue of the above Dedimus to us directed, we have examined Ann,
wife of the said John McClane apart from her said husband, and she
relinquished her right of dower. January 15, 1787
s/ Jno Wilson, Wm Harrison
April 16, 1787

Page 23   McCubbins Deed from McClane
January 11, 1787 between John McClaine of P and William McCubbands
of P for 150 pounds current money of Virginia a parcel of land on both
sides of Rutledge's Creek containing 335 acres more or less
Bounded: Samuel Bynum's corner, Richard Gibson's corner, said
Gibson's line
s/ John (X) McClaine
Wit: Thomas Duncan, Richard Gibson, Jeney Duncan, Jno Wilson, Wm
Harrison
April 16, 1787

Page 25   Harrison's Deed from Hall
March 17, 1787 between George Hall and William Harrison Junr both of P
for 60 pounds current money of Virginia certain parcel of land on the water
of Upper Double Creek containing 153 acres
Bounded: Thomas Hardy's line, George Robert's line, Nimrod Scott's
line, said Hall's former line, Nathaniel Murrey's line
s/ George Hall
Wit: none
April 16, 1787

161

Page 26   Cook's Deed from Witcher
April 2, 1787 between John Witcher of P and Harmon Cook of P for 20
pounds current money of Virginia a certain tract of land containing by
estimation 100 acres lying on the north branch of Pigg River
Bounded: William Atkinson's corner on Pigg River, James Carr's line,
William Young's line, crossing the Corn branch, straight line to the river
s/ John Witcher
Wit: Wm Witcher, Jillian Jurery, William Leekey
April 16, 1787

Page 27   McDonald's Deed from Lay
April 1, 1787 between David Lay of P and James McDonald for 5 pounds
current money of Virginia, a tract of land in the county of P and parish of
Granvil on the south side of Sandy Creek of Dan River containing 10
acres.
Bounded: at a branch where the said McDonald and Lays line crosses on a
beech to a great Rock including the spring
s/ David Lay
Wit: Richard Fain, Absalum McDonnalld, William Lynch
April 16, 1787

Page 27   Fowlks' Deed from Wimbish
December 27, 1786 between John Wimbish and Mary his wife of P and
John Fowlkes of Amelia County for 200 pounds current money of
Virginia, a certain parcel of land on both sides of Sandy Creek containing
by estimation 400 acres
Bounded: Billings line
s/ Jno Wimbish
Wit: Christopher Robertson, Joseph Carter, Samuel Thompson
April 16, 1787

Page 28   Motley from Markham Relinq of Dower
To Benjamin Lankford, Stephen Coleman and Joshua Stone of P,
Gentlemen:
Whereas John Markham by his certain Indenture of sale dated March 1,
1780 hath conveyed unto David Motley 234 acres of land and whereas
Mary, wife of the said John Markham, cannot conveniently travel to our
said county Court to make acknowledgement of the said Indenture, we do
therefore command you, or any two or more of you, that you do personally
repair to the said Mary and take her acknowledgement of the said
Indenture. March 22, 1787
s/ Will Tunstall
Pittsylvania County

162

By virtue of the above Commission to us directed, we have examined
Mary, the wife of the said John Markham, apart from her said husband.
We do hereby certify that the said Mary volunterely relinquished
her right of Dower. March 22, 1787
s/ Ben Lankford, Stephen Coleman
April 16, 1787

Page 29   Clark's Deed from Todd as Sheriff
April 17, 1787 between William Todd Gent Sheriff of the County of P and
William Clark of P by virtue of an Act of Assembly passed in the October
session 1786 directing him the said William Todd, Sheriff of the county of
P to convey anew for all lands sold by John Owen, deceased, late Sheriff of
the said P that he, the late John Owen, deceased, Sheriff did not make
deeds for or convey to the purchasers in his life time that he exposed to
sale for the public taxes and by virtue of the clause in the Revenue Act of
Assembly, directing him then sheriff to seize and sell for so much the land
within his county as will pay the taxes thereon where there is no other
property to be found in the said county belonging to the owners thereof.
He, the said John Owen, deceased hath at public auction sold unto the said
William Clark, he being the lowest bidder, 300 acres part of 900 acres
charged by the Commissioners of the said county to Amos Thompson for 3
pounds, 7 shillings taxes and cost due thereon for the year 1782 on
Sweeting fork of Sandy Creek
Bounded: Benja Terry's corner in said Thompson line, along said old line,
crossing said Sweetings fork to Terry's line, Payne's line, crossing Old
Field Branch and said Sweeting fork
s/ Will Todd
Wit: Abra Shelton, Daniel Tompkins, Fred Shelton
April 17, 1787

Page 30   Walker's Bill of Sale from Walker
I, Joseph Walker of P for 100 pounds paid by William Walker of P have
sold unto the said William Walker three Negroes named Lucy, Lenier, and
Lenney
s/ Joseph (X) Walker
Wit: Caleb Hundley, Maridith (X) Walker, Nancey (X) Walker, Daniel
Witcher, Junr, Jeremiah Ward, William Southerland
April 16, 1787

Page 31   Motley from Markham
To Benjamin Lankford, Stephen Coleman, and Joshua Stone, Gent,
Justices of the County of P Greetings: Whereas John Markham by his
Indenture of sale dated February 29, 1780 hath conveyed unto Joseph
Motley of P a tract of land containing by estimation 281 acres and whereas

163

Mary, the wife of the said John Markham, cannot conveniently travel to and from our County Court of P, we trusting to your faithful and provident circumspection in examining Mary the wife of the said John Markham from and apart from her said husband whether she does freely relinquish her rights of dower. November 17, 1786
s/ Will Tunstall
Pittsylvania County
By virtue of the above commission to us directed we have examined Mary, the wife of John Markham, and she relinquished her right of dower. March 22, 1787
s/ Ben Lankford, Stephen Coleman
April 16, 1787

Page 31   Dix's Deed from Hendrick delivered to Thomas Barnett, admr of William Dix, deceased
February 20, 1786 between Humphrey Hendrick of P and William Dix of P for 150 pounds current money of Virginia, all the messuage, plantation and tract of land whereon the said Humphrey Hendrick now dwells containing by estimation 528 acres being a part of 3 several land grants from the Land Office of the State of Virginia dated June 21, 1784.
s/ Humphrey Hendrick
Wit: Wm Durrett, Wm Wilkinson, Robt Wynne, Nathaniel (X) Wooton, Bezaleul Wier
April 16, 1787

Page 33   Rowland's Deed from Rowland
April 14, 1787 between Simon Rowland of P and John Rowland of P for natural love he bears to the said John Rowland his son, 100 acres whereon the said John now lives
Bounded: beginning at Tunstall and Irby's Corner
s/ Simon (X) Rowland
Wit: Francis Irby, Richard (X) Terrell, Edward (X) Flowers
April 16, 1787

Page 33   Rowland's Deed from Rowland
April 11, 1787 between Simon Rowland of P and Jesse Rowland of P for natural love he bears to the said Jesse Rowland his son, 102 acres whereon the said Jesse now lives
Bounded: John Rowland' corner, Dunings line, David Irby's line, Tunstall's line, John Rowland's line
s/ Simon (X) Rowland
Wit: Fran's Irby, Richard (X) Terrel, Edward (X) Flowers
April 16, 1787

Page 34 **Mays Deed from Cunningham**
1787 between Bridget Cunningham of P and Mattox Mays of P for 70
pounds current money of Virginia a parcel of land on the south side of
Bannister River containing by estimation 70 acres
Bounded: Henry Blanks corner, Henry Farguson's line
s/ Bridget (X) Cunningham
Wit: Stephen Coleman, William Shelton, Gabriel Shelton
April 16, 1787

Page 36 **Jones' Deed from Griffith**
April 17, 1787 between Jonathan Griffith of P and William Jones of P for
30 pounds current money of Virginia a certain parcel of land containing
100 acres on the waters of Little Cherry stone Creek
s/ Jonathan Griffith
Wit: None
April 16, 1787

Page 37 **Clopton's Deed from Parrish**
January 31, 1787 between David Parrish of Halifax County Virginia and
Robert Clopton of P for 150 pounds current money of Virginia, a parcel of
land containing 160 acres by estimation on branches of Sandy Creek
Bounded: Walker's line, Elijah King's line, Henry Terry's line
s/ David (X) Parrish
Wit: Elijah King, William Russell, Phillimon Russell
April 16, 1787

Page 38 **Wright's Deed from Chambers delivered to F Wright**
December 21, 1786 between Thomas Wright of P and Thomas Chambers
of County of Halifax for 50 pounds current money of Virginia, a tract on
the south side of White Oak Mountain containing by estimation 85 acres
Bounded: Abraham Adams line, top of the Mountain, Jas Burks line
s/ Thomas (X) Chambers
Wit: John Wright Senr, James Lawless, James Birks, Henry Hardin, John
Wright Junr, Absalum Adams
April 16, 1787

Page 39 **Bradley's Deed from Chattin**
April 16, 1787 between John Chattin and Frances his wife of P and John
Bradley of County of Cumberland for 70 pounds current money of
Virginia , parcel of land on both sides of Indiafield of Cherrystone Creek
containing by estimation 300 acres
Bounded: Hutchings Road, crossing Indian field branch, Thomas
Watson's line, William Easley's line, Francis More Petty's line
s/ Joh Chattin

Wit: none
April 16, 1787
(Examined & delivered to Jno Bradley)

Page 40   Calland's Deed from Black
December 7, 1786 between Thomas Black of P and Samuel Calland of P
for 75 pounds, 9 shillings, 2 pence current money of Virginia 100 acres on
both sides of Snow Creek, part in P and other part in Henry County
Bounded: said Samual Calland's line formerly belonging to Arc'd
Graham, Snow Creek to George Jefferson's line, said Calland's corner
s/ Thos Black
Wit: L Tuggle, Sam'l Tompkins, W Young, Joseph King Junr, John
Campbell
April 16, 1787

Page 42   Vest's Deed from Pattey
October 6, 1786 between Jesse Pattey of P and George Vest of P for 15
pounds current money of Virginia a parcel of land on branches of Bucktree
Creek containing by estimation 400 acres
Bounded: James Doss's corner, Thomas Mustain's line, William Alford's
line, Bucktree Creek, John Cook's line, Doss's corner, James Doss's line
s/ Jesse Patty
Wit: Ambrose Doss, Benja Terrell, John Haster, Charles Haster
April 16, 1787

Page 43   Hall's Deed from Dudgeon
February 19, 1787 between James Dudgeon of Charlotte and Benjamin
Hall of Halifax County for 200 pounds current money of Virginia, a parcel
of land containing by estimation 430 acres being in P County formerly
Halifax
Bounded: Roger Atkersons by W Robert's Spring, Richard Lain's line,
corner of James Roberts, it being the same parcel that was conveyed to
Richard Dudgeon from James Terry by Deed dated March 19, 1767 and
recorded in the county of Halifax
s/ James Dudgeon
Wit: Ephraim Hill, William Hill, James Bruce, Charles Bruce, Will Todd,
Crispin Shelton Junr, Jos Motley
April 16, 1787

Page 44   Pruntey's Deed from Finney
October 14, 1786 between Peter Finey of Franklin County and Robert
Prunty for 300 pounds current money of Virginia lying near the mouth of
Turkey Cock Creek containing by estimation 400 acres lying on both sides
of said creek

s/ Peter Finney
Wit: Thos Terry, L Tuggle, Thomas Terry Junr, George Tuggle
April 16, 1787

Page 44   Morris's Deed from Gardner &c
January 20, 1787 between Heth Garner and Theodrick McDaniel of P and
Benj Morris of P for 45 pounds current money of Virginia a parcel
containing 100 acres
Bounded: Moor's line where Dodson's line meets it, north to Moors
Corner, Hankeses Spring Branch, Terry's Order line near Creels, side of
the Mill Pond
s/ Heath Gardener, Theoderick McDaniel
Wit: Gideon Ragland, James (X) Donilson, Samuel (X) Morris
April 16, 1787
Susanna, wife of the said Heath, she being first privately examined,
relinquished her right of dower.
s/ Will Tunstall

Page 46   Farrar's Deed from Young
December 15, 1786 between John Young of P and Seth Farrar of P for 100
pounds current money of Virginia, a parcel of land containing 200 acres on
the Smith fork of Sandy River
Bounded: Clay's order, lands of John Young, Isaiah Morton, William
Hewlett, Jesse Delosier, Entry of Capt Roberts
s/ John Young
Wit: Arthur Nash, James Young, William Nance, Lenard (X) Farrar
April 16, 1787

Page 47   Russell's Deed from Rice delivered John Barry
February 17, 1787 between William Rice of P and William Russel of P for
35 pounds current money of Virginia, a parcel of land on branches of Fall
Creek containing by estimation 300 acres it being the remainder of 504
acres that was patented to Robert Walters bearing date the 13th day of June
1780
Bounded: Orlander Smith's corner, William Russel's line, said Smith's
line
s/ William Rice
Wit: none
April 16, 1787

Page 48   Chelton's Deed from Walters
April 16, 1787 between John Walters of P and Thomas Chelton of P for
46 pounds good and lawful money of Virginia, a parcel of land on
branches of Sandy Creek containing by estimation 157 acres

167

Bounded: Robert Walter's Sr line, said John Walter's land
s/ John Walters
Wit: Wm (X) Chelton, Champ (X) Madding, Jesse (X) Runnalds
April 16, 1787

Page 49   Gibson's Deed McClain
January 11, 1787 between John McLain of P and Richard Gibbson of P for
20 pounds current money of Virginia a parcel of land on both sides
Rutlages Creek containing 100 acres more or less
Bounded: Robert Payne's corner, Henry Dixon's line, Thomas McLains
corner, crossing Rutledges Creek, Henry Dixon's line, Dixon's corner
s/ John (X) McLain
Wit: Thomas Duncan, William McCubbin, Jno Wilson, Wm Harrison
April 16, 1787

Page 50   Jefferson's Deed from Calland
October 13, 1786 between Samuel Calland of P and Peter Field Jefferson
of P for 450 pounds current money of Virginia certain parcel of land
containing 729 acres
Bounded: James Smith's corner, John Childles line, John Ball's line,
Harmon Cook's corner, said Calland's corner, Harmon Cook's line,
crossing Little Tomahawk, crossing Crooked Creek, John Campbell's line
s/ Sam'l Calland
Wit: Benja Bailey, Bowker Smith, Sam'l Tompkins Junr, Daniel Witcher
Senr
April 16, 1787

Page 51   Calland's Deed from Jefferson
October 10, 1786 between Peter Fields Jefferson of P and Samuel Callands
of P for 825 pounds current money of Virginia a parcel of land containing
875 acres on both sides of Turkey Cock Creek
Bounded: Foot of Turkey Cock Mountain in old patent line, Turkey Cock
Creek, Pearson and Wooten's lines, crossing Turkey Cock Creek to the
mouth of a branch, Wooten's line, old order line including the manor
plantation
s/ Peter F Jefferson
Wit: Bowker Smith, Daniel Witcher Senr, Sam'l Tompkin Junr, Benja
Bailey
April 16, 1787

Page 53   Calland Exor of Hopkins' Deed from Walker
September 6, 1786 between Elisha Walker of P and Samuel Calland
Executor of Arthur Hopkins estate of P for 59 pounds 6 shillings, 6 pence

168

current money of Virginia, a parcel of land containing 200 acres by estimation on Turkey Cock Creek
Bounded: Berry Mountain, crossing Turkey Cock Creek to old order line, Jefferson's line, crossing Turkey Cock creek to McGoodes line including the mill and plantation.
s/ Elisha Walker
Wit: Sam'l Tompkins Junr, Bowker Smith, Thos Clift
April 16, 1787

Page 54   Walker's Deed from Seale and Martin
April 16, 1787 between James Seal and Peter Martin of P and Samuel Walker of P for 52 pounds of good and lawful money of Virginia, a certain parcel of land containing 78 acres on waters of Sandy Creek
Bounded: Cook's corner, Harrison's line, Cook's line, Murray's line, Butts line, Waddler's line
s/ James (X) Seal, Peter (X) Martin
Wit: none
April 16, 1787

Page 55   Rice's Deed from Brewer
March 20, 1787 between James Brewer of P and John Rice of the county of Charlotte for 50 pounds current money of Virginia a certain parcel of land near the old Court House containing by estimation 173 acres
Bounded: George Elliott's line, Wm Devins line
s/ James Brewer
Wit: Sam'l Calland, Jno Wilson, Constt Perkins, Daniel Tompkins, Thomas Hoskins
April 16, 1787

Page 56   Stratton's Deed from Adams
February 17, 1787 between John Adams Senr of P and William Stratton of P for 10 pounds current money of Virginia a parcel of land containing 160 acres by estimation on the south side of Bannister River
Bounded: Robert Martin's line on the said river, Rocky Branch, a new line marked by said Adams and Stratton and Allen Adams, said river
s/ John Adams Senr
April 16, 1787

Page 57   Reynold's Deed from Neal and Perkins
June 15, 1786 between Benjamin Neal and Peter Perkins of P and Henry Counties and George Reynolds of P for 200 pounds good and lawful money of Virginia, part of two tracts of land containing 350 acres more or less
Bounded: Harris line, Mountain Run

s/ Benjamin (X) Neal, Peter Perkins
Wit: John Reynolds, Charles Oakes, Phillip Jenkins, John Briscoe, Joseph Reynolds
October 16, 1786

Page 59   Parrot's Deed from Doss
January 15, 1787 between James Doss of P and Curtis Parrott of P for 50 pounds, a tract of land on north side Volintines Creek containing 40 acres
Bounded: said Dosses corner
s/ James (X) Doss
Wit: Benjamin Terrell, Jemima Boe, Jesse Boe
April 16, 1787

Page 60   King's Deed from King Gift
I, James King of P, for the affection I bear to my loving son Joel King and daughter Salley King and Nancy King give and grant all my household goods and stocks of all kinds, also my plantation utensils
s/ James King
Wit: none
June 18, 1787

Page 60   Shelton's Deed from Shelton
June 18, 1787 between Abraham Shelton Gent, late Sheriff of the County of P, and Vincent Shelton of P That the said Abraham Shelton, late Sheriff of the county of P agreeable to a clause in the Revenue Act of Assembly directing him the said sheriff to seize and sell so much of all tracts of land within his county as will pay the taxes due thereon (where there is no other property to be found in the said county belonging to the owners thereof), sold at public auction to the said Vincent Shelton 275 acres which was charged by commissioners of said county to John Robertson of Hanover County for the sum of 5 pounds, 4 shillings and 7 pence, taxes due on the said land for 1785 and cost on both sides of Harping Creek
Bounded: said creek, Rocky Fork of said Creek
s/ Abra Shelton
Wit: none
June 18, 1787

Page 61   Watson's Deed from Watson
November 7, 1786 between William Watson of P and Samuel Watson of Prince William for 80 pounds current money of Virginia a parcel of land on both sides of a branch of Sandy River containing 100 acres more or less, it being part of a larger tract granted to the said William Watson by patent dated October 24, 1785
Bounded: Adam's corner

170

s/ William (X) Watson
Wit: Harris Gammon, John Gammon, William Gammon
June 18, 1787

Page 63   Maples Deed from Sweeney
June 18, 1887 between John Sweeney of P and Joseph Maples of P for 40
pounds current money of Virginia, a parcel of land containing by
estimation 357 acres more or less on both sides of Cherry stone Creek
Bounded: John Donelson's corner, south side of the creek, John
Donelson's order line, crossing the road, Donelson's line
s/ John (X) Sweney
Wit: None
June 18, 1787

Page 64   Parks Deed from Adams
June 18, 1787 between Elkanah Adams of P planter and John Parks of P
for 110 pounds current money of Virginia a parcel of land containing by
estimation 175 acres being the same land the said Elkanah Adams
purchased of John Adams Junr and by said John Adams Junr conveyed to
said Elkanah Adams dated September 16, 1785
Bounded: Robert Woodings line, said John Parks line, William P Martin's
line
s/ Elkanah (X) Adams
Wit: none
June 18, 1787
Mary wife of Elkanah Adams relinquished her right of dower
s/ Will Tunstall

Page 65   Duncan's Deed from Robertson
December 10, 1786 between Alexander Robertson of state of South
Carolina and Cheran District and John Duncan of P for 140 pounds current
money of Virginia a parcel of land on north side of Pigg River containing
322 acres more or less
Bounded: Peyton Smith's line, Pigg River, Rode ford to Peyton Smith's
line
s/ Alexander (X) Robertson
Wit: L Tuggle, Peyton Smith, Pey'n T Smith
April 16, 1787

Page 66   Wimbish's Deed from Lyle
April 3, 1787 between James Lyle of the County of Chesterfield and John
Wimbish of P for 80 pounds current money of Virginia, nine lots or half
acres of land in the town of Peytonsburg in P formerly Halifax numbered

in the plan of the said town as followeth: Lot 109, 110, 111, 122, 123, 124, 136, 137, 138
s/ James Lyle
Wit: Abra Shelton, Rubin Pain, Crisping Shelton Junr
June 18, 1787

Page 68   James' Power from Grimes
I, David Grimes of the County of Spartinburg in state of South Carolinia appoint Thomas James of P my lawful attorney to recover for me a tract of land lying in the County of Charlotte, Virginia which is withheld by a certain Williams from me the said David Grimes being heir at law to a certain Francis Grimes
s/ David Grimes
December 4, 1786
Wit: Haynes Morgan, Nancey (X) Yeats
June 16, 1787

Page 68   Morrison's Deed from Todd
July 16, 1787 between William Todd Gent Sheriff of P County and Mercer Morrison, merch't ,late of said county, in obedience to an act of assembly passed at the October session 1786 entitled An Act directing conveyances to be made for lands sold under the Revenue Law by John Owen, deceased late sheriff of the county of P and for 5 pounds current money of Virginia paid by Mercer Morrison to Daniel Tompkins for John Owen, deceased, late sheriff for 80 acres of land, part of 400 acres charged by the said Commissioners of P to Chamberlains Orphans and sold by the said sheriff for taxes due for 1783 in P on both sides of the Bannister River
Bounded: Weatherford's corner, John Emmerson's line, crossing the river, Hickeys Road, William Thomas line
s/ Will Todd
Wit: none
July 16, 1787

Page 69   Robert's Deed from Allen &c
November 17, 1786 between George Allen and Frances his wife and Moses Hall and Mary his wife of P and Daniel Roberts of P for 40 pounds current money of Virginia a parcel of land 38 acres of land on the draughts of Straitstone Creek
Bounded: George Allen's line, Davis line, a conditional line run by the consent of parties, Chick's line
s/ Moses (X) Hall, Mary (X) Hall, George (X) Allen, Frances (X) Allen
Wit: Richard Chick, Wm Ramey, Presley Ramey
July 16, 1787

172

Page 71   **Robert's Deed from Alford**
March 10, 1787 between William Alford and Martha Alford his wife of
Cambell and Daniel Roberts of P for 80 pounds current money of Virginia
a parcel of 170 acres on both sides of Nicks Creek
Bounded: dividing line run between Jesse Paty and Thomas Mustain on
said Patty's line now John Wargs, line for the old patent, crossing said
Nix's Creek
s/ William Alford, Martha Alford
Wit: William Jones, Joseph Roberts Junr, James (X) Doss Junr
April 16, 1787

Page 73   **Callands Deed from Kezee Trust**
May 12, 1787 between Arthur Keezee of P and Samuel Calland of P for
200 pounds current money of Virginia a parcel of land containing 943
acres being the land whereon Jeron? lives, four Negroes to wit: Jack, a
young fellow, Joe, a young fellow, also Moll, a middle aged wench, Lucy a
middle aged wench, also eight head horses to wit: one English blooded
filly three years old blaz'd face and white feet, an glass eyed black horse,
one bay mare colt three years old, one bald eagle mare branded with two
dots on the flank, one bald eagle horse four years old past branded on the
buttock, one black horse with a large stare in his forehead, one bald eagle
mare eleven or twelve years old, one bay mare with white feet and a stare
in her forehead, 17 head of cattle of different marks, ages and sizes, four
feather beds and furniture, 14 puter plates, 6 ditto dishes, 6 ditto basons, 6
chairs including all my household furniture, also my last years crop of tobo
susposed to be about 5000 weight
s/ Arthur (X) Keezee
Wit: Sam'l Tompkins junr, Sam'l Smith
July 16, 1787

Page 75   **Pendleton's Deed from Motley**
March 2, 1787 between Daniel Motley and Sarah, his wife, of P and Sarah
Pendleton of P for 170 pounds current money of Virginia, a parcel of land
on the branches of Sandy Creek containing 125 acres
Bounded: Joseph Motley and Floyd Tanner's corner, crossing a cold
branch in said Motley's old line, Daniel Motley's line formerly Tanners
s/ Daniel Motley
Wit: Ben Terry, Thos Linthicum jun, David Motley, John Parker
July 16, 1787

Page 76   **Dupree's Deed from Motley and Hall**
May 5, 1787 between Joseph Motley of P and Benjamin Hall of Halifax
and Peter Dupree of Amelia County for 400 pounds lawful money of

Virginia a tract of land on the waters of Sandy Creek containing by estimation 473 acres
Bounded: East side Echol's fork, Thomas Tanner's former line, Samuel Motley's line
s/ Joseph Motley, Benjamin Hall
Wit: John Camp, Mildred Hall, Newbill (X) Pucket
July 16, 1787

Page 77   Shelton's Deed from Shelton
April 13, 1787 between Benja Shelton Senr late of P and Leonard Shelton of P for 50 pounds current money of Virginia a parcel of 170 acres on the Glady fork of Panther Creek
Bounded: Beverley Shelton's line, Vincent Shelton's line, Crispin Shelton jurn line, Abra Shelton (Mill tract) line, Jno Grant's line and the lines that was formerly Wades
s/ Benja Shelton
Wit: Benja Bailey, Vincent Shelton, Gabriel Shelton, Armstead Shelton
July 16, 1787

Page 78   Shelton's Deed from Shelton
April 13, 1787 between Benja Shelton Senr late of county of P and Vincent Shelton of P for 90 pounds current money of Virginia a tract of land containing 400 acres on Panther Creek and Buck branches
Bounded: Beverley Shelton's line, Crispin Shelton's lines, Abraham Shelton's lines, Joel Shelton's line, Crispin Shelton junr's line, Leonard Shelton's line
s/ Benja Shelton Senr
Wit: Benja Bailey, Gabriel Shelton, Leonard Shelton, Armistead Watlington
July 16, 1787

Page 79   Campbell's Deed from Hoskins
July 16, 1787 between Thomas Hoskins and Mary his wife of P and Archibald Campbell of P for 55 pounds current money of Virginia, a parcel of land on the branches of Little Cherry stone creek containing by estimation 100 acres
Bounded: Parson's old line, Richard Farthings patent line
s/ Thomas Hoskins, Mary Hoskins
Wit: John Adams
July 16, 1787

Page 80   Tate's Deed from Watson

174

July 9, 1787 between James Watson of Caswell County North Carolina and
Nathan Tate of P for 25 pounds a parcel of land on the drafts of Double
Creek and Burches Creek containing by estimation 100 acres
Bounded: John Bennet's corner, Thomas Dodson's line, James Watson's
line, Spring branch, Stamp's line, Thomas Hill's line, Chanies line, said
James Watson's line, part of it being in a patten granted to James Watson
dated September 1, 1780
s/ James (X) Watson
Wit: None
July 16, 1787

Page 81   Cox's Deed from McBee
November 20, 1786 between William Macbee and Mary Ann his wife of
Washington County, North Carolina and James Cox of P for 75 pounds
current money of Virginia a parcel of land containing 137 ½ acres on both
sides of the east fork of Cascade Creek
Bounded: Russell's line
s/ William McBee, Mary Ann (X) McBee
Wit: William Short, John Parks, Aaron Hutchings
January 15, 1787
Mary Ann wife of William McBee relinquished her right of dower.
November 21, 1786
s/ Will Tunstall

Page 83   Hodges Sale from Brown
I Henry Brown of P for 20 pounds of lawful money of Virginia to see unto
Jesse Hodges 210 acres of land being the tract I now live on joining Gilbert
Hunt and Edward Flowers, seven head of Nutt cattle
s/ Henry (X) Brown
Wit: Isaac Clement, Jesse Rowland
September 16, 1787

Page 84   Taylor's Deed from Taylor
September 17, 1787 between James Taylor of P and Edmund Taylor of P
in consideration for the tender regard and affection I have for my son
Edmund Taylor and for five shillings I give him a certain parcel of land on
both sides of Mill Creek below the Court House Road containing by
estimation 46 acres
Bounded: Thomas Payne's line, Spencer Shelton's line, crossing Mill
Creek, Court House Road
s/ Jas Taylor
Wit: Spencer Shelton, Griffith Dickinson, Henry Kay
September 16, 1787

Page 85   **Faris Deed from Davis**
April 16, 1787 between Thomas Davies of P and Jacob Faris of P for 14
pounds current money of Virginia, a parcel of 80 acres lying on north
branches of Stinking River
Bounded: Jacob Faris' line, up the said creek, John Martin's line to
Richard Kezee
s/ Thos Davis
Wit: Jesse Mustain, Bardill Roach, James Lewis
September 16, 1787

Page 86   **Wright's Deed from Claybrook**
June 15, 1787 between William Claybrook of county of Hanover and
George White of P for 20 pounds, a parcel of 225 acres between Rocky
Branch and the branches of Sandy Creek of Banister River
Bounded: Dividing between Thomas Adams and said Claybrook, line of
the said pattern that was granted to said Claybrook, line of the said pattern
to a corner
s/ Wm Claybrook
Wit: None
July 16, 1787

Page 87   **Hodges's Deed from Ward**
September 17, 1787 between John Ward of county of Halifax and Jesse
Hodges of P for 100 pounds current money of Virginia a parcel of land on
both sides of Camping Branch of Straightstone Creek containing by
estimation 150 acres.
Bounded: John Ballinger's line, Thomas Collins line, said Jesse Hodges
former line,
s/ John Ward
Wit: None
September 16, 1787

Page 88   **Shelton's Deed from George**
August 1, 1787 between John George of County of Halifax and Abraham
Shelton of P for 500 pounds current money of Virginia a parcel of land
containing by estimation 1400 acres lying on both sides of south fork of
Allens Creek
Bounded: William Dosses Spring Branch, Haynes Morgan's line, Charles
Crenshaw's line, Richard Todd's line, William Todd's line, Daniel Jenkins
line, Peter Pickets line, William Humblet's line, James Henderson's line,
Joseph Farris line, Joseph Farris Junr line, said Morgan's line, said William
Dosses line
s/ John George
Wit: Vincent Shelton, James George Junr, W Shelton, Fred Shelton

176

September 16, 1787

Page 89   Calland's Sale from Brewer
I James Brewer of P am firmly bound unto Samuel Calland of P for 100
pounds current money of Virginia, do sell unto the said Samuel Callands
one dark bay horse about 4 ft eight or nine inches, ten or eleven years old,
brand not remembered if any, one bright bay horse four years odd about
four feet five or six inches high, and branded thus S, eight head of cattle
marked with an underkeel and a crop in the left, one feather bed and
furniture together with all my household furniture and plantation utensils.
June 21, 1787
s/ James Brewer
Wit: Bowker Smith
September 16, 1787

Page 90   Hutcherson's Deed from Tucker
May 1787 between William Tucker of P and Walter Hutcherson of P in
consideration of (Blank) a parcel of land containing 100 acres
Bounded: said Tucker's line, William Payne's line, Edmund Payne's line,
Pigg River Road
s/ William Tucker
Wit: None
September 16, 1787

Page 91   Smith's Sale from Bailey
I Benjamin Bailey of P am bound unto Bowker Smith of P for the sum of
60 pounds current money of Virginia have this day sold unto Bowker
Smith the following: one Dun colored horse six years old which horse I
had of Daniel Witcher Senr and is now in the hands of Seth Culwell and
his brand forgot, also one dark bay mare seven years old past brand not
perceivable about four feet seven or eight inches high likewise in the hands
of the said Caulwell, one wagon and gear, one two year old yearling which
I had of Gabriel Shelton, one red heifer that I had of Moses Hurt marks
forgot, five heads of hogs marked with a slit in each ear, one large old
table, one large pot, one dutch oven, one middle sized pott together with all
my household furniture and plantation utensils.
s/ Benja Bailey
Wit: James Calland, Sam'l Smith
September 16, 1787

Page 92   Croff's Deed from Bennett
1786 between Reuben Bennett of state of Georgia and Henry Croff of P for
60 pounds current money of Virginia a parcel containing 275 acres on the
branches of Frying Pan Creek

Bounded: His and William Bennett's corner, said Goad's former line
s/ Reuben (X) Bennett
Wit: Daniel Crider, Caty (X) Crider, Daniel Crider Junr
September 16, 1787

Page 93   Taylor's Deed from Hudson
February 14, 1787 between John Hudson of P and John Taylor of P for 30
pounds current money of Virginia a parcel of land containing 150 acres on
the waters of Cedar Creek
Bounded: Polly's corner, David Rosses line, Ephraim Witcher and John
Taylor
s/ John (X) Hudson
Wit: Melton Young, Daniel Witcher Junr, John Sweeney
September 16, 1787

Page 94   John's Deed from Rork
September 17, 1787 between Charles Rork of Campbell County Virginia
Executor to the estate of James Karr, deceased and Thomas Johns of P for
consideration of the sum of (Blank) a parcel of land on both sides of Pigg
River
Containing 50 acres
s/ Charles Rork
Wit: None
September 16, 1787

Page 95   Barron's Deed from Wooton
September 17, 1787 between Nathaniel Wooten of P and Josiah Barron of
P for 60 pounds current money of Virginia a parcel of land containing by
estimation 166 acres being part of another dividend purchased by the said
Nathaniel Wooton of Humphrey Hendrick containing 252 acres as by the
records of the Court of the county. One hundred fifty five acres part of the
166 acres is bounded as follows: Hendrick's line. Ten acres other part is
bounded as followeth: Wooten's old line and one acre, the residue thereof
is bounded as follows: Dixes Ferry Road
s/ Nath'l (X) Wooten
Wit: None
September 16, 1787

Page 97   Mays from Tweedwell
September 17,1787 between William Tweedwell of P and Gabriel May of
P, said Gabriel May heretofore purchased of Silvanus Stokes 186 acres of
land as by a deed recorded in the court of P being part of a patent granted
to the said William Twedwell July 10, 1767 and may more fully appear for
400 acres and whereas it is discovered by a resurvey of the said 186 acres

178

of land that there is a manifest error in the boundaries thereof by the conveyance of the said Silvanus Stokes to the said Gabriel May is rendered invalid. Therefore in order to avoid disputes the same said William Tweedwell has agreed to convey the said 186 acres to the said Gabriel May as being the first proprietor by virtue of the patent foresaid.
Bounded: William Twedwell's old line, crossing Cargill fork of Fall Creek
s/ William Twedel
Wit: None
September 16, 1787

Page 98   Tunstall from Mays release of dower
l, Margaret Mays, widow and relict, of Joseph Mays, late of the county of Pittsylvania, deceased do freely and volunterely release and quit claim to all rights, title, or demand of dower in and to 187 ½ acres of land on Stinking River which was sold by my said husband to Samuel Cox and him sold to Thomas Tunstall for which my right of dower therein l have received full satisfaction.
s/ Margaret Mays
Wit: None
October 15, 1787

Page 99   Tanner from Terry Dedimus and Report
To Reubin Payne and Jeremiah White, Gentlemen, Justices of the County of Pittsylvania:
Whereas Benjamin Terry by his certain Indenture have conveyed unto Floyd Tanner of P a certain tract of land containing by estimation 61 acres and whereas Elizabeth the wife of the said Benjamin Terry cannot conveniently travel to the court house to acknowledge the same, we trusting to your faithful and provident circumspection in examining Elizabeth apart from her said husband, whether she does freely relinquish her right of dower. November 17, 1786
s/ Will Tunstall
Pittsylvania
By virtue of the above Commission to us directed, we have examined Eliza, the wife of the said Benja Terry apart from her said husband and she relinquished her right of dower. August 14, 1787
s/ Rubin Pain, Jere White
October 15, 1787

Page 99   Stockton's Deed from Roberts
October 15, 1787 between William Roberts and John Roberts and John Stockton for 100 pounds current money of Virginia a parcel of land containing by patent 246 acres on both sides of Wet Sleve Creek
s/ William Roberts, John Roberts

Wit: None
October 15, 1787
Sarah wife of the said William and Elizabeth the wife of the said John being privately examined as the law directs relinquished their right of dower.
s/ Will Tunstall

Page 101   Smith's Deed from Flanaghan
August 1, 1787 between James Flannigan of county of Bedford and Thomas Smith of P for 30 pounds current money of Virginia a parcel of land containing 330 acres on both sides of Sycamore Creek and Ralph's Branch
Bounded: William Evans line, crossing Ralphs Branch, Crossing Sycamore Creek, William Smiths line
s/ James Flanaghan
Wit: None
October 15, 1787
Ann, the wife of James Flanagan, being privately examined, relinquished her right of dower.
s/ Will Tunstall

Page 102   Galloway and Co Deed from Casey
October 5, 1787 between Thomas Casey of P and James Galloway of P for 70 pounds a tract of land containing 282 acres agreeable to a deed made to me by Sarah Duncan relict of Charles Duncan and oldest son John Duncan of him the said Charles Duncan, deceased, and her the said Sarah
Bounded: land on which Charles Duncan's family lived upon, joining the land where James Duncan us'd to live, joining Nathaniel McGrifford's land where he now lives, Constant Perkins land
s/ Thomas Casey, James Galloway
Wit: James Macfarland, David Owen, Nathaniel Magoford, Jonathan Montg Church
October 15, 1787

Page 104   Alexander's Deed from Faris
March 19, 1786 between Charles Faris of the county of Henry and William Alexander of P for 100 pounds a parcel of land whereon the said William Alexander now lives on Fly Blow Creek containing 105 acres
Bounded: By the lines of James Bruce, Charles Crenshaw, Richard Todd, William Todd, Robert Farguson
s/ Charles (X) Faris
Wit: Thos Tunstall Junr, John Griggory
September 16, 1787

Page 105   Bradley's Deed from Hardin
September 19, 1787 between Henry Hardin of P and Daniel Bradley of P
for 95 pounds current money of Virginia a parcel of land on branches of
Banister River the north side of the mountain containing by estimation 230
acres
Bounded: By the lines of Thomas Hardy, Jesse Carter, Zachariah Waller,
Henry Hardin jr, said Theo Carter
s/ Henry Hardin
Wit: Jesse Carter, George Prosise, W Wallin, Thomas Chapwin Carter,
Joseph Carter
October 15, 1787

Page 106   Motley's Deed from Motley
October 15, 1787 between Joseph Motley of P and John Motley of P for
five shillings a parcel of land the said Joseph Motley bought of Hugh
Henry and David Qwinn lying on both sides Shocko Creek containing 670
acres adjoining William Willis, Laurance Duff, Tucker Woodson, Jeremiah
Ellington, Thomas Jones and Corbin, it being the place where the said
Joseph Motley now lives
s/ Joseph Motley
Wit: None
October 15, 1787

Page 107   Lansford Deed from Jones
March 26, 1787 between George Jones of Surry County, North Carolina
and Henry Lansford of P for 20 pounds Virginia Currency, a parcel of land
containing by estimation 50 acres on both sides of Cascade Creek, being
part of a tract of land formerly surveyed by Henry Lansford, deceased, and
bounded by the lands of said Henry Lansford, Isham Lansford, David
Stevens, Morias Jones &c
s/ George S S/L? Jones, Elizabeth Jones
Wit: Robert Bullington, Clement Nance, William (X) Mitchell, Thomas
(X) Harris, Isham Williams
October 15, 1787
Elizabeth wife of George Jones was privately examined and relinquished
her right of dower.
s/ Will Tunstall

Page 108   Jones Deed from Moreland
October 10, 1787 between Joseph Moreland of Dinwiddie County and
John Jones of P for 80 pounds current money of Virginia, a parcel of land
containing 250 acres, it being part of a large tract purchased of David
Walker of P of James Terry of Orange County, North Carolina as will
appear by the deed recorded in P dated December 4, 1773 and conveyed by

said David Walker to the said Daniel White by Deed and conveyed as follows
Bounded: Motley's line, Walker's old line
s/ Joseph Moreland
Wit: Reubin Pain, Barton (X) Terry, Randolph Corbin, Thomas Linthicum
October 15, 1787

Page 110 (No title given)
At a court held 15 day of October 1787, James Flanagan acknowledged his deed and Ann his wife relinquished her right of dower
s/ Will Tunstall

Page 110 Jones Deed from Terry
October 9, 1780 between William Terry of P and John Jones for 60 pounds current money of Virginia a parcel of land whereon the said William Terry now dwells
Bounded: David Crawford's dividing line, Brown's line
s/ William (X) Terry
Wit: Reubin Pain, Jere White, Thos Linthicum, George White
October 15, 1787

Page 111 Jones Deed Terry Dedimus &c
To Reubin Payne and Jeremiah White, Gentlemen, Justices of the County of Pittsylvania:
Whereas William Terry by his certain Indenture have conveyed unto John Jones of P a certain tract of land and whereas Mary the wife of the said William Terry cannot conveniently travel to the court house to acknowledge the same, we trusting to your faithful and provident circumspection in examining Mary apart from her said husband, whether she does freely relinquish her right of dower October 12, 1787
s/ Will Tunstall
Pittsylvania
By virtue of the above Commission to us directed, we have examined Mary, the wife of the said William Terry apart from her said husband and she relinquished her right of dower. October 9, 1787
s/ Rubin Pain, Jere White
October 15, 1787

Page 112 Clark's Deed from Todd
October 15, 1787 between William Todd, Gentleman, Sheriff of P and William Clark of P, by nature of a clause in the Act of Assembly passed in the October Session 1786 directing him, the Sheriff of P, to make deeds and convey all lands sold by John Owen, deceased, late sheriff of P, that the said John Owen, deceased, Sheriff did not make deeds for and convey

in his lifetime. By virtue of a claim in the Revenue Act of Assembly directed him, the said John Owen, deceased, then Sheriff of the county, to seize and sell so much of all lands in the county as will pay the tax due thereon (where there is no other property to be found in the said county belonging to the owners thereof) and did at public auction sell unto William Clark, being the lowest bidder, 400 acres of land charged to James Gray for the sum of five pounds, four shillings and six pence, taxes and cost due thereon for the year 1783 on the branches of Middle Creek of Banister River
Bounded: Said Creek near Legrand's line, Thos Dosses line, crossing Miery Branch, said Clark's corner
s/ Will Todd
Wit: None
October 15, 1787

Page 113   Boatman's Deed from Pace
February 5, 1787 between William Pace of P and Robert Boatman of P for 60 pounds current money of Virginia a parcel of land on both sides of White Thorn Creek containing 150 acres
Bounded: Mouth of a small branch in Armstead Shelton's line, corner on William Payne's line, William Goodman's line, crossing the creek to corner on William Hopwood's line, crossing a branch to Armstead Shelton's line
s/ W Pace
Wit: Dan'l Shelton, Gabriel Shelton, Moses Hurt
September 16, 1787

Page 114   Hardin's Deed from Hardin
June 8, 1783 between Henry Hardin of county of Wilks, North Carolinia and Martin Hardin of P for consideration for the natural love and affection he beareth to his son Martin Hardin and for five shillings a parcel of 229 acres of land
Bounded: Wright's line, Carter's line, Tanner's line, Murrics line
s/ Henry Hardin
Wit: James Lawless, John Taleaferro, Wm Hardin
October 15, 1787

Page 115   Pickral's Deed from Medkiff
August 13, 1787 between Joseph Medciff of P and Henry Pickrel of P for 100 pounds current money of Virginia a parcel of 200 acres
Bounded: West's line, an old West's line
s/ Joseph (X) Madciff
Wit: James Blackburn, Jos Robinson, Abel Marlow
October 15, 1787

Page 116   Burch Junr's Deed from Clark
May 19, 1787 between Spencer Clark of the county of Franklin and John
Burch Junr of Henry County for 40 pounds current money of Virginia a
parcel of land containing 294 acres by survey on the branches of Frying
Pan Creek
Bounded: Smith's line, Cedar Pond fork of Frying Pan Creek
s/ Spencer Clack
Wit: Sam'l Calland, James George Junr, Bowker Smith
October 15, 1787

Page 119   Dix's Deed from Shelton
September 17, 1787 between Abraham Shelton, Gentleman, late Sheriff of
P and William Dix of P. The said Abraham Shelton late Sheriff of P
agreeable to a Clause in the Revenue Act of Assembly directing him, the
said Sheriff, to seize and sell so much of all tracts of land within the county
as will payable tax due thereon (where there is no other property to be paid
on the said county belonging to the owner thereof) hath sold at public
auction to William Dix 189 acres of land being part of a greater tract
charged by the Commissioners of P to John Whealer for the sum of 30
shillings taxes due on the said land and cost for 1785 lying on both sides
the Old Womans Creek
Bounded: Edward Bybee's corner, said Whealer's old line
s/ Abra Shelton
Wit: None
December 17, 1787

Page 120   Moore's Deed from Bates
May 18, 1787 between Daniel Bates and Elizabeth his wife of P and John
Moore of P for 25 pounds current money of Virginia, a parcel of land on
the waters of Little Cherry Stone Creek containing 40 acres
Bounded: Parson's line, Hoskins line
s/ Daniel Bates, Elisabeth (X) Bates
Wit: John Hammond, Richard Farthing, John Farthing, William Moore
October 15, 1787

Page 121   Parrish's Deed from Dyer
December 17, 1787 between John Dyer of the county of Henry and Abram
Parrish of P for 160 pounds current money of Virginia, a parcel of land on
the head branches of Little Bareskin Creek, it being part of a great tract of
land granted unto the said George Dyer by John Bosley by deed dated
April 18, 1784 containing 300 acres

184

Bounded: Edward Adkinson's line, 200 yards below the plantation, up the branch on the south side, Jesse Robinson's line, Samuel Emmerson's line, Henry Atkinson's path, crossing John Pigg's road
s/ George (X) Dyer
Wit: None
December 17, 1787
Rachel, wife of George Dyer, being privately examined, relinquished her right of dower.
s/ Will Tunstall

Page 123   Simpson's Deed from Owen
November 19, 1787 between Uriah Owen of P and Loyd Simpson of P for 30 pounds lawful money of Virginia, a tract of land near Sandy Creek, being part of a tract where the said Uriah Owen now lives, of which is a parcel of land containing 100 acres
Bounded: Said Simpson's line, Elijah Cook's line, Waller's line, John Stamps's line, Simpson's old spring branch
s/ Uriah Owen
Wit: Jer Simpson, Elijah Cook, Erasamus Simpson
December 17, 1787

Page 124   Jones Deed from Crawford
January 20, 1788 between David Crawford of P and John Jones of P for 30 pounds current money of Virginia a parcel of land containing by estimation 65 acres beginning on waters Shocko Creek
Bounded: a dividing line between the tract of land that the said John Jones purchased of William Terry
s/ David (X) Crawford
Wit: Benja Shelton, Thos Linthicum
January 21, 1788
Christain, wife of David Crawford, relinquished her right of dower
s/ Will Tunstall

Page 126   Ward's Deed from Mitchell
January 21, 1788 between James Mitchell of P and Jeremiah Ward of P for 160 pounds current money of Virginia, a parcel of land on both sides of Potters Creek containing 252 acres
Bounded: Bryant Ward Nowlins line, by William Thompson's heirs, Harmon Cook's line, by survey made by Joshua Stone for the said Mitchell
s/ James Mitchell
Wit: None
January 21, 1788
Aggathy, wife of James Mitchell, relinquished her right of dower
s/ Will Tunstall

Page 127   Covington's Deed from Austin
October 1, 1787 between Joseph Austin of P and Edmond Covington of P
for 60 pounds current money of Virginia a parcel of land on the forks of
Sandy River containing 172 acres
Bounded: David Hankins corner, Wm Payne's line, Yarringtons or
Hankins line, James Morton's line, on the fork of Sandy River, Daniel
Hankins line
s/ Joseph Austin
Wit: William Austin, John Austin, Champness Austin
January 21, 1788

Page 129   Adkins Deed from Gorman
November 7, 1787 between John Gorman of state of South Carolina and
Edward Adkins of P for 100 pounds current money of Virginia, a parcel of
land lying on both sides of Barskin Creek containing by estimation 169
acres
Bounded: Great Road, John Jackson
s/ John (X) Gorman
Wit: Edw's Nunnele, Jesse Hodges, Abner Adkins, Joseph Morton, Joseph
Austin
January 21, 1788

Page 131   Hammond's Deed from Persons
September 15, 1786 between John Person and Sarah, his wife, and John
Hammond of P for 20 pounds current money of Virginia a parcel of land
on the waters of Mill Creek containing 100 acres
Bounded: Persimmon Branch of Mill Creek, Martin's line, Roches line,
head of the south fork of the Persimmon Branch of Mill Creek, Roaches
line
s/ John (X) Persons, Sarah (X) Persons
Wit: Daniel Bates, Thomas (X) Rock, Richard Farthing, William Moore
April 16, 1787

Page 133   Lausett's Deed from Cox
August 18, 1787 between John Cox of county of Henry and John Andrew
Lausett and Company of P for 15 pounds current money of Virginia a
parcel of land on Little Bearskin on the waters thereof containing by
estimation 265 acres
Bounded: the Road
s/ John Cox
Wit: Arch Campbell, A? Bardett , Stephen Yates
January 21, 1788

Page 135   **Smith's Bill of Sale from Green**

I, William Green, of P for the sum of 30 pounds have sold to John Smith of
P one gray mare branded on the near shoulder and buttock thus V, one cow
and calf, one feather bed and furniture, one sow marked with a staple for h
in the left ear and the aforesaid cow marked with a smooth crop in the right
ear, a quanitity of pewter viz: two dishes, four basons and eight plates, the
whole of the plantation tools together with the crop new made or growing.
s/ William Green
Wit: Ra Smith, Sam Smith
January 21, 1788

Page 135   **Ward's Bill of Sale from Watkins**

Joseph Walker & William Walker of P for 250 pounds current money of
Virginia or 500 acres of land to us in hand paid by Jeremiah Ward of P
have sold unto Jeremiah Ward one Negro woman named Luce, one Negro
girl named Linny and their future Increase, and one Negro boy named
Squire. June 30, 1787
s/ Joseph (X) Walker, William (X) Walker
Wit: James Mitchell, Jeremiah Ward Junr, Daniel Witcher Junr, John (X)
Hudson
February 18, 1788

Page 136   **Yates Deed from Medkiff**

February 18, 1788 between John Medkiff Senr and Agnes his wife of P and
Stephen Yates of P for 50 pounds current money of Virginia a parcel of
land on the upper part of Mill Creek containing 70 acres
Bounded: John Williams line, John Cox's line, Sawpit Branch, said John
Medkiff's line
s/ John Medkiff
Wit: None
February 18, 1788
Agnes, wife of John Midkiff, released her right of dower
s/ Will Tunstall

Page 138   **Callands & Smith's Deed from Brewer**

February 16, 1788 between James Brewer of P and Calland & Smith of P
for 75 pounds current money of Virginia a parcel of land formerly
purchased by James Smith and Company of George Jefferson, divided by
Sailors Creek lying on the south side of said Creek containing by
estimation 250 acres being the land where on the said Smith & Company
formerly resided near Pittsylvania's old Courthouse whereon the Store
House now occupied by the said Calland & Smith stands and the plantation
thereunto adjoining which land was decreed to the said James Brewer in

the High Court of Chancery in Richmond December 3 last as will appear
by the said records of the said Court of Chancery.
s/ James Brewer
Wit: Jno Tompkins, Will Shelton, Tavenor Shelton, Jam Tompkins Jr
February 18, 1788

Page 139   Denton's Deed from Cox
October 12, 1787 between James Cox and Elizabeth, his wife, and James
Denton of P for 90 pounds, 137 ½ acres on both sides of Cascade Creek
s/ James Cox, Elizabeth Cox
Wit: John (X) Cox, Robert (X) Gilmore, Wm (X) Worsham
February 18, 1788

Page 141   Robert's Bill of Sale from Roberts
I, Daniel Roberts, for consideration of the sum of 100 pounds paid by
Joseph Roberts of P, have sold unto the said Joseph Roberts six Negroes:
Grace, Dice, Ned, Steven, Milly and Lonnon, also two horses, five head
cattle, 20 head of hogs, five feather beds and furniture, and one desk, two
chests &c, one wagon and gear, 18 chairs, two cubards and three furniture
and all my pewter, also all working tools
s/ D Roberts
Wit: Joseph Roberts Junr, Harrod Roberts
February 18, 1788

Page 142   Price's Deed from Tomlin &c
September 18, 1787 between John Tomlin Senr and Mary, his wife, and
Jasper Tomlin and Alice, his wife, of P and William Price of P for 150
pounds current money of Virginia a parcel of land containing by estimation
270 acres on the Sandy Creek of Dan River
Bounded: fork of said Sandy in said Tomlin's line
s/ John (X) Tomberling, Jasper (X) Tomberling, Alice (X) Tomberling,
Wit: John May, Daniel Price, Cuthburd Price
February 18, 1788

Page 143   Dunn Junr Deed from Cantrell &c
October 6, 1787 between Joshua Cantrall and Jesse Vinson of P and John
Dunn Junr of P for 30 pounds, all that tract of land on the branches of
Strawberry and Sandy Creek containing by estimation 150 acres being part
of a greater tract of 250 acres granted to the said Joshua Cantrall by patent
bearing date April 17, 1784 and was conveyed to the said Jesse Vinson by
said Joshua Cantrall by deed dated July 13, 1786 & that the same is invalid
and insufficient in law to convey a title and the same is bounded as in and
by the said deed is expressed
s/ Joshua Cantrall, Jesse (X) Vincent

Wit: Joseph Morton, John (X) Dunn, James Cunningham, Edward (X)
Popjoy
February 18, 1788

Page 145   Midkiff Junr's Deed from Yates
February 18, 1787 between Stephen Yates of P and John Midkiff of P for
50 pounds current money of Virginia, a certain parcel of land containing
50 acres
Bounded: Jesse Robertson's corner, Wm Short's line, Curry's line, Joseph
Parson's line, John Rowland's line, Jesse Robertson's corner, Richard
Farthing and Rowlands, said Robertson's line
s/ Stephen Yates
Wit: None
February 15, 1788

Page 146   Clark's Deed from Todd
February 16, 1788 between William Todd, Gentleman, late Sheriff of P
and William Clark of P. That the said William Todd, late Sheriff of P,
agreeable to a Clause in the Revenue Act of Assembly, directing him, the
said Sheriff, to seize and sell so much of all tracts of land within his county
as will pay the tax due thereon (where there is no other property to be paid
on the said county belonging to the owner thereof) hath sold at public
auction to William Clark 200 acres of land it being part of 690 acres
charged by the Commissioners of P to Peter Legrand of the county of
Prince Edward for the sum of four pounds, 2 shillings and nine pence
taxes due on the said land and cost
Bounded: Wm Jones lines, crossing two branches & the Meadow Road,
Armstead Shelton's line, Meadows Road, Middle Creek, said Clark's line
s/ Will Todd
Wit: None
February 18, 1788

Page 147   Shelton Junr Deed from Todd delivered
October 10, 1787 between William Todd, Gentleman, late Sheriff of P and
Crispin Shelton Junr of P. That the said William Todd late Sheriff of P in
obedience to a Clause in the Revenue Law which directs him the said
Sheriff to seize and sell as much of all tracts of land lying within his
county that will pay the tax due thereon (where there is no other property
to be paid on the said county belonging to the owner thereof) hath sold at
public auction to Crispin Shelton Junr 280 charged by the Commissioners
of P to Amos Thompson for the sum of two pounds, 8shillings and one
penny half penny taxes due on the said land and cost for the year 1786
lying on both sides of Sweetings fork of Sandy Creek being the residue of
a greater tract of 900 acres

Bounded: Jeremiah White's line, Sweetings fork, old field branch
s/ Will Todd
Wit: None
February 18, 1788

Page 149   Wimbish's Deed Trust from Mitchell
I James Mitchell of P, am bound unto John Wimbish of P in the sum of 36
pounds current money of Virginia with legal interest thereon from this
date. I have this day have sold to the said Jno Wimbish the following
personal estate, to wit: three feather beds and furniture, six heads of cattle
to wit: one cow branded the marked not remembered, also the said cow
yearling branded one pied cow red and white, one red cow with a white
back, one pied yearling red and white, the last a last afore mentioned
marked with a swallow fork in the right ear and a crop and slit in the left
ear, one stone colt two years old last spring of a black colored intermixed
with white hairs, branded on the near shoulder and off buttock with a
stirrup iron and one bay horse with a star in his forehead, some saddle
spots branded on the near shoulder 3, on the near buttock RC, and on the
off buttock an H I, also all my household furniture.
s/ James Mitchell
Wit: None
February 18, 1788

Page 150   Self's Deed from Lattimore
August 21, 1787 between Samuel Lattimore of P and Thomas Self of P for
50 pounds current money, a parcel of land on both sides of Squirrel Creek
containing 100 acres of land.
s/ Samuel Lattimore
Wit: Haynes Morgan, Rich'd Anderson, Thoms Anderson
February 18, 1788

Page 152   Calland's Bill of Sale from King
I, Joseph King Senr of P, am firmly bound unto Samuel Calland, merchant
of P for 72 pounds, 15 shillings and three pence current money of Virginia,
and honestly desiring to pay the same hath sold unto Samuel Calland one
Negro wench named Jane and her increase now left in the hands of my son
Joseph King Jurn and all my crop of tobacco I made on my plantation this
year, also 25 barrels of corn left in the hands of Thomas Ramsey.
s/ Joseph King
Wit: John Smith, Abra Frisse
April 18, 1788

Page 153   F Shelton's Deed from Todd

February 18, 1788 between William Todd, Gentleman, late Sheriff of P and Frederick Shelton of P. The said William Todd, sheriff of P, hath in obedience to a clause in the Revenue Law which directs him the said Sheriff to seize and sell so much of all tracts of land within his county as will pay the taxes due thereon (where there is no other property to be found in the said county belonging to the owner thereof) sold unto said Frederick Shelton for two pounds, five shillings taxes due for 1786, a parcel of 200 acres of land charged by the Commission of the said county to Thomas Made, that being the last quanity of land that any person present at the sale would pay. Said land lies on the branches of Cherry stone and Banister River
Bounded: Thomas Hardy's line, George Myers line
s/ Will Todd
Wit: None
February 18, 1788

Page 154   W Shelton's Deed from Todd

February 18, 1788 between William Todd, Gentleman, late Sheriff of P and William Shelton of P. The said William Todd, sheriff of P, hath in obedience to a clause in the Revenue Law which directs him the said Sheriff to seize and sell so much of all tracts of land within his county as will pay the taxes due thereon (where there is no other property to be found in the said county belonging to the owner thereof) sold unto said William Shelton for two pounds taxes due for 1786, a parcel of 96 acres of land charged by the Commission of the said county to Richard Ryan, that being the last quanity of land that any person present at the sale would pay. Said land lies on the draughts of the north fork of Straightstone Creek
Bounded: David Hunt's corner, Blanks Moody's line, Nat Hunt's line, Moody's line
s/ Will Todd
Wit: None
February 18, 1788

Page 155   W Shelton's Deed from Shelton

October 10, 1787 between Abraham Shelton, late Sheriff of P and William Shelton of P. The said Abraham Shelton, sheriff of P, hath in obedience to a clause in the Revenue Law which directs him the said Sheriff to seize and sell so much of all tracts of land within his county as will pay the taxes due thereon (where there is no other property to be found in the said county belonging to the owner thereof) sold unto said William Shelton for twelve pounds, five shillings, five pence, one farthing being taxes due for 1784 and 1785, a parcel of 300 acres of land being part of a tract of 900 acres charged by the Commission of the said county to Amos Thompson, that being the last quanity of land that any person present at the sale would pay.

Said land lies on the sides of Old Field Branch of Sweeting Fork of Sandy Creek
Bounded: Jeremiah White's line, Wm Clark's line, crossing the Old Field Branch, Jeremiah White's line
s/ Abra Shelton
Wit: None
February 18, 1788

Page 157   Shelton's Deed from Shelton
February 18, 1788 between Armistead Shelton of P and Leroy Shelton of P for five pounds, a parcel of land containing 60 acres lying on the drafts of White Thorn Creek
Bounded: Daniel Shelton's line, Gabriel Shelton's line, Benja Bailey's line, Spencer Shelton's line
s/ Armested Shelton
Wit: None
February 18, 1788

Page 158   Handcock's Deed from Mcleroy
May 19, 1787 between Hugh Mckleroy of the county of Campbell and Joseph Hendcock of the county of Halifax for 130 pounds current money of Virginia, a parcel of land containing 106 acres being part of a tract of land formerly granted to Dutton Layne lying on both sides of Sugar Tree Creek bounded on the west by John Mack's line and on the east by James Cox's line and on the south by lands entered by John Oakes, also onother tract of land containing 252 acres and bounded by the heirs of John Mack, James Burnett and John Cox and by the lines of above mentioned tract of land
s/ Hugh McKleroy
Wit: Jesse Rowden, John Rowden, Jeremiah Echols, James McKleroy
December 17, 1787

Page 159   Cody's Deed from Allen
December 15, 1787 between William Allen of P and Redmond Cody of P for 120 pounds current money of Virginia, a parcel of land on the head branches of Allens Creek containing by estimation 190 acres
Bounded: George Allen's corner now Gilbert Hunt's on Buckley line, Joseph Faris, Ben Lankford's line, George Allen on Gilbert Hunt's line
s/ Wm Allen Senr
Wit: James George Junr, Wm George, John (X) Solomon, James (X) Bruce, Owen Wish
February 18, 1788

Page 162   Oakes Deed from Payne

192

August 14, 1787 between Edmund Payne and Stephen Payne of Henry County Virginia and Charles Oakes of P for 80 pounds good and lawful money of Virginia a parcel of land willed to them by John Payne, deceased, in P lying on both sides of Mountain Creek containing 133 acres
Bounded: James Oakes line
s/ Edmond (X) Payne, Stephen (X) Payne
Wit: William Murphy, David (X) Stephens, William (X) Oakes, Phil Perkins
February 18, 1788

Page 164 Stone's Deed from Watlington
November 20, 1787 between John Watlington and Elizabeth, his wife, of the county of Halifax and Joshua Stone of P for 300 pounds current money of Virginia, a tract of land on both sides of both forks of Allen Creek containing by estimation 300 acres
Bounded: Wm Epperson's corner, Epperson's line, Haynes Morgan's line, Joseph Farris Junr temporary line, mouth of the said Farris junr spring branch, Buckley's dividing line, Allens Creek, said Stone's old line, old line surveyed for James Farris
s/ John Watlington, Betsy Watlington
Wit: Thomas Hoskins, Will Todd, James George Junr, Dan'l Tompkins
February 18, 1788

Page 167 George Junr and Shelton's Deed from Todd
February 18, 1788 between William Todd, Gentleman, late Sheriff of P and James George Junr and William Shelton both of P. The said William Todd, sheriff of P, hath in obedience to a clause in the Revenue Law which directs him the said Sheriff to seize and sell so much of all tracts of land within his county as will pay the taxes due thereon (where there is no other property to be found in the said county belonging to the owner thereof) sold unto said James George Junr and William Shelton for three pounds taxes due for 1786, a parcel of 208 acres of land charged by the Commission of the said county to Henry Burch, that being the last quanity of land that any person present at the sale would pay. Said land lies on the south fork of Sycamore Creek
s/ Will Todd
Wit: None
February 18, 1788

Page 169 W Shelton's Deed from Todd
February 18, 1788 between William Todd, Gentleman, late Sheriff of P and William Shelton of P. The said William Todd, sheriff of P, hath in obedience to a clause in the Revenue Law which directs him the said Sheriff to seize and sell so much of all tracts of land within his county as

will pay the taxes due thereon (where there is no other property to be found in the said county belonging to the owner thereof) sold unto said William Shelton for five pounds, thirteen shillings taxes due for 1786, a parcel of 490 acres of land charged by the Commission of the said county to Peter Puckett of Prince Edward County, that being the last quanity of land that any person present at the sale would pay. Said land lies on the south fork of Allens Creek
Bounded: John George's line of the land he bought of John Terrell crosses the said fork, John George's new line
s/ Will Todd
February 18, 1788

Page 170   F Shelton's Deed from Todd
February 18, 1788 between William Todd, Gentleman, late Sheriff of P and Frederick Shelton of P. The said William Todd, sheriff of P, hath in obedience to a clause in the Revenue Law which directs him the said Sheriff to seize and sell so much of all tracts of land within his county as will pay the taxes due thereon (where there is no other property to be found in the said county belonging to the owner thereof) sold unto said Frederick Shelton for two pounds, three shillings taxes due for 1786, a parcel of 400 acres of land charged by the Commission of the said county to John Robertson of Hanover County, that being the last quanity of land that any person present at the sale would pay. Said land lies on both sides of Wheeler's Branch of Sycamore Creek
Bounded: Ralph Smith's line, crossing Pocket Road, Charles Calloway's line, crossing Pocket Road
s/ Will Todd
February 18, 1788

Page 174   W Shelton's Deed from Todd
February 18, 1788 between William Todd, Gentleman, late Sheriff of P and William Shelton of P. The said William Todd, sheriff of P, hath in obedience to a clause in the Revenue Law which directs him the said Sheriff to seize and sell so much of all tracts of land within his county as will pay the taxes due thereon (where there is no other property to be found in the said county belonging to the owner thereof) sold unto said William Shelton for eleven shillings, ten pence half penny taxes due for 1786, a parcel of 50 acres of land charged by the Commission of the said county to Edward Munford, that being the last quanity of land that any person present at the sale would pay. Said land lies on the head branches of Fly Blow Creek
Bounded: Francis Irby's line, John Gregory's line, David Hunt's line, a new line run for the said Wm Shelton, Francis Irby's line, fish station
s/ Will Todd

Wit: None
February 18, 1788

Page 173   F Shelton's Deed from Todd
February 18, 1788 between William Todd, Gentleman, late Sheriff of P
and Frederick Shelton of P. The said William Todd, sheriff of P, hath in
obedience to a clause in the Revenue Law which directs him the said
Sheriff to seize and sell so much of all tracts of land within his county as
will pay the taxes due thereon (where there is no other property to be found
in the said county belonging to the owner thereof) sold unto said Frederick
Shelton for one pound, ten shillings and three pence taxes due for 1786, a
parcel of 230 acres of land being part of a greater tract charged by the
Commission of the said county to Abram Allen, that being the last quanity
of land that any person present at the sale would pay. Said land lies on the
Head branches of Banister River
Bounded: Beaver's corner, Emmerson's line, Brown's line, Wm Devan's
line, crossing the said river several times, Emmerson's line
s/ Will Todd
Wit: None
February 18, 1788

Page 174   Yates Deed from Shelton
February 18, 1788 between Abraham Shelton, Gentleman, late Sheriff of P
and Stephen Yates of P. The said Abraham Shelton, sheriff of P, hath in
obedience to a clause in the Revenue Law which directs him the said
Sheriff to seize and sell so much of all tracts of land within his county as
will pay the taxes due thereon (where there is no other property to be found
in the said county belonging to the owner thereof) sold unto said Stephen
Yates for one pound, five shillings taxes due for 1785, a parcel of 50 acres
of land being part of a greater tract charged by the Commission of the said
county to John Williams, deceased, that being the last quanity of land that
any person present at the sale would pay. Said land lies on the head
branches of Mill Creek
Bounded: Madcaps line, John Coxes line
s/ Aba Shelton
Wit: None
February 18, 1788

Page 175   Hunt's Deed from Andrews
April 1, 1787 between James Andrews and Sarah, his wife, of P and David
Hunt of P for 60 pounds current money of Virginia parcel of land on the
head of Allens Creek and both sides of Camp Branch containing 300 acres
Bounded: Mackberry's line, Ballinger's line

s/ James (X) Andrews, Sarah (X) Andrews
Wit: Jos Roberts, Joseph Roberts Junr, Joel Shelton, Harrod Roberts
October 15, 1787

Page 178   Kezee's Deed from Duncan
September 13, 1784 between Benjamin Duncan of P and Jeremiah Kezee
of P for 100 pounds current money of Virginia, a parcel of land on the
branches of Tomahawk Creek containing 182 acres
Bounded: Robert Neley
s/ Benjamin Duncan, Elizabeth (X) Duncan
Wit: Noton Dickinson, Jussus (X) Dyer, George Smith, John Ball
February 25, 1785

Page 180   George Jun's Deed from Todd
February 18, 1788 between William Todd, Gentleman, late Sheriff of P
and James George Junr of P. The said William Todd, sheriff of P, hath in
obedience to a clause in the Revenue Law, which directs him the said
Sheriff to seize and sell so much of all tracts of land within his county as
will pay the taxes due thereon (where there is no other property to be found
in the said county belonging to the owner thereof) sold unto said James
George Junr for two pounds, twelve shillings and eleven pence half penny
taxes due for 1786, a parcel of 122 acres being part of a greater tract of
land charged by the Commission of the said county to Frances Moore
Petty, that being the last quanity of land that any person present at the sale
would pay. Said land lies on Green Rock Creek
Boudned: Wm Easley, Said Petty's line, Jo Farguson, John Watson's line,
Easley's line aforesaid, Easley's dividing line
s/ Will Todd
Wit: None
February 18, 1788

Page 181   Lovell's Deed from Todd
March 17, 1788 between William Todd, Gentleman, late Sheriff of P and
Daniel Lovell of P. The said William Todd, sheriff of P, hath in
obedience to a clause in the Revenue Law which directs him the said
Sheriff to seize and sell so much of all tracts of land within his county as
will pay the taxes due thereon (where there is no other property to be found
in the said county belonging to the owner thereof) sold unto said Daniel
Lovell for two pounds, eight shillings taxes due for 1785 & 1786, a parcel
of 130 acres of land charged by the Commission of the said county to
William Davenport it being a part of a larger tract of land 404 acres
charged to William Davenport, that being the last quanity of land that any
person present at the sale would pay lying on both sides of Cherry Stone
Creek

196

Bounded: John Watson Senr's line
s/ Will Todd
Wit: None
March 17, 1788

Page 183   Hopwood from Innis Dedimus
To John Dickinson and Hugh Martin, Esquire or any two Justices of the
county of (Blank): Hugh Innes by his certain Indenture hath conveyed
unto William Hopwood of P a tract of land containing 400 acres and
whereas Hannah, wife of the said Hugh Innes cannot conveniently travel to
the said county court of P, Know ye that we trusting in your faithful and
prominent circumspection in examining Hannah, wife of the said Innes,
apart from her said husband, whether she does voluntarily relinquish her
right of dower.
Will Tunstall
Henry County
By virtue of the above dedimus to us directed we have examined Hannah,
the wife said Hugh Innes and she relinquished her right of dower.
September 24, 1787
John Dickerson, Hugh Martin
Martin 17, 1788

Page 184   Coleman's Deed from Lumpkin
June 13, 1787 between Robert Lumpkin of P and Spilsby Coleman of
Caswell County, North Carolina for 100 pounds a parcel of land on the
south side of Dan River containing 126 ½ acres part of a larger tract of
land whereon the said Lumkin now lives   May 16, 1786
Bounded: Falls Road, Spil Coleman's old line, south side of Jackson's
Creek
s/ Robt Lumkin
Wit: Robert Payne, Henry Campbell, Robert Payne Junr, Wm Dix,
Nathaniel Thomas, Wm B Burton, Thomas (X) Richard
March 17, 1788

Page 185   Doss's Deed from Buckley
March 18, 1788 between John Buckley of P and James Doss Junr for 50
pounds current money of Virginia, a parcel of land on Beach tree
containing 200 acres
Bounded: James Dosses line, crossing Dry Creek
s/ John Buckley
Wit: Joshua Stone, Luther (X) Hopper, Jas Craine
March 18, 1788

Page 187   Burnett's Deed from Denton

197

October 27, 1787 between James Denton and Nancy, his wife, and Gilbert Burnett, both of P, for value received a parcel of land containing 142 acres on the branches of south fork of Sandy River and the branches of Sugar tree Creek
Bounded: Lumkins corner, Lumkins line, Thomas corner, branch of Sugar Tree Creek, Grasham's line, south fork of Sandy River
s/ James Denton, Nancy Denton
Wit: James Burnett, Henry Burnett, John Cox, John Burnett
March 17, 1788

Page 189   Barksdale's Deed from Pigg
November 3, 1787 between Wm Pigg of P and Beverley Barksdale of P for 150 pounds current money of Virginia a parcel of land containing by estimation 264 acres lying on the south side of Banister River
Bounded: South side of Banister River, Rawley Corbin's corner
s/ William Pigg
Wit: Reubin Pain, Wm Clark, Reubin Pain Jr
April 21, 1788

Page 191   Cox's Deed from Hencock
March 17, 1788 between Joseph Hencock of the county of Halifax and John Cox of P for 60 pounds current money of Virginia a parcel of land containing 106 acres and being part of a tract of land formerly granted to Dutton Lane on both sides Sycamore Creek, bounded on the west by John Mack's line, on the east by James Cox's land, on the south by land entered by John Oakes. Also one other parcel of land containing 252 acres and bounded by the lines of John Mack, James Burnett, James Cox and by lines of the above mentioned tract of land
s/ Joseph (X) Hancock
Wit: Wm Short, John Davis, Henry Burnett, Gilbert Burnett, James Cox
April 21, 1788

Page 192   Baker's Deed from Latimore
October 4, 1787 between Samuel Lattimore of P and James Baker of P for 70 pounds current money of Virginia a parcel of land containing 75 acres on the south side of Banister River
Bounded: River Banister on the north, A Campbell on the west and Glascow on the south
s/ Samuel Lattimore, Liddy (X) Lattimore
Wit: Clem't McDaniel, Wm Jones, Meridith Compton, Wm Doss
April 21, 1788

Page 194   Gardner's Deed from Dodson and

April 21, 1788 between Lazrus Dodson, George Hardey of P and Silvany Gardner of P for 25 pounds good and lawful money of Virginia a parcel of land containing 75 acres by estimation on the waters of Sandy Creek
Bounded: Said Dodson's corner, said Dodson's line, said Hardy's land
s/ Lazerus Dodson, George Hardey
Wit: John Chelton, George Dodson, Bennet Chelton
April 21, 1788

Page 196   Duncan's Deed from King
November 9, 1787 between Joseph King of P and Field Allen Dunkan of P for 100 pounds current money of Virginia a parcel of land containing 185 acres on north side of Pigg River
Bounded: mouth of Rocky Branch, north side of Pigg River
s/ Joseph King
Wit: John Bobbitt, Pey'n Smith, William Young, John Duncan, Joseph King Junr
April 21, 1788

Page 198   Davis' Deed from Watson
November 16, 1787 between Nathan Watson Senr of P and George Davis of P for 500 pounds good and lawful money of Virginia a parcel of land containing 220 acres on the lower ford of Beans Creek
Bounded: Watson's old corner
s/ Nathan Watson
Wit: Daniel Tompkins. Reubin Pain, Leroy Shelton, Samuel M Lovell, Jere White
April 21, 1788

Page 200   Gardner's Deed from Dodson
April 16, 1788 between Thomas Dodson of Halifax and Heath Gardner of P for 10 pounds current money of Virginia a parcel of land on Burch Creek containing by estimation 40 acres
Bounded: said Dodson's line where it crosses a branch that emptys into Burch Creek on the south side of Neas below John Creel's mill, Burches Creek, mouth of the said branch
s/ Thomas Dodson
Wit: Jno Chelton, John Johnson, Silvanny Gardner
April 21, 1788

Page 202   Gammon's Deed from Wilson
April 21, 1788 between Peter Wilson of P and John Gammon of P for 40 pounds current money of Virginia a parcel of land containing by estimation 131 acres on Rocky Run
Bounded: Gammon's line, Owen's line, Givens line to Rocky Branch

s/ Peter Wilson
Wit: None
April 21, 1788

Page 205   Payne's Deed from Pigg
November 3, 1787 between Wm Pigg of P and Reubin Payne of P for 54 pounds current money of Virginia a parcel of land containing by estimation 54 acres on the south side of Banister River
Bounded: Martin's line
s/ William Pigg
Wit: Wm Clark, Edmund Pain, Reubin Payne Junr, Laban Payne
April 21, 1788

Page 206   Walker's Deed from Walker
1787 between Elisha Walker of P and Wm Walker of P for 100 pounds a parcel of land containing 250 acres, being part of 500 acres surveyed for said Elisha Walker on Turkey Cocke Creek
s/ Elisha Walker
Wit: Caleb Hundley, Joel Walker, Sally (X) Hundley
April 21, 1788

Page 208   Southerland's Deed from Billings
April 14, 1788 between James Billions of P and John Southerland of P for 100 pounds a parcel on Sandy Creek containing 75 acres
Bounded: James Burton's fork of Sandy Creek, Runson Fallins line, James McDaniel's line, main fork of Sandy Creek
s/ James (X) Billings
Wit: None
April 21, 1788

Page 210   Shelton's Deed from Shelton
April 21, 1788 between Daniel Shelton of P and Young Shelton for 10 pounds current money of Virginia a parcel of land containing 100 acres, part of the land the said Daniel Shelton now lives on
Bounded: Spencer Shelton's line, Lightfoot's former line
s/ Daniel Shelton
Wit: None
April 21, 1788

Page 211   Womack's Deed from Hailey
March 22, 1788 between Ambrose Hayley of P and Charles Womack and the Baptist Society for one shilling sterling a parcel of land containing one acre near the line that divides the said county from Halifax on the waters of Johns Run

s/ Ambrose Haley
Wit: Wm Ryburn, Thomas Shaw
April 21, 1788

Page 212   Shelton's Deed from Shelton
April 21, 1788 between Gabriel Shelton of P and Vincent Shelton of P for
nine pounds current money of Virginia, a parcel of land containing 30
acres it being part of the land the said Gabriel Shelton now lives on
Bounded: Hickeys Road
s/ Gabriel Shelton
Wit: None
April 21, 1788

Page 214   Burnett's Deed from Robertson
January 1, 1788 between Thomas Roberson and Keaty his wife and Henry
Burnet, both of P, for value received a parcel of land containing 162 acres
on Stewarts Creek
Bounded: Pattern line, crossing the Tenhought Branch, Stewarts Creek
s/ Thomas Roberson, Catherine (X) Roberson
Wit: Gilbert Burnett, George (X) Hankins, Mary (X) Hankins, John
Cunningham, Wm Cunningham, Wm Shields
March 17, 1788

Page 215   Hankins Bill of Sale from Worsham
We, Jeremiah Worsham and Ann, his wife, of P for sum of 45 pounds
current money of Virginia, have sold Daniel Hankins a Negro girl named
Lucy about twelve years old. March 19, 1788
s/ Jeremiah (X) Worsham, Ann (X) Worsham
Wit: John Cox, Joseph Morton
April 21, 1788

Page 216   Ryburn's Deed from Barksdale
March 18, 1787 between Bevereley Barksdale of P and Ann, his wife and
William Ryburn of P for 45 pounds current money of Virgina, a tract of
land on branches of Sandy Creek on or near the head of Eagles Fork of the
said Creek containing 60 acres
Bounded: Branch where the said Ryburn's line crosses the branch,
Motley's path
s/ B Barksdale
Wit: None
April 21, 1788

Page 218   Nelson's Deed from Willis

February 18, 1788 between Sterling Willis of P and William Nelson of P for 30 pounds current money of Virginia a tract of land containing 80 acres lying on the drafts of White Thorn Creek
Bounded: Wm Pace's line, Armistead Shelton's line, Wm Payne's line, Henry Keys line, Edmund Taylor's line, Wm Pace's line
s/ Sterling Willis
Wit: None
April 21, 1788

Page 219   Nunnelee's Deed from Stockton
April 21, 1788 between John Stockton of P and Edward Nunnelee of P for 170 pounds current money of Virginia a parcel of land on Sandy River containing by estimation 525 acres being part of a grant granted to Richard Swepson
Bounded: Coxes former line
s/ John Stockton
Wit: None
April 21, 1788

Page 220   Devins Deed from Biswell
November 27, 1787 between John Biswell Senr of P and Robert Devin of P for 200 pounds lawful money a parcel of land containing 230 acres
Bounded: Jenkins line, Little Strawberry Creek
s/ John Biswell
Wit: Wm Devin, James Biggars, Jubs (X) Nuchsum
April 21, 1788

Page 222   Morton's Deed from Smith
October 15, 1787 between Drury Smith of Rockingham, North Carolina and Joseph Morton of P for 150 pounds current money of Virginia, a parcel of land on both sides of Sandy River on Crooked Creek
Bounded: 400 acres bounded by Clouds and Wallins corner and 104 acres bounded by Yarrington's corner, Hickeys Road, John Morton's line
s/ Drury Smith
Wit: None
April 21, 1788

Page 224   Tompkins Deed from Shelton
1788 between Abra Shelton, Gentleman, late Sheriff of P and Daniel Tompkins of P. The said Abra Shelton, sheriff of P, hath in obedience to a clause in the Revenue Law which directs him the said Sheriff to seize and sell so much of all tracts of land within his county as will pay the taxes due thereon (where there is no other property to be found in the said county

belonging to the owner thereof) sold unto said Daniel Tompkins for 32 pounds 2/10 taxes due for 1785 & 1786, a parcel of 2843 acres of land charged by the Commission of the said county to Miss Clay and Co, to wit: Henry Clay 1000 acres, Green Clay 1000 acres, Mathew Clay 843 acres lying part in P and part in Henry County that being the last quanity of land that any person present at the sale would pay lying on the south fork of Sandy River and Cascade Creek
Bounded: Clay's order line, crossing Charles Clay's dividing line, fork of Caskade Creek, Thomas Clay's dividing, Henry Clay's dividing line, Mathew Clay's dividing line, crossing the south fork of Sandy River
s/ Abra Shelton
Wit: None
April 21, 1788

Page 226   Calland's Deed of Trust from Bobbitt
I John Bobbitt of P am firmly bound unto Samuel Calland of P for the sum of 40 pounds current money of Virginia and desiring to pay have sold to said Samuel Calland my crop of tobacco being about 4000 tobo, also 60 barrels of corn, two small black mares, nine or ten years old, also six head of cattle marked with two swallow forks and underked in the right ear together with all my household furniture. October 7, 1787
s/ John Bobbitt
Wit: Wm Jenkins, Bowker Smith, Sam Tompkins, Sam Tompkins Jur, Sam'l Smith
May 19, 1788

Page 228   Nash's Power of Attorney from Nash
I, Marvel Nash of Lincoln County Virginia appoint my son William Nash my true and lawful attorney to sell the legasee that is coming Edmond Hodges estate as he shall think proper to do. March 1, 1786
s/ Marvel Nash
Wit: Jabus Townsen, John Jackson, John Allen, John Bailey
May 19, 1788

Page 229   Coleman's Bd for collecting the specie tax of 1788
We, Stephen Colemam, Abraham Shelton, Wm Todd, John Markham, Beverley Barksdale, Wm Dix, Wm Short, & Joshua Stone of P are bound unto Jacquilin Ambler, Treasurer of the Commonwealth of Virginia for 10,000 pounds current money of Virginia. May 19, 1788
The condition of the above obligation is such that if the above bound Stephen Coleman do, shall, will and truly collect, account for and pay unto the said Treasurer according to law all the taxes which may become due and payable in specie from each and every taxable person in the county for 1788 which are imposed by an Act of Assembly

s/ Stephen Coleman, Abram Shelton, Will Todd, Jno Markham, Wm Dix, B Barksdale, Wm Short, Joshua Stone   Taken in open court
May 19, 1788

Page 230   Mathis from Dyer
October 15, 1787 between Joseph Dyer of P and Nehemiah Matthews of P for 75 pounds current money of Virginia, a parcel of land whereon the said Joseph Dyer now dwells containing by estimation 390 and is the land which was granted to Samuel Emmerson by a grant from the Land Office of this state dated October 26, 1779 and by said Samuel Emmerson by deed conveyed to said Joseph Dyer
s/ Joseph (X) Dyer
Wit: Thomas Dyer, James Dyer, Peter F Jefferson, John Rigney
May 19, 1788

Page 232   Hunts Deed from Allen
November 17, 1787 between George Allen of P and Gilbert Hunt of P for 200 pounds current money of Virginia, a parcel of land containing by estimation 374 acres on both sides of Allens Creeks
Bounded: Old patent line
s/ George (X) Allen
Wit: Joshua Stone, William Roach, Will Todd, Isaac Clement, Joseph Wish
December 17, 1787
Frances, wife of said George Allen, being privately examined, relinquished her right of dower.
Will Tunstall

Page 234   Mustain's Deed from Shelton
June 16, 1788 between Leonard Shelton and Susannah, his wife, of P and Avery Mustain of P for 70 pounds current money of Virginia a parcel of land containing 200 acres and lying on Panther Creek on a branch called the Glady Fork
Bounded: Vincent Shelton's line, Beverley Shelton's line, Jere Kezee's line, John Grant's line, Crispin Shelton Junr's line
s/ Leonard Shelton
Wit: None
June 16, 1788

Page 236   Jones Deed from Oakes
November 7, 1787 between James Oakes of Henry County, Virginia and John Jones of P for 50 pounds current money of Virginia a parcel of land on both sides of Sugar Tree Creek containing 112 acres
s/ James Oakes

Wit: Robert Bullington, Preston Hampton, Wm (X) Mitchell
December 17, 1787

Page 239   Jones Deed from Nance
October 29, 1787 between Giles Nance of Amelia County and John Jones
of P for 110 pounds, a parcel of land containing by survey 300 acres on
Sugar Tree Creek
Bounded: Robert Ballington's line, north side of Sugar tree fork, James
Oakes line, John Payne's line
s/ Giles Nance
Wit: Robert Bullington, Willliam (X) Mitchell, David Scales
December 17, 1787

Page 240   Shelton's Deed from Shelton
March 19, 1788 between Crispin Shelton of P and Vincent Shelton of P for
15 pounds current money of Virginia, a parcel of land containing 438
acres, the plantation whereon the said Vincent Shelton now lives being a
part of the said tract of land and lying on both sides of White Thorn
Creek
Bounded: Gabriel Shelton's line, Mrs Clark's line, John Shelton's line,
Gabriel Shelton's line
s/ Crispin Shelton
Wit: Griffith Dickinson, Spencer Shelton, Gabriel Shelton
June 16, 1788

Page 243   Gray's Deed from Wooten
November 17, 1787 between Nathl Wooten of P and Andrew Gray of P for
50 pounds current money of Virginia, a parcel containing by estimation
150 acres
Bounded by the lines of William Dix, Josias Barron, Jesse Reynolds, Wm
Twedell
s/ Nathaniel (X) Wooten
Wit: W Wright, George Hardy, Ann Wright, Robert (X) Wright
June 16, 1788

Page 245   Slate's Deed from Henry
December 31, 1787 between James Henry of the county of
Northumberland and Samuel Slate of P for 115 pounds, ten shillings
current money of Virginia, a parcel of land lying in the county of Halifax
and P containing and now laid out for 206 acres of land
Bounded: Medciff's old line
s/ Jas Henry
Wit: B Barksdale, Wm Ryburn, Chas McLaughlan
June 16, 1788

Page 246   Ferguson's Deed from Worsham delivered to Wm B Giles

March 25, 1788 between Jeremiah Worsham of P and Josiah Farguson of P for 4 pounds current money of Virginia a parcel of land containing 30 acres on the north side of Green Rock

Bounded: Little below the said Ferguson's house, said Worsham's line, Hickeys old road crosses said branch, Worsham and Devins posts line, Davenport's line

s/ Jeremiah (X) Worsham

Wit: Dan'l Lovel, Hannah Hoskins, Sam'l M Lovel

June 16, 1788

Page 248   Tharp's Deed from Christain

October 29, 1787 between John Christain of P and Wilson Thorp of Franklin County did cook a deed for the same and proved by two witnesses only, upon which recantation of the whole bargain has ensued. Therefore, in consideration of the above recantation of the former tract, he the said Christain, for his part, doth by those present give up and return to said Thorp all the land that he the said Christain received of said Thorp containing 170 acres on waters of White Oak Creek

Bounded: Adam's line, near Pigg Road

s/ John (X) Christain

Wit: Thomas Elliot, James Elliot, Benj Williams Junr

June 16, 1788

Page 250   West's Deed from Ramey

To David Hunt, Joshua Stone and William Todd, Justices of the County of P: Whereas Absalom Ramey Junr by his Indenture of Sale dated December 20, 1787 hath conveyed unto Joseph West Junr 163 acres of land and whereas, Elizabeth, the wife of the said Absalom cannot conveniently travel to the court house to relinquish her right of dower, we do therefore command you or any two of you to personally go to the said Elizabeth and examine her apart from her husband. December 20, 1787 Pittsylvania County

In pursuant to the above Commission to us directed we did personally go to Elizabeth Ramey, wife of the said Absalom Ramey and examined her privately. She examined her right of dower. December 20, 1787

s/ D Hunt, Joshua Stone

Wit: None

June 16, 1788

Page 251   Kings's Deed from Allen

206

December 20, 1787 between George Allen of P and James King, son and heir of James King deceased of P for 6 pounds current money of Virginia, a parcel of land on the branches of Straightstone Creek containing by estimation 80 acres
Bounded: Thomas Davis line, Little Straightstone, said James King's former line, Wm Betterton's line
s/ George Allen
Wit: Joshua Stone, Cornelius McHaney, John West, Hardin Chick
June 16, 1788

Page 253   Fowlks Deed from Clay
March 6, 1787 between Eleazor Clay of county of Chesterfield and Jennings Fowlks of Amelia for 123 pounds, ten shillings current money of Virginia a parcel of land on both sides of Dry Fork of Great Sandy Creek containing by estimation 247 acres
Bounded: Murray's corner, Murray's line
s/ Eleazar Clay
Wit: Christopher Robertson, Thomas Davis, Avery Mustain
April 18, 1787

Page 255   McHaney's Deed from Allen
December 20, 1787 between George Allen of P and Cornelius Machaney for 50 pounds current money of Virginia a parcel of land on branches of Straightstone Creek containing by estimation 100 acres being part of a greater tract granted to the said George Allen by patent dated September 1, 1780
Bounded: Thomas Davis line, a new line of chopted trees, Little Straightstone Creek, Thomas Davis corner
s/ George Allen
Wit: Joshua Stone, John West, Hardin Chick, William Chick
June 16, 1788

Page 257   Tharp's Deed from Hamblin
October 23, 1785 between George Hamblin of P and William Thorp for 70 pounds a parcel of land containing 167 acres
Bounded: Hock Branch
s/ George (X) Hamblin
Wit: Moses Vinson, Thomas Elliot, James Elliot
January 16, 1786
Pearsey, wife of George Hamblin relinquished her right of dower
s/ Will Tunstall

Page 258   Spencer's Deed from Farmer

November 3, 1787 between Mathew Farmer of Halifax and John Spence of
P for 60 pounds current money of Virginia a parcel of land containing 282
acres on the branches of the Double Creek and Burches Creek
Bounded: James Adams corner, Weatherford's order line, Giddion
Ragland's line, Anderson's line, crossing Nippers Branch, Adams line
s/ Mathew Farmer
Wit: Gidion Ragland, Wm Herring, Wm Madding, Hugh Kelly
June 16, 1788

Page 260   Tennison's Deed from Stone
April 21, 1788 between Joshua Stone of P and Ignatious N Tennison for 5
pounds current money of Virginia a parcel of land containing 200 acres
lying on the Rocky Branch of Sandy Creek formerly the property of the
said Ignatious N Tennison which was sold by the sheriff of P to said
Joshua Stone for taxes
Bounded: John Bruce's corner in Thomas Clay's line, Charles Clay's line,
John Bruce's corner
s/ Joshua Stone
Wit: None
June 16, 1788

Page 261   West Junr Deed from Ramey
December 20, 1787 between Absalom Ramey and his wife Elizabeth of P
and Joseph West Junr of P for 50 pounds current money of Virginia, a
certain tract of land on the drafts of Straightstone Creek containing by
estimation 163 acres
Bounded: Wm Collins line, Tribelis line, Gilbert Hunt's line, Donelson's
line, Camp branch, John Ballinger's line
s/ Absalom Ramey, Elizabeth (X) Ramey
Wit: D Hunt, Joshua Stone, William Betterton, John Craddock
June 16, 1788

Page 263   Hodges Deed from Hopper &c
October 26, 1780 between Luther Hopper and William Adkinson of P and
Thomas Hodgers of P for 80 pounds current money of Virginia, two
parcels of land, they being both in one survey divided by the said William
Atkinson's father and Oen Atkinson. The said Oen Atkinson sold the one
part to Luther Hopper and Wm Atkerson, deceased and willed the other
part to his son William Atkinson, they containing by estimation 130 acres
on Bearskin Creek
Bounded: Bank of the creek, Roberson's line, Hopper's spring, Hopper's
plantation just below the ford
s/ Luther Hopper, William (X) Atkinson
Wit: George Robinson, Moses Hodges, Haman Dyer

June 21, 1788

Page 265   Cook's Deed from Nowlin
June 15, 1788 between Bryant W Nolin of P and Harmon Cook of P for 85
pounds current money of Virginia, a parcel of land on both sides of Potters
Creek containing 126 acres
Bounded: Roberson's corner, Roberson's line, dividing line formerly
made by John Henslee and Bryant W Nolin, crossing a branch
s/ Bryan W Nolin
Wit: Thos Dyer, James Dyer, David Dalton
July 21, 1788
Lucy the wife of Bryant Ward Nowlin relinquished her right of dower
s/ Will Tunstall

Page 267   Watson's Bill of Sale from Mitchell
I, James Mitchell of P, for the sum of 75 pounds current money of Virginia
have sold unto John Watson one Negro wench named Fanny and her future
Increase. March 29, 1788
s/ James Mitchell
Wit: Mary (X) Wheat, Nancy Mitchell
July 21, 1788

Page 267   Hodges Deed from Dyer
1788 between John Dyer of P and Thomas Hodges of P for 25 pounds
current money of Virginia a parcel of land containing by estimation 100
acres on both sides Bearskin Creek
Bounded: Owen Atkinson's corner, new dividing line, line of the Pattant,
Atkinson's line
s/ John Dyer
Wit: None
July 21, 1788

Page 268   Cook's Deed from Swinney
October 21, 1785 between James Swinnney of the county of P and Harmon
Cook of P for four pounds, fourteen shillings and eight pence a parcel of
land lying on Cherry stone waters containing 150 acres by supposition
adjoining Chs Rigney and Linthicum and Joseph Swinney
s/ James (X) Swinney
Wit: Jere Kezee, James Dyer, John Dalton
January 19, 1787

Page 270   Davis's Deed from Chatwin

July 21, 1788 between John Chatwin and Fanny, his wife, of P and John Davis of P for 50 pounds, a parcel containing 200 acres on both sides of Green Rock Creek
Bounded: the order line, John Pigg's line, Patty's line, Washam's line, Robertson's line
s/ John Chatwin, Fanny Chatwin
Wit: None
July 21, 1788
Frances, the wife of John Chatwin, relinquished her right of Dower

Page 272   Vincent's Deed from Brewer
July 18, 1788 between James Brewer of P and William Vincent of P for 100 pounds current money of Virginia, a parcel of land containing by estimation 500 acres on the Waters of Turkey Cock Creek being part of Windson Forest which Joseph Walker purchased of John Philpot dated December 17, 1782
Bounded: Little Roundtop Mountain in the old line
s/ James Brewer
Wit: Abram Parish, John Smith, John Hodges, Elisha Walker
July 18, 1788

Page 273   Lewis's Deed from Taylor
December 29, 1787 between James Taylor of P and Charles Lewis Junr of P for the sum of 120 pounds lawful money of Virginia, one certain tract of land containing 145 acres
Bounded: Court house road, Edm'd Taylor and Thos Payne's corner, Payne's line, the Road, Tucker's line, Henry Kay's line to Mill Creek, Kays and Burton's corner, Burton's line, Spencer Shelton's line
s/ James Taylor
Wit: Edm'd Taylor, Henry Kay, Thos Payne, Edw'd Lewis
August 19, 1788

Page 274   Dyer's Deed from Atkinson
August 18, 1788 between Jesse Atkerson of P and William Dyer for 30 pounds, a parcel of land on Bearskin Creek containing 110 acres
Bounded: Said Creek, the old Pathway to the head of Mill Pond, Hump fork of the said Barskin Creek by the head of the Mill Pond, mouth of a gut, Mill path near the pond, Luther Hoppers, crossing said Bareskin Creek
Jesse (X) Atkerson
Wit: None
August 19, 1788

Page 276   Cook's Deed from Laws

210

December 15, 1787 between Joseph Laws and Tabitha, his wife of P, and
Harmon Cook of P for 100 pounds, a certain tract of land of the south side
of Pigg River containing 40 acres
Bounded: Jeremiah Ward and Peyton Wade's line on the north side of
Pigg River, crossing the river to Jacob Bayer's line, James Mitchell's line,
survey made by Robert Dalton, William Thompson's line to the river
s/ Joseph (X) Laws, Tabitha (X) Laws
Wit: Thos Dyer, John Wright, John Ball, Harmon Cook junr
July 21, 1788

Page 277   Lumkin's Deed from Stillwell
December 21, 1787 between Jacob Stillwell Senr and Anne Stillwell of P
and Joseph Lumpkin of P for 250 pounds, a tract of land containing 200
acres lying on the south side of Dan river
Bounded: at the Mill, John Worsham's line and Charles Wynne's line,
corner of Jacob Stillwell Junr, along a branch to Rutledges Creek, cross the
said Creek, along said Stillwell's line to Thomas Tiffin's line which is
between Charles Wynne and myself to Rutledges Creek, up said Creek
near the Mill
s/ Jacob Stillwell, Anne (X) Stillwell
Wit: John Worsham, John Lumpkin, Jno Dix, Jacob Stillwell, Pitman
Lumpkin
August 18, 1788

Page 278   Worham's Deed from McCubbins
February 16, 1788 between William McCubbin of P and John Worsham of
P for 130 pounds, a parcel of land on the south side of Dan River
containing 435 acres
Bounded: Samuel Bincims corner on the south side of Rutledges Creeks, a
new line, Binum's line
s/ William (X) McCubbins
Wit: Joseph Lumpkin, Mathew Wynne, Robt Farguson, John Lumpkins
August 18, 1788

Page 280   Coleman's sale from Markham
I, John Markham of P, for 100 pounds have sold Stephen Coleman two
Negroes, to wit: Charles and Dick.
s/ John Markham
Wit: Daniel Coleman
August 21, 1788

Page 280   Hubbard's Deed from Emmerson

June 25, 1788 between Samuel Emmerson of the county of Lincoln, and
John Hubbard of P for 110 pounds, a parcel of land on both sides of Little
Bairskin Creek containing by estimation 400 acres
Bounded: Edm'd Hodges corner, east fork of Bearskin creek, Pig's Road,
said Hodges corner, crossing the creek
s/ Samuel Emmerson
Wit: None
August 18, 1788

Page 282   T Shelton's Deed from Todd
April 21, 1788 between William Todd, Gentleman, late Sheriff of P and
Tavinor Shelton of P, by virtue of a clause in the Revenue Law which
directs the said Sheriff to seize and sell as much of all lands within his
county that will pay the taxes due thereon (where there is not property
sufficient in the said county belonging to the owners of the said land to pay
the taxes thereof) hath sold unto the said Tavinor Shelton 333 acres of land
which was charged by the Commissioners of the County to Jesse Clay for
the sum of two pounds and three pence for taxes cost etc for the year 1786
lying on the Beaver Pond branch of Dan River
Bounded: Harris's old road, Clay's order line, crossing the said Beaver
Pond branch, Clay's dividing line, Daniel Clay's dividing line, Henry
Mickleberry's line
s/ Will Todd
Wit: None
September 15, 1788

Page 283   T Shelton's Deed from Todd
April 21, 1788 between William Todd, Gentleman, late Sheriff of P and
Tavinor Shelton of P, by virtue of a clause in the Revenue Law which
directs the said Sheriff to seize and sell as much of all lands within his
county that will pay the taxes due thereon (where there is not property
sufficient in the said county belonging to the owners of the said land to pay
the taxes thereof) hath sold unto the said Tavinor Shelton 794 acres of land
which was charged by the Commissioners of the County to Mathew Clay
for the sum of five pounds, eight shillings and 9/ pence for taxes cost etc
for the year 1786 lying on the branches of Fall Creek and Sandy Creek
Bounded: Christopher Robertson's corner, Henry Clay's line, crossing
several branches of Sandy Creek, the Road in Clay's order line, Alexander
Murrey's line
s/ Will Todd
Wit: None
September 15, 1788

Page 284   T Shelton's Deed from Todd

April 21, 1788 between William Todd, Gentleman, late Sheriff of P and
Tavinor Shelton of P, by virtue of a clause in the Revenue Law which
directs the said Sheriff to seize and sell as much of all lands within his
county that will pay the taxes due thereon (where there is not property
sufficient in the said county belonging to the owners of the said land to pay
the taxes thereof) hath sold unto the said Tavinor Shelton 285 acres of land
which was charged by the Commissioners of the County to Peter Clay for
the sum of one pound, six and three pence taxes and cost due on the said
land for 1786 lying on the branches of Dan River and Sandy Creek
Bounded: Daniel Clay's corner, Eleazar Clay's line, Clay's order line,
Ann McDaniel's line, crossing several branches of Sandy Creek, Daniel
Clay's dividing line
s/ Will Todd
Wit: None
September 15, 1788

Page 284   C Shelton's Deed from Todd
April 21, 1788 between William Todd, Gentleman, late Sheriff of P and
Crispin Shelton, jr of P, by virtue of a clause in the Revenue Law which
directs the said Sheriff to seize and sell as much of all lands within his
county that will pay the taxes due thereon (where there is not property
sufficient in the said county belonging to the owners of the said land to pay
the taxes thereof) hath sold unto the said Tavinor Shelton 1000 acres of
land which was charged by the Commissioners of the County to Alexnder
Murrey for the sum of two pounds, 19 shillings and two pence taxes and
cost due on the said land for 1786 lying on the head branch of Fall Creek
Bounded: Christopher Robertson's corner, Clay's order line, crossing
Lawless's Spring Branch, said Murrey's dividing line, crossing two forks
of Fall Creek
s/ Will Todd
Wit: None
September 15, 1788

Page 285   Woody's Deed from May
September 13, 1788 between Gabriel May and Thomas Woody, both of P,
for 250 pounds, a certain parcel of land on Fall Creek containing by
estimation 420 acres
Bounded: Tweedales line, West side of Cargill's fork of Fall Creek, mouth
of Wagons Fork of Fall Creek, Tweedle's line, Pistole's corner, branch of
Great Fall Creek
s/ Gabriel May
Wit: None
September 15, 1788
Susanna, wife of Gabriel May, relinquished her right of Dower

Page 286 **Gray's Power from Gray**
I, Adin Gray of P, have appointed my trusty friend and brother, Jeremiah
Gray of the county of Montgomery, Maryland to be my lawful attorney to
deliver to Charles Cattron of Montgomery County, Maryland such deed as
said Charles shall reasonably require for conveyance of 59 ½ acres of land
and to collect all such debts due and owing in any part of the state of
Maryland. September, 1788
s/ Adin Gray
Wit: None
September 15, 1788

Page 287 **F Shelton's Deed from Todd**
April 21, 1788 between William Todd, Gentleman, late Sheriff of P and
Frederick Shelton of P, by virtue of a clause in the Revenue Law which
directs the said Sheriff to seize and sell as much of all lands within his
county that will pay the taxes due thereon (where there is not property
sufficient in the said county belonging to the owners of the said land to pay
the taxes thereof) hath sold unto the said Tavinor Shelton 224 acres of land
which was charged by the Commissioners of the County to William Baber
for the sum of one pound, 13 shillings and three pence, taxes due on the
said land for 1786 lying on the branches of Stanton River
Bounded: Crossing Great Branch, a branch of Sycamore
s/ Will Todd
Wit: None
September 15, 1788

Page 288 **F Shelton's Deed from Todd deliv'd to Edw'd
Nunnelee parden**
April 21, 1788 between William Todd, Gentleman, late Sheriff of P and
Frederick Shelton of P, by virtue of a clause in the Revenue Law which
directs the said Sheriff to seize and sell as much of all lands within his
county that will pay the taxes due thereon (where there is not property
sufficient in the said county belonging to the owners of the said land to pay
the taxes thereof) hath sold unto the said Tavinor Shelton 210 acres of land
which was charged by the Commissioners of the County to James Carr for
the sum of 11/13/7 ½ lying on both sides of Pigg River
Bounded: said River, Kook's line, Jo King's corner, Daniel Witcher's line
Will Todd
Wit: None
September 15, 1788

Page 289 **F Shelton's Deed from Todd**

214

April 21, 1788 between William Todd, Gentleman, late Sheriff of P and Frederick Shelton of P, by virtue of a clause in the Revenue Law which directs the said Sheriff to seize and sell as much of all lands within his county that will pay the taxes due thereon (where there is not property sufficient in the said county belonging to the owners of the said land to pay the taxes thereof) hath sold unto the said Tavinor Shelton 116 acres of land which was charged by the Commissioners of the County to John Robertson of Hanover County for the sum of 15 shilling taxes, cost due on the said land for 1786 lying on both sides of Fallen Creek, a branch of Stanton River
Bounded: Joseph Toaler's corner, Mackendrees and Hoskins lines, Toaler's line
s/ Will Todd
Wit: None
September 15, 1788

Page 290   Wilson's Deed from Parr &c
March 28, 1788 between William Parr and Robert Lumpkin of P and John Wilson of P for 60 pounds, a parcel of land containing 400 acres
Bounded: Weddy's corner, Floyd's line, Whitehead's corner, Weady's line
s/ Will'm Parr Senr, Robt Lumpkin
Wit: William Dix, Thomas Fearn, Peter Wilson junr, James Burton, William Parr jr
July 21, 1788

Page 291   Wilson's Deed from Lay
February 15, 1788 between David Lay Senr of P and John Wilson of P for 150 pounds current money of Virginia, a tract of land whereon the said David Lay now lives containing 90 acres part of 100 acres the said Lay purchased of Jasper Billings and also 50 acres which Redmond Fallin made me a Deed too and 127 acres by patent granted to said David Lay by this Commonwealth, the Survey dated January 17, 1786 which amounts to 267 acres of land and lies on both sides of Sandy Creek and adjoins James McDaniel which is the lower side and Stokes on the upper side on the Creek now said to be Atkinson
s/ David (X) Lay
Wit: James Fitzgarald, Peter Wilson, Robt Lumpkin, John Wilson jr, Peter Wilson jr
April 21, 1788

Page 293   Roaches Deed from Hendrick

March 5, 1788 between Obediah Hendrick and Dorcus, his wife of P, and
Thomas Roch of P for 20 pounds, a tract of land on the Waters of Banister
River containing 60 acres
Bounded: Pigg's Road joining Thomas Made, Thomas Made's line,
Nathaniel Thacker's line, Pigg's Road, Thomas Hardey
s/ Obediah Hendrick, Dorcus Hendrick
Wit: Arch'd Campbell, Randole Thacker, Gidion Roach, Joseph Thacker
September 15, 1788

Page 294   Lovell's Deed from Shelton Sheriff
October 1, 1788 between Abraham Shelton, late Sheriff of P and Daniel
Lovell of P, by virtue of a clause in the Revenue Law which directs the
said Sheriff to seize and sell as much of all lands within his county that
will pay the taxes due thereon (where there is not property sufficient in the
said county belonging to the owners of the said land to pay the taxes
thereof) hath sold unto the said Daniel Lovell 100 acres of land on Cherry
Stone Creek which was part of a greater tract of land which was charged
by the Commissioners of the County to William Davenport for the sum of
two pounds, 10 shilling taxes, cost due on the said land for 1785
Bounded: Said Creek, Snelson's old line north, crossing said creek
s/ Abra Shelton
Wit: None
October 20, 1788

Page 294   Walpool's relingq of Dower to Jefferson Ded's &
Report
To Thomas Garland and Edward Brodnax of the county of Lunenburg:
Whereas George Jefferson, deceased in his life time by an Indenture dated
May 12, 1774 and another July 12, 1776 and another dated May 12. 1774
and April 30, 1778. The first deed conveying 409, other 141 acres, 321
acres and 1459 acres to Peter Field Jefferson and whereas the said George
Jefferson having since passing and leaving, Elizabeth, his widow who has
since intermarried with Edward G Walpole and said Elizabeth cannot
conveniently travel to our Court to relinquish her right of Dower to the said
several tracts of land, we do command you or any two of you that you do
go to the said Elizabeth and examine her privately apart from her husband.
September 30, 1788
s/ Will Tunstall
Lunenburg County
By virtue of the above Commission to us directed, we have examined
Elizabeth, the wife of Edward G Walpole and examined her apart from her
husband. She relinquished her right of Dower. October 16, 1788
s/ Thos Garland, Edw'd Brodnax
October 20, 1788

Page 295   Cox's Power from Cleaver
I John Cleaver of the county of Henry appoint my friend John Cox of the county of Henry my lawful attorney to act for me to recover for me and my heirs all sums of money that may appear to be due to me from the Estate of William Lightfoot, deceased of the county of Gloucester. Also from the estate of William Lightfoot, deceased of the county of Charles City to recover for me from the exors or admrs of the Estates. October 20, 1788
s/ John Cleaver
Wit: Dan'l Thompkins, Robertson Shelton
October 20, 1788

Page 296   Muse's Deed from Jefferson
October 20, 1788 between Peter Jefferson of the county of Lunenburg and John Muse of the county of Franklin for 100 pounds current Money of Virginia, a tract of land containing 500 acres lying on both sides of Sailors Creek
Bounded: Samuel Calland's line, Elijah Walker's line, Hamlet's line
s/ Peter Jefferson
Wit: None
October 20, 1788

Page 297   Cunagem's Deed from Cox
March 15, 1788 between John Cox of Henry and Bridget Cunagem of P for 50 pounds paid to John Parsons and John Cox, a parcel of land containing 300 acres of land
Bounded: Edmond Gray's line, Philimon Payne's line, Pigg River Road, Donelson's order line, crossing a branch, Polley's line
s/ John Cox
Wit: Moses Hunt, D Roberts, John Cleaver
October 20, 1788

Page 298   Twedell's Deed from Twedell taken out
May 17, 1788 between William Twedell of P and John Twedell, son of the said William of P, in consideration of the natural love and affection for John Twedell and also sum of 5 shillings, a parcel of land on the Waters of Sandy Creek of Dan River, being part of a greater tract of 400 acres granted to Humphrey Hendrick containing by estimation 250 acres
Bounded: lines of William Dix formerly said Humphrey Hendrick, Roger Atkinson, Thomas Wilkinson, James Johnson and William Wright
s/ William Twedel
Wit: W Wright, William (X) Twedel, Ann Wright
October 20, 1788

Page 299   **Henderson's Deed from Roberts**
September 20, 1788 between Daniel Roberts of P and James Henderson of
P in consideration of 20 pounds, a parcel of land on branches of
Straightstone Creek containing by estimation 138 acres
Bounded: Gilbert Hunt's line, Thomas Davis's line, head of the said
branch
s/ D Roberts
Wit: Joshua Stone, William Henderson, Ben Lankford
October 20, 1788
Mary, wife of said Daniel Roberts, relinquished her right of Dower

Page 300   **Jones Deed from Williams**
March 15, 1788 between Lewis Williams of P and John Jones of P for 59
pounds, 17 shillings, a parcel of land containing by Survey 117 acres on
branches of Shocko Creek
Bounded: David Motley and Richard Brown's line, said Motley's new
line, Thos Williams line, said Jones line purchased of Crawford and Terry,
crossing three branches, Pigg River, old Road, Richard Brown's line,
Brown's old patent line called Williams
s/ Lewis Williams
Wit: Laurence Duff, Wm Webb
October 20, 1788

Page 301   **Jones's Deed from Barksdale**
October 1788 between Beverley Barksdale of P and John Jones of P in sum
of 62 pounds, 12 shillings, 4 pence current money of Virginia, a parcel
containing by Survey 221 acres
Bounded: Ellington's line, up the branch, Ryburn's line
s/ B Barksdale
Wit: None
October 20, 1788

Page 302   **Hendrick from C Wynne**
November 13, 1788 between Charles Wynne of the county of Dunwiddee
and Humphrey Hendrick of P for 37 pounds, ten shillings, a parcel of land
containing 100 acres lying on the south side of Dan river
Bounded: Stillwell's corner, Thomas Fearn's corner, Fearn's line to
Fearns and Hendricks corner
s/ Charles Wynee
Wit: Thos Fearn, William Dix, Lusey Runnals, Daniel (X) Askew, Joseph
Lumpkin, Harrison Lumpkin, Mathew Wynne, John Worsham
November 17, 1788

Page 303   **Hendrick's Deed from R Wynne**

218

February 20, 1787 between Robert Wynne of P and Humphrey Hendrick of P for 300 pounds, a parcel of land on the south side of Dan River containing by estimation 300 acres being part of a greater tract of 1810 acres which was granted to William Wynne, deceased, by Setters Patent dated June 13, 1760
Bounded: by the lines of Thomas Fearn, Charles Wynne, Jacob Stillwell, John Worsham
s/ Robt Wynne
Wit: William Dix junr, William Dix, W Wright, Ann Wright, Elis'a (X) Hancock
June 18, 1787

Page 305   Hankin's Deed from Morton
November 17, 1788 between Joseph Morton of P and Daniel Hankins of P for 150 pounds, a parcel of land on Crooked Creek and both sides of Sandy River bounded by Clouds and Wallins corner, new line, crossing two forks of Sandy River including 400 acres, the other of which said parcel of land bounded by Yarrington's corner, Hickie's Road, John Morton's line, Yarrington's line including 104 acres
s/ Joseph Morton
Wit: David Hodges, W Wright, Jos Akin
November 17, 1788

Page 306   Worsham's Deed from Hendrick
November 17, 1788 between Humphrey Hendrick of P and John Worsham of P for 337 pounds, ten shillings current money of Virginia, a parcel of land on the south side of Dan River and Rutleges Creek containing 400 acres
Bounded: beginning on the said river at the mouth of a gut, Thomas Fearn's line, Mill Branch, Rutleges Creek, Dan river it being he same land the said Hendrick bought of Robert Wynne and Charles Wynne
s/ Humphrey Hendrick
Wit: Robt Lumkin, Daniel Worsham, Jacob Stillwell, Robt Farguson
November 17, 1788

Page 307   Elliott's Bond for celebrating marriages
We, Richard Elliott and Thomas Hardy of P are bound unto Edmund Randolph, Esq. Governor of Virginia for the sum of 500 pounds current money.
November 17, 1788
The Condition of the above Obligation is such that if the above bound Richard Elliott, who is a minister of the Gospel of the Society of Christians called Baptists, shall well and truly celebrate the rites of Marriage between

all persons applying to him for that purpose, then the Obligation to be void.
Taken in Open Court
Richard Elliot, Thos Hardy
November 17, 1788

Page 308   Munford's Deed from Shelton

November 16, 1788 between William Shelton and Edward Munford for 12 pounds, a parcel of land containing by Estimation 400 acres, it being the tract of land formerly possessed by said Munford, 350 acres of which was sold for taxes under Abraha Shelton, Sheriff, acres, the balance of the said 400, was sold for taxes under William Todd.
s/ Will Shelton
Wit: Rich'd N Venable, Geo Craghead, Jos Akin, D C Poly
November 20, 1788

Page 308   Fearn's Deed from Wynne

November 13, 1788 between Charles Wynne of the county of Dunwiddie and Thomas Fearn of P in consideration of 180 pounds current money of Virginia, a tract of land containing 514 acres and on the south side of Dan River.
Bounded: new line to Thomas Fearn's corner according to the patent
s/ Charles Wynne
Wit: William Dix, Joseph Lumpkins, Humphrey Hendrick, Lucy Runnalds, Daniel Askew, Mathew Wynne, Harrison Lumpkin, James Dix Senr
November 17, 1788

Page 309   De Laforest's Deed from Piat

July 27, 1787 between Claud Piat and Mary his wife of the Town of Petersburg and Aubin de Laforest of (Blank) in consideration of 25 poundsm a parcel of land on the head braches of Allin's Creek containing by estimation 150 acres
Bounded: James Mackleen' s line where it crosses Clement's old road, new line till it strikes Daniel Jenkins line, Thomas Vaughan's line, Chissums line, crosses Clement's old road, it being the land purchased by the said Piat of James Moore October 9, 1784
s/ Claud Piat, Mary Piat
Wit: Daniel Roberts, Will George, D Bardet
October 15, 1787

Page 311   Clark's Deed from Adams

October 30, 1788 between Alin Adams of P and William Clark of P for conisideration of 60 pounds current money of Virginia, a parcel of land containing 3 acres and on both sides of Banister River and including the

mill built by William Pigg on the land of the said Allen Adams cross the said Banister river and 2 acres of the said land being a part of the said land the said Allin Adams now lives, and one acre being part of the land James Mead now lives one
Bounded: Robert Martin's branch, Banister river
s/ Allin (X) Adams
Wit: John Thompson
November 17, 1788

Page 311   Terrell's Deed from Perkins
November 15, 1788 between Phillimon Perkins and Molly his wife of P an Benjamin Terrell of P in consideration of 100 pounds, a parcel of land containing 150 acres being part of James Doss Senr pattented land, it being the place the said James Doss gave to his son Thomas Doss which land was conveyed by Thoms Doss to Henry Mullins and said Mullins to the above mentioned Phillimon Perkins lying on both sides of Valentine's Creek
s/ Phillimon Perkins, Molly Perkins
Wit: William Dudley, Archer (X) Perkins, James (X) Doss, Armstead Dudley
November 20, 1788

Page 312   Lovell's Deed from Davenport
August 2, 1788 between William Davenport of the county of Cumberland and Daniel Lovell of P for 100 pounds, a tract of land containing 440 acres
Bounded: by Jeremiah Worsham, John Watson, junr, Daniel Lovell, Jesse Robinson, Charles Hutchings lines
s/ William (X) Davenport
Wit: William Watson, John Hall, George Watson, John Watson
November 19, 1788

Page 313   Calland and Smith's Deed from Oliver
July 31, 1788 between Thomas Oliver of P and Calland and Smith, Merchants, of P for sum of 30 pounds, a parcel of land containing by estimation 200 acres on the Waters of Banister River which said tract of land was sold by the Sheriff for taxes due thereon and willed by Drury Oliver, deceased to the said Thomas Oliver, his son
Bounded: Mitchell and Roberts lines above and a pease formerly surveyed for Richard Yates below (willed by the said Drury Oliver, deceased to son John) lying on both sides of the road leading from P Old Court House to P present Court House whereon the said Thomas Oliver's mother, Mary Oliver, now lives
s/ Thomas Oliver
Wit: Sam Tompkins jr, James Mitchell, Elsiha Walker

December 15, 1788

Page 314   **Walker's Deed from Brewer**
August 6, 1788 between James Brewer of P and Elisha Walker of P for the
sum of 90 pounds current money of Virginia, a parcel of land containing
by estimation 250 acres adjoining the lands of William Vincent, Callands
and Smith, a dividing line, William Hamblet, John Elgins, it being
susposed to be one half of 500 acres that I obtained by a decree in the High
Court of Chancery vs James Smith and Co and Edm'd Randolph, Esquire,
Atto General and Abraham Shelton, Escheator dated December 3, 1787
lying on the north side of Sailors Creek and is the remaining half of the
said 500 acres that I sold Mesr Calland and Smith, 250 of theirs lying on
the south side of Sailors Creek
s/ James Brewer
Wit: Sam Tompkins, John Smith, James Mitchell, Bo Smith
December 15, 1788

Page 316   **Sever's Deed from Cook**
December 5, 1788 between Harmon Cook of P and John Sever of P for 50
pounds, a parcel of land containing by Survey 100 acres
Bounded: Christian Turk and Henry Croff's line, David Dalton's line,
Cook's new line, Croff's line, Elander Hampton's line, crossing the
Hunting Camp branch, Christian Turk's line
s/ Harmon Cook
Wit: Thos Dyer, Philip Debo
December 15, 1788
Mary, wife of said Harmon Cook, relinquished her right of Dower

Page 316   **Turk's Deed from Cook**
June 21, 1788 between Harmon Cook of P and Christian Turk of P for 30
pounds current money of Virginia, a parcel of land on the branches of
Potters Creek containing 66 acres beginning in Henry Croff's line, crosses
the spring branch, William Mitchell's line
s/ Harmon Cook
Wit: Thos Dyer, James Dyer, Jonathan (X) Rigney
December 15, 1788
Mary, wife of Harmon Cook, relinquished her right of Dower
Delivered to Jno Rorer(written on side)

Page 317   **Debo's Deed from Cook**
December 8, 1788 between Harmon Cook of P and Philip Dibo of P for 30
pounds, a parcel of land on the branches of Potters Creek containing by
survey 64 acres
Bounded: John Sever's corner, William Smith's line

s/ Harmon Cook
Wit: Thos Dyer, George Hannah
December 15, 1788
Mary, wife of Harmon Cook, relinquished her right of Dower

Page 318   Crymer's Deed from Cook
December 8, 1788 between Harmon Cook of P and Christian Crymer of P
for 50 pounds, a certain tract of land containing 62 acres by survey lying
on the branches of Potters Creek
Bounded: Christian Turk's corner, William Mitchell's line, Turk's line
s/ Harmon Cook
Wit: None
December 15, 1788
Mary, wife of Harmon Cook, relinquished her right of Dower

Page 319   Shield's Deed from Hall
December 4, 1788 between Joseph Hall of P and Pleasant Shields of P for
80 pounds Virginia currency, a parcel of land on the north fork of the
upper Double Creek containing by estimation 135 acres
Bounded: William Harris's line, Jonathan Hill's line, John Watkin's line,
new dividing line crossing said creek
s/ Joseph Hall
Wit: Daniel L Farley, Thomas Hill, Nimrod Scott
December 15, 1788
Presiller, wife of Joseph Hall, relinquished her right of Dower

Page 320   Shields Deed from Scott
December 13, 1788 between Nimrod Scott of P and Pleasant Shields of P
for 28 pounds, two shillings and six pence, a parcel of land on the upper
Double Creek containing by estimation 22 ½ acres
Bounded: the old Road upon William Richerson's line, said Shields line,
said Scott's line, fork of the branch
s/ Nimrod Scott
Wit: None
December 15, 1788

Page 320   Hart's Deed from Cook
May 13, 1788 between Harmon Cook of P and Henry Hart, Senr of Orange
County, North Carolina for 25 pounds, a parcel of land containing 360
acres on both sides of the Cold Branch of Cherry Stone creek
Bounded: Wright's corner, John Sweney's line, Taylor's line
s/ Harmon Cook
Wit: Thos Dyer, Christian Keen, Abraham Rohrer
December 15, 1788

Mary, wife of Harmon Cook, relinquished her right of Dower

Page 321   Keezee's from Atkerson

March 11, 1788 between Joseph Atkerson and Rachel of P and Jeremiah Keesee of P for 100 pounds, a parcel of Land being part of a tract of land which William Nealy did live on lying on Tomahawk Creek on the north side containing 100 acres.
Bounded: crossing said Creek, George Smith's line, joining said Keezee's land that he bought of Benja Duncan, the line that George Smith bought of Cook, along said Smith's line to said Creek
s/ Joseph (X) Atkson, Rachel Atkson
Wit: William Blear, Hugh Rennolds, Rich'd Keesee, William Baber
May 19, 1788

Page 323   Watlington's Relinquish of Dower to Stone

To William Terry, Michael Roberts and Jos Newman Haynes of the county of Halifax whereas John Watlington hath conveyed unto Joshua Stone 300 acres of land and whereas, Elizabeth, wife of the said John Watlington, cannot conveniently travel to the P Court to relinquish her right of Dower, we do therefore command you or any two of you to go the the said Elizabeth and examine her privately. July 15, 1788
s/ Will Tunstall
Halifax County
In pursuant of the above Commission to us directed we did personally go to the said Elizabeth and she did relinquish her right of Dower. October 30, 1788
s/ Wm Terry, Mich'l Roberts
December 15, 1788

Page 324   Gammon' s Deed from Norton

January 19, 1789 between Jacob Norton of P and Harris Gammon of P for 25 pounds, a parcel of land on both sides of Stone's Branch containing 100 acres
Bounded: Thomas Spark's line, George Adam's line, said Norton's line
s/ Jacob (X) Norton
Wit: Geo Adams, Walter Guild, Ignatius Wilson, Geo Davis
January 19, 1789

Page 325   Headrick's Deed from Ward

December 24, 1788 between Jeremiah Ward of P and Jacob Headrick of P for 200 pounds, a parcel of land on both sides of Potters Creek containing 360 acres

Bounded: Brian Ward Nowlin's line, William Tomson's line, Harmon Cook's line, new line to Toches line, Jacob Bargar's line, William Mitchell's line, Brian Ward Nowlin's line
s/ Jeremiah (X) Ward
Wit: Thos Ward, Daniel Witcher, Jeremiah Ward, jr
January 19, 1789

Page 326   Short's Deed from Ragsdale
January 15, 1789 between Daniel Ragsdale of P and William Short of P for 50 pounds, a parcel of land on White Oak Creek containing by estimation 100 acres
Bounded: said Ragsdale's line, Moses Hutching's line, Joseph Richard's line, passing White Oak Creek
s/ Daniel (X) Ragsdale
Wit: Thomas Ragsdale, Obediah Ragsdale, William Short
January 19, 1789
Pheby, wife of Daniel Ragsdale, relinquished her right of Dower

Page 327   Cook's Sale from Dyer
I, John Dyer, Planter of P, for 25 pounds have sold to Harmon Cook of P, Merchant, one Negro woman named Nan
s/ John Dyer
Wit: None
January 19, 1789

Page 328   Hick's Deed from Blair
January 19, 1789 between William Blare of P and Nathaniel Hicks of P for 45 pounds, a parcel of land on the branches of Tomahawk Creek containing 284 acres
Bounded: Maghan's line
s/ William Blare
Wit: None
January 19, 1789
Sarah, wife of William Blare, relinquished her right of Dower

Page 329   Cook's Sale from Wickard
I, Barlet Wickard of P, for the sum of 15 pounds sell Harmon Cook of P the following articles: to wit, two beds and furniture and all my pewter, and household furniture, one cow and one stone sledge and mason tools and all my stone augers
s/ Bartlet Wickart
Wit: Thos Dyer, James (X) Dyer
January 19, 1789

Page 330   **Tucker's Deed of Gift from Tucker**
January 15, 1789 between William Tucker of P and Robert Tucker, his son
of P, for love and affection he bears his son and five shillings, one certain
Negro woman named Jenny and her future increase
s/ William Tucker
Wit: Nelson Tucker, William Shelton, Thos Payne
January 19, 1789

Page 330   **Morgan's Deed from Shelton**
November 3, 1788 between Abraham Shelton of P and Haynes Morgan of
P for 120 pounds a parcel of land on the west fork of Allen Creek
containing by estimation 400 acres being part of a greater tract conveyed
from John George to the said Abraham Shelton
Bounded: William Doss's line, Doss's old line, said Morgan's former line,
Joseph Faris's line, Hickey's Road, to a line adjoining a tract lately
purchased of Richard Anderson
s/ Abra Shelton
Wit: Joshua Stone, T Tunstall, Will Doss
January 19, 1789

Page 332   **Thomas's Deed from Bizwell**
August 18, 1788 between John Biswell, Planter, and Jonathan Thomas,
both of P for 60 pounds, a parcel of land containing about 375 acres on the
Waters of Strawberry Creek
Bounded: Strawberry Creek, Bynums line
s/ John Biswell
Wit: William Devin Senr, Robert Devin, George Thomas
February 16, 1789

Page 333   **Duncan's Deed from Welch**
February 10, 1789 between Joshua Welch of P and Jesse Duncan of P for
38 pounds, 15 shillings current money of Virginia, a parcel of land
containing 62 acres on the Waters of Cherry Stone
Bounded: Jesse Duncan's line, Burton's line, Chattins line, Allens line,
said Duncan's line
s/ Joshua Welch
Wit: Joseph Carter, John Chattin, Elisha (X) Nuckles
February 16, 1789
Jemima, wife of Joshua Welch, relinquished her right of Dower

Page 334   **Cook's Deed from Razor**
January 14, 1789 between Paul Reiser of P and Harmon Cook for 60
pounds a parcel of land containing 148 acres on Potters Creek
s/ Paul Reiser

Wit: Thos Dyer, Leonard Rise, George Haack, Paul Reaser
February 16, 1789

Page 335   May's Deed from Hall
February 9, 1789 between John Hall and Lucy Hall of Amelia County and
John May of P for 90 pounds a parcel of land containing 200 acres
Bounded: said May's spring, crossing two forks of Sandy Creek, Price's
line, Burnt Cabbin line, crossing Middle Creek to Ash branch, Astin's line,
Astin's fork of Sandy Creek, Astin's line, along said May's line
s/ John Hall, Lucy (X) Hall
Wit: Peter Kendall, James (X) Billings, David (X) Lay
February 16, 1789

Page 336   Todd and Shelton's Deed from Markham
January 19, 1787 between John Markham of P and William Todd and
Crispin Shelton Junr for 350 pounds, a parcel of land lying on the north
side of White Thorn Creek and Banister River, also seven Negroes to wit:
Squire, Toby, Bassell, Beck, Amy, John, and Syphy, also seven horses and
30 head of Neat cattle.
s/ John Markham
Wit: None
February 16, 1789

Page 337   Yates's Deed from Medkiff
February 16, 1789 between John Medkiff of P and John Yates of P for 60
pounds, a parcel of land on Mill Creek containing 100 acres
Bounded: Old line crossing a branch, below the mouth of the Otter
Branch, new dividing line
s/ John Medkiff
Wit: None
February 16, 1789

Page 338   LeGrande's Deed from Owen
February 16, 1789 between William Owen of P and Abraham Legrand of P
in consideration of 400 pounds, a parcel of land containing 100 acres
Bounded: John Owen, deceased line, on the side of a branch, John Owen's
line chopt four sides
s/ William Owen
Wit: None
February 16, 1789
Eddy, wife of William Owen, relinquished her right of Dower

Page 339   Hardy's Deed from Allen

February 16, 1789 between Frances Allen of P and Thomas Hardy of P for 70 pounds, a parcel of land on Strawberry Creek containing by estimation 165 acres
Bounded: Bank of the Creek, Edward Long's line, Jonathan Thomas's line, James Meghan's line
s/ Frances (X) Allen
Wit: Jacob (X) Mires, John (X) Mires, William Mires
February 16, 1789
Rachel, wife of Francis Allen, relinquished her right of Dower

Page 340   Hardy's Sale from Hardy
I, George Hardy of P, for 17 pounds, 6 shillings and 8 pence half penny paid by George Hardy Senr and John Lewis of P have sold unto them two beds and furniture, one loom, six plates and two dishes, three basons, one woman's saddle and two chests, one black walnut one and the other a pine one, also two mares and two cattle
s/ George Hardy
Wit: John Jones, Tho Linthicum
February 16, 1789

Page 341   Anderson's Deed from Shelton
October 31, 1788 between Abraham Shelton of P and Richard Anderson of P for 32 pounds, 15 shillings, a tract of land on branches of Allens Creek and Stinking River containing by estimation 231 acres
Bounded: Crenshaw's corner in Todd's line on Hickeys Road, Todd's line, Shelton's line formerly John Georges, crossing Hickey Road and a branch of Allen Creek, Crenshaw's line
s/ Abra Shelton
Wit: Will Todd, Haynes Morgan, Joshua Stone
February 16, 1789

Page 342   Muse's Deed from Pearson
1789 between Sherwood Pearson of P and John Muse of Franklin County for 150 pounds, a parcel of land containing 359 acres on both sides of Turkey Cock Creek
s/ Sherwood Peerson
Wit: None
January 16, 1789
Elizabeth, wife of Sherwood Pearson, relinquished her right of Dower

Page 343   Lewis's Deed from Taylor
August 19, 1788 between Edmund Taylor of P and Charles Lewis of P of 46 pounds a parcel of land containing 46 acres

Bounded: Thomas Payne's corner, it being the corner on James Taylor's line sold to the above, said Payne's line to Spencer Shelton's line, crossing Mill Creek to Hickeys Road
s/ Edmund Taylor
Wit: None
February 16, 1789

Page 344   Pearson's Deed from Muse
February 16, 1789 between Sherwood Pearson of P and John Muse of Franklin County for 200 pounds, a parcel of land on the Camp branch containing 409 acres
s/ John Muse
Wit: None
February 16, 1789
Lucy, wife of John Muse, relinquished her right of Dower

Page 345   Allen's Deed from Weatherford
February 16, 1789 between David Weatherford and his wife Mary of P and Francis Allen Junr of P for 70 pounds a parcel of land containing by estimation 100 acres
Bounded: Branch of the head of what is called the Little Meadow on Cherrystone Creek, Jesse Duncan's line, John Welch's line, John Chattin's line, George Miers line, Thomas Hardy's line, said Meadow's branch
s/ David Weatherford, Mary Weatherford
Wit: None
February 16, 1789
Mary, wife of David Weatherford, relinquished her right of Dower

Page 346   Farmer's Deed from Yates &c
February 16, 1789 between John Yates and James Farmer of P and Marlin Farmer of P for 210 pounds, a parcel of land on both sides of Elkhorn Creek containing 200 acres
Bounded: James Farmer's line, Woodson's line, a branch of Elkhorn Creek
s/ John Yeats, James Farmer
Wit: None
February 16, 1789

Page 347   Sartain's Deed from Hundley
January 16, 1786 between Caleb Hundley of P and John Sertain of P for 30 pounds a parcel of land containing by estimation 50 acres on the branches of Bareskin Creek
Bounded: crosses a branch of Bearskin Creek
s/ Caleb Hundley

Wit: None
January 16, 1786

Page 348   Turner's Sale from Terry
I, Stephen Terry of P, in consideration of the sum of 65 pounds, 9 shillings
in gold or silver, have sold unto Abednego Turner of P one Negro woman
slave named Peg and her children of the names of Jim and Ned July 27,
1786
s/ Stephen Terry
Wit: John Turner
March 17, 1787

Page 348   Robert's Deed from Epperson
March 27, 1787
Between William Epperson of P and Daniel Roberts of P for 250 pounds,
hath sold one Negro woman by the name of Tiller, one Negro girl by the
name Luce, three horses, six head of cattle, three feather beds and all the
rest of the household furniture with all the purtainances belonging in any
way to the premises
s/ Wm Epperson
Wit: None
October 15, 1787

Page 350   Collin's Deed from Atkerson
January 14, 1786 between Joel Atkinson of the county of Henry and Daniel
Collings of P for 100 pounds, a parcel of land containing by patent 294
acres on both sides of Cold Branch on Cherry stone Creek
Bounded: William Right's line
s/ Joel Atkinson
Wit: None
January 16, 1786

Page 350   Worsham's Deed from Worsham
I, Jeremiah Worsham of P, for the sum of nine pounds, six shillings and
four pence half penny paid by John Worsham of P have sold unto him one
Negro woman slave called and known by the name of Vina
s/ Jeremiah (X) Worsham
Wit: W Wright, Aaron Hutchings
Marach 19, 1787

Page 351   Cook's Sale from Quarles
I, Francis Quarles of P have sold unto Harmon Cook of P one wagon and
two pairs of hind geers, two beds and furniture, one saddle, working tools,

two spinning wheels, two iron pots, chest, one pow and one pewter dish
and eight pewter plates
s/ Francis Quarles
Wit: Thomas Dyer, Abraham Arron junr
January 15, 1787

Page 352   Parrot's Deed from Parrot deliver'd to Luke Parrot
July 29, 1785 between Thorp Parrot of the county of Henry and Nathaniel
Parrott Senr of the same county for 33 pounds, a parcel of land containing
220 acres
Bounded: Barber's path
s/ Thorp (X) Parrot
Wit: Peyton Smith, Henry Atkinson, George Ramsle
January 16, 1786

Page 352   Dyer's Deed from Duncan
April 12, 1784 between Jesse Duncan of P and John Dyer of P for 40
pounds, a parcel of land on both sides of Bearskin Creek, being part of a
greater tract of 400 acres granted unto John Pigg and by said John Pigg
conveyed the aforesaid 100 acres of land to the said Daniel McKensey by
Deed dated November 22, 1773 lying at the lower end of the said 400 acres
s/ Jesse Duncan
Wit: Jos Akin, Will Shelton, Thos Terry
November 15, 1784

Page 353   Ellington's Deed from Ellington
January 24, 1787 between Enoch Ward Ellington of P and Jeremiah
Ellington of P for 200 pounds, tract of land on branches of Elkhorn Creek,
it being the same land that Jeremiah Ellington foremerly bought of Thomas
Terry containing by estimation 200 acres
Bounded: Atkinson's line, Stephen Coleman's line, Joseph Terry's line,
Atkinson's line
s/ Enoch W Ellington
Wit: Floyd Tanner, Anthony Wilkinson, Elizabeth Tanner
September 16, 1787

Page 355   Wright's Deed from Collie
April 13, 1787 between William Collie of the county of Washington and
William Wright of P for 80 pounds, a parcel of land on the branches of
Sandy Creek containing by estimation 304 acres which was granted to the
said William Collie by a grant from the Land Office of the state of Virginia
s/ William Collie
Wit: Charles Collie, William Sladen, Jesse Mann, John (X) Johnson
April 16, 1787

Page 356   Watkins power from Laws &c
We, John Laws and Ann Miller of the county of Wilkes, North Carolina, appoint our truly friend Isaiah Watkins of P our true and lawful attorney and in our names and to our use to ask, demand and receive of and from any and all persons living or being in Bedford County, Virginia that is indebted to us or doth hold in his possession anything, goods, chattels, lands or money, to follow legal courses for the recovery of the same as touching the lands granted to us by law some other movable property being of the estate of John Miller, deceased May 15, 1785
s/ John Laws, Ann Miller
Wit: Adam Poor, Nathaniel (X) Poor, Lydall (X) Watkins
May 16, 1785

Page 357   Taylor's Deed from Burton
August 19, 1788 between William Burton of P and Edmund Taylor of P for 50 pounds, a parcel of land containing 156 acres
Bounded: Spencer Shelton's line, Parhan's line, William Pace's line, Henry Kay's line
s/ William (X) Burton
Wit: Will Todd, Gabriel Shelton, Moses Hurt, William Shelton, Jas Taylor, Wm Griggory, Lem Shelton
March 16, 1789

Page 358   Tunstall's Sale from Tunstall
I, William Tunstall of Henry County, for 120 pounds paid by Edmund Tunstall of P have sold him one Negro wench Polly and child called Armistead and a boy Sandy October 1, 1788
s/ Will Tunstall
Wit: Barna Wells junr, W Tunstall junr
March 19, 1789

Page 358   Todd's Sale from Greggory
I, John Greggory of P, for the sum of 120 pounds current money of Virginia, am indebted to William Todd of P have sold unto William Todd two bay mares, and a bay mare colt, the oldest mare is branded thus, CI, has a star on her face and three white feet. The second mare has no brand, has a star in her forehead and three white feet, the young bay mare colt, two years old this spring, has a star and snipe and four white feet, also ten head of cattle, nine of which are marked with a crop and overkeel in the right ear and underkeel in the left ear, the other is a pided cow and marked with a slit in the right ear and underkeel in the left, also two feather beds and furniture, one black walnut chest, one hair trunk, one pine table, chairs, a quanity of pewter, two iron pots, one dutch oven, one iron skillet and

sundry earthern ware, one gun, one woman's saddle and two spinning wheels
s/ John Griggory
 Wit: Isaac Griggory, Walter Lamb
March 16, 1789

Page 359   Easley's Deed from Hutchinson deliver'd to John Giles
March 16, 1789 between Christopher Hutchins of P and Pirant Easley of P for 60 pounds, a parcel of land containing 171 acres on the north side of Banister River
Bounded: John Hutchinson's line, crossing Pigg's Road, Pigg's line, Carter's line, Courthouse road, Pigg's road
s/ Christopher Hutchings
Wit: None
March 16, 1789

Page 360   Thomas's Deed from Thomas
April 6, 1789 between William Thomas of P and Peyton Thomas of P in consideration of the love and affection, one tract of land containing 400 acres on both sides of Strawberry Creek
Bounded: line of Richard Chamberlayne's patent, being part of Richard Chamberlayne's Order of Counsel, new dividing line
s/ Wm Thomas
Wit: None
April 20, 1789

Page 361   Boyd's Deed from Lumpkin
August 29, 1788 between Robert Lumpkins of P and William Boyd of Halifax County for 40 pounds, a parcel of land containing 102 acres on the south side of Dan river
Bounded: Larkin Dix's line, William Wynn's line, crossing the road
s/ Robt Lumkin
Wit: Jos Lumpkin, Stith Wynne, John Lumkin, Pittman Lumpkin, Thomas Whitlock
April 20, 1789

Page 362   Dix's Deed from Dix
April 18, 1789 between William Dix, Gentleman, of P and James Dix of P for 100 pounds, a parcel of land containing by estimation 200 acres, a part of a tract whereon the said William Dix now dwells
Bounded: at a beach near the branch called the Great Branch, about 50 or 60 yards from Dan River, William Dix's back line, said James Dix's old line

s/ William Dix
Wit: James Burton, Simon Adams, W Wright, John Wier, Bezl Weir
April 20, 1789

Page 363   Johnson's Deed from Watson
April 20, 1789 between Thomas Watson of P and James Johnson of P for
300 pounds, a parcel of land containing 266 acres
Bounded: north side of Cherrystone Creek between the said Watson
Currey's order, William Easley's line, crossing Cherrystone Creek,
Hardy's line, crossing Cherrystone Creek, corner on Currrey's order
s/ Thos (X) Watson
Wit: None
April 20, 1789

Page 364   Potter's Deed from Mosley
August 29, 1788 between Samuel Mosley of Henry County, Virginia and
Henry Potter of P for 200 pounds Virginia currency, a parcel of land
containing by estimation 263 acres on the south fork of Sandy River
Bounded: lands of Jesse Robertson, David Harris, and James Curry, being
the land and plantation whereon Henry Lansford lived and died
s/ Samuel Mosley
Wit: David Harris, Isham Williams, Seth Farrar, Peter (X) Rigg, James
Cary, Sarah (X) Maddox
April 20, 1789

Page 365   Creel's Deed from Hughes
November 3, 1788 between James Hughes of the county of Aberville,
South Carolina and Rosenah Creel of P for 60 pounds, a parcel of land
containing 100 acres by estimation lying on the Waters of Burches Creek
Bounded: said Creek line at a branch, Terry's line
s/ James Hughs
Wit: John Chelton, Michjah Creel, Thos Creel, John Creel
April 20, 1789

Page 367   Quinn's Deed from Wier
April 4, 1789 between John Wier and Sally his wife of P and William
Quinn of P for 100 pounds, a parcel of land containing by estimation 205
acres
Bounded: Wilson's line, Wilson's spring branch, new line
s/ John Wier, Sally (X) Wier
Wit: Daniel Price, Wm Price, Maraday Price
April 20, 1789

Page 367   Purcel's Deed from Hoyl

April 20, 1789 between Charles Hoyl of Halifax County and Charles Purcel of the city of Richmond in consideration of 200 pounds Virginia currency, a parcel of land on waters of Upper Double Creek and Wolfe Hill branch containing by estimation 300 acres.
Bounded: Gabriel Richard's line, Dan'l Allen's line, William Waddell's line, Daniel Farley's line, Nimrod Scott's line, James Woody's line, Gabriel Richards line
s/ Chas Hoyl
Wit: None
April 20, 1789

Page 368   Prewett's Deed from Wier
April 4, 1789 between John Wier of P and John Prewitt of P for 15 pounds, a parcel of land containing by estimation 15 acres
Bounded: Rocky Branch, Wilson's spring branch, Wilson's line
s/ John Wier
Wit: Daniel Price, Wm Price, Maraday Price
April 20, 1789

Page 369   Hoyl's Deed from Farley
April 18, 1789 between Daniel L Farley of Halifax County and Charles Hoyl of Halifax for 100 pounds Virginia currency, a parcel of land on the waters of the upper Double Creek and Wolf Hill Branch containing by estimation 300 acres
Bounded: Gabriel Richard's line, David Allen's line, William Waddell's line, Said Farley's line, Nimrod Scott's line, James Woody's line, Gabriel Richards' line
s/ Daniel L Farley
Wit: William Harrison, Nimrod Scott, William Richardson
April 20, 1789

Page 370   Birches's Deed from Gray
October 10, 1788 between Andrew Gray of P and John Birch of P for 25 pounds, a parcel of land which the said Andrew Gray purchased on Nathaniel Wooten by deed
s/ Andrew (X) Gray
Wit: Thomas Shelton junr, William (X) Runnelds, Bird (X) Lawless, Sarah (X) Shelton
April 20, 1789

Page371   Craddock's power from Hendrick
I, Nathaniel Hendrick of P; have appointed John Craddock of P my attorney to sue, arrest any person owing to me in any sum of money at his discreation   March 14, 1789

s/ Nathaniel Hendrick
Wit: Thos Davis, John Craddock
April 20, 1789

Page 371   Price's Deed from Adams
January 15, 1789 between George Adams of P and William Price Senr of P
for 40 pounds containing 40 acres which Francis Ross purchased of
Charles Burton together with the land and plantation that the said Ross
formerly lived on containing in the whole 100 acres
Bounded: south side of Sandy Creek, Thomas Deakes line
s/ Geo Adams
Wit: D Price, Robert Price, Maraday Price
April 20, 1789

Page 372   Devin's Deed from Boaz
November 4, 1788 between Abednego Boaz of the county of Buckingham
and Robert Devin of P for 75 pounds, a parcel of land containing 293 acres
Bounded: Thomas Boaz's line on the west side of Strawberry, Long
branch, Chamberlain's line
s/ Abednego Boaz
Wit: Shadrack Boaz, James Fulton, William Daniel, Edmund Boaz
April 20, 1789

Page 373   Burnett's from Devin
April 20, 1789 between Robert Devin of P and Benjamin Burnett Senr of P
for 100 pounds, a parcel of land containing 293 acres
Bounded: Thomas Boaz's line on the west side of Strawberry, Long
Branch, Chamberlin's line
s/ Robert Devin
Wit: None
April 20, 1789

Page 374   Farley's Deed from Pettit
October 29, 1788 between John Pettit of Caswell County, North Carolina
and Daniel L Farley of Halifax County Virginia for 150 pounds Virginia
currency, a tract of land on the waters of Upper Double Creek and Wolfhill
Branch containing by estimation 362 acres
Bounded: Gabriel Richards' line, David Allen's line, Waddil's line, said
Daniel L Farley's line, William Richardson's and Pleasant Shields corner,
Nimrod Scott's line, James Woody's line
s/ John Pettit
Wit: Robert Walters, John Walters, William Harrison
April 17, 1789

Page 374 Price's Deed from Chelton
April 10, 1789 between Mark Chelton of P and William Price of P for 60
pounds, a parcel of land containing 60 acres by estimation
Bounded: Murray's line, corner of Robert Williams near the creek,
Williams line, old road, the old field
s/ Mark (X) Chelton
Wit: M Clay, George Chelton, Orlando Smith
April 20, 1789

Page 375 Chaney's Deed from Chaney
April 17, 1789 between Jacob Chaney Senr of P and Jacob Chaney junr of
P for 40 pounds, a parcel of land containing 140 acres on the draughts of
Birches Creek
Bounded: Jacob Chaney Senr's line, Colo Henry's order, on a line of a
tract of land the said Jacob Chaney Senr sold to John Atkinson
s/ Jacob Chaney
Wit: None
April 20, 1789

Page 376 Price's Deed from Wier
April 4, 1789 between John Wier of P and William Price of P for 50
pounds, a parcel of land containing by estimation 70 acres
Bounded: Rocky branch, Adkerson's corner, Adkerson's line, Burton's
former line
s/ John Wier
Wit: Daniel Price, John (X) Pruit, Marady Price
April 20, 1789

Page 376 Glascock's Deed from Baker
April 20, 1789 between James Baker of P and William Glascock, John
Glascock and George Glascock, the lawful children of William Glascock.,
deceased of the county of Northumberland in consideration of 100 pounds,
a parcel of land on both sides of Squirrel Creek containing by estimation
100 acres
Bounded: said Baker's lower corner, said Glascock's line
s/ Jas Baker
Wit: None
April 20, 1789

Page 378 Perkins's Deed from Smith
April 10, 1788 between Lemuel Smith of Surry County, North Carolina
and Phillimon Perkins of P for 200 pounds, a parcel of land containing 254
acres on both sides of Cascade Creek bounded by George Russell's
dividing line, hill near the Russell's field, also 400 acres adjoining the tract

above mentioned granted by patent to Isaiah Watkins beginning in
Russell's line on the east side of Cascade Creek, head of Mill Pond on said
Creek, Brown's line to where it strikes Russell's old line
Bounded: George Russell's dividing line, hill near the Russell's field, also
s/ Lem'l Smith
Wit: Edw'd Warren, Philip Perkins, Thomas Perkins, Joseph (X) Harris
July 21, 1788

Page 379   Adams's Deed from Sparkes
November 1, 1788 between Thomas Sparkes Senr and Simon Adams for
150 pounds, a parcel of land on the north side of Sandy River, being the
tract of land whereon Mathew Sparks now lives containing 300 acres
Bounded: river mentioned, on the river, crossing two branches
s/ Thos Sparkes
Wit: Dan'l Tompkins, Thos Smith, John Baggerly, Leonard Murray
February 16, 1789

Page 380   Smith's power from Black
I, Thomas Black of Willis County, Georgia, appoint my truly friend John
Smith of P my true and lawful attorney to make a good and lawful rite in
fee simple clear of any incumbrances to Samuel Calland of P unto a certain
tract of land on both sides of Snow Creek and joining the said Calland's
plantation and containing 100 acres, the bounds will be fully appear by
deed made by Archibald Young to me and recorded June 5, 1783.
October 25, 1788
s/ Thomas Black
Wit: James Cowdon, William Cowdon, Loa'k Tuggle, Geo Tuggle
February 15, 1789

Page 381   Shelton's Deed from Hurt
November 10, 1788 between Moses Hurt of P and Beverly Shelton of P for
10 pounds, 10 shillings, three Negroes named Daniel, Ritta and Lucy and
one sorrel mare, three feather beds and furniture, 8 head of neat cattle, 45
barrels corn, one ox cart, all other of my household furniture, one hogshead
tobacco
s/ Moses Hurt
Wit: Armistead Shelton., Benja Shelton, Thos Payne
April 20, 1789

Page 382   Price's Deed from Wright
April 8, 1789 between John Wright Senr of P and William Price of P for 70
pounds, a parcel of land on the head branches of Sandy Creek containing
by estimation 133 ½ acres
s/ John Wright

Wit: Lucius Tanner, George Chelton, James (X) Martin, William Price
April 20, 1789

Page 383   Keatt's Deed from Tucker
September 13, 1787 between William Tucker of P and Charles Keatt for
150 pounds, a parcel of land on both sides Mill Creek, Pigg River Road
and Courthouse Road, being the upper part of land John Cox formerly
lived on and conveyed by said Cox to said Tucker dated September 21,
1779 containing by estimation 300 acres
Bounded: Thomas Payne's corner, Courthouse Road, Robert Tucker's
corner, said William Tucker's line, crossing the creek to Pigg River Road,
said Tucker's upper line, Edmund Payne's line, Thomas Jones' corner, Ben
Shelton's corner, Courthouse Roas
s/ William Tucker
Wit: James Taylor, Edm'd Taylor, Marlisha Thurnston
April 20, 1789

Page 384   Bennett's Deed from Bennett
1789 between Reuben Bennett of Willis County, Georgia and Thomas
Bennett of P for natural love and affection for the said Thomas Bennett, a
parcel of 85 acres of land being part of 650 acres granted by patent to
Benjamin Tarrant, assignee of Leonard Tarrant (his father), assignee of
William Lynch lying on the south side of Stanton River
Bounded: River between Lynch's Little Creek and Big Creek, old line
s/ Reubin (X) Bennett
Wit: James Arther, William (X) Bennett, Elizabeth (X) Bennett, Charity
(X) Wheeler
April 20, 1789

Page 385   McDonald's Deed from Clay
April 1, 1787 between Charles Clay of county of Potan in Virginia and
Jams McDonald of P for 7 pounds current money of Virginia, a parcel of
land on the waters of Sandy Creek being part of his order containing 100
acres
Bounded: M McDoanld's upper corner, Jasper Billings's corner, Scool
house branch, William Price's line, Stoksis line
s/ Charles Clay
Wit: Richard Gain, Absolom McDonalld, David Laye
December 17, 1787

Page 386   Hammock's Deed from Vincent
April 20, 1789 between William Vincent of P and Peter Hammock of P for
47 pounds, a parcel of land containing 250 acres on the north side of

239

Sailors Creek, suspose to be one half of 500 acres said Vincent purchased of Brewer
Bounded: Said Vincent's lower line, Sailors Creek up to the fork, said Vincent's east line
s/ Will Vincent
April 20, 1789

Page 387   Cook's Deed from Wright
February 10, 1789 between William Wright of P and Harmon Cook of P for 100 pounds, a parcel of l and containing by estimation 800 acres as by a patent duly recorded in the Land Office of this state dated May 7, 1786
s/ W Wright
Wit: Thos Dyer, James (X) Dyer, Robert Dalton, James (X) Bennett
April 20,1 1789

Page 388   Thomas's Deed from Thomas
April 6, 1789 between William Thomas of P and Jacob Thomas of P for love and affection to Jacob Thomas, a parcel of land containing 400 acres on both sides of Strawberry Creek
Bounded: line of Richard Chamberlain being part of Richard Chamberlain's order of Council, said Patern line
s/ Wm Thomas
April 20, 1789

Page 389   Cook's Deed from Shelton
April 20, 1789 between Frederick Shelton of P and Harmon Kook of P for 10 pounds, a parcel of land containing 50 acres of land lying on both sides of Pigg River which said land was formerly charged by the said Commissioners to James Carr and sold by the sheriff for taxes
Bounded: said river, Cook's line, said river bank, corner of George Peak's patent
s/ Fred Shelton
April 20, 1789

Page 390   Cook's Deed from Shelton
April 20, 1789 between Frederick Shelton of P and Harmon Cook of P for 15 pounds, a parcel of land containing 116 acres which was formerly the property of John Robertson of Hanover County and sold to the said Frederick Shelton by the Sheriff for taxes lying on both sides of Falling Creek
Bounded: Joseph Toaler's corner, crossing the said creek, along Mackendree and Hoskins line, Toaler's line
s/ Fred Shelton
April 20, 1789

Page 390   Cook's Deed from Todd, Sheriff
April 20, 1789 between William Todd, Gentleman, late Sheriff of P and
Harmon Cook of P by virtue of a clause in the Revenue Law which directs
him the said sheriff to seize and sell as much as all tracts of land within
said County that will pay the tax due thereon hath sold at public auction
unto the said Harmon Cook 200 acres of land charged by the said
Commissioners to Elenor Hampton in the consideration of 1 pound, 5
shillings and one pence due for 1786 lying on both side of the Hunting
camp branch of Frying Pan Creek
Bounded: Arthur Keezee's line, James Downey's line
s/ Will Todd
April 20, 1789

Page 391   Dyer's Deed from Atkins
February 15, 1788 between Richard Atkins of P and John Dyer of P for 25
pounds, a parcel of land on the branches of Bearskin Creek containing by
estimation 50 acres, being part of a great tract of 266 acres the property of
the said Richard Atkins
Bounded: Line of Luther Hopper, Noton Dickinson, Moses Hodges and a
dividing line between George Dyer and the said Richard Atkins
s/ Richard (X) Adkins
Wit: Jesse (X) Adkins, Joshua (X) Mullins, Abram Parrish
September 15, 1788

Page 392   Willard's Deed from Payne
February 10, 1789 between Edmund Payne of P and Beverly Willard of P
for 105 pounds, a parcel of land containing by estimation 294 acres lying
on the branches of White Thorn and Mill Creek
Bounded: William Payne's line, crossing Sullings branch, William
Tucker's line, Thomas Jones line, Hameses line, Gray's corner,
Goodman's corner, William Payne's line
s/ Edmund Payne
Wit: Reubin Pain, William Parks, Pyrant Easley
April 20, 1789

Page 393   Twedell's sale from Wright
I, William Wright of P, for 20 pounds have sold to William Twedell one
chestnut sorrel mare, unbranded, the right hind foot white a little above the
buttock, one sorrel horse colt, and two cows and calves, all which I
purchased of Harmon Cook, also nine other head of cattle, young and old
s/ W Wright
Wit: John Twedel
April 20, 1789

I Reubin Bennett of Wilkes County, Georgia do constitute my trusty
friend, William Bennett of P to be my lawful attorney to sue for levy and
receive all and every sums of money that are now due to me on which shall
be due belonging to me by any manner of means especially to survey
patent and sell all my land and claims for land of P and Bedford and to
make conveyances in fee simple to the purchasers thereof as well as such
lands that I have already sold and have not conveyed
s/ Reubin Bennett
Wit: Wm Ward, James Arther, William Ellis
April 20, 1789

Page 394   Snow's Deed from Hunt &c

June 7, 1788 between William Hunt and Dolly his wife, Stephen Collins
and Caty, his wife, Nipper Adams and Lucy his wife and James Hoskins
and John Stone, executors of William Hoskins, deceased, of the county of
Halifax and Thomas Snow of P for 10 pounds, a parcel of land on the
branches of Stanton River being part of a great tract granted to the above
named parties containing by estimation 150 acres
Bounded: John Dalton's corner, new dividing line run by the said Snow
and Thomas F Bennett, order line, John Dalton's corner, Dalton's line
s/ William Hunt, Dolly D Hunt, Stephen Collins, Caty Collins, Nipper
Adams, Lucy (X) Adams, James Hoskins, John Stone
Wit: Joshua Stone, John Buckley, Thos Lankford
December 15, 1788

Page 396   Bennett's Deed from Hunt &c

June 7, 1788 between William Hunt and Dolly his wife, Stephen Collins
and Caty, his wife, Nipper Adams and Lucy his wife and James Hoskins
and John Stone, executors of William Hoskins, deceased, of the county of
Halifax and Thomas F Bennett of P for 80 pounds, a parcel of land on the
branches of Stanton River being part of a greater tract granted to the above
named parties containing by estimation 300 acres
Bounded: Thomas F Bennett and Joseph Toler's corner, new line of chopt
trees, about 650 yards crossing Challis Road to John Dalton's corner,
Dalton's line, new line to divide between the said Thomas F Bennett and
Thomas Snow, William Ward's line
s/ William Hunt, Dolly D Hunt, Stephen Collins, Caty Collins, Nipper
Adams, Lucy (X) Adams, James Hoskins, John Stone
Wit: Joshua Stone, John Buckley, Thos Lankford
December 15, 1788

Page 398   Farmer's Deed from Neal

May 18, 1789 between Stephen Neal of P and Isham Farmer of P for 109 pounds, a parcel of land on the lower of Byrd Creek containing by estimation 365 acres
Bounded: said Isham Farmer's upper corner on the said Byrd Creek, his former line, crossing two branches, Terry's order line, crossing several branches, Cherry branch
s/ Stephen Neal
Wit: None
May 18, 1789

Page 399   Morton's Deed from Strong
October 25, 1788 between John Strong of county of Gilford, North Carolina and Joseph Morton of P for 40 pounds, a parcel of land on the south fork of Sandy River containing 80 acres
Bounded: south of said fork of Sandy River, William Howlett's line, fork of Sandy River, Zarachiah Groom's line, Glady fork of Sandy River
s/ John Strong
Wit: A Nash, Thos Richardson, Zack (X) Groom, Jesse Robinson, Isaiah Morton, Stephen (X) Macmillion, Jacob Coalley, Stephen Watkins
May 18, 1789

Page 400   Beggarly's Deed from Sparks
November 2, 1788 between Thomas Sparks Senr of P and John Beggarly of P for 100 pounds, a parcel of land on the south side of Sandy River containing 94 acres
Bounded: Kennon's old line, crossing a branch, the river
s/ Thos Sparks
Wit: Samuel Harvey, Thomas (X) Norton, Leonard Sparks
May 18, 1789

Page 401   Norton's Deed from Sparks
October 13, 1788 between Samuel Sparks of P and Thomas Norton of P for 30 pounds a parcel of land containing 100 acres of patented land on Reeds Spring branch
Bounded: Robertson's old tract, old line
s/ Samuel (X) Sparks, Rachel Sparks
Wit: Samuel Harvey, Leonard Sparks, Mathew Sparks, John Beggarley
May 18, 1789

Page 401   Burnet's Deed from Dunn
May 1789 between John Dunn of P and Godfrey Burnet of P for 30 pounds, a parcel of land on the north side of Long branch containing by estimation 100 acres

Bounded: Spring branch, old road, John Smith's line, to a drean, crossing
the road
s/ John Dunn
Wit: none
May 18, 1789

Page 402   Cook's Deed from Dyer
March 1789 between John Dyer of P and Harmon Cook of P for 100
pounds, a parcel of land on Bearskin Creek containing 100 acres
Bounded: Luther Hoper's line, Noton Dickerson's line, Moses Hodges
line, Haystack branch, Atkerson's line
s/ John Dyer
Wit: Thos Dyer, John Cook, John Wright, Leonard Rise
May 18, 1789

Page 403   Shelton's Deed from Sparks
September 22, 1788 between Thomas Sparks of P and David Shelton for
40 pounds, a tract of land on both sides of Stewart's Creek containing 80
acres
Bounded: Stewart's Creek, dividing line between Thomas and William
Robison, James Fulton's line
s/ Thos Sparks, Elizabeth (X) Sparks
Wit: James Garner, William Vincent, Leonard Sparks
May 18, 1789

Page 403   Allen's Deed from Clay
October 6, 1788 between Mathew Clay of Henrico county and David Allen
of P for 600 pounds, a parcel of land containing 1000 acres bounded by
James Burton's line on the road, Henry Clay's line, Eleazar Clay, head of
Fall Creek, old order, James Burton's line. Also one other tract of land
containing 1000 acres bounded by Harris, Henry Clay, George Young
s/ M Clay
Wit: John Lewis Junr, Robt Lewis, John Walters, Archer Walters, Abra
Shelton, Edm'd Samuel, Tav'r Shelton, John Ball, Dan'l Tompkins
May 18, 1789

Page 404   Hinton's Deed from Shelton
May 19. 1789 between Crispin Shelton junr of P and James Hinton of P for
33 pounds, a parcel of land containing 280 acres lying on both sides
Sweelings fork of Sandy Creek
Bounded: Jere White's line
s/ Crispin Shelton junr
Wit: None
May 18, 1789

Page 405   **Sparks Deed from Sparks**
November 22, 1788 between Thomas Sparks of P and Leonard Sparks of P
for 100 pounds, a parcel of land
Bounded by a dividing line between Leonard Sparks and David Sutton
s/ Thos Sparks
Wit: Samuel Harvey, Thomas (X) Norton, John Baggerely
May 18, 1789

Page 406   **Hewlett's Deed from Strong**
178- between John Strong of Gilford County North Carolina and Anna
Hewlett of county of Henry, Virginia for 25 pounds, a parcel of land on the
south fork of Sandy River containing 138 acres
Bounded: south side of said fork of said Sandy River. Wm Hewlett
s/ John Strong
Wit: Jesse Robinson, Stephen McMillion, Jacob Cooley, Isaiah Morton,
Stephen Watkins
May 18, 1789

Page 407   **Bays Deed from Neal**
May 18, 1789 between Stephen Neal of P and John Bays junr of P for 30
pounds, a parcel of land on the upper of Byrd Creek containing by
estimation 90 acres
Bounded: along Daniel Robert's line, said Byrd Creek, John Buckley's
line
s/ Stephen Neal
Wit: None
May 18, 1789
Lucy, wife of said Stephen Neal, relinquished her right of Dower

Page 407   **Burgesses Deed from Stratton**
June 15, 1789 between William Stratton of P and William Burgess of P for
600 pounds, a parcel of land containing by estimation 213 acres, it being
the said Elisha Arnold purchased of Francis Wright
Bounded: Mark Chelton's corner
s/ William (X) Stratton
Wit: None
June 15, 1789

Page 409   **Robinson's Deed from Atkinson**
June 15, 1789 between William Atkinson and Jesse Atkinson of P and
George Robinson of P for 75 pounds, a parcel of land containing by
estimation 50 acres on both sides the Hemp fork of Bearskin Creek

Bounded: Hodges corner, Hopper's spring, Mill pond, small dreen that comes in the Mill Pond, Nathaniel Atkinson's line, crossing the creek
s/ William Adkins, Jesse Adkins
Wit: None
June 15, 1789

Page 409   W Gammon's Deed from Gammon
November 29, 1788 between John Gammon junr of P and William Gammon of P for one shilling current money of Virginia, a parcel of land on the waters of the Rocky Branch
Bounded: Harris Gammon's line
s/ John Gammon
Wit: None
June 15, 1789

Page 410   J Gammon's Deed from Gammon
May, 20, 1789 between John Gammon Senr and John Gammon junr for five pounds, a parcel of land containing 100 acres
Bounded: Harris Gammon's line, mouth of a branch, William Gammon's line
s/ John Gammon
Wit: None
June 15, 1789

Page 411   Finley's Deed from Chamberlayne
June 15, 1789 between William Chamberlayne of the county of New Kent and Robert Finley of P for 25 pounds, a certain parcel of land on both sides of Strawberry Creek, it being part of an Order of Council of Richard Chamberlayne, deceased and bounded by the lines of Etathroditus White, James Blakley, Joshua Cantrill, and along the new line
s/ Wm Chamberlayne
June 15, 1789

Page 411   Claps Deed from Croff
December 1, 1788 between Henry Croff of P and Lawrence Clap of P for 25 pounds, a parcel of land on the waters of Frying Pan Creek containing by estimation 100 acres
Bounded: David Ross's line, William Mitchell's line, Christian Turk's line, and said Henry Croff's line which divides his line from the said Claps
s/ Henry Croff
Wit: James Mitchell, Agatha Mitchell, Nancy Mitchell
June 15, 1789

Page 412   George's Deed from Ballinger

246

December 10, 1788 between John Ballinger of P and Jonadab George of Halifax County for 100 pounds, a parcel of land on the waters of Straightstone Creek containing by estimation 263 acres
Bounded: Jesse Hodges corner, William Bederton's line, John Buckley's line, new line made between the said Ballinger and the said George, Jesse Hodges line
s/ John (X) Ballinger
Wit: John George, Cornelius McHaney, Richard Craddock, Richard George
June 15, 1789

Page 413   Morton's Deed from Isaac
June 15, 1789 between Jacob Isaac of P and Capt John Morton of P for 150 pounds, a parcel of land containing 240 acres on the branches of Strawberry bounded by Smith's line, John Biswell's line, Thomas Hill's line. Also one other parcel of land containing 100 acres, it being laid off by marked lines on the branches of the Little Fork of Strawberry bounded by fork of Hickeys and Joseph Austin's Roads
s/ Jacob Isaac
Wit: Edw'd Nunnelee, Isaiah Morton, Abraham McMillion, John Nash
June 15, 1789

Page 414   H Gammon's Deed from Gammon
February 17, 1789 between John Gammon of P and Harris Gammon of P for one horse valued to six pounds lawful money of Virginia, a parcel of land containing 130 acres
Bounded: north side of the Rocky Branch
s/ John Gammon
Wit: None
June 15, 1789

Page 414   Parson's Deed from Medcalf
October 28, 1787 between Joseph Medcalf and John Parsons of P for 50 pounds, a parcel of land containing 60 acres
Bounded: Slowns Branch, crossing Cheriston Creek, John Midkiff's line which is a dividing line between Parsons and said Midkiff
s/ Joseph (X) Midkiff
Wit: John Cleaver, Henry (X) Pickrill, Able Marlow, John Midkiff
May 19, 1788

Page 415   Midkiff's Deed from Midkiff
October 20, 1787 between Joseph Midkiff of P and John Midkiff of P for 20 pounds, a parcel of land containing 40 acres
Bounded: old north line, Slones branch

Joseeph (X) Midkiff
Wit: John Cleaver, Henry (X) Pickrill, Able Marlow, John (X) Pasins
May 19, 1788

Page 416   Cook's Deed from Roberts
June 11, 1789 between William Roberts of Bottetot County and Harmon
Cook of P for 90 pounds, a parcel of land on branches of Sandy River and
Banister containing 200 acres
Bounded: John Cook's line, Robert's line, crossing the Courthouse Branch
of Sandy River, branch of Banister River, Cook's line
s/ William Roberts
Wit: Thos Dyer, Joshua Stone, George Smith, John Wright, Jo McCool
June 15, 1789

Page 417   Cook's Deed from Sweney
May 12, 1789 between Joseph Swenney of P and Harmon Cook of P for 50
pounds, a parcel of land on branches of Middle fork of Cherrystone
containing 130 acres as appears by patent dated September 5, 1780
Bounded: Hire line, Charles Rigney's line, Hixes corner
s/ Joseph Swenney
Wit: Thos Dyer, Jacob Goollmer?, Joseph McCool
June 15, 1789

Page 419   McDaniel from Dodson &c release
We, Fortunatus Dodson and Rawley Dale, sons and heirs at law of Samuel
Dodson and Alice Dodson both of county of Richmond in consideration of
77 pounds, ten shillings, paid by Henry McDaniel of the county of
Greenbryer, hath sold to said McDaniel all their claim, right, title, interest,
and demand whatsoever under the will of William Dodson, later of the
county of Richmond to any slaves with all their increase and in particular
the the Negro slave Winney and her increase
s/ Fortun Dodson, Rawleigh Dale
Wit: B Barksdale, Lewis Haley, Thomas Shaw
June 15, 1789

Page 420   Wilson's Deed from Todd
June 15, 1789 between William Todd, Gentleman, late sheriff of the
county of P and Ignatius Wilson of P by virtue of a clause in the late
Revenue Law which directs him, the said sheriff, to seize and sell as much
of all tracts of land within his county as will pay the tax due thereon, hath
sold at public auction 100 acres charged by the Commissioners of P to
Zadock Barnett for one pound, two shilling and 6 ¾ taxes and cost due for
1785 and 1786 lying on the branches of Mountain Creek

Bounded: William Mitchell, Presley Thornton and Joseph Conn's corner, Mitchell's line
s/ Will Todd
June 15, 1789

Page 420   Keezee's Deed from Phillips
October 1787 between Jonathan Phillips and Elizabeth his wife of P and Arthur Keezee of P for 75 pounds, a parcel of land containing 267 acres
Bounded: Barnett's corner, Pigg River Road, aforesaid Barnett's line
s/ Jonathan Phillips
Wit: Able Marlow, John (X) Keezee, Roland (X) Martin
May 19, 1788

Page 422   Thompson's Deed from Blackburne
August 2, 1787 between James Blackburn of P and John Thompson of P for 40 pounds, 100 acres of land
Bounded: Thomas Lackey's line
s/ James Blackburn
Wit: Able Marlow, John Cleaver, William Porter
June 15, 1789

Page 422   Cook's Sale from Dyer
I, John Dyer of P, have sold unto Harmon Cook of P, all my good wares and merchandize to wit: one Negro child, four horses and five head of cattle and all my household furniture together with all my beds and all my movable that I now possess for the first claim of any persons whatsoever, but said Cook is not to remove any of the property until such time that Cooks rents is due from him of said Dyer. January 29, 1789
s/ John Dyer
Wit: Thos Dyer, Nathan (X) Dyer
July 20, 1789

Page 423   Cook and Wright's Sale from Cook
Harmon Cook of P, I am merchant for and in consideration of the sum of 450 pounds paid by John Cook and John Wright have sold the said John Cook and John Wright one Negro man of the name of Rubin and one Negro wench, 13 head of horses, 25 head of cattle, 5 head of sheep, one wagon and 4 pair gears, two stills and set of blacksmith tools, two jack screws, four feather beds, two plows and axes, two iron wedges, one grind stone, one cask, all my pewter pots and kitchen furniture and all my riding saddles, two chests and all other household furniture, all my still vessels and 3000 pounds of loos tobacco, two cros cut saws, one broad ax, one abds and all my augers and small tools. March 4, 1789
s/ Jon (can't read)

Wit: Thos Dyer, James (X) Dyer, Obrasarre C (can't read)
July 20, 1789

Page 424   Anderson's Deed from McDaniel

January 1, 1789 between Rotherick McDaniel of Caswell County, North Carolina and Mathew Anderson of Hanover County, Virginia for 60 pounds, a parcel of land on the branches of Birches Creek containing by estimation 298 acres
Bounded: Robert Walters corner, Samuel Harris's line, Gray's corner, Robert Walters's line, Dodson's corner, Dodson's line, William Walters corner, crossing a branch
s/ Rotherick McDaniel
Wit: Mathew Tanner, Creed Tanner, William Bennett, Nathan Tate
July 20, 1789

Page 426   Robinson's Deed from Irvine

July 2, 1789 between William Irvine and his wife Patsy of Campbell County and Nicolas Robinson and Arthur Hobson Robinson of the county of Bedford for 500 pounds, a parcel of land containing by estimation 630 acres
Bounded: William Bardett's line
s/ William Irvine, Patsy Irvine
Wit: None
July 20, 1789

Page 426   Pannill's Deed from Roberts

June 19, 1789 between Joseph Roberts and Sarah his wife of P and (Blank) Parrish and John Pannill of the county of Halifax and Atrim Parrish, Joseph Roberts and Judith, his wife, for 374 pounds, a parcel of land containing by late survey 375 acres on Stinking River, it being part of a tract of land containing 454 acres which the said Roberts purchased of William Short together with the mill &c
Bounded: south side of said river on Acholses line, Litefoot's line, crossing Hickies Road, Crenshaw's line, crossing the Lick branch, Haley's line, Thomas Tunstall's line, crossing Stinking River Road, north side of the river, Acholses line
s/ Joseph Roberts, Sarah Roberts
Wit: James Bruce, William Keene, James Welles, Daniel Parker, Joshua Stone
July 20, 1789

Page 427   Bagby's Deed from Irvine

July 20, 1789 between William Irvine and his wife Patsy of Campbell County and William Bagby of the county of Bedford in consideration of

100 pounds, a tract of land on the south side of Stanton River containing 267 acres
Bounded: mouth of a small branch of Stanton River, Irvine's new line at the foot of Smith's Mountain
s/ William Irvine
July 20, 1789

Page 428   Woodson's Deed from Farmer
July 20, 1789 between Marlin Farmer of P and Allen Woodson of P for 96 pounds, a parcel of land on both sides of Elkhorn Creek containing 100 acres
Bounded: James Farmer's line, the dividing line between the said Marlin Farmer and James Farmer, a new line
s/ Marlin Farmer
July 20, 1789

Page 428   Watkins's Deed from Hewlett
December 5, 1788 between Anna Hewlett of Henry County and Stephen Watkins of P for 60 pounds, a parcel of land on both sides of the south fork of Sandy River it being the tract of land deeded from John Strong to said Anna Hewlet containing 137 acres
Bounded: Isaiah Morton's line, Joseph Morton, William Hewlet
s/ Anna Hewlet
Wit: Jesse Robinson, Samuel Shumate, Isaiah Morton, John (X) Nash
June 15, 1789

Page 429   Motley's Deed from Terry
January 19, 1789 between Benjamin Terry of P and Daniel Motley of P for 65 pounds, a parcel of land containing by estimation 184 acres on the branches of Johns Run adjoining the lands of the said Daniel Motley which he purchased of Floyd Tanner
Bounded: Daniel Motley's old corner, Sarah Pendleton's line to Edmund Fitzgerald's line, Linthicum's line, Edmund Fitzgerald's line, said Daniel Motley's corner
s/ Ben Terry
Wit: Benjamin Hall, David Tanner, Samuel Motley
August 17, 1789

Page 430   Owen's Deed from Blagrave
January 1, 1789 between Henry Blagrave of P and William Owen of P for 100 pounds, a parcel of land on north side of Banister River and Bearskin Creek containing by estimation 152 acres
Bounded: Echoles corner on Bearskin Creek, John Hutching's line, John Chatings corner, Banister River, mouth of Bearskin Creek

251

s/ Henry Blagrave
Wit: Hezekiah Pigg, William Leaniay, Harrison Blagrave, John Holland
Owen
May 18, 1789

Page 431　　　Williams's Deed from Robinson

June 13, 1789 between Jesse Robinson and Betty Robinson, his wife of P
and Robert Williams of P for 75 pounds, a parcel of land on both sides of
Youngs Creek, it being 200 acres taken of 300 acres which was patented
by Edward Wade and conveyed from him to George Young by deed and
then conveyed by Young to Seth Farrar by deed and then conveyed by Seth
Farrar to Jesse Robinson containing 200 acres
Bounded: Clay's order line, John Young's line, Isaiah Morton's corner,
William Hewlet's line, Delosers Entery, the old line then to Roberts line,
Clay's order
s/ Jesse Robinson, Betty Robinson
Wit: Isaiah Morton, Abraham Mackmillion, Field Robinson
August 17, 1789

Page 432　　　Dodson's Power of Attorney from Thomas

I, Elisha Thomas of the county of Mercer in Virginia, made my beloved
friend Joshua Dodson of Mercer County my true and lawful attorney to act
and dispose of all the premises hereafter mentioned to all interests and
purposes especially all debts, dues and demands, accounts, legacies, notes,
bonds and other settlements made and contracted in P, to plead in any court
of record that may appear necessary, to sell and disperse of all my estate
whether real, personal or mixed that is or may be found in P especially all
that mesuage and tract of land in P on Long Branch of Stewarts Creek
bounded by the lands of Bernard McCullough, James Boaz and Heirs of
John Smith, Moses Vincent and James Fulton containing 284 acres
s/ Elisha Thomas
Wit: None
Mercer County July 17, 1789 Elisha Thomas came before me and
acknowledged this instrument of writing
s/ Hugh McGary, Samuel Taylor
August 20, 1789

Page 433　　　Emmerson's Power of Attorney from Emmerson

I, John Emmerson of P, do authorize my brother, Samuel Emmerson in
Kaintucky to claim on my behalf a certain parcel of land containing 100
acres conveyed from a certain Montgomery to one Newton and from him
to John Certain and from him to me and I have hereby authorized my
brother to claim and demand a deed for said land as my attorney according
to law. August 19, 1789

s/ John Emmerson
Wit: None
August 19, 1789

Page 434   Stockton's Deed from Cooley

April 6, 1789 between Jacob Cooley of P and John Stockton of P for 85
pounds a parcel of land containing 270 acres on the head branches of
Sandy River
Bounded: Elisha Welling's? line, crossing two branches, crossing a branch
and is included by the lines called John Warren's part of the said tract
given by the said Fuller to the said Warren, also by the lines of Daniel
Hankins
s/ Jacob (X) Cooley
Wit: Daniel Hankins, Joseph Morton, Dan'l Tompkins, James
McAchrand, Daniel Hankins, junr
July 20, 1789

Page 435   Stockton from Cooley Dedimus

To Daniel Hankins and Joseph Morton, Gentlemen, Justices of P. Whereas
Jacob Cooley by his Indenture hath conveyed unto John Stockton of P 270
acres and whereas Sarah, the wife of the said Jacob Cooley, cannot
conveniently travel to our county court to relinquish her right of dower, we
ask that you examine Sarah Cooley apart from her said husband. April 4,
1789
s/ Will Tunstall
Pittsylvania County   By virture of the above Commission to us directed,
we have examined Sarah Cooley, wife of Jacob Cooley, and she
relinquished her right of Dower. April 6, 1789
s/ Daniel Hankins, Joseph Morton
Wit: None
August 17, 1789

Page 435   Crenshaw's Deed from Muse

1789 between John Muse of Franklin County, Virginia and William
Winston Crenshaw of P for 220 pounds, a parcel of land containing 521
acres of land on both sides of Turkey Cock Creek
Bounded: Arthur Hopkins corner, Hopkins line
s/ John Muse
Wit: None
August 17, 1789
Lucy, wife of John Muse, relinquished her right of Dower

Page 436   Calland and Smith Deed of Trust from Jefferson

August 3, 1789 between Peter Field Jefferson Senr of P and Calland and Smith, merchants of P, for 263 pounds, four shillings current money of Virginia which said Jefferson is indebted to them and honestly desires to secure and pay and in further consideration of five shillings, six Negroes, viz: Austin, Poll, Moll, Jacob, Charles and Edith, five head of horses to wit: one roam mare, one black horse, one black mare and colt, one black sorrel filie, four cows and calves and four other cattle of different sexes, marks, and ages, five feather beds and furniture, a desk and bookcase, one chester drawers, three chests, two cases and bottles together with all my household furniture and plantation utensils and all the appurtances. Callands and Smith shall after the 25th day of December 1790, shall sell for the best price after giving ten days notice the said Negroes and other recited premises and out of that money discharge the above sum with lawful interest.
s/ Peter F Jefferson
Wit: Elisha Walker, Sa Tompkins Junr
August 17, 1789

Page 437   Harris &c release from Wright &c
William Wright of P hath made and given a Bill of Sale to William Twedel of P for one large chestnut sorrel mare, a sorrel horse colt and two cows and calves which the said William Wright bought of Harmon Cook as per Bill of Sale of record. And the said William Wright having exchanged the said mare with Samuel Harris of P for a grey horse which the said Harris purchased of Thomas Cicell of P and the said sorrel horse colt with Harrison Carter for a sorrel horse with a small blaze on his face and branded on the near buttock thus WS, the said William Wright and the William Twedel doth release and quit claim to the said Samuel Harris and Harrison Carter all rights, title, interest or advantage which the said William Twedel or William Wright may claim
s/ W Wright, William Twedel
Wit: Ben Harris, Solomon Taylor
August 17, 1789

Page 438   Gilbert's Deed from Clement Exors
June 10, 1789 between Isaac and Adam Clements, Executors of Benjamin Clement, deceased, of P and Campbell County and John Webster Gilbert of Cambell for 650 pounds, a parcel of land containing by estimation 375 acres on the south side of Stanton River and on both sides of Sycamore Creek
Bounded: said river, said Clement's former patent, Joshua Abston's line, Hallaway's corner, Ralph Smith's corner, on the said creek, Clement's old line, opposite to the end of Persimmon Island
s/ Isaac Clement, Adam Clement

Wit: Haynes Morgan, Thomas East, John Ward junr, Preston Gilbert
September 21, 1789

Page 439   Hodges Deed from Todd, Sheriff
September 21, 1789 between William Todd, Gentleman, late Sheriff of P,
and David Hodges of P, sold at public auction 90 acres being part of a
greater tract charged by the Commissioners to Richard Chamberlain for
four pounds, 13 shillings, 9 pence, taxes and cost for 1786 lying on both
sides of Bannister River and Hickeys Road
Bounded: Mercer Morrison's corner in Weatherford's line, Thomas line,
Morrison's corner
s/ Will Todd
Wit: None
September 21, 1789

Page 440   Brown's Deed from Vest
September 15, 1789 between George Vest and Sarah, his wife of P and
John Brown of Campbell County for 25 pounds, a parcel of land
containing by estimation 200 acres lying on the waters of Beech Tree
Creek
Bounded: Alford's line, Beech Tree Creek, John Cook's line
s/ George (X) Vest
Wit: Thomas East, Ezekiel East, John Hister
September 21, 1789
Sarah, wife of said George Vest, relinquished her right of Dower

Page 440   Thacker's Deed from Hutchings
September 14, 1789 between Christopher Hutchings and Elizabeth, his
wife of P and Nathaniel Thacker of P for 25 pounds, a parcel of land on
the waters of Banister and Cherrystone containing by estimation 200 acres
Bounded: Easley's corner, said Carter's line to old order line, Short's line,
Chattin's line, John Hutchings line, Easley's line
s/ Christopher Hutchings
Wit: None
September 21, 1789

Page 441   Shelton from George Ded's
To William Todd, Joshua Stone, Benjamin Lankford, Gentlemen:
Whereas John George hath conveyed to Abraham Shelton of a parcel of
land containing 1400 acres and whereas Frances, wife of the said John
George cannot conveniently travel to County Court, we ask that you
examine the said Frances apart from her husband. September 14, 1789
s/ Will Tunstall

Pittsylvania County: By virtue of the above Commission to us directed, we have examined Frances, the wife of John George. She relinquished her right of Dower. September 14, 1789
s/ Will Todd, Joshua Stone
September 21, 1789

Page 442   Pannill from Roberts Ded's
To William Todd, Joshua Stone, Benjamin Lankford, Gentlemen:
Whereas Joseph Roberts hath conveyed to John Pannill of P a parcel of land containing by estimation 375 acres and whereas Sarah, wife of the said Jos Roberts cannot conveniently travel to County Court, we ask that you examine the said Sarah apart from her husband. August 18, 1789
Pittsylvania County: By virtue of the above Commission to us directed, we have examined Sarah, the wife of said Joseph Roberts. She relinquished her right of Dower. September 21, 1789
s/ Will Todd, Joshua Stone
September 21, 1789

Page 443   Neal's Deed from Stewart
September 21, 1789 between John Stewart and Mary, his wife of P, and Stephen Neal of P for 400 pounds, a parcel of land on both sides of Elkhorn Creek including the plantation whereon the said John Stewart now lives and containing by estimation 420 acres
Bounded: said Creek, Neal's former line, William Rice's and Benjamin Brawner's line, John Wimbish's line
s/ John Stewart, Mary Stewart
Wit: None
September 21, 1789
Mary, wife of the said John Stewart relinquished her right of Dower

Page 444   Rice's Deed from Stewart
May 18, 1789 between John Stewart of P and William Rice of P for 100 pounds, a parcel of land joining Elkhorn Creek containing by estimation 100 acres
Bounded: Elkhorn Creek in Fisher's line, Farmer's corner, Farmer's line, Stewart's line, Elkhorn
s/ Jno Stewart
Wit: None
September 21, 1789
Mary, wife of the said John Stewart relinquished her right of Dower

Page 445   Irby's Deed from Irby
September 21, 1789 between Charles Irby, Gentleman of Halifax and John Irby of P for 20 pounds, a parcel of land containing by estimation 173

acres being part of a larger quanity granted to Nathaniel Terry by patent it
being the plantation whereon the said John Irby now lives
Bounded: Leaks line, crossing the fork branch of Elkhorn Creek,
Glascock's line, Leak's line, fork of Elkhorn Creek
s/ Charles Irby
Wit: None
September 21, 1789
Susanna, wife of Charles Irby, relinquished her right of Dower

Page 446   Griggory's Bond for building bridge
We, John Griggory and William Todd of P are bound to the justices of the
county for 50 pounds. October 3, 1789
The condition of the above Obligation is such that whereas the above
bound John Griggory hath this day undertaken to build a bridge across
Stinking River near the house of Daniel Roberts where Hickeys Road
crosses the said river, to keep the bridge in good repair for the term of
seven years.
Wit: D Hunt
s/ John Griggory, Will Tod
October 19, 1789

Page 446   Wilson's Deed from Bostick
October 8, 1788 between Absalom Bostick of Surry County, North
Carolina and John Wilson of P for 50 pounds, a parcel of land containing
81 acres
Bounded: Wilson's line, Little's line, Little and Bostick's corner
s/ Absalom Bostick
Wit: Reubin Wright, Pearce (X) Turner, N Perkins, P Wilson junr
October 19, 1789

Page 447   Womack's Deed from Smith &c
June 18, 1789 between Wm Sterling Smith and Paulina, his wife, and
Joseph Price and Martha, his wife of the county of Henrico and Allen
Womack of P for 4000 weight of neat and inspected crop Tobacco, a parcel
of land containing 400 acres on the north side of Banister River
Bounded: Lightfoot's line, Banister river
s/ Wm Sterling Smith, Paulina Smith, Joseph Price, Martha Price
Wit: William Womack, James Allen junr, Joseph Watson, Samuel Watson
October 19, 1789

Page 448   Waller's Sale from Tucker
I John Waller of P do hereby give unto Nelson Tucker of P one Negro boy
named James, one mare colt in consequence of a provision made for his
wife Martha Tucker by the Last Will and Testament of her father, Thomas

257

Clark, deceased, being deficient and that it appears he will not be benefited thereby agreeable to the intent and meaning of the said deceased will. May 22, 1789
s/ John Waller
Wit: James Keatts, Martha (X) Keatts, John Keatts
October 19, 1789

Page 449   Charles Clark's Bill of Sale from Keatts
I Charles Keatts of P do sell unto William Clark of P one Negro girl named Anica in consideration of 49 pounds. July 22, 1789
s/ Charles Keatts
Wit: John Keatts, James Katts
October 19, 1789

Page 449   Waller &c release of Charles Clark's estate
We John Waller, Charles Keatts, and Nelson Tucker of P and William Barber Price of the county of Henry do hereby relinquish all future claims which may arise from the estate of Thomas Clark, deceased which is now is possession of Martha Clark, widow of the said decedent which by the Last Will and Testament of the said decedent, provision is made for portion of a dividend of a residuum to our wives respectively, daughters of said decedant, we considering our shares already received respectively agreeable to the tenor of the said will to be a better proportion. May 2, 1789
s/ John Waller, Charles Keatts, Nelson Tucker, William B Price
Wit: John Keatts, James Katts, Martha Keatts
October 19, 1789

Page 450   Keatt's release from Clark
I, William Clark of P, in consequence of having received of Charles Keatts, a Negro girl named Annica at the valuation of 49 pounds current money do hereby exhonerate the executors of my father, Thomas Clark, deceased, from any further payment of my legacy of 100 pounds which was provided for me by the Last Will and Testament of the said decedant and furthermore that for myself do resign all claim to every other part of my deceased father's estate but that which is assigned to me by his said will, the residue of the said estate now in the possession of my said mother, the whole of which I am to have at her decease which has been resigned by several other claimants. October 19, 1789
s/ William (X) Clark
Wit: John Keatts, James Keatts
October 19, 1789

Page 450   Waller's Deed from Clark

October 19, 1789 between William Clark of P and John Waller of P for 5 shillings, a parcel of land on both sides of George's Creek alias Panter Creek containing by estimation 100 acres
Bounded: Isaac Coles' line by William Lewis' line, John Shelton's line, dividing line between William Clark and said Waller
s/ William Clark, Martha (X) Clark, Anna (X) Clark
Wit: Nelson Tucker, James Keatts, John Keatts
October 19, 1789

Page 451   **Stimson's Deed from Owen**
December 6, 1788 between Uriah Owen of the county of Wilks, Georgia and Erasmus Stimson of P for 40 pounds, a parcel of land near Sandy Creek where the said Uriah Owen formerly lived containing 100 acres
Bounded: Stimson's old spring at Lloyd Stimson's corner, Lloyd Stimson's line, John Stamps line, Basel Hawker's line, Wilson's old road, said Hawker's field, Dupries line, Jeremiah Stimson's line
s/ Uriah Owen
Wit: Jer Stimson, Benjamin Burgess, Lloyd Simpson
April 20, 1789

Page 452   **Davis Deed from Keesee**
June 12, 1789 between Richard Keesee of P and Thos Davies of P for 50 pounds, a parcel of land containing 100 acres on the draughts of Stinking River, it being part of the tract of land that said Richard Keesee now lives on
Bounded: Thos Davis' line, Jacob Farris line, John Martin's line, Charles Keesee's line
s/ Rich'd Keesee
Wit: Charles Keesee, Samuel Irby, Nathaniel Faris
November 16, 1789

Page 453   **Walters Deed from Walters**
August 30, 1789 between Robert Walters of state of Georgia and county of Franklin and Elijah Waters of state of Virginia for 100 pounds, a parcel of land containing 200 acres on Birch Creek
Bounded: On the road in Tanner's line, Mathew Tanner's line, Bennett's line, crossing the creek, Anderson's line
s/ Robt (X) **Walters**
Wit: Robert Walters junr, John Madding, William Walters
October 19, 1789

Page 454   **Madding's Deed from Tanner**

November 15, 1789 between Lucias Tanner of P and William Madding of
P for 25 pounds, a parcel of land containing by estimation 25 acres lying
on the Waters of Birch Creek
Bounded: on the road in the said Madding's line, Harris's line
s/ Lucius Tanner
Wit: None
November 16, 1789

Page 455   Wimbish's Sale from Markham
I, John Markham of P for 75 pounds, do sell John Wimbish a Negro slave
known by the name Aaron
s/ Jno Markham
Wit: Floyd Tanner
November 16, 1789

Page 455   Rice's Power from Aaron
I, Daniel Arron of P, appointed my trusty friend, Leonard Rice, my true
and lawful attorney to demand of any and from Christian Toler and
Daneless Rorer, executors the sum of 22 pounds due with interest from
date till paid
s/ Daniel Aaron
Wit: Thos Dyer, Joseph Raynolds, Jere Keesee
November 16, 1789

Page 456   Smith's Deed from Smith
October 30, 1789 between Thomas Smith junr of P and Thomas Smith senr
of P for 50 pounds, a parcel of land which was willed to me by my
grandfather, Thomas Smith the Older, deceased on the north side of Sandy
River containing by estimation 100 acres
Bounded: Mouth of the said Thomas Smith, deceased, spring branch,
mouth of the Haw Branch, old line of said land
s/ Thomas Smith
Wit: Hezekiah Smith, John Gover, Jacob Dodson, William Smith
November 16, 1789

Page 457   Stamps Deed from Johnson
May 28, 1789 between James Johnson and Rebecca, his wife of P and
William Stamps of P for 100 pounds, a parcel of land containing 200 acres
lying on Sandy Creek
Bounded: Musick's line, crossing two branches and the said Creek,
Adkerson's line
s/ James (X) Johnson, Rebecca Johnson
Wit: John Stamps, Billy Holloway, George Spratten
November 16, 1789

Rebecca, wife of James Johnson, relinquished her right of Dower

Page 458   Motley from Overseers of the Poor Indenture for P Ellington
October 20, 1789 between William White and Mathew Tanner, Overseers of the Poor of P and John Motley of P agreeable to an Order of the county of P September Court ordering the Overseer to bind our Pleasant Ellington, son of David Ellington who has left this county without leaving a proper support for the said Pleasant Ellington. The aforesaid William White and Mathew Tanner have bound as an apprentice Pleasant Ellington unto John Motley until he arrive at age 21 to be taught the science or occupation of shoemaker which the said John Motley agrees to teach or cause to be done.
s/ John Motley, Wm White, Mathew Tanner
Wit: Peter Dupuy
November 16, 1789

Page 458   Rorer's Deed from Price
December 19, 1789 between William Price Senr and Susanna, his wife of P, and Francis Rorer for 100 pounds, a parcel of land in county of P and parish of Trinity? containing by estimation 112 acres
Bounded: Smith's line, Price's line
s/ Wm Price, Susannah (X) Price
Wit: Abraham Daverson, William W Quinn, Daniel Price
December 21, 1789

Page 459   Parrish's Deed from Smith
April 20, 1789 between John Smith of P and Abraham Parrish of P for 100 pounds, a parcel of land containing 400 acres on the Waters of Little Bearskin Creek
Bounded: north side of said creek, Atkins line, Dunn's line, Price's line
s/ John Smith
Wit: Thos Hodges, Hammon (X) Dyer, John Hodges
November 19, 1789

Page 460   Cox's Bill of Sale from Farguson
Robert Farguson of P for consideration of 200 pounds paid by John Cox of the county of Henry hath granted and sold to John Cox three Negroes to wit: Nann, Nutt, Philis, two head of horses, all my stock of howes, cattle, hogs and household furniture August 22, 1789
s/ R Farguson
Wit: Will Todd, Isaac Greggory, Milly Farguson
October 19, 1789

Page 460   Wright's Deed from Birk delivered to Tho Wright

April 7, 1789 between James Birk of P and John Wright Senr of P for 50
pounds, a parcel of land on the south side of the White Oak Mountain
containing by estimation 182 acres
Bounded: Carter's corner, south side of Swetens fork, crossing the said
creek, said Carter's line to the top of the mountain
s/ James Birk
Wit: William Price, Thomas (X) Wright, James (X) Martin
August 20, 1789

Page 461   Bardett's Deed from Doss
September 18, 1789 between Thomas Doss and Saray, his wife, of P and
Charles A Bardet of the county of Halifax for 40 pounds a parcel of land
containing 150 acres
Bounded: Simmon's corner, John Adams corner, Meadow Road, Francis
Sampson's corner, Richard Farthing line, Rowland's corner
s/ Thomas (X) Doss, Sarrah (X) Doss
Wit: Arch'd Campbell, Stephen Yates, Daniel Lovell junr
November 16, 1789
Sarah, wife of Thomas Doss, relinquished her right of Dower

Page 463   Roach's Deed from West
December 21, 1789 between Owen West of P and Burdett Roach of P,
Owen West and Elizabeth, his wife, for 19 pounds, eight shillings, a parcel
of land containing 100 acres on the south fork of Stinking River
Bounded: said Owen West line
s/ Owen West, Elizabeth West
Wit: John Skinner, Judith Skinner, Judith Roach
December 21, 1789

Page 463   Love's Deed from West
December 18, 1789 between Owen West of P and James Love of the
county of Fairfax, Owen West and Elizabeth, his wife, in consideration of
the sum of 38 pounds, 16 shillings, a parcel of land containing by
estimation 200 acres on the south fork of Stinking River
Bounded: Burdet Roach's corner
s/ Owen West, Elizabeth West
Wit: John Skinner, Judith Skinner, Judith Roach, Bardet Roach, Jesse
Kessee
December 21, 1789

Page 465   Calland's Deed from Smith atto for Black
December 21, 1789 between John Smith of P attorney for Thomas Black of
the state of Georgia and Samuel Calland for 75 pounds, a parcel of land

transferred from Archibald Young unto said Thomas Black containing 100
acres on both sides of Snow Creek, part in P and part in Henry County
Bounded: said Black's line formerly belonging to Archibald Graham,
George Jefferson's line, Archibald Graham's corner
s/ John Smith
Wit: none
December 21, 1789

Page 465   Theric's Deed from Roberts
November 25, 1789 between Daniel Roberts and Mary Roberts, his wife of
P and Francis Theric of the county of Charlotte for 100 pounds, a parcel of
land on both sides of Nix's Creek containing 170 acres
Bounded: Dividing corner of a dividing line run between Jesse Paty and
Thomas Mustain on said Pety's line, crossing the said creek
s/ D Roberts, Mary Roberts
Wit: C A Bardet, J Parnell, Joshua Stone, Will Todd

Pittsylvania County: To William Todd, Joshua Stone, David Hunt,
Justices of P, whereas Daniel Roberts of P hath conveyed unto Francis
Theric of Charlotte County a parcel of land and whereas, Mary wife of the
said Daniel Roberts cannot conventiently travel to our said county court,
we ask that you privately examine Mary apart from her husband whether
she does freely relinquish her right of dower. November 28, 1789
s/ Will Tunstall
By virtue of the Commission to us directed we have examined Mary, the
wife of said Daniel Roberts and she relinquished her right of dower.
November 28, 1789
s/ Will Todd, Joshua Stone
December 21, 1789

Page 467   Theric's Deed from Roberts
November 25, 1789 between Daniel Roberts and Mary Roberts, his wife of
P and Francis Theric of the county of Charlotte for 150 pounds, a parcel of
land on branches of Stinking River and George Creek containing 380 acres
Bounded: William Lester's corner, Owen West's line, crossing two
branches of Stinking River, John Buckley's line, John Byrd's line, John
Doss's line, Branch of George's Creek, William Lester's line
s/ D Roberts, Mary Roberts
Wit: C A Bardet, J Parnell, Joshua Stone, Will Todd

Pittsylvania County: To William Todd, Joshua Stone, David Hunt,
Justices of P, whereas Daniel Roberts of P hath conveyed unto Francis
Theric of Charlotte County a parcel of land and whereas, Mary wife of the
said Daniel Roberts cannot conventiently travel to our said county court,

we ask that you privately examine Mary Roberts apart from her husband whether she does freely relinquish her right of dower. November 28, 1789
s/ Will Tunstall
By virtue of the Commission to us directed we have examined Mary, the wife of said Daniel Roberts and she relinquished her right of dower.
November 28, 1789
s/ Will Todd, Joshua Stone
December 21, 1789
(delivered to Col George Townes December 21, 1834)

Page 468   Shelton's sale from Hurt
I Moses Hurt of P in consideration of 25 pounds paid by Thomas Shelton of P hath sold him one yoke of draughts steers, one six head of cattle four feather beds with furniture to each bed, seven chairs and three whicles
s/ Moses Hurt
Wit: Edm'd Taylor, Chas Lewis Junr, Wm Nelson
January 18, 1790

Page 469   Kennon's Deed from York
December 28, 1789 between William York of Surry County, North Carolina and Charles Kennon of Halifax County, Va for 50 pounds, a parcel of land on both sides of the Double Creek, which creek was so called at the time of the survey dated November 14, 1750 agreeable to a patent granted to the said William York dated October 21, 1788 containing 150 acres
s/ William (X) York
Wit: Elijah Ayres, Thomas (X) Ayres junr, Jacob Ayres
January 18, 1790

Page 469   (Title torn)
December 28, 1789 between William York of Surry County, North Carolina and Charles Kennon of Halifax County, Va for 50 pounds, a parcel of land on both sides of the upper Double Creek, which creek was so called at the time of the survey dated October 19, 1749 agreeable to a patent granted to the said William York dated October 21, 1788 containing 150 acres
s/ William (X) York
Wit: Elijah Ayres, Thomas (X) Ayres junr, Jacob Ayres
January 18, 1790

Page 470   Ragsdale's Deed from Thaxton
December 22, 1789 between William Thaxton of county of Halifax and Frederick Ragsdale of P for 11 pounds, 10 shillings, a parcel of land on branches of White Oak Creek containing 73 acres

Bounded: said Ragsdale's line, Joseph Richards line
s/ William Thaxton
Wit: Thos Ragsdale, Jen Thompson, Charles Carter
January 18, 1790

Page 471   Lipford's Deed from Chattin
November 4, 1789 between John Chattin of P and Anthony Parr Lipford of
P for 100 pounds, a parcel of land containing by estimation 112 acres on
the north side of Banister River
Bounded: on Banister river at William Owen's line formerly Davis's line,
John Hutchings' deceased line which said land the said John Chattin
purchased of Thomas Hardy as appears by deed date March 21, 1780
s/ John Chatten
Wit: Jeduthun Carter, Thos Carter, Jesse Carter
January 18. 1790

Page 472   Hurt's Bill of sale from Hurt
I Moses Hurt of P for sum of 50 pounds paid by Dandridge Hurt of P have
sold unto him one Negro man slave named Daniel about 22 years of age.
January 11, 1790
s/ Moses Hurt
Wit: Adm'd Taylor, Chas Lewis junr, Wm Nelson
January 18, 1790

Page 472   Shelton's Deed of Trust from Bardet
December 23, 1789 between Charles Andrew Bardet of Halifax and
Gabriel Shelton of P, a parcel of land on the waters of Banister River,
formerly the land of Thomas Doss containing 150 acres for 100 pounds
s/ C A Bardet
Wit: Fred Shelton, Thos Shelton, Moses Hurt, Young Shelton, Beverly
Shelton
January 18, 1790

Page 473   Elliot's Deed from Poyner and others
January 12, 1790 between William Poyner, Pleasant Waller and Agge
Waller of county of Caswell North Carolina and Charles Lewis of P and
Richard Elliott of P for 50 pounds, a parcel of land containing 100 acres
Bounded: Abraham Campbell's corner, Henry Hardins, Henry Hawls,
Polly's Branch, Campbell's line
s/ William Royner, Pleasant (X) Waller, Agge (X) Waller, Charles Lewis
Wit: M Clay, William Price, Mathew (X) Orender, John (X) Burgis,
William Price
January 18, 1790

Page 474   Shelton's Deed from West

August 5, 1789 between Owen West and Elizabeth, his wife, of P and Clayburn Shelton for 40 pounds, a parcel of land containing 217 acres on south fork of Stinking River
s/ Owen West, Elizabeth West
Wit: Joel Shelton, Jesse Mustain, Sam'l Irby, Vincent Shelton, Fred Shelton, Stephen Yates
January 18, 1790

Page 476   Hammock's Deed from Witcher

January 15, 1790 between Ephriam Witcher of P and John Hammock of P for 9 pounds, a parcel of land containing by estimation 30 acres on both sides of Reads Creek
Bounded: William Goads line, Reades Creek, David Ross's line, William Goad's corner
s/ Ephrum Witcher
Wit: Marlin Young, Wm Young, Milton Young
January 18, 1790

Page 477   Dunn's Deed from Peak

February 15, 1790 between William Peak of P and William Dunn of P for 70 pounds, a parcel of land on branches of Bearskin Creek containing 110 acres
Bounded: Robbins Branch, John Pigg's Road
s/ Will Peek
Wit: None
February 15, 1790

Page 479   Polly's Deed from Polly

February 15, 17 90 between Agnes Polly of P and David Polly of P for 20 pounds, a parcel of land, it being the plantation where the said Agnes Polly formerly lived on the south side of the Corn branch containing by estimation 100 acres
Bounded: James Kerr's corner, William Young's land, new line to John Reece's line
s/ Agnes Polly
Wit: None
February 15, 1790

Page 480   Johnson's Deed from Payne

February 15, 1790 between Rubin Payne of P and James Johnson of P for 220 pounds, a parcel of land containing 378 acres on both sides of Banister River

Bounded: south side of Banister River on Barksdale line, crossing Middle Creek to Simmon's corner
s/ Rubin Pain
Wit: None
February 15, 1790
Agnes, wife of the said Rubin Payne relinquished her right of dower

Page 482   Mabry's Deed Gift from Mabry
I Braxton Mabry of P for natural love and affection which I bear to my beloved children, Robert Smith Mabry, Polly Braxton Mabry, Jane Stanback Mabry have given the following Negro slaves and a feather bed and furniture to wit: to my son Robert S Mabry, Robert and Armstead, to my daughter Polly B Mabry, Biddie and Amy, to my daughter Jane S Mabry, Mary and her increase
s/ Braxton Mabry
Wit: Wm White, Jere White, John White
February 15, 1790

Page 483   Jefferson's Deed from Jefferson
October 24, 1788 between Peter Jefferson of the county of Lunenburg and Peter F Jefferson of P for 85 pounds, a parcel of land on the Mill Branch containing 613 acres
Bounded: Callands and Muses lines, Elgans line, crossing the head branches of Mill Creek, David Ray and Piesums Lines
s/ Peter Jefferson
October 24, 1788
Wit: Samuel Calland, Field Jefferson, Richard N Veneable
May 18, 1789

Page 484   Callands Deed from Walker
February 15, 1790 between Elisha Walker of P and Samuel Calland of P for 60 pounds, a parcel of land containing by survey 75 acres on the west side of Turkey Cock Creek being part of the land I bought of Benjamin Maniese?
Bounded: said Callands line, William Walker's line, Turkey Cock Creek
s/ Elisha Walker
Wit: John Smith, Robertson Shelton, Sam'l Johnson
February 15, 1790

Page 487   Grains Deed from Croff
February 2, 1790 between Henry Croff of P and Koonrod Grain of P for 30 pounds, a parcel of land containing by estimation 100 acres
Bounded: Laurence Clapp's line, Henry Croff's line, John Severs line, Christian Turks line, Laurence Clapp's line

s/ Samuel Geoff, Eleazibeth (X) Geoff
Wit: Jos Robinson, Philip Dibo
February 15, 1790

Page 488   **Legrand from Legrand Deed of Gift d'd Jesse Wilson**
October 10, 1789 between Abrabram Legrand of P and Jesse Legrand,
Sally Wilson, Polly Legrand, Betsy Legrand and George Legrand of P for
good causes and consideration and love for son Jesse and daughters, Sally
Wilson, Polly Legrand, Betsy Legrand, and son George Legrand. I give to
my son Jesse one bed and furniture, one cow and calf, to daughter Sally
Wilson one bed and furniture, also a mare and colt, one cow and calf, one
chest, one cotton wheel, one Flax wheel, also to my daughter Polly
Legrand one Negro boy named Isaac, also two year old horse colt, bridle
and saddle called Duck, also a bed and furniture, cow and calf, one large
chest, one cotton wheel and one flax wheel, also I give to my daughter
Betsy Legrand one Negro girl named Dinah, also one horse named Jordan,
one saddle and bridle, one bed and furniture, also one cow and calf, one
large trunk, one cotton wheel, flax wheel, also I give to my son George
Legrand my cash and the rest of my cattle, my hogs and stock of all kinds,
one bed and furniture and all my household and kitchen furniture of all
kinds, all my plantation tools and other tools whatever, also one Negro
woman named Dafney. If the said Negro woman Dafney and Negro girl
Dinah should have any children before the decease of me, the said
Abraham Legrand and my wife, Agnes Legrand, that their children shall be
equally divided among all my children that survives me and my wife. And
the said Jesse Legrand, Sally Wilson, Betsy Legrand, George Legrand or
any one of them should die without an heir then the goods given above
should be equally divided among all my surviving children.
s/ Abm Legrande
Wit: Jesse Legrand, George Legrand, Betsy Legrand
February 15, 1790

Page 489   **Walker's Deed from Maddin**
February 13, 1790 between Robert Maddin of P and Samuel Walker of P
for 52 pounds, a parcel of land on waters of the Lower Double Creek
containing by estimation 100 acres
Bounded: said Maddins corner, John Bennett deceased line to Nathan
Tate's line, Terry's line, John Spencer's line, John Harris' line, said
Maddin's line
s/ Robert (X) Maddin
Wit: Robert Walters, Archer Walters, John Bennett
February 15, 1790

Page 490   **Logan's Deed from Cody**

268

February 28, 1789 between Redmond Cody of county of Halifax and
David Logan of Halifax for 38 pounds, a parcel of land on the head
branches of Allen's Creek containing by estimation 190 acres
Bounded: Daughertys corner now Buckleys, Joseph Faris's line, Benjamin
Lankford's line, Gilbert Hunt's line
s/ Redmond Cody
Wit: Joshua Stone, John Stone, Joshua Stone junr
October 19, 1789

Page 492   Bardett's Deed from Hopwood
December 4, 1789 between James Hopwood and Joyce, his wife of P and
Charles A Bardet of county of Halifax for 16 pounds, a tract of land on
both sides of Long Branch of Whitethorn Creek including 260 acres
Bounded: William Hopwood's line, Isaac Motley's line, said Long
Branch, Edmond Payne's line, Jere Kesee's line, Doss's path, John Payne's
corner, Hugh Jennings' corner, crossing the Little Long branch, John
Buckley's line, William Hopwood's line
s/ James Hopwood, Joyce (X) Hopwood
Wit: John Stone, Wm Keatt, John Wyatt
February 15, 1790

Page 494   Duff's Indenture from Jennings
January 23, 1790 between Mathew Tanner and Will White, Overseers of
the Poor of P, and Laurence Duff of P. Whereas the Court of P December
last did make and order that the Overseers should bind Sherod Jennings
according to law, do place and bind the said Sherod Jennings to said
Laurance Duff until the said Sherod Jennings shall arrive at the full age of
21 years, being now about 13 years. The said Laurence Duff shall provide
sufficient drink, washing and lodging.
s/ Laurence Duff, Mathew Tanner, Wm White
Wit: Jeremiah White
February 15, 1790

Page 495   Walters' Deed from Shields
November 6, 1789 between Pleasant Shields of P and Robert Walters of P
for 23 pounds, a parcel of land on the waters of the upper Double Creek
containing by estimation 22 ½ acres
Bounded: William Richardson and said Shields and Nimrod Scott and
John Scott's line, being the tract of land deeded by Nimrod Scott to said
Shields
s/ Pleasant Shields
Wit: Mic'h Pinder, Chas Hoyle, Presely Carter, Samuel Walker, John
Bennett, Archer Walters
February 15, 1790

Page 496   Bardet's Deed from Hopwood

December 4, 1789 between James Hopwood and Joyce his wife of P and
Charles A Bardett for 10 pounds, a tract of land on the sides of Whitethorn
Creek including 100 acres
Bounded: Colwell's corner in William Hopwood's line, John Thompson's
line, Pickrall's corner, Coldwell's line
s/ James Hopwood; Joyce (X) Hopwood
Wit: John Stone, William Keatt, John Wyatt
February 15, 1790

Page 498   Walters' Deed from Thrasher

August 5, 1789 between Benjamin Thrasher of county of Pennelton South
Carolina and John Walters of P for 175 pounds, a parcel of land on the
draughts of Cane and Sandy Creek, it being a parcel of land granted to the
said Thrasher in a patent dated July 20, 1787 containing 376 acres
Bounded: Ayres corner, Robertson's corner, Cargil's line, crossing the
meadow fork of Cane Creek
s/ Benja Thrasher
Wit: Robert Walters, Samuel Walker, Archer Walters
February 15, 1790

Page 500   Cugneau's Deed from Bardett

February 15, 1790 between Charles A Bardet of the county of Halifax and
Henry Cugneau of county of Dinwiddie for 120 pounds, a parcel of land on
both sides of Long branch of Whitethorn Creek including 270 acres
Bounded: William Hopwood's line, Isaac Motley's line, crossing said
Long Branch, Edmund Payne's line, Jesse Keesee's line, John Payne's
corner, Hugh Innes's corner, crossing Little Long Branch, Main Long
Branch, said Innes' line, John Buckley, William Hopwood's line
s/ C A Bardet
Wit: Dan'l Lovell Senr, Sam'l M Lovel, Daniel Lovell
February 15, 1790

Page 502   Tanner Junr's Deed from Walters

November 16, 1789 between Elijah Walters of P and Mathew Tanner Junr
of P for 55 pounds, a parcel of land on Birches Creek containing by
estimation 200 acres being part of a patent granted to Robert Walters
Bounded: Road in Tanner's line, Mathew Tanner's line, Bennett's line,
Anderson's line, the Road
s/ Elijah (X) Walters
Wit: Wm White, Floyd Tanner, Jno Markham, Wm Maddin
March 15, 1790

Page 503   Astin's Deed from Mims
October 21, 1789 between Robert Mims of Goochland County and
William Astin of P for 14 pounds, a parcel of land on branches of Sandy
Creek containing 218 acres
Bounded: Charles Burton's corner, Charles Clay's order line, Burton's
former line, Wm Astin's line, crossing two branches, John Asworth's line,
Clay's order line forsaid
s/ Robert Mims
Wit: Christopher Robertson, William May, James Givins
March 15, 1790

Page 505   Wooding's Deed from Wooding
February 27, 1790 between Robert Wooding of Halifax County and
Thomas H Wooding of P for of divis good causes and 5 shillings, a parcel
of land containing by estimation 200 acres on the draughts of Great
Cherrystone Creek
Bounded: John Davis' corner in Finney's line, Courthouse road, said
Robert Wooding's line
s/ Ro Wooding
Wit: Haynes Morgan, J Panill, D'd Clark, H Townes
March 15, 1790

Page 506   Hankins' Bond for his Sheri atty
We Dan'l Hankins, Jos Morton, William White, William Clark, David
Clark, Jere White, Crispin Shelton, junr, Rich'd Brown, Benjamin Shelton
and Thomas Tunstall of P are bound unto the Justices of P in the sum of
500 pounds. March 15, 1790
The condition of the above Obligation is such that the above bound Daniel
Hankins is appointed Sheriff of P by Commission from the Governor.
s/ Daniel Hankins, Joseph Morton, Wm White, Wm Clark, David Clark,
Jere'h White, Crispin Shelton, Junr, Benja Shelton, Rich'd Brown, T
Tunstall
Taken in open court
March 15, 1790

Page 507   Hankins's bd from his sheriff XXX
We Dan'l Hankins, Jos Morton, Wm White, Wm Clark, David Clark, Jere
White, Crispin Shelton, junr, Rich'd Brown, Benjamin Shelton and
Thomas Tunstall of P are bound unto the Justices of P in the sum of 1000
pounds. March 15, 1790
The condition of the above Obligation is such that the above bound Daniel
Hankins is appointed Sheriff of P by Commission from the Governor. If
above bound Daniel Hankins shall collect all official fees and dues put into

his hands and truly account for and pay to the offices unto such fees are due, then the above obligation to be void
s/ Daniel Hankins, Joseph Morton, Wm White, Wm Clark, D'd Clark, Jere'h White, Crispin Shelton, Junr, Benja Shelton junr, Rich'd Brown, T Tunstall
Taken in open court
March 15, 1790

Page 508   Collie's Deed from Watkins
April 14, 1790 between John Watkins and Mary his wife of P and William Collie of P for 32 pounds, a parcel of land containing 126 acres on waters of Sandy Creek
Bounded: James Collie's corner on Weatherford's order line, James Collie's line, crossing a branch
s/ John Watkins, Mary (X) Watkins
Wit: Charles Collie, Samuel Watkins, Obediah Walters, Daniel Slaydon
April 19, 1790

Page 509   Young's Deed from Young
April 19, 1790 between William Young of P and Archibald Young of P for 100 pounds, a parcel of land containing 201 acres on waters of Redes Creek
Bounded: on Lee Road
s/ William Young
Wit: None
April 19, 1790

Page 509   Harris' Deed from Harris
April 19, 1790 between David Harris of P and Joseph Harris of P for 100 pounds, a parcel of land containing by estimation 100 acres on the Great Fork of Cascade Creek
Bounded: said Joseph Harris' land on east, Mosias Jones' land on west, vacant land on north and south
s/ David Harris
Wit: None
April 19, 1790

Page 510   Tucker's Deed from Keatts
September 4, 1789 between Charles Keatts of P and Robert Tucker of P for 15 pounds, 15 shillings, a parcel of land containing by estimation 25 acres
Bounded: Robert Tucker's corner, on the Courthouse Road, Pigg River Rode, Carthow Rode
s/ Charles Keatts
Wit: Thomas B Jones, Em'l Jones, Rebecca Jones

April 19, 1790

Page 511   Hailey's Deed from Hailey
March 3, 1790 between Ambrose Hailey and Ambrose Hailey Junr for 5
pounds, a parcel of land on branches of Sandy Creek containing 50 acres
Bounded: Mire Branch, Hailey's old plantation, Johns Run, mouth of a
branch, Louis Hailey's line, Henry's line, Raccone Branch, crossing Johns
Run, Henry's line, George Thompson's line, said Mier Branch
s/ Ambrose Hailey
Wit: B Barksdale, Jos Terry, Thos Dodson, Thos Shaw
April 19, 1790

Page 512   Goad's Deed from Goad
March 14, 1790 between William Goad of P and John Goad of P for 10
pounds, a parcel of land containing 50 acres on the waters of Red Eye
creek
Bounded: David Ross's corner, fork of Rodeys Creek, William Goad's
line, crossing the Lick Fork of Redey's Creek, Rodey's Creek
s/ William Goad
Wit: William Young, Milton Young, John (X) Hammock
April 19, 1790

Page 512   Young's Deed from Young
April 19, 1790 between William Young of P and Marlin Young of P for
100 pounds, a parcel of land on waters of the Corn Branch containing 196
acres
Bounded: on the Road
s/ William Young
Wit: None
April 19, 1790

Page 513   Young's Deed from Young
April 19, 1790 between William Young of P and Milton Young of P for
100 pounds, a parcel of land on waters of the Corn Branch containing 246
acres
Bounded: the Road, up the Corn Branch
s/ William Young
Wit: None
April 19, 1790

Page 514   Lewis's Deed from Hardy &c
April 17, 1790 between George Hardy senr, George Hardy junr, Lazarus
Dodson of P and William Lewis of P for 50 pounds, a parcel of land on
waters of Mire Branch containing by estimation 100 acres

273

Bounded: Charles Lewis' line, Hardey's field, said Dodson's line
s/ George Hardey senr, George Hardy junr, Lazarus Dodson
Wit: Charles Lewis, William Dodson, Joshua (X) Hardey
April 19, 1790

Page 515   Payne's Deed from Payne
March 22, 1790 between Reubin Pain of P and Phillimon Payne of P for
love and affection he has for his son Phillimon Paynes, does give unto
Reubin Payne a parcel of land containing by estimation 70 acres
Bounded: mouth of a branch on Banister River, William Clark's corner,
Martin's line, mountain
s/ Reubin Pain
Wit: Allen Addams, Jas Johnson, Edmond Fitzgerrald, Langston Johnson
April 19, 1790

Page 516   Paynes' Deed from Martin
March 22, 1790 between Robert Martin of P and Phillimon Payne of P for
30 pounds, a parcel of land containing by estimation 58 acres lying on the
south side of Banister River
Bounded: Reubin Payne's corner, William Clark's line
s/ Robert (X) Martin
Wit: Jas Johnson, Edmond Fitzgerrald, Thomas Shelton, Allen Addams
April 19, 1790

Page 516   Easley's Deed from Lester
November 24, 1789 between Jesse Lester of Surry County North Carolina
and William Easley of P for 5 pounds, a parcel of land on both sides of the
south fork of Straightstone Creek containing 28 acres, being part of a
larger tract of land of 340 acres whereon Thomas Lester, deceased,
formerly lived
Bounded: south side of said Creek in the old line
s/ Jes Lester
Wit: Jno (X) Ballinger, Thomas Lester, Will Todd
April 19, 1790

Page 518   Phillips Deed from Hunt and all
April 10, 1790 between William Hunt and Dolly, his wife, Stephen
Collins, and Catey, his wife, Niper Adams and Lucy, his wife, James
Hoskins and John Stone, executors of Wm Hoskins, deceased of county of
Halifax and Tobias Phillips of P for 10 pounds, a parcel of land containing
100 acres being part of a greater tract granted to Mackendree's heirs and
Hoskins exors on Pigg River
Bounded: Jeremiah Ward's line, Tobias Phillips corner on Pigg River,
along his former line, Harmon Kook's line

s/ William Hunt, Dolly Hunt, Stephen Collins, Caty Collins, Niper Adams,
Lucy Adams, James Hoskins, John Stone
Wit: Joshua Stone, Joseph Farris senr, Daniel Jenkins, Amos Farris
April 19, 1790

Page 519   Shelhorse's Deed from Goodman
April 19, 1790 between William Goodman of P and Barnett Shelhorse of P
for 50 pounds, a parcel of land containing 160 acres on both sides of Pigg
River Road
Bounded: said William Goodman's corner, William Hayme's line,
crossing Pigg River Road
s/ Wm Goodman
Wit: None
April 19, 1790
Jemima, wife of said William Goodman, relinquished her right of dower

Page 520   Nance's Deed from Perkins
March 29, 1790 between Peter Perkins of P and Clement Nance of P for
100 pounds, a parcel of land containing by estimation 254 acres on the east
side of Cascade Creek
Bounded: Walton's line, crossing the creek
s/ Peter Perkins
Wit: Robt Harrison, Butler Stonestreet, Jno Carter, Jno Biscoe, D
Coleman
April 19, 1790

Page 521   Hughes' Deed from Lynch
August 22, 1789 between William Lynch of P and Joseph Hughes of P for
35 pounds, a parcel of land containing by estimation 134 acres on waters of
Fall Creek which said land was granted to said William Lynch by patent
dated November 6, 1783
Bounded: William Tweedwell's corner, Charles Harris's corner,
Wilkerson's line, Twedwell's corner
s/ William Lynch
Wit: William Summers, Wm Lynch, Jacob Rhodes, Abner Lynch, Joseph
Lynch
April 19, 1790

Page 522   Cisill's Deed from Twedel
17—between William Twedell of P and Thomas Cisell of P for 50 pounds,
a parcel of land on branches of Fall Creek containing by estimation 125
acres
s/ William Twedell
Wit: None

April 19, 1790

Page 523   Wilson's Deed from Glasgow
August 31, 1789 between John Glasgow of P and John Wilson of P for 23
pounds, 4 shillings and 5 pence, a parcel of land on branches of Fall Creek
containing 300 acres
Bounded: Harris and Clay's line, Finnes Branch, Clay's corner
s/ John (X) Glasgow
Wit: P Wilson junr, D Coleman, James Thompson, John Wilson junr
April 19, 1790

Page 524   Hamack's Deed from Goad
April 1;8, 1785 between William Goad of P and John Hamack of P for 10
pounds, a parcel of land containing 40 acres on waters of Redeys Creek
Bounded: William Young's corner, dividing line between Ephriam
Witcher and William Goad, Redeys Creek, William Goad's back line
s/ William Goad
Wit: Jno Goad, Milton Young, William Young
June 20, 1785

Page 525   Gammon's Deed from Norton
April 19, 1790 between Jacob Norton of P and William Gammon of P for
30 pounds, a parcel of land on waters of Sandy River containing 200 acres
by survey dated April 19, 1790
Bounded: Spark's corner, Harris Gammon's line
s/ Jacob (X) Norton
Wit: Dozier Brawner, Harris Gammon, John Gammon
April 19, 1790

Page 525   Harris's Deed from Rainey
April 18, 1790 between Mathew Rainey of county of Henry Virginia and
Geo Fuller Harris of P for 3 pounds, ten shillings, a parcel of land
containing 50 acres
Bounded: Clay's line, crossing the creek, meeting house spring branch,
said Rainey's line, Clay's line, in the fork of the creek joining the said
Harris
s/ Mathew Rainey, Judith (X) Rainey
Wit: Lucy (X) Rainey, Alice (X) Watkins, Nat Durham
April 19, 1790

Page 526   Crider's Deed from Cornelius &c
January 30, 1790 between Anne Cornelius and Jones William Cornelius
and Jephtha Cornelius of P and Daniel Creyter of P for 100 pounds, a

276

parcel of land containing 202 Acres on both sides of Buck branch of
Frying Pan Creek adjoining the lands of Jacob Barger, David Ross
s/ Ann (X) Cornelius, William Cornelius, Jeptha Cornelius
Wit: Jos Robinson, James (X) Henson, Jacob Barger
April 19, 1790

Page 527   Campbell's Deed from Williams
December 15, 1789 between Lewis Williams of county of Mecklenburg
and James Campbell of county of Brunswick for divers good causes and
consideration and 66 pounds, 12 shillings a parcel of land containing 222
acres by survey on both sides of Open Ground fork of Brins? Creek
Bounded: Constant Perkins line, said fork, Perkins corner, crossing the
said Open Ground fork
s/ Lewis Williams
Wit: Ishmael Dunn, Thomas Dunn, Benja Williams, Geo Adams, William
Ross, Tav'n Shelton
April 19, 1790

Page 528   Watkins' Deed from Walker
February 13, 1790 between Samuel Walker of P and John Watkins of P for
50 pounds, a parcel of land on branches of the Double Creek and branches
of Sandy Creek containing 100 acres
Bounded: George Cook's corner on William Harrison' line, Murray's line,
Dupuy's line, Butt's line, Waddill's line
s/ Samuel Walker
Wit: William Collie, Asa Thomas, Charles Collie, Robert Walters
April 19, 1790

Page 529   Rhodes' Deed from Lynch
August 22, 1789 between William Lynch of P and Jacob Rhodes of P for
30 pounds, a parcel of land containing 126 acres lying on the waters of Fall
Creek which said land was granted to said William Lynch by patent dated
November 6, 1783
Bounded: Wilkerson's line, Wilkerson's path, Tweedwell's corner
s/ William Lynch
Wit: Wm Summers, Wm Lynch, Joseph Hughes, Joseph Lynch, Abner
Lynch
April 19, 1790

Page 529   Dodson's Deed from Dodson
April 19, 1790 between Lazararus Dodson of P and William Dodson of P
for 30 pounds, a parcel of land on the branches of Sandy Creek containing
152 acres
Bounded: the order line, Charles Lewis' line

s/ Lazarus Dodson
Wit: Charles Lewis
April 19, 1790

Page 530   Pemberton's Deed from Keeling
July 29, 1789 between Leonard Keeling of the county of Halifax and
William Pemberton of P for 40 pounds, a parcel of land containing 108
acres
Bounded: Mchaney's line
s/ Leonard Keeling
Wit: Haynes Morgan, John Buckley, Jeremiah Elliott
February 15, 1790

Page 531   Blakeley's Deed from Blakeley
December 3, 1785 between John Blakeley of P and James Blakeley Senr
hath given unto said James Blakely Senr a parcel of Land containing by
estimation 161 acres
Bounded: Hickey's Road, crossing Strawberry Creek
s/ John Blackley, Jenne Blackley
Wit: William Devin, James (X) Blackley, Benjamin (X) Blackley
January 16, 1786
(Also call her Jane)

Page 532   Waddill's Deed from Seal
March 8, 1790 between James Seal of P and Noel Waddill Junr of P for
100 pounds, a parcel of land containing 124 acres
Bounded: Noel Waddill's line, branch in James Seal's line, new dividing
line to Harrison, along Harrison's line, Samuel Walker's line
s/ James (X) Seale
Wit: None
April 19, 1790

Page 533   Thomas' Deed from Lumkin
September 21, 1789 between George Lumpkin Junr and Joseph Lumpkin
of P and William Thomas junr of P for 545 pounds, a parcel of land
whereon the said George Lumkin junr now lives on the south side of Dan
River containing 194 acres including all the land shown by said George
Lumkins junr when sold to the said Thomas
Bounded: River bank, at the corner of a fence just above the fishing place,
William Boyd's line, Larkin Dix's line
s/ George Lumpkins, Joseph Lumpkin
Wit: Jacob Thomas, Bereman Watkins, John Worsham, Thomas
Worsham, Robt Farguson
September 21, 1789

Page 534   Buckley's Deed from Bruce
April 10, 1790 between Robert Bruce and Jane his wife of P and John
Buckley of P for 100 pounds, a parcel of land containing 247 acres
Bounded: onb both sides of main branch of Straitstone Creek, John Jones'
corner
s/ Robert (X) Bruce
Wit: Answorth Harrsison, J A Buckley, John Twedell, David Hamerick,
James Henderson junr, D Tunstall, Jno Chisnhall, Nathan Rowland
April 19, 1790

Page 535   Nance's Bond for marriages
We Clement Nance and Joseph Akin of P are held unto Beverley
Randolph, governor of the Commonwealth of Virginia for 500 pounds.
April 19, 1790
The condition of the above Obligation is such that if the above bound
Clement Nance who is minister who is minister of the Society of Christians
called Babtists shall well and truly celebrate the rites of marriage between
all persons applying to him, then the above Obligation to be void. Taken
in open court
s/ Clement Nance, Jos Akin
April 19, 1790

Page 536   Pannill's Deed from Roberts
November 22, 1789 between Joseph Roberts and Sarah, his wife, and
Daniel Roberts and John Pannill for 150 pounds, a parcel of land
containing by late survey 107 acres lying on the north side of Stinking
River being part of a tract of 464 acres which said Joseph Roberts
purchased of William Short being the whole of the land Joseph Roberts
and Daniel Roberts possessed on Stinking River
Bounded: North side of Stinking River and Echol's line, Thomas
Tunstall's line
s/ Jos Roberts, Sarah Roberts, D Roberts
Wit: Will Shelton, Will Todd, Crispin Shelton junr
Sarah, wife of said Joseph Roberts, relinquished her right of dower
February 15, 1790

Page 538   Toler's Deed from Hunt and Company
April 10, 1790 between William Hunt and Dolly, his wife, Stephen
Collins, Caty his wife, Nipper Adams, and Lucy his wife, James Hoskins
and John Stone, executors of Williams Hoskins, deceased, of the county of
Halifax and Joseph Toler of P for 40 pounds, a parcel of land containing
600 acres being part of a greater tract granted to James Mckendree's heirs
and William Hoskins, executor, lying on Linches Kents and Falling Creek

Bounded: said Toler and Thomas Bennett's corner, said Bennett's new line, John Dalton's corner, Dalton's plantation, crossing the road, crossing Kents Creek and Falling, crossing the said road, Chinquepin Branch, Daniel Kryder's new line, Harmon Cook's line, Roarers line, crossing the road, Linches Creek, said Joseph Toler former line near Falling Creek, near Kents Creek
s/ William Hunt, Dolly Hunt, Stephen Collins, Caty Collins, Nipper Adams, Lucy Adams, James Hoskins, John Stone
Wit: Joshua Stone, Joseph Faris sen, Daniel Jenkins, Amos Faris
April 19, 1790

Page 541   Kryder's Deed from Hunt and Company
April 10, 1790 between William Hunt and Dolly, his wife, Stephen Collins, Caty his wife, Nipper Adams, and Lucy his wife, James Hoskins and John Stone, executors of Williams Hoskins, deceased, of the county of Halifax and Daniel Kryder of P for 25 pounds, a parcel of land containing 400 acres being part of a greater tract granted to James Mckendee's heirs of William Hoskins, executor, lying on draughs of Frying Pan Creek
Bounded: Harmon Cook's corner, Ann Phillips line, crossing Green Branch, Jacob Barger's line, Rayney Goods line, Jeremiah Ward's line, Tobias Phillips new line
s/ William Hunt, Dolly Hunt, Stephen Collins, Caty Collins, Nipper Adams, Lucy Adams, James Hoskins, John Stone
Wit: Joshua Stone, Joseph Faris sen, Daniel Jenkins, Amos Faris
April 19, 1790

Page 544   Lewis from Kennon sent by AsaThomas
March 3, 1788 between Charles Kennon and Mary his wife of county of Halifax and John Lewis Senr (Byrd) of P, for 300 pounds, a parcel of land on waters of Dan River and Sandy Creek containing by estimation 152 acres
Bounded: Mouth of Sleep Hill branch on north side of Dan River, branch between said Lewis and Kennon to Sandy Creek, Dan River
s/ Charles Kennon
Wit: Will Peters Martin, John Lewis senr, Jno Lewis junr, James Lucas, Will Thomas, James Woody
June 16, 1788

Page 545   Atkinson from Certain
July 12, 1787 between John Certain of P and Moses Atkinson for 30 pounds, a parcel of land containing 50 acres on waters of Bearskin Creek
Bounded: where the old line crosses branch of Bearskin Creek, up the branch to fork, new line on the ridge to the old line
s/ John Certain

Wit: None
July 16, 1787
Hanna, wife of John Certain, relinquished her right of Dower

Deeds & Wills No 11
1780-1820

This transcription includes only pages 1-113 of the Book which covers the Deeds of Pittsylvania County, Virginia May 1790 to April 1791

Page 1
Lewis's Deed from Perkins
September 25, 1789 between Nicholas Perkins of County of Hawkins, North Carolina and Samuel Lewis of P for 100 pounds, a parcel of land containing 340 acres on Moberless Creek and branches of Mountain Creek. Bounded: Harris and Comp, Moberless Creek, Harris and Co Line
s/ Nicholas Perkins
Wit: N Perkins, Phil Perkins, lgnatius Wilson, Const Perkins, Rich'd Farrar, James Sneed
May 17, 1790

Page 1
Ware's Deed from Perkins
October 11, 1789 between Nicholas Perkins of P and William Ware of P for 300 pounds, a parcel of land containing by estimation 81 acres
Bounded: Dan River on North side at the dividing line between William Stone and David Chadwell, Silvester Adams line, now George Adams line, it being the middle lott of Land that Henry Stone formerly sold to David Shadwell which was granted to Henry Green by Patent, the said tract of land Henry Stone Deeded to David Chadwell
s/ Nicholas Perkins
Wit: Wm Harrison, N Perkins, Anna Harrison, James Oakes, Const Perkins
May 17, 1790

Page 3
Ware's Deed of Gift from Harrison
I, William Harrison of P, for five shillings together with the love and affection I bear to my loving Son in Law William Ware, give the following Negros, Viz: John, Silvey, Sarah, Molley, Bettey, Moll, Lavina and Will, also one Horse, one feather bed and furniture, one chest of drawers, two Tables.   Decem 25, 1788
s/ Wm Harrison
Wit: None
May 17, 1790

Page 3
Davidson's Deed from Chelton
May 13, 1790 between Mark Chelton and John Davidson, both of P, for 25
pounds, a parcel of Land containing 50 acres .
Bounded: Maurey's Side line and William Price's corner, Cannons line
s/ Mark (X) Chelton
Wit: M Clay, George (X) Miers, William Meirs, George Chelton
May 17, 1790

Page 4
Clark's Bond for 87 tax
We, Dav'd Clark, Tho Clark, Nath'l Hunt, Jas Legrand, Wm Owen, Joel
Clark, Wm White, Daniel Hankins, Ben Hall, Dav'd Powell, Jno McCraw,
Wm Clark, Noell Waddill, Vincent Shelton, Beverley Shelton and Wm
Shelton of P, are bound unto Jacquelin Ambler, Treasurer of the
Commonwealth for 10,000 pounds
May 17, 1790
The Condition of the above Obligation is such that the above bound David
Clark shall collect and pay unto the said Treasurer all the Taxes which
shall become due in specie from each and every taxable person in P for the
year 1787.
s/ David Clark, Joel Clark, Thos Clark, Noel Waddill, Nath'l Hunt,
Vincent Shelton, James Legrand, David Powell, Wm Owen, Wm Clark,
Beverley Shelton, Wm White, Will Shelton, Daniel Hankins, James
MCraw, Benja Hall
Wit: None
May 17, 1790

Page 4
Hankin's Bond for the 1790 Tax
We, Daniel Hankins, Joseph Morton, Edward Nunnellee, William Hankins,
Gilbert Dear and William Clark of P, are bound unto Jacquelin Ambler,
Treasurer of the Commonwealth for 10,000 pounds. May 17, 1790
The Condition of the above Obligation is such that the above bound Daniel
Hankins shall collect, account for and pay unto the Treasurer all the taxes
which shall become due and payable for the year 1790.   Taken in Open
Court.
s/ Daniel Hankins, Joseph Morton, Edw'd Nunnelee, William Hankins,
Gilbert Dear, Wm Clark
Wit: None
May 17, 1790

Page 5
Hankins's Bond for the 1789 Tax

We, Daniel Hankins, Benj Lankford, Wm Dix, Joshua Stone, Wm White, Crispin Shelton jr, John Markham, Mathew Tanner, Gabriel Shelton, John Keatts, Charles Lewis jr, David Clark and William Clark of P, are bound unto Jacquelin Ambler, Treasurer of the Commonwealth for 10,000 pounds. May 17, 1790

The Condition of the above Obligation is that the above bound Daniel Hankins shall pay to the said Treasurer all the taxes due and payable from each and every taxable person in P for the Year 1789.

s/ Gabriel Shelton, John Keettes, David Clark, John Markham, Chas Lewis, Mathew Tanner, Wm Clark, Daniel Hankins, Ben Lankford, William Dix, Joshua Stone, Wm White, Crispin Shelton jr

Wit: None

May 17, 1790

Page 5
Smith's Bill of Sale from Smith

I Orlando Smith Senear of P, Planter, in the consideration of 65 pounds paid to Col John Wilson, Marchant of P, at the ensealing and delivery of these presents by ous Jesse Smith and Orlando Smith Junr of P, the receipt of wich I do hereby acknowledge by these present having Sold, transferred and setover unto the said Jesse Smith and Orlando Smith junr fore feather Beads and furniture, one chestnut Sorel hors branded on the shoulder N D, one white iron bound trunk, one Dun mar about fore foot six inches big, a dosen black warnet chars, ten pots, one Dutch Oven, one frier pan, one brindle Cow, one pute heffer, twenty heads of hogs, one looking glass

s/ Orlando Smith

Wit: Elizabeth Smith, Casader Smith, Martha Smith

May 17, 1790

Page 6
Tanner's Deed from Watkins

April 19, 1790 between John Watkins of P and Creed Tanner of P for 40 pounds, a parcel of land lying on the branches of Burches Creek containing by estimation 100 acres, being part of a greater Tract of 150 acres granted to the s'd Watkins by Pattern

Bounded: Robt Walters Line, Weatherfords Order line

s/ John Watkins

Wit: Thos Shelton jr, William Colle, John (X) Lawless

May 17, 1790

Page 7
Hendrake's Deed from Duncan

September 7, 1789 between William Duncan of P and Humphrey
Hendrake of P for 140 pounds, a parcel of land on the South side of Dan
river containing by Estimation 135 acres.
s/ William (X) Duncan
Wit: John Wilson, Geo Adams, P Wilson jr, John Wilson jr
February 15, 1790

Page 8
Walters Deed from Watkins
April 19, 1790 between John Watkins of P and Robt Walters Sen of the
State of Georgia for 20 pounds, a parcel of land on the branches of Burches
Creek containing by Estimation 50 acres, being part of a greater tract of
150 acres granted to the said Watkins by Patern
Bounded: s'd Walters corner
s/ John Watkins
Wit: Thomas Shelton, William Collie, John (X) Lawless
May 17, 1790

Page 9
Perkins Deed from Gwin
October 25, 1789 between Rich'd Gwinn, Son and heir of Rich'd Gwinn
deceased of Wilks County, North Carolina and Peter Perkins of P for 100
pounds, a parcel of land containing 400 acres on Panthur Creek.
Bounded: Said Creek, Timber fork, Glady fork, a boald Branch
s/ Rich'd Gwyn
Wit: George Adams, William Astin, John Spencer
February 15, 1790

Page 10
Harrison's Deed from Perkins
October 24, 1789 between Nicholas Perkins, late of P, and William
Harrison of P for 30 pounds, a parcel of land containing by Estimation 56
acres
Bounded by the lines of said Nicholas Perkins, Butler Stone Street and said
William Harrison.
s/ Nicholas Perkins
Wit: Constt Perkins, Wm Ware, Zach Sneed, John (X) Poor
May 17, 1790

Page 11
Brown's Deed from Moore
June 16, 1790 between Thomas Moore and Anne, his wife, of P and
George Brown of (Blank County) North Carolina for 16 pounds, a parcel
of land containing 112 acres on the Camp branch and Allins Creek

Bounded: Jno Donelson's line, Pemberton's line, the old road, Chisam line, Mathew Vance's line
s/ Thomas More, Anne More
Wit: None
June 21, 1790
Anne Moore relinquished her Right of Dower

Page 11
Fitzgerald's Deed from Pain
March 22, 1790 between Reubin Pain of P and Edmund Fitzgerrald of P for 50 pounds, a parcel of land containing by estimation 212 acres
Bounded: James Johnson corner, Banister River
s/ Reubin Pain
Wit: Jas Johnson, Philimon Payne, Thomas Shelton, Allan Adams, Langston Johnson
July 19, 1790

Page 12
Fitzgerald's Deed from Payne
March 12, 1790 between Reubin Pain of P and Edmund Fitzgerald of P for 120 pounds, a parcel of land containing by Estimation 233 acres, being part of a Tract granted to the s'd Reubin Pain by Setters pattant dated June 1, 1782 lying on both sides of John Chapmans Run.
Bounded: Benjamin Terry's corner, Watkins line, Dudging's line, John Chapman's Run, Gwynes line, the old mill
s/ Reuben Pain
Wit: William Pigg, William Parks, Allen Adams, Ambros Corbin, Wm Goodman, Thomas Shelton, Philimon Payne, Jas Johnson
July 19, 1790

Page 13
Goodman's Deed from Haymes
April 19, 1790 between William Haymes of P and William Goodman for 13 pounds, a parcel of land containing 13 acres on the Horse Shoe Branch
Bounded: William Hayme's old line, said Goodman's Mill pond
s/ William Haymes
Wit: None
July 19, 1790

Page 14
Dunn's Deed from Burnet
1790 between Godfrey Burnett of P and John Dunn Jr of P for 22 pounds, a parcel of land containing by estimation 50 acres being part of a greater Tract of 100 acres whereon the said Godfrey Burnett now dwells.

Bounded: John Dunn Senr's line, John Weatherford's path, Long Branch,
William Easley's line
s/ Godfrey Burnett
Wit: None
July 19, 1790
Elizabeth Burnett, wife of said Godfrey Burnett, relinquished her Right of
Dower.

Page 15
William's Deed from Durrett
July 19, 1790 between William Durrett of P and Robert Williams for 58
pounds, a parcel of land containing by estimation 118 acres adjoining the
said William Durret's line
Bounded: Spring Branch that Benjamin King live on, the said William
Durret's line, Wynn's line
s/ William Durrett
Wit: Dr Williams, Thos Hammack, John H Hendrick
July 19, 1790

Page 15
Mottley's Deed from Dupuy
May 2, 1790 between Peter Dupuy of State of Virginia and Joseph Motley
of the state of North Carolina for 300 pounds, a parcel of land containing
476 acres by Estimation on both sides of Eacolses fork Branch of Sandy
Creek
Bounded: Joyning the Lands of William Riborn, Samuel Motley, Lacy,
Adkinson and Ellington
s/ Peter Dupy
Wit: Ben Terry, Daniel Motley. Samuel Motley
July 19, 1790

Page 16
Hutchings's Deed from Hutchings
May 17, 1790 between Christopher Hutchings of P and James Hutchings of
P for 100 pounds, a parcel of land containing 297 Acres
Bounded: Cap Pigg's Line, Hutchins's Order Line
s/ Christopher Hutchings
Wit: None
July 19, 1790

Page 17
Wimbish's Deed from Neal
January 16, 1790 between Stephen Neal of P and John Wimbish of P for
12 pounds, a parcel of land adjoining the Land of the said John Wimbish

287

on both sides of his Spring Branch and on both sides of one other small branch containing 12 acres
Bounded: said Wimbish's line, said Stephen Neal's line, crossing the Spring Branch
s/ Stephen Neal
Wit: Allen Woodson, John Martin, John Wimbish jr, Rich'd N Venable, Sam'l McCraw, James McCraw jr
May 20, 1790

Page 18
Coleman's Bill of Sale from Tunstall
I, Edmund Tunstall of P, for the sum of 100 pounds paid by Philip Coleman, Merchant of P, hath sold him five Negroes, to wit: Bristol, Titus, Sandy, Armistead and Spencer. Also three feather beds and furniture, together with all my Household and kitchen furniture, two Horses and five head of Cattle
s/ E Tunstall
Wit: T Tunstall, Will Tunstall jr, Thos Lankford
August 16, 1790

Page 18
Muse's Deed from Muse
August 17, 1790 between John Muse and Lucy Muse, his wife, of the County of Franklin and Thomas Muse of the county of Fairfax for 100 pounds, a parcel of land on both sides of Salors Creek containing be estimation 500 acres.
Bounded: Samuel Callands Line, Elisha Walker's Line, Hamblet's line
s/ John Muse, Lucy Muse
Wit: None
August 17, 1790
Lucy Muse relinquished her right of Dower.

Page 19
Hinton's Deed from Twedell
July 28, 1790 between William Twedell of P and Richard Hinton of P for 50 pounds, a parcel of land containing by estimation 88 acres, being part of a greater tract of 440 acres granted to said William Twedall by Patent dated June 21, 1784
Bounded: By the lines of John Reynolds, Jacob Rhodes, William Matherley, Foulis's Order and a dividing line between the said Richard Hinton and Thomas Cecill
s/ William Twedel
Wit: Robert (X) Wright, Martha (X) Wright, W Wright
August 17, 1790

Page 20
Anderson's Power of Atto from Morton
I, Joseph Morton of P, appoint Robert Anderson of Bedford County,
Virginia my attorney for the special purpose of Settling and Conveying a
certain Tract of land granted me as Assignee of Patrick Henry by the Land
Office Treasury Warrant Numbered 10,084 issued December 1, 1781,
containing 290 acres by Survey, being in Washington County in Powell's
Valley on the East side of Chisman's land on both sides of the branch that
runs down past the Rock Spring Station
s/ Joseph Morton
Wit: Jos Akin
August 17, 1790

Page 21
Constable's Deed from Twedell
July 28, 1790 between William Twedell of P and Samuel Constable of P
for 50 pounds, a parcel of land on the branches of Falls Creek containing
by estimation 125 acres
s/ William Twedel
Wit: Benja'm Twedwell, Thomas Cecill, W Wright, Martha (X) Wright,
Robert (X) Wright
August 17, 1790

Page 22
Bryant's Deed from Barsell
November 30, 1789 between Matthew Bussell of P and Susanna his wife
and Edward Bryant of P. Whereas Thomas Hardy, late of P, decea'd,
Grandfather of the said Susannah, by his last Will and Testament did give
to his Daughter Sarah (Mother of said Susannah) during her widowhood
100 acres of land on the South side the double Creek with the Plantation
she is now possessed of, but after her death to fall to her daughter
Susannah. The said Matthew Bussell and Susannah his wife for 250
pounds sells the 100 acres to Edward Bryant.
s/ Matthew (X) Bussell, Susannah (X) Bussell
Wit: W Wright, John (X) Carrell, Wm Wilkinson, John (X) Carrell,
Pleasant (X) Waller, William Hardy
February 15, 1790

Page 23
Marr's Deed from Barker
August 18, 1790 between William Barker of P and John Marr of Henry
County for 36 pounds, a parcel of land on the South side of Sandy River
containing 150 acres, it being part of a Tract of 334 acres Surveyed to
Thomas Oliver

Bounded: Sandy River, John Gammon, Shadrak Lewis's?
s/ William Barker
Wit: None
August 18, 1790

Page 23
Lovell's Power of Attorney from Tunstall
I, William Tunstall of P, have appointed Samuel M Lovell of P my lawful
attorney to demand and recover all clerks Tickets due to said William
Tunstall from the different persons as will appear by the Tickets State of
South Carolina and Georgia.
August 19, 1790
s/ Will Tunstall
Wit: None
August 20, 1790

Page 24
Bobinson's from Irvine Ded's & Rept
To William Harrison, Jesse Burton, Justices of the County of Campbell:
Whereas William Irvine hath conveyed unto Nicholas Robinson and
Arthur H Robinson of P a parcel of Land containing by Estimation 630
acres and whereas Patsy, wife of said William Irvine, cannot conveniently
travel to and from our said County Court, we trusting to your faithful and
provident circumspection in examining Patsy Irvine whether she does the
same freely and volentarily
September 21, 1789
s/ Will Tunstall
Campbell County: Patsy Irvine relinquished her right of Dower.
November 13, 1789
s/ Wm Henderson, Jesse Burton
August 19, 1790

Page 25
Willes's Deed from Jefferson
April 24, 1790 between Peter Jefferson of Lunenburgh County and David
Willes of Franklin county for 30 pounds, a parcel of land on Snow Creek
containing by Estimation 75 pounds
s/ Peter Jefferson
Wit: Sam'l Calland, Field Jefferson, John Smith, Dan'l Sayre
April 24, 1790

Page 26
Morton's Deed from Rieger

August 16, 1790 between Jacob Rieger of P and Isaiah Morton of P for 200 pounds, two parcels of land on both sides of the South fork of Sandy River containing by estimation 107 acres
Bounded: George Young's line, crossing south fork of Sandy River
The other tract containing 100 acres bounded: said Jacob Rieger's line, John Morton's corner, crossing the Mill Pond, George Young, Zachariah Grooms line
s/ Jacob Rieger
Wit: None
August 16, 1790
Nancy, wife of Jacob Rieger, relinquished her right of Dower

Page 27
Turner's Deed from Conn
1790 between Joseph Conn of P and Pierce Turner of P for 500 pounds, a parcel of land containing 175 acres on the Waters of Mountain Creek, it being the said Land whereon Zaddock Barnord did formerly live
Bounded: Mitchell's line, branch of Caskade, Mountain Creek
s/ Jo Conn
Wit: John Carter, Mel Spragins, Will Shelton
August 17, 1790

Page 28
Gresham's Power of Atto from Layne
I, Isaac Layne, Son and heir of John Fuller Lane deceased, late of Washington County, North Carolina, appoint my trusty friend, Thomas Gresham of the county and State aforesaid, my Lawful Attorney and to the use? of Joseph Conn of P to use and prosecute all that tract of land which my Father John Lane sold to Conn for which the said John Fuller Lane gave his obligation to convey the same and finish for me and in my Name all and singular things which shall be necessary.
s/ Isaac Lane
Wit: Caleb Shields, Joseph Crouch, Zachariah McCubbin
August 16, 1790

Page 29
Conn's Deed from Gresham
August 5, 1790 between Thomas Gressom Attorney in fact for Isaac Lain, Son and Heir of John T Lain dec'd of Green County, N. C. and Joseph Conn of P for 300 pounds, a parcel of land on the Waters of Mountain Creek containing 433 acres by Survey dated April 4, 1770
Bounded: Cargile's Line, Strong's Line, Kerkland's Line
s/ Thos Gresham
Wit: Jno Wilson, Will White, Richard Conn, Geo Adams

August 16, 1790

Page 30
Crittenden's Deed from Bullington
September 18, 1790 between Robert Bullington of P and William
Crittendon of Heneries County, Virginia for 100 pounds, a parcel of land
containing by Estimation 100 acres on the North side of Sugar tree Creek,
it being the land that the said Bullington holds on the North side of said
Creek belonging to the tract whereon he now lives
Bounded: Cox's old line
s/ Robert Bullington
Wit: William (X) Bullington, William Crittenden Junior, Jarrot (X)
Crittenden
September 20, 1790

Page 31
Morton's Bill of Sale from Morton
I, John Morton Senr of P, have sold unto Isaiah Morton of P 17 Negroes
nam'd as follows, Viz: Dogra, Tillis, Abraham, Sall, Dinah, Luce, Bob,
Luce, David, Ruth, Will, Sabe, Bartlett, Reuben, David, Solomon, Cloey
for 850 pounds
s/ John Morton
Wit: John Harvey, John Morton Jnr, John Allsup
September 20, 1790

Page 31
Bullington's Deed from Nance
November 20, 1789 between Giles Nance of Amelia County, Virginia and
Robert Bullington of P for 20 pounds, a parcel of land containing by
Estimation 75 acres on the Waters of Sugar tree Creek
Bounded: said Bullington's line, fork of Young's Road, Bullington's old
line, Jones's line, Bullington's old line
s/ Giles Nance
Wit: Clement Nance, John Jones, William (X) Mitchell, Michael (X) Hiler
April 19, 1790

Page 32
Pannill's Deed from Echolls
September 14, 1790 between Elkanah Echolls, Elizabeth his wife and Joel
Echolls of P and John Pannill of P for 150 pounds, a parcel of land
containing, by a late Survey made by Griffith Dickerson, 229 acres on
Stinking River, it being part of a tract of Land containing 400 acres which
the said Echols purchased of Joseph Echols
Bounded: Crossing Stinking River, crossing the dry fork

s/ Elkanah Echols, Joel Echols
Wit: E Tunstall, Griffith Dickinson, John Rowland, R Farguson, John Griggory
September 20, 1790
Elizabeth, wife of said Elkanah Echols, relinquished her right of Dower

Page 34
Henry's Deed from Barksdale
October 28, 1789 between Beverly Barksdale of P and Anne his wife and James Henry of Northumberland County for 50 pounds, a parcel of land on Sandy Creek hereafter described unto the said Martin Palmer in fee simple, but the said Palmer is willing to Mortgage the same to the said Henry for securing the payment of the said debt and interest and the Costs of the Suit accruing thereon, securing the equity of redemption in the premises unto the said Palmer on his paying the said Sum of money and Interest, the Costs of the Suit now depending which is to be entered agreed and the Cost of this Deed, a parcel of land containing 196 acres
Bounded: North Easterly by the Lands of the said Henry, North Westerly by the Lands of Roger Atkinson Gen't , lands now in possession of Charles Terry, Sandy Creek
s/ B Barksdale, Anna Barksdale, Jas Henry, Martin Palmer
Wit: Henry H Barksdale, Fortan Dodson, Martan (X) Palmer
January 18, 1790

Page 35
Kezee's Deed from Handley
February 16, 1790 between Caleb Hundley of P and Jeremiah Keesee of P for 50 pounds, a parcel of land containing 50 acres on the Waters of Bareskin Creek
Bounded: William Persize's line, Jeremiah Keesee line, Richard Kesee line, Joseph Dyer dividing line
s/ Caleb Hundley
Wit: Thos Dyer, John Watson Jur, William Griffith, Jonathan Rigney
June 21, 1790

Page 36
Anderson's Deed from Morton
May 25, 1790 between John Morton and Joseph Morton and Richard N Venable, Trustee, for 180 pounds, a parcel of land with interest from the November 17, 1789 which the said John Morton is justly indebted to David Anderson and Company, a parcel of land lying on both sides Sandy River containing 400 acres, which is the same which John Morton purchased of Robert Peck who purchased of Richard Womack, recorded in Halifax Court

Also a tract of land supposed to be 300 acres purchased by s'd John
Morton of Sam'l Shields lying on Hutchersons branch and adjoining the
Land afores'd
s/ John Morton, Joseph Morton
Wit: Jno Carter, Jos Carter, Daniel Hankins, John Harvey
October 18, 1790

Page 37
Coleman's Deed from Terry
October 18, 1790 between David Terry of Louisa and Stephen Coleman of
P for 125 pounds, a parcel of land containing by Estimation 179 acres,
being the same land Nathaniel Terry dec'd, in his lifetime conveyed to the
said David Terry as part of a larger Tract conveyed to the said Nathaniel
Terry by John Robinson Esq dec'd in his lifetime
s/ David Terry
Wit: Wm Dix, Edmund (X) Beadles, W Wright
October 18, 1790
Ellenor, wife of said David Terry, relinquished her right of Dower

Page 38
Malicot's Deed from Atkins
January 31, 1788 between Richard Atkins of P and John Mallicot of P for
50 pounds, a parcel of land on Bearskin Creek containing by Estimation
116 acres, being part of a greater Tract of 266 acres which was granted to
the s'd Richard Atkins by a Grant dated November 2, 1779
Bounded by the lines of Jesse Atkins and Noton Dickerson, s'd Jesse
Atkins
s/ Richard (X) Atkins
Wit: Thos Dyer, James Dyer, William Dyer, Joab Watson
July 21, 1788

Page 39
Calland's Deed from Prunty
June 10, 1790 between Robert Prunty of Franklin county and Samuel
Calland of P for 60 pounds, a parcel of land on both sides of Turkey Cock
Creek containing 400 acres
Bounded: said Calland's own land which he purchased of Archibald
Graham, David Willis's Corner, mouth of a Drean, Cap Lod'k Tuggle's
line, Thomas Terry's line, crossing Turkey Cock Creek, said Calland's
own line in the Land that formerly belonged to William Young
s/ Robert Prunty
Wit: Sam Tompkins jr, R'd Johnson, John Smith
June 10, 1790

Page 41
Dix's Deed of Gift from Dix
October 9, 1790 between William Dix of P and his three children, Namely
Patsy Booker Dix, Edward Dix and Henieritta Dix in consideration of the
natural love and affection that I bear to my s'd three children and for the
consideration of 50 pounds the following articles, Viz: one Negro Man
named Joe, one ditto named Minos, one ditto named Chester, one ditto
named Daniel, one Negro Girl named Nancey, all my stock of Horses,
Cattle, Sheep, & hogs, all my Household and Kitchen furniture, one wagon
and team with the Plantation Utencils
s/ Wm Dix
Wit: Jas Burton, Robt Payne, Will White, Wm Wilkinson, Thos Fearn
October 18, 1790

Page 41
Shackleford's Deed from Young
October 18, 1790 between James Young of P and John Shackleford of P
for 130 pounds, a parcel of land containing by Estimation 150 acres
Bounded: Stephen McMillion, James Curry's line, Jesse Robinson
s/ James Young
Wit: None
October 18, 1790

Page 42
Stamps's Deed from Wynne
February 16, 1785 between Thomas Wynne of P and John Stamps of P for
200 pounds, a parcel of land on both sides of Sandy Creek containing by
Estimation 300 acres
Bounded: Edward Burgesses
s/ Thos Wynne
Wit: Benjamin Burgess, Edward (X) Burgess, William Stamps
October 18, 1790

Page 43
Hopper's Deed from Dyer
December 20, 1790 between John Dyer of P and Luther Hopper of P for
six pounds, a parcel of land containing by estimation 50 acres on the
Waters of Barskin Creek
s/ John Dyer
Wit: None
December 20, 1790

Page 44
W Shelton's Deed from V Shelton

July 21, 1790 between Vincent Shelton of P and William Shelton of P for 20 pounds, a parcel of land containing 356 acres (by Grant dated November 13, 1779) lying on both sides of the Cattail fork of Georges Creek
Bounded: James Farris corner, Armistead Shelton's line, James Farris old line
s/ Vincent Shelton
Wit: John Shelton, Frances Shelton, Abraham Shelton, Nancy Shelton, Letey Shelton
December 20, 1790

Page 45
Williams's Deed from Williams
October 22, 1790 between John Williams of Greenvil County, South Carolina and James M Williams of P for 70 pounds, a parcel of land containing by estimation 200 acres on the Waters of Elkhorn Creek.
Bounded: Corner agreeable to a Deed made from Nathaniel Terry to William Dickerson and from Dickerson to Richard Brown being bounded by Atkinson's Line, Joseph Terry's and John Jones's lines
s/ John Williams
Wit: John (X) Adams, William Williams, Nathan Adams
December 20, 1790

Page 45
Cox's Deed from McCraw
July 5, 1790 between James McCraw of Halifax County and John Cox of Henry County for 200 pounds, a parcel of land on Cherry Stone Creek and the branches thereof, being one mority of 2020 acres Granted to said James McCraw by Paten dated February 22, 1785, containing by Estimation 1010
Bounded: Cherry Stone Creek, Hatters branch, branch of the Middle fork, said Taylor's Survey
s/ James McCraw
Wit: Rich'd N Venable, R Williams, John C McCraw, Wm McCraw, Halcott Townes, Jno Wimbish, Thos Jer Williams, William Phelps, Haynes Morgan
December 20, 1790

Page 47
Sampson's Deed from Morton
Between Joseph Morton and Clarey his wife of P and Benjamin Sampson of P for 60 pounds, a parcel of land containing 195 acres on the draughts of Sandy River
Bounded: Thomas Hargate's Corner in Morton's line
s/ Joseph Morton, Clary Morton

Wit: James Blakley, Mathew Wells, Joel Morton
January 17, 1791
Clarey, wife of said Joseph Morton, relinquished her right of Dower

Page 48
Kirby's Deed from Burgess
January 17, 1790 between Thomas Burgess and Henry Kirby of P for 60
pounds, a parcel of land on the head branches of Sandy Creek containing
216 acres.
Bounded: Thomas Burgess corner line below the Cattail Pond (the upper
end of the s'd land is for this s'd Henry Kirby), to Walkers Order, William
Cottrels corner
s/ Thos Burgess
Wit: John Wright, John Dawson, Joseph Rogers
January 17, 1791

Page 48
Lovett's Deed from Davenport
Sept 17, 1790 between William Davenport of Cumberland County and
Daniel Lovell of P for 250 pounds, a parcel of land containing 404 acres on
both sides of Cherry Stone Creek and on both sides of Hickeys Road which
said land was Conveyed to said William Davenport by two Deeds, one
from the said Daniel Lovell for 332 acres dated Oct 15, 1782 and 70 acres
from Jeremiah Worsham dated April 6, 1784
Bounded: First tract-Watson's line, crossing the said creek, line of John
Lovings Patent, lines of Townsends Survey, Swetson's Survey
s/ Will (X) Davenport
Wit: Benjamin Burton, Thomas Carter, Winefred Carter, Thomas Nash
Dec 20, 1790

Page 50
Smith's Deed of Gift from Morton
I, Joseph Morton of P, in consideration of the Love and good will which I
bare towards Elijah Smith of P have given, after the death of his Father
Edward Smith and his wife Martha, one Negro Girl named Cate, one
horse, two feather Beds, three head of Cattle, nine Hoggs and Household
and Kitchen Furniture, now in Edward Smith's possession
s/ Joseph Morton
Wit: Robert Devin, James Blakley, James M Achran
Jan'y 17, 1791

Page 51
Spraggins's Deed from Morton etc

January 12, 1791 between Joseph Morton and Archer Weatherford of P
and William Spragen of P for 100 pounds, a parcel of land on both sides of
the South fork of Sandy River including five hundred acres of land
Bounded: John Weatherford's line, Glady fork, referring to the Deed from
Arthur Nash to Weatherford and Morton and John Strong to Morton and
the balance of Joseph Alsup to said Spragen
s/ Joseph Morton, Archer Weatherford
Wit: Jeremiah White, Money Weatherford, William Spraginns
January 17, 1791

Page 52
Weatherford's Deed from Morton
January 17, 1790 between Joseph Morton of P and Money Weatherford of
P for 100 pounds bought of Joseph Alsop containing 170 acres on both
sides of the Glady fork of Sandy River
Bounded: Jacob Rigers corner, Yarrington Order Line, crossing said
Glady fork, Gibson's old road, Thomas Alsup's Survey, Jacob Rigers old
line
s/ Joseph Morton
Wit: Arche Weatherford, Money Weatherford, William Spragen
January 17, 1791

Page 53
Calland's Deed from Morton
November 5, 1790 between Joseph Morton of P and Samuel Calland of P
for 650 pounds, on both forks of Sandy River containing 1053 acres, 400
acres of which was willed to me by my Father Joseph Morton, deceased,
400 acres of the said Tract of Land I purchased of my Brother John Morton
which was also willed to him by our said Father and also 253 acres which I
purchased of Thomas Harget adjoining the same
Bounded: Joseph Ostain's fence, Sandy River near Matthew Wells's
fence, Hickeys Road, crossing Sandy River
s/ Joseph Morton
Wit: Edw'd Nunnellee, James Blakley, John Smith, Sam'l Tompkins jr,
Joseph Austin
January 17, 1791
Clarey, wife of Joseph Morton, relinquished her right of Dower

Page 54
Wimbishes Deed of Trust from Shelton
July 24, 1790 between Beverley Shelton of P and John Wimbish of P for
32 pounds, 13 shillings and seven pence, half penny, sell the following five
Negro Women Slaves, to wit, Polley, Sarah, Ritter, Patty, Tiller, also one

bay Mare, one Sorrel Horse, stock of Cattle, Hogs, Household and Kitchen furniture and plantation utencils
s/ Beverley Shelton
Wit: John G? Martin jur, Jno Wimbish jr
January 17, 1791

Page 56
Shackelford's Deed from Shelton
January 3, 1791 between Da'd Shelton of P and Henry Shackelford for 20 pounds, a parcel of land on both sides of Stewards Creek containing 80 acres
Bounded: Stewards Creek, dividing line between Thom's Robison and Wm Robison, James Fulton's line
s/ David Shelton, Elizabeth Shelton
Wit: George (X) Hankins, Abraham Frizzell, William Vincent
February 21, 1791

Page 56
Burnet's Deed from Sparks etc
February 14, 1791 between Leonard Sparks, Polley Sparks, his wife, and Samuel Harvy of P and Barnett Burnatt, for satisfaction made to each of them by the said Burnatt, a parcel of land containing 109 acres
Bounded: James Fulton's line, dividing line between said Leonard Sparks and David Shelton
s/ Leonard Sparks, Polley Sparks, Samuel Harvey
Wit: David Shelton, William Vincent, Jesse Vincent
February 21, 1791

Page 57
Davis's Deed from Westbrook
February 21, 1791 between Henry Westbrook and Mary his wife of P and Thomas Davis of P for 36 pounds, a parcel of land containing by Estimation 100 acres
Bounded: Mill Creek, Hammons's line, old Survey line, Thomas Jones's line
s/ Henry (X) Westbrook
Wit: None
February 21, 1791

Page 58
Vincent's Deed from Dunn
September 1790 between John Dunn junr and his wife Nansay of P and Jere Vincent Juner of P for 30 pounds, a parcel of land being on the branches Strawberry and Sandy Creeks containing by estimation 150 acres,

being part of a Tract of 250 acres joining Edward Atkinson's lines, granted unto Joshua Canterill by patent dated April 11, 1784 and was convaid by the s'd Joshua Cantrill by deed dated July 13, 1786.
s/ John Dunn junr
Wit: None
February 21, 1791

Page 59
Mottley's Deed From Payne
January 4, 1790 between Reuben Payne Senr of P and Daniel Mottley of P for 80 pounds, a parcel of land containing 340 acres on and near the head of Shocko Creek and on Johns Run
Bounded: Willis line on Shocko Creek, Linthicom's line, Johns Run, Hicks line, Shocko Creek
s/ Reuben Pain
Wit: Floyd Tanner, Benj'a Shelton, Edmund Fitzgerald
June 21, 1790

Page 60
Williams's Power of Atto from McCraw etc
We, William McCraw and Susannah his wife, Elizabeth Walker, Wilmoth Williams, wife of James Mastin Williams, Thomas T Williams and Tabitha his wife of P and Halifax do appoint James Mastin Williams of P our lawful attorney to sell and dispose of a certain tract of Land lying in the County of Brunswick, it being the Land conveyed by Indenture from John Robertson and wife to James Walker which said Land descended to the above Co heirs by the death of the said James Walker and containing by estimation 160 acres
s/ Wm McCraw, Susanna McCraw, Elizabeth Walker, Wilmoth Williams, Thomas T Willilams, Tabitha Williams
Wit: Wm Waldron, Bartlet Nunnery, Barton Terry
February 21, 1791

Page 60
Foust's Deed from Hodges
December 20, 1790 between Thos Hodges and Salley his wife of P and Antony Foust of P for 30 pounds, a parcel of land containing by Estimation 180 acres on the branches of Bareskin Creek
Bounded: Edmund Hodges corner, Emmerson's line
s/ Thos Hodges
Wit: None
February 21, 1791

Page 61

300

Southerland's Deed from Lumkin

February 21, 1791 between Robert Lumkin and his wife Drucillar of P and John Sutherlin of P for 200 pounds, a parcel of land containing 500 acres by estimation

Bounded: Larkin Dix corner, Boyd's line to the Fauls Road, Coleman's corner, Butler's line, George Sutherlin's line

s/ Robt Lumkin, Drucillar (X) Lumkin

Wit: None

February 21, 1791

Drucilla, wife of said Robert Lumkin, relinquished her right of Dower

Page 62

Southerland's Deed from Lumkin

Feby 16, 1791 between Robert Lumkins and his wife Drucillar of P and George Sutherlin of P for 70 pounds, a parcel of land containing 200 acres by estimation.

Bounded: said Lumkin's upper corner on the River, William Durkin's line, Dixon's line

s/ Robt Lumkins, Drucillar (X) Lumkins

Wit: None

February 21, 1791

Drucilla, wife of said Robert Lumkin, relinquished her right of Dower

Page 63

Dears Deed from Hankins

February 8, 1791 between Daniel Hankins of P and Gilbert Dear of P for 10 pounds, a parcel of land on both sides of Sandy River containing by estimation 100 acres, it being the land the said Daniel Hankins purchased of William Graham and said William Graham purchased of John Austin

s/ Daniel Hankins

Wit: Edw'd Nunnellee, Drury Cross, William Cross

March 21, 1791

Page 64

Perkins's Deed from Tunstall

March 21, 1791 between William Tunstall of Henry County and Peter Perkins of Henry County for 200 pounds, a parcel of land being on both sides the South fork of Sandy River containing by Estimation 200 acres, being the same land which the said William Tunstall purchased of Samuel Moseley and was by said Samuel Moseley by Indenture dated March 1, 1785 conveyed to the said William Tunstall

s/ Will Tunstall

Wit: Nathan Hall, Geo Hairston, David (X) Mays, James (X) Elkins

March 21, 1791

Page 65
Johnson's Deed from Watkins
December 17, 1790 between Samuel Watkins of P and John Johnson of P
for 37 pounds, a parcel of land lying on the head of Middle Sandy Creek
containing 150 acres
Bounded: Joseph Fliping line, Ann Daniel's line, Wm Dix's line, new
Road
s/ Samuel Watkins
Wit: Joseph Flippin, Josiah Atkinson, Jonathan Hill
March 21, 1791

Page 66
Lumkins Deed from Thomas
September 14, 1790 between William Thomas jr of P and George Lumkins
jurn of P for 545 pounds, a parcel of land whereon the said Lumkin now
lives on the South side of Dan River
Bounded: River bank at the Corner of a fence just above the fishing place,
Jones old line, William Boyd's line, Larkin Dix's line
s/ Will Thomas jr
Wit: Geo Adams, Richard Conn, Peter Wilson, Crispin Shelton jr, Wm
Lynch
February 21, 1791

Page 67
Seal's Deed from Johnson
November 19, 1790 between James Johnson of P and James Seal of P for
110 pounds, a parcel of land containing 290 acres on the Waters of Sandy
Creek
Bounded: William Stamps, Musick's line, Roger Atkinson's line
s/ James Johnson
Wit: William Dix, Wm Seal, Wm (X) Seal junior, John (X) Hall, William
Stamps
March 21, 1791

Page 68
Muse's Deed from Tuggle
September 25, 1789 between Lodowick Tuggle of P and John Muse of
Franklin County for 250 pounds, a parcel of land containing by estimation
1200 acres
Bounded: Willis's line, Samuel Calland's line, Francis Henry's Line, Pigg
River, mouth of Snow Creek
s/ Lodowick Tuggle
Wit: John Duncan, Field L Duncan, Arch Weatherford, Robt Tuggle
March 21, 1791

Page 69

Thomson's Deed from Perkins

February 15, 1791 between Peter Perkins of P and John Thomson of P for 5 pounds, a parcel of land on White thorn Creek and being part of 400 acres the said Perkins had of Richard Gwinn deceased called by Savorys Meadow

Bounded: Timber'd ford, crossing the Glady fork, crossing White thorn creek

s/ Peter Perkins

Wit: Crispin Shelton jr, Wm Ware, Tav'r Shelton

March 21, 1791

Page 70

Pickrals' Deed from Perkins

February 15, 1791 between Peter Perkins of P and Henry Pickral of P for 5 pounds, a parcel of land containing 200 acres lying on Whitethorn Creek (being called Savorys Meadow) and being one half of four hundred acres the said Peter Perkins had of Richard Gwin, deceased

s/ Peter Perkins

Wit: Crispin Shelton jr, Wm Ware, Tav'r Shelton

March 21, 1791

Page 71

Coleman's Deed from Lumpkin

September 18, 1790 between Jos Lumpkin of P and Daniel Coleman of P for 70 pounds, a parcel of land on the South side of Dan River containing 140 acres

Bounded: Jackson's Creek, Sam'll Jones, Nathan Jones, his son, George Lumpkins, Robt Lumpkins, Charles Wynne's lines

s/ Joseph Lumpkin

Wit: Robt Lumpkin, Jn'o Dix, Robt Farguson, Thos Fearn, George Lumpkin

March 21, 1791

Page 72

Marshall's Deed from McCraw

January 25, 1791 between James McCraw Senr and Mary his wife of Halifax County, Virginia and Humphrey Marshall of Fayette County, Virginia for ten shillings, a parcel of land on the lower side of the North fork of great Cherry Stone Creek containing 110 acres

Bounded: on a branch of the said fork, crossing the Road, Hatters Branch, upper line of James Taylor's Survey

s/ James McCraw

Wit: Rich'd N Venable, Geo Craghead, J Pannill, D C? Clarke

March 22, 1791

Page 73
Wimbish's Deed of Trust from G Shelton
July 24, 1790 between Gabriel Shelton of P and John Wimbish of P for
120 pounds, four shillings and four pence which said Gabriel Shelton is
justly indebted unto said John Wimbish, said Shelton sells unto Said
Wimbish the following seven slaves, to wit, Vilet, Patt, Larry, Easter,
Liller, James and Delphy, one bay horse, one black mare, one sorrel mare,
stock of cattle, hogs and sheep, also Household and Kitchen furniture and
Plantation Utensels
s/ Gabriel Shelton
Wit: John O? Martin, John Wimbish jr, Jas Johnson, Fred Shelton
March 21, 1791

Page 74
Fitzgerald's Power of Atto from Hightower
I, Thomas Hightower of P, appoint by tusty friend Francis Fitzgarald of
Nottoway County my Lawful Attorney to collect and receive of and from
such person as shall be authorized to pay the same, the Sum of 24 pounds
due to me from the publick of Virginia as Pensioner   March 22, 1791
s/ Thomas Hightower
Wit: Rich'd N Venable, W Wright
March 22, 1791

Page 75
Report of the Inspection of the Clks Office
The Clerk Office of Pittsylvania County
Pursuant to an Order of Pittsylvania Court to us directed, we whose Names
are hereunto subscribed, have proceeded to examine the Clerks Office of
said County and find the State of it as follows. We find the Docket and
Execution Book in good Order, and also the papers in the Office properly
fil'd away. We fine the Wills Recorded to September 1780 from June
1767 the commencement of the County, and since September 1780 none
have been recorded. We find the Deeds recorded from the commencement
of the County to January 1787 and none since. We find the Inventories
recorded and also the Guardian Accounts till the present time. We find the
Order Book in the Office and we find that no Orders Court Judgments or
decrees have ever been recorded since the Commencement of the County.
Except from April 1777 till November 1779. And lastly we find that no
Rules taken in the Office have ever been recorded. Given under hands
Jany 21, 1791
s/ Jas Johnson, Sam'l Calland
March 22, 1791

Page 75
McDaniel's Negro Emancipated
I, Anne McDaniel of P, being conscience that the Doctrine of Christ
teacheth us to do unto others as we would they should do to us and having
a Negro Woman Slave in my possession named Caroline, I do now set free
and Emancipate the said Slave and her increase, and do for myself my
Heirs etc resign and relinquish all my right and title to the said Slave
Caroline and her increase. Signd with my Seal this 11th day of November
1790
s/ Anne (X) McDaniel
Wit: B Williams, Jno Call
March 21, 1791

Page 75
L Shelton's Deed from Pace
December 29, 1790 between William Pace of Henry County and Lemuel
Shelton of P for 46 pounds, a parcel of land containing 270 acres on the
North side of White Thorn Creek containing 270 acres
Bounded: head of the South fork of Rackoon branch, Motley's line,
Hamlet's line, J Parhams line, White Thorn Creek, mouth of the Rackoon
branch, south fork of said Rackoon branch
s/ W Pace
Wit: Vincent Shelton, Wyatt Shelton, Gregory Shelton, Benja Shelton,
Gabriel Shelton
April 18, 1791

Page 76
R Shelton's Deed from Pace
December 29, 1790 between William Pace of Henry County and Reddick
Shelton of P for 32 pounds, a parcel of land containing 110 acres on the
South side White thorn Creek
Bounded: White Thorn Creek on Edmund Taylor's line, Bowlins line,
Armistead Shelton's line to the aforesaid Creek opposite the mouth of the
long branch
s/ W Pace
Wit: Vincent Shelton, Wyatt Shelton, Grigory Shelton, Benj'a Shelton,
Gabriel Shelton
April 18, 1791

Page 77
Ab Shelton's Deed from Pace
December 29, 1790 between William Pace and Susanna his wife of Henry
County and Abraham Shelton of P for 72 pounds, a parcel of land on
Whitethorn Creek containing 312 acres

305

Bounded: Head of the South fork of the Rackoon branch, Motley's line, Long Branch, White thorn Creek, mouth of the Rackoon branch, up the main South fork of said branch
s/ W Pace
Wit: Vincent Shelton, Wyatt Shelton, Grigory Shelton, Benj'a Shelton, Gabriel Shelton
April 18, 1791

Page 78
Elliott's Deed from Thorp
January 16, 1791 between William Tharp of Franklin County and Thomas Ellitt of P for 70 pounds, a parcel of land on the Waters of White Oak containing 167 acres
Bounded: White Oak, Hawk's Nest branch
s/ William (X) Tharp
Wit: William Ross, Jno Dupuy, James Elliot, Allen Stokes
February 21, 1791

Page 79
Witcher's Deed from Duncan
February 28, 1791 between Field Allen Duncan of P and Daniel Witcher of P for 100 pounds, a parcel of land on the south side of Pigg River containing by Estimation 185 acres
Bounded: mouth of Rockey branch, north side of the river
s/ Field A Duncan
Wit: John Bobbitt, Milton Young, Merlin Young, Ephraim Witcher
April 18, 1791

Page 79
Ragland's Deed from Kelley
April 16, 1791 between Hugh Kelley of P and Gidion Ragland of P for 17 pounds, fifteen shillings, a parcel of land containing by Estimation 17 ¾ acres on Birches Creek
Bounded: Prestridge's branch
s/ Hugh (X) Kelley
Wit: Thomas Shelton, Barton Terry, John Harris, John Spencer
April 18, 1791

Page 80
Collie's Deed from Watkins
April 15, 1791 between Mary Watkins and Samuel Watkins, Heirs of John Watkins dec'd of P, and William Collie of P for 75 pounds, a parcel of land containing 124 acres on the Waters of Burches Creek and North side of Dixes Road

Bounded: Robert Walters Jr line,
s/ Samuel Watkins, Mary Watkins
Wit: Pey'n Thomas, Robert Walters, Wm Durratt
April 18, 1791

Page 81
Hodges Deed from Hopper
November 12, 1790 between Luther Hoper and Thos Hodges of P and
Moses Hodges of P for 50 pounds, a parcel of land containing by
estimation 71 acres
s/ Luther (X) Hopper, Thos Hodges
Wit: Richard Elliott, Sam'a (X) Hughes, John (X) Nash, William Dyer
April 18, 1791

Page 82
Foust's Deed from Hodges
April 18, 1791 between Thos Hodges and Salley his wife of P and Jacob
Foust of P for 30 pounds, a parcel of land containing 182 acres on the
Waters of Barskin Creek
Bounded: Hodges's new line
s/ Thos Hodges
Wit: None
April 18, 1791

Page 83
Orrender's Deed from Poyner
October 21, 1790 between John Poyner of Halifax County and Matthew
Orrander of P for 35 pounds, a parcel of land containing 100 acres
Bounded: Walker's Order Line, the road, M Hardin's line, H Kelley's line
s/ John Poynor
Wit: David Poynor, Josiah Rogers, John Owen
April 18, 1791

Page 84
Smith's Deed from Watson
October 7, 1790 between Samuel Watson of Prince William County and
Hezekiah Smith of P for 50 pounds, a parcel of land on the Waters of
Sandy River containing 100 acres
Bounded: George Adam's corner on the south side of Stone's branch,
Norton's old line, said Hezekiah Smith's line, Merrick's line
s/ Sam'l Watson
Wit: Geo Adams, Jno Wilson, Harris Gammon, John Stone
March 21, 1791

Page 85

Wilson from Lay Ded's & Report

To Constant Perkins and William Harrison of P, Whereas David Lay of P by his certain Indenture dated Feby 15, 1788 hath conveyed to John Wilson 267 acres And whereas Catherine Lay, Wife of said David Lay, is not able to travel to the Court to relinquish her right of Dower in the said Land, We do therefore Command you or any two or more of you that you personally go to the said Catherine Lay and examine her privately . Feby 10, 1789

s/ Will Tunstall

Pittsyl'a County

In Obedience to the above Commission, we the Subscribers did go to Catherine Lay, wife of the above named Dav'd Lay and examined her privately. She relinquished her right of Dower   Feby 13, 1789

s/ Constt Perkins, Wm Harrison

(No recording date given)

Page 86

Thomas from Lumpkins Ded'o & Report

To John Wilson and George Adams, Gent, Justices of P: Whereas Geo Lumkin and Jos Lumkin, by his certain Indenture, hath conveyed unto William Thomas junr of P a certain Tract of land containing by estimation 194 acres. And whereas Mary, the wife of the said George Lumpkin junr, cannot conveniently travel to and from our said Court House. Know ye that we trusting to your faithful and provident circumspection in examining Mary apart from her said Husband whether she does voluntarily relinquish her right of Dower   August 17, 1790

s/ Will Tunstall

By virtue of the above Commission to us directed, we have examined Mary, wife of said George Lumkin, and she relinquished her right of Dower. Sept 3, 1790

s/ Jno Wilson, Geo Adams

April 18, 1791

Page 87

Wilson from Whitby Ded's and Report

To William Harrison and Geo Adams, Gent, Justices of P: Whereas Richardson Whitby by his certain Indenture hath conveyed unto John Wilson of P a certain Tract of land containing by estimation 260 acres. And whereas Sary Whitby, the wife of the said Richard Whitby, cannot conveniently travel to and from our said Court House. Know ye that we trusting to your faithful and provident circumspection in examining Sary apart from her said Husband whether she does voluntarily relinquish her right of Dower   March 3, 1791

s/ Will Tunstall
By virtue of the above Commission to us directed, we have examined
Sarah, wife of said Richardson Whitby, and she relinquished her right of
Dower. March 3, 1791
s/ Wm Harrison, Geo Adams
(No recording date given)

Page 88
Hardey's Deed from Hardey
1790 between Thomas Hardey Senr of P and Thomas Hardey Junr of P for
the sum of five pounds and for the love and affection the said Thomas
Hardey Senr doth bear to his son Thomas, doth sell a certain Parcel of land
on Strawberry Creek containing by Estimation 165 acres
Bounded: Edward Long's line, Jonathan Thomas' line, James McGehee's
line
s/ Thomas Hardey
Wit: Peter J Bailey, Welcom W Allen, Isham Hardey
April 18, 1791

Page 89
Pulliam's Deed from Watson
April 16, 1791 between Nathan Watson of P and Drury Pulliam of P for
100 pounds, a parcel of land containing 250 acres being part of two
Surveys of the s'd Watson
Bounded: Norton's corner, Davis's line
s/ Nathan Watson
Wit: Randolph McDonall, Absel McDonald, Anderson Watson
April 18, 1791

Page 90
Slayden's Deed from Mann
March 7, 1791 between Jesse Mann of P and Joseph Slayden of P for 15
pounds, a parcel of land on the lower Double Creek containing by
Estimation 37 acres
Bounded: William Slayden line, old dividing line between said Jesse
Mann and Joseph Slayden, Daniel Slayden's line, William Slayden's line
s/ Jesse Mann
Wit: Lemuel Hogpeth, Larkin Mading, John Mading
April 18, 1791

Page 91
Bailey's Deed from Hardey

December 1, 1790 between Thomas Hardey of P and Peter J Bayley of P for 60 pounds, a parcel of land on the South branches of Banister river containing 200 acres
Bounded: Jesse Carter's line, Dan'l Bradly's line, Thos Carter's line, Welcom W Allens line
s/ Thomas Hardey
Wit: Welcom W Allen, Isham Hardey, Elisha (X) Nuckels
April 16, 1791

Page 92
Hardin's Deed from Poynor
Oct 21, 1790 between John Poynor of Halifax County and Martin Hardin of P for 20 pounds, a parcel of land containing 71 acres
Bounded: Orrender's line, said Hardin's line, T Carter's line
s/ John Poynor
Wit: John Owen, Josiah Rogers, David Poynor
April 18, 1791

Page 93
Wamock's Deed from Watkins
January 1790 between Samuel Watkins and Mary Watkins of P and Elizabeth Womack of P for 51 pounds, a parcel of land on the Waters of Sandy Creek of Dan River containing by Estimation 102 ½ acres
Bounded: William Harrison's line, George Cook's corner, John Clark's line, Zacheriah Butts line, Noell Waddell Junr line
s/ Samuel Watkins, Mary (X) Watkins
Wit: Noel Waddill junr, Wm Durrett, Charles Waddill, Noel Waddill
April 18, 1791

Page 94
Wray's Deed from Jefferson
April 18, 1791 between Peter Field Jefferson of P and David Wray of P for 50 pounds, a parcel of land on the head of Camp Branch of Turkey Cock Creek containing by Estimation 140 acres
Bounded: said Peter Field Jefferson's own corner, the old Pattent line
s/ Peter F Jefferson
Wit: Sam'l Tompkins jr, G Tunstall, John Stockton
April 18, 1791

Page 95
Hardin's Deed from Bradley
January 1, 1791 between Daniel Bradley of P and Henry Hardin of P for 95 pounds, a parcel of land on branches of Banister River on the North side of the Whiteoak Mountain containing 230 acres

310

Bounded; By the lines of Peter Bailey, Jesse Carter, Richard Elliott, Abram
Cambell, John Wright Senr and John Wright Junr and Theodorick Carter
s/ Daniel (X) Bradley
Wit: Charles Carter, George Prossise, John Wright Senr
April 18, 1791

Page 96
Hatker's Deed from Stamps
December 17, 1790 between John Stamps of P and Ambross Halker of P
for 120 pounds, a parcel of land on both sides of Sandy Creek containing
150 acres
s/ John Stamps
Wit: Nathan Riddle, Basil Hucker, Ambrose Hucker
April 18, 1791

Page 97
Owens Deed from Beckham
February 9, 1791 between Elijah Beckham of Culpeper County and David
Owen of P for 200 pounds, a parcel of land on the South side of Banister
River and both sides of Polecat Creek containing 267 acres
Bounded: on the river on William Short's line, Christopher Hutchings old
Order line, Polecat Creek
s/ Elijah Beckham
Wit: John Wilson, Geo Adams, Obadiah Owen, Peter Wilson, Jos Carter
April 18, 1791

Page 99
Burnett's Deed from Cunningham
March 12, 1791 between John Cunningham and Saly his wife and Henry
Burnett both of P, a parcel of land containing 84 acres on both sides Sandy
River
Bounded: Fork of Sandy River on the south side of said river, bounded on
the Norwest and weste by the Land and plantation that was formerly James
Shields, said Burnett line, bounded on the east by the Lands of said
Burnett, James Galoway and John Begerly, then the river, Simon Adams
Land, the said Land lying on the north side of Sandy River, Begerly's on
the South, William Shealds line, said Adams land on the East, William
Shealds Land and plantation bounding the said Land on the North.
s/ John Cunningham, Sarah Cunningham
Wit: James Burnett, Gilbert Burnett, Patrick Shields
April 18, 1791

Page 100
Brown's Deed from Duncan

December 4, 1790 between John Duncan and Francis his wife and Tarlton Brown for 150 pounds, a parcel of land containing by Estimation 322 acres lying in P and Franklin County
Bounded: Peyton Smith's line formerly John Kerby's line, Pigg River
s/ John Duncan, Frances Duncan
Wit: Robt Tuggle, Robt Napier, Ashford Napier, Lodo'k Tuggle
April 18, 1791
Frances, wife of John Duncan, relinquished her right of Dower

Page 101
Conn's Deed from Conn
March 14, 1791 between Joseph Conn of P and Samuel Conn of P for 150 pounds, one certain parcel of land where the said Joseph Conn now lives at the Cross Roads which Land the said Joseph Conn purchased of John Fuller Laine lying on both sides of Mountain Creek containing by Estimation 107 ½ acres
Bounded: East side line of that Land Dutton Lain sold to the said Joseph Conn
s/ Jo Conn
Wit: Rich'd Conn, Elizabeth (X) Conn, Ara (X) Conn
April 18, 1791

Page 103
Weatherford's Deed from Tuggle
April 18, 1791 between Lodowick Tuggle of P and John Weatherford of P for 65 pounds, a parcel of land containing by Estimation 150 acres
Bounded: William Justice's line on Pigg River, Thomas Ramsy's corner, Rockey Creek, Pigg River
s/ Lodowick Tuggle
Wit: None
April 18, 1791

Page 103
A Southerland Deed from Southerland
April 12, 1791 between George Southerland of P and Adams Southerland of P for the love I have for my son Adams Southerland, a parcel of land on both sides of Sandy Creek containing 255 acres
Bounded: Wm Southerland's corner, mouth of the long branch, up Sandy Creek, crossing said Creek, mouth of William Southerland's Spring branch
s/ George (X) Southerland
Wit: Thomas Duncan, John Gwin, William Southerlin
April 18, 1791

Page 105

W Southerland's Deed from Southerland
April 12, 1791 between George Southerland of P and William Southerland of P for the love I have for my said Son, William Southerland, a parcel of land on the North side of Sandy Creek containing 250 acres
Bounded: mouth of a Spring branch on said Creek, Ann McDaniels and Clay's lines, the long branch, George Southerland's corner
s/ George (X) Southerland
Wit: Thomas Duncan, John Gwin, Adams Southerland
April 18, 1791

Page 107
Smith's Deed from Stockton
April 18, 1791 between John Stockton of P and John Smith of P for 350 pounds, a parcel of land on both sides of Turkey Cock Creek and containing by Estimation 520 acres
s/ John Stockton
Wit: None
April 18, 1790

Page 108
Shelton's Deed from Kelly
April 16, 1791 between Hugh Kelly of P and Thomas Shelton of P for 101 pounds, a parcel of land containing by estimation 106 acres on Burches Creek
Bounded: Mill branch
s/ Hugh (X) Kelly
Wit: Gidion Ragland, Barton Terry, Jno Harris, John Spencer
April 18, 1791

Page 109
Hodges Bill of Sale from Owen
William Owen of P for 100 pounds paid by Jesee Hodges of P for one Negro Woman named Amey about 16 years old, and one grey Horse
s/ William Owen
Wit: Jer White
April 18, 1791

Page 109
Potter's Deed from Witcher
April 18, 1791 between Ephraim Witcher of P and Stephen Potter of P for 50 pounds, a parcel of land containing 50 acres on the Waters of Readeys Creek
Bounded: John Hammock's line on the ridge path, Ephaim Witcher's new line, Taylor's field, Rosses corner, Hammock's line

s/ Ephraim Witcher
Wit: John Hammock, Richard Shockley, William Young, William (X)
Clement, Milton Young
April 18, 1791

Page 110
Stockton's Deed from Stockton
April 18, 1791 between John Stockton of P and Peter H Stockton of P for
love and affection he has for his Son Peter H Stockton, a parcel of land
containing by estimation 270 acres on the head Branches of Sandy River
Bounded: Elisha Walling line, John Warrons line and part of the said Tract
given by Arthur Fuller to the said Warron, also Capt Daniel Hankins line
s/ John Stockton
Wit: Sam'l Tompkins jr, David (X) Wray, Peter F Jefferson
April 18, 1791

Page 112
Wilson's Deed from Whitby
March 3, 1791 between Richardson Whidby of P and John Wilson of P for
100 pounds, a parcel of land containing 260 acres
Bounded: William Southerlin's line
s/ Richesson Whitbey
Wit: Wm Harrison, Geo Adams, P Wilson jr, John Wier, Bezalul Wier,
John Stone, Silv Stokes, Henry Lansford
April 18, 1791

314

Index to Pittsylvania County, VA. Deeds

Index to Pittsylvania County, VA, Deeds

Index to Pittsylvania County, VA. Deeds

Index to Pittsylvania County, VA. Deeds

Index to Pittsylvania County, VA. Deeds

Index to Pittsylvania County, VA. Deeds

Index to Pittsylvania County, VA. Deeds

Index to Pittsylvania County, VA. Deeds

Index to Pittsylvania County, VA. Deeds

Index to Pittsylvania County, VA. Deeds

Index to Pittsylvania County, VA. Deeds

Index to Pittsylvania County, VA. Deeds

Index to Pittsylvania County, VA. Deeds

Index to Pittsylvania County, VA. Deeds

Index to Pittsylvania County, VA, Deeds

Index to Pittsylvania County, VA. Deeds

Index to Pittsylvania County, VA, Deeds

Index to Pittsylvania County, VA. Deeds

Index to Pittsylvania County, VA. Deeds

Index to Pittsylvania County, VA. Deeds

Index to Pittsylvania County, VA. Deeds

Index to Pittsylvania County, VA. Deeds

Index to Pittsylvania County, VA. Deeds

Benj 167
Samuel 83,167
MORRISON
Mercer 172,255
MORTON 71
Capt John 247
Clarey 296,297,298
Hezekiah 100
Isaiah
147,159,167,243,245,247,251,252,291,292
Isiah 159
James 186
Joel 297
John
28,49,80,133,147,202,219,291,293,294,298
John Jnr 292
John Senr 292
Jos 57,271(2)
Jos Esq'r 9
Joseph
30,31(2),80,91,140(2),144,159,186,189,201,202,219,
243,251,253(2),272,283,289,293,296,297(2),298(3)
Joseph dec'd 298
Joseph Junr 158
Pertin 40
MOSELEY/MOSLEY/MOSLY
Samuel 1,3,33,79,82,147,234,301
MOTLEY/MOTTLEY
11,53,54(2),117,182,201,305,306
Daniel
11,90,132(3),133(2),133,173,251,287,300
David 109,132,162,173,218
Elizabeth 132,133(2)
Isaac 51,269,270
John 181,261
Jos 168
Joseph
11,51,53,54,67,83,89,91,132(3),133,160,161,163,173(2),174,181,287
Samuel
11,91,95,110,132,133,174,251,287
Sarah 132,133(3),173
MOUNTAIN
Banister/Bannister 77,109,130
Berry 169
Little Round 64
Little Roundtop 210
Smith 251
Turkey Cock 168
White Oak 35,125,136,145,165,262,310
MOUSTON 73
MOWN
Thos 83
MULINAY
Hugh 16
MULLINGS/MULLINS
Henry 221
John 32,104

Joshua 241
MUMFORD/MUNFORD
Edward 134,157,194,220
MURDOCK
Thoms 137
MURPHY
James 114
William 193
MURRAY 169,207,237,277
Leonard 238
Nathaniel 46
William 45
MURREY
Alexander 212,213
Nathaniel 161
MURRIC 183
MURTAIN
Thomas 134
MUSE 267
John 24,43,217,228,229,253,288,302
Lucy 229,253,288
Thomas 288
MUSICK 260,302
Electus 20
Eleclious 144
MUSTAIN
Avery 204,207
Jesse 176,266
Thomas 77,147,166,173,263
MYERS
George 191
NAKINS
Daniel 294
NANCE
Clement 21,85,98,181,275,279,292
Giles 85,205,292
William 158,159,167
NAPIER
Ashford 312
Robt 312
NASH 74
A 243
Arther 147
Arthur 33,167,298
Isbell 79
John 48,141,247,251,307
Marvel 203
Wm 140(2),203
NEAL/NEEL 138,141
Benjamin 143,169,170
Eliz'a 143
John 69
Lucy 245
Stephen
119,134,138,141,243,245,256,287,288
NEALY/NEELEY/NEELY/NELEY 41
Robert 25,196
William 41,224
NECK?
John 70
NEGRO
Alley 137

Index to Pittsylvania County, VA. Deeds

Index to Pittsylvania County, VA. Deeds

Mary 25,75,267
Mesheck 82
Nane 11
Patt 304
Patty 298
Peter 11,65
Phillis 51
Pinn 11
Polley 298
Priss 82
Rachal 11
Ritter 298
Robert 267
Rubin 120,249
Sall 11
Sam 75,82
Sarah 298
Shadrick 82
Solomon 292
Spencer 288
Syphy 227
Tener 51
Tiller 298
Tillie 292
Timmy 51
Titus 288
Tom 75
Toney 82
Vilet 304
William 82
Winney 248
NEGRO WENCH
Fanny 209
Jane 190
Polly 232
NEGRO WOMAN
Amey 313
Beck 35
Dafney 268
Deley 115
Jenny 226
Luce 187
Lucy 51
Nan 225
Peg 230
Tiller 230
Vina 230
NELSON 110(2),144
Baswell 144
Bazel 86,140
James 14,107,109
John 123
Joshua 9
William 66,140,202,264,265
NEWTON 252
NICKOLS
Jacob 22
NORFOLK BOUROGH 97
NORTH CAROLINA 53,121,285,287
NORTH CAROLINA COUNTIES
Anson 112

Gilford/Guildford/Guilford10,13,23,32,67,1
22, 243,245
Granville 159
Green 291
Hawkins 282
Lincoln 42(2)
Notochuckey 87
Orange Cnty 181,223
Rockingham 202
Sullivan Cnty 53
Surry Co
5,18,72,181,237,257,264(2),274
Washington 8,116,119,175,291
Washington Sylivan 21
Wilks/Wilkes 102,183,232,285
NORTON 307,309
Jacob 224,276
John 9
Nehemiah 82,135
Thomas 243(2),245
NOWLIN/ NOLIN
Bryan Ward 40,122,85,225
Bryant W 209
Bryant Ward 125
Lucy 125,209
Nuchsum
Jubs 202
NUCKELS/NUCKLES
Elisha 226,310
NUNNELE/NUNNELEE/NUNELLEE
Edward 186,202,247,283,298,301
NUNNERY
Bartlet 300
OAKES
Charles 82,83,170,193
Daniel 47
James 56,98,193,204,205,282
John 16,192,198
William 193
OAR
Jean 113
Robert 113
OLD COURT HOUSE 221
Old Wagon Ford 16,91
OLIVER/OLLIVER
Drury Dec'd 221
John 221
Mary 221
Thomas 221,289
William 10,43,89
ORENDER/ORRANDER/ORRENDER 310
Mathew 265,307
ORR
Jane 47,113
Jean 47
Robert 47,61,64
OSTAIN
Joseph 298
OWEN/OWENS 199
David 122,180,311
Edey/Eddy 66,73,130,138,227

Index to Pittsylvania County, VA. Deeds

Index to Pittsylvania County, VA. Deeds

John 82
PRESTON
  J 68
PRICE 227,261
  Cutburd 188
  D 236
  Daniel 188,234,235,237,261
  Joseph 257
  Maraday 234,235,236,237
  Martha 257
  Robert 236
  Susanna 261
  Thomas 129,148(2),149
  William
38,50,118,188,234,235,237(2),238,239(2),
262,265,283
  Wm B 67
  William Barber 258
  William Junr 109,125
  William Senr 109,236,261
PRIER
  Edward 23
PRISE
  Mary 95
PROSISE/PROSIZE,PROSSISE/PERSIZ
E
  George 157,181,311
  William/Wilm 62,63,293
PRUIT/PRUITT/
PREWET/PREWETT/PREWITT 10
  Daniel 10
  John 15,23,235,237
  Richard 80
  Samuel Junr 120
  Zackariah 120
PRUNTY
  Robert 166,294
PRUR
  Edward 23
PRYOR/PRIOR
  Edward 48,119
  Mary 48
  Samuel 137
PUCKET
  Newbill 174
  Peter 98,154,194
PULLIAM
  David 131
  Drury 9,57,309
PURCEL
  Charles 235
  James 97,110
PYEARS
  Elijah 6
QUARLES
  Francis 230,231
QUILLE
  Thomas Junr 137
QUIN/QUINN/QWINN 39
  Ann 109
  David 181
  William 15,92,109,234

William W 261
RAGLAND
  Gideon/Giddion/Gidion 167,208,306,313
RAGSDALE 49,136,265
  Daniel 225
  Fred 86
  FredrickFrederick/Frederic
11,35,144,264
  John 49
  Obediah 225
  Pheby 225
  William 49,51
  Thomas 225,265
  William 49,51
RAINEY/ RANEY
  Jno 134
  Judith 276
  Lucy 276
  Mathew 159,276
  John 44
RAMEY/RAMCY
  Absalom 208
  Absalom Junr 206
  Elizabeth 206,208
  Jno 94,119
  John 44
  Presley 172
  Wm 172
RAMSEY/RAMSY/RAMSLE
  George 231
  Thomas 33,190,312
RANDOLPH
  Beverley 279
  Edm'd 222
  Edmund Esq 219
RAY
  David 267
READ/REED 73
  Elizabeth 28,159
  Samuel 135
  Thomas 152
  Reaser,Paul 227
REDMOND
  John 157
REECE/REESE,REES
  John 104,160(2),266
REISER
  Paul 226
RENFRO/RENTFROE
  Jno 58
  John 58
REPEIN
  Anthony 129
REYNOLDS/RENNOLDS/RAYNOLDS/RU
NNALDS/RYNOLD
  George 143,169
  Hugh 1,25,61(2),94,224
  Jesse 160,168,205
  John 137,170,288
  Joseph 61,170,260
  Lucy/Lusey 218,220
  William 108,160,235

Index to Pittsylvania County, VA. Deeds

Index to Pittsylvania County, VA. Deeds

Index to Pittsylvania County, VA. Deeds

Index to Pittsylvania County, VA. Deeds

Thomas Senr 238,243
SPEED
  John 93
SPENCE
  John 208
SPENCER
  John 268,285,306,313
SPRAGEN/SPRAGGINS/SPRIGINNS/SPRAGINS
  Mel 13,14,291
  William 298(2)
SPRATTEN
  George 260
STAMPS 47,129,175
  John 55,86,144,185,259,260,295,311
  Timothy 144
  William 86,260,295,302
STANTON
  Sally 145
STARLING
  William Esq 93
STEGALL
  William 115
STEPHENS/STEVENS
  David 83(2),181,193
  Sarah 83
  Thomas 82
STEWART 26
  Jno Jr 141
  John 26,258(2)
  Mary 256(2)
STILLWELL/STILWELL 218
  Anne 211
  Jacob 42,211,219(2)
  Jacob jr 4,211
  Jacob Senr 211
  Nance 42
STIMSON
  Benjamin 86
  Erasmus 259
  Jeremiah 86,90,259 Lloyd 259
  Rosamon 90
STITH
  Drury 87
STOCKTON
  John
10,20,43,51,61,73,179,202,253(2),310,313
,314
  Peter H 314
STOKES 29,39(2),49,118,160,215
  Allen/Allin 23,49,306
  Evins 38
  Sylvanus/Silvanus/Silv
29,33,34,49(2),81(2),118,178,179,314
STOKSIS 239
STONE 11,122,124(2)
  Dolly 102
  Henry 282
  John
102,242(2),269(2),270,274,275,279,280,3
07,314

Joshua
22,37,42,43,69,76,86,94,95,102,119,136,1
37,141,143,148,149,153,155,157,162,163,
185,193,197,203,204(2),206,207(2),208(2)
,218,224,226,228,242(2),248,250,255,256
(2),263(2),264,269,275,280(2),284
  Joshua junr 269
  Joshua Senr 152
  Mary 43
  William 282
STONESTREET
  Butler 275,285
  Butler Edelen 84
STOTT
  Solomon 120
STRATON/STRATTON
  Benja 7,21
  Thomas 7(2)
  William 169,245
STRAWBERRY 107,131,236(2),247
STRONG 291
  John 243,245,251,298
STROTHER/STROTHERS
  G 7,12,29,32
  Geo 21
STUART 141
SUGAR TREE 98
SUMMERS 27
  William 56,275,277
SUMTERS
  General 102
SUTTON
  David 245
  William 57
SWAN
  George 120,121
  SusannahSusanna 120,121
SWANSON
  Nathan 17
SWEENEY/SWENEY/SWENNEY/SWINNEY
  James 209
  John 50,171,178,223
  Joseph 92,209,248
  Moses 18
SWELINS 85
SWEPSON/SWETSON/SWIPSON
  Richard 20(2),202
SYCAMORE 84,214
SYMMOND 57
TALBOT 23
  John 61,152
TALEAFERRO
  John 183
TANNER 95,183,259
  Creed 39,250,284
  David 76,86,251
  Elizabeth 160,161,231
  Floyd
39,95,132(2),133,1,161,173,179,231,251,2
60,270,300
  Joel Senr 39

Index to Pittsylvania County, VA. Deeds

Index to Pittsylvania County, VA. Deeds

195,196,197,204(2),228,232,256,261,263(
2),264,274,279
  William
5,12,30,31(2),106,110,111(2),150(2),151,1
63,172,176,180,182,189(2),191(2),193(2),
194(2),195,196(2),206,212(2),213(2),214(
2),215,220,227,232,241,248,255(2),256,2
57
TOLBART/TOLBERT 84
  Charles 84
TOLER 280
  Christian 260
  Joseph 242,279,280
TOMBERLING
  Alice 1
  Jasper 188
  John 188
TOMLIN/TOMLINS/TOMKIN 104,105
  Alice 188
  Jasper 188
  John 38
  John Senr 188
  Joseph 37
  Mary 188
  Sam'l Junr 168
TOMPKINS
  D 125,130,155
  Daniel
81,84,119,150(2),163,169,172,193,199,20
2,203,238,244,253
  Jno 188
  Sam 203,222
  Samuel 119,154,166
  Sam'l Junr
92,105,117,168,169,173,188,203,221,254,
294,298,310,314
TOMPSON 110
  John 128,156
  William 225
TORROR 22
TOST
  Jacob 77
TOWLER
  Joseph 128
TOWNES
  George Col 264
  H 271
  Halcott 296
TOWSEN/TOWSEND/TOWSON 297
  Benjamin 90
  Jabus 203
  Thomas 97(2)
TRAVESES
  William 4
TREBELIS 208
TRIGG
  William 123,124
TUCKER 177,210
  Gabriel 106
  Martha 257
  Nelson 226,257,258,259
  Phoebe 6

  Robert 6,71,226,239.272
  William/Will
6,22,36,53,71,78,113,177,226,239,241
TUGGLE/TOGGLE
  Cap Lod'k 294
  George 167,238
  L 166,167,171
  Lodowick,Lodwick,Lodock,Lodd'r,Lou'k
,Lodo'k
30,31(3),54,63,92,104,115,121,145(2),146
(2),153,238,302(2),312(2)
  Rob't 121,302,312
  Thos 121
TUNSTALL 164(2)
  D 279
  E 293
  Edmund 232,288
  G 310
  Jno 134
  T 30,134,226,272,288
  Thomas 30,65,139,179,250,271(2),279
  Thomas Junr 30,101(2),134,180(3)
  Thos Senr 12
  Will
9,21,31,35,43,58,75,76(2),94,96,104,111,1
18,123,143,144,161,162,164,167,171,175,
179,180(2),181,182(2),185(2),187,197,204
,207,209,216,224,253,255,263,264,308,30
9
  Will jr 288
  William 134,232,290,301
TURK
  Christian 222,223,246,267
TURKEY COCK 105
TURLEY
  John 14
  John Sen 146
TURNER 55,68
  Abedmego 230
  John 5,230
  Meshach 68(2),76
  Pearce,Pierce 257,291
  Rebecca 76
  Shadrick 65
**TWEDEL/TWEDELL/TWEDWELL/TWEED
ALE/TWEEDWELL/TWIDWELL**
15,71,112,213(2),277
  Benjamin 14(2),61,289
  John 217,241,279
  William
14(2),107,109,138,154,178,179(2),205,21
7(2),241,254,275,288,289,275
ULIAS
  Philip 37
URQUART
  Walter 85
VALLEY
  Powell's 289
VANCE 19
  Anne 18
  Mathew 18,285
VASON

Index to Pittsylvania County, VA, Deeds

Index to Pittsylvania County, VA. Deeds

Index to Pittsylvania County, VA. Deeds

Index to Pittsylvania County, VA. Deeds

WORSHAM
  Ann 201
  Daniel 219
  Henry 11
  Jeremiah
57,65,95,117,201,206,221,230,297,221,23
0,297
  John 4,26,27,211(2),218,219(2),230,278
  Sarah 12
  Thomas 278
  Wm 188
WORTHY 67,89
  Elizabeth 149
  Richard 67,89,138
  Thomas 39,88(3),110,111(2),149
WRAY
  David 310,314
WRIGHT 183,223
  Ann 205,217,219
  Charles 145
  Fanny 158
  Francis 245
  George 77, 110,135,157
  John
76,79,94,127,158,211,244,248,249,297
  John Jr 145,165,311
  John Senr 145,156,165,238,262,311
  Joseph 114
  Martha 288,289
  Mary 84,127
  Reubin 257
  Robert 205,286,289
  Thomas 145,165,262
  W
107,109,160,205,217,219(2),230,234,288,
289(2),294,304
  William
14,50,81,84,108,217,231,240,241,254
WYATT
  John 269,270
WYER
  John 38
WYNN/WYNNE 40,287
  Charles 211,218,219(2),220,303
  John 29,42
  Mathew 211,218,220
  Robert 12,27,29,122,136,164,219(2)
  Stith 233
  Thomas 46,86,295
  William 42,233
  William Dec'd 219
YARINGTON/YARRINGTON 49,
186,202,219,298
YATES/YEATS 49,50
  Elizabeth 56,57
  John 51,78,89,227,229
  Nancey 172
  Richard 221
  Stephen 70,186,187,189,195,262,266
YILLIE
  Barksdale & Co 137
YORK/ YOURK

  William 72,264(2)
YOULCE
  Philip 62
YOUNG/YONG/YUNG
  Archibald,Archerball 17(2),31,238,272
  George 44,82,159,244,252,291
  George Sen 147,158
  Irvin 63
  James 158,159,167,295
  John 44,158,167,252
  Marlin 266,273(2)
  Melton 178
  Merlin 306
  Milton 17,104,266,273(2),276,306,314
  Sarah 31
  W 122,166
  William
33,104,160,162,199,266(2),272,273(3),27
6(3),294,314
YUILLE
  Thomas Junr 137